D0409751

Praise for *The Resilience Dividend*

"Dr. Rodin's extraordinary leadership has helped introduce the world to the concept of resilience—the critical strategy for breaking the endless cycle of emergency response and relief for millions of people. From supporting our nation's recovery in the aftermath of Hurricane Sandy to helping megacities in Asia protect their most vulnerable citizens, Dr. Rodin has made resilience a global priority at home and abroad. Rigorously analytical and powerfully argued, Dr. Rodin's book challenges us to work smarter and more collaboratively to predict disasters before they strike and enable citizens to build stronger communities and thriving economies."

—Dr. Rajiv Shah, administrator of USAID

"With heartbreaking stories and practical examples, Judith Rodin makes a timely and much needed contribution for creating a better world in an increasingly volatile environment. Turning volatility into advantage is a skill that leaders at all levels of any organization can use in building resilience into business models."

—Paul Polman, CEO of Unilever

"This book makes a compelling case, drawing on stories from countries and communities across the world, that resilience is not just a defense mechanism but a positive gain or dividend, with added value in economic and social terms. The message is timely, given the increasingly disruptive force of climate change and the need to encourage communities to respond positively. It is also a highly readable account because it relies on actual human experience."

—Mary Robinson, president of the Mary Robinson Foundation-Climate Justice, and UN Special Envoy on Climate Change

"Judith Rodin is a world-class entrepreneurial philanthropist. In *The Resilience Dividend*, she brings her life's work to bear on the subject, drawing on her deep and personal experiences from around the world. She uses every tool available (including the world's most advanced technologies) to understand the urban terrain and to deploy real-world solutions. All with the goal of saving and improving human lives."

—Dr. Alex Karp, cofounder and CEO, Palantir

"In a world where disruption is a fact of life and uncertainty is guaranteed, Judith Rodin draws on years of experience to offer an inspiring look at how we can prepare for the unexpected—and by doing so make our communities stronger, more prosperous and more connected in the process."

—Bill Clinton, former President of the USA

"From climate change, to economic adjustment, to the breakdown in political governance, the scale and complexity of threats and challenges in today's interconnected world are immense. This timely and insightful book by Judith Rodin, president of The Rockefeller Foundation, reminds us that we urgently need to build greater resilience to enable individuals, businesses, and communities to prepare for both systemic disruptions and new opportunities in the world order."

—Kofi Annan, former Secretary-General of the UN and chairman of the Kofi Annan Foundation

"Judith Rodin's ground-breaking work at The Rockefeller Foundation is helping cities adapt to a changing climate—and a changing world. In her new book, *The Resilience Dividend*, she lays out a powerful case for why governments and companies should prepare for—and not just react to—disruptions to business as usual."

—Michael Bloomberg, founder of Bloomberg LP & Bloomberg Philanthropies, and 108th mayor of New York City

"Positive, pragmatic, and powerful, Judith Rodin's *The Resilience Dividend* is precisely the innovative thinking we need. By focusing on the ways individuals, businesses, and communities can build a foundation for resilience, Rodin gives us a blueprint for a future where we are stronger, more adaptable, and better equipped to meet the world's greatest challenges."

—**Arianna Huffington, president and editor-in-chief,**
The Huffington Post Media Group

"Embracing and driving change is key to adapting to our customers' needs and is a big part of what enables us to deliver great service. Every company must adapt and change in order to grow and succeed. *The Resilience Dividend* makes a powerful case for doing business differently in a dynamic and disruptive world."

—**Tony Hsieh,** *New York Times* **best-selling author of**
Delivering Happiness **and CEO of Zappos.com, Inc.**

"Humanity has long celebrated those able to avoid, overcome or bounce back from adversity. And, in an increasingly interdependent and volatile world, resilience has never been more valuable—or seemed in shorter supply. Indeed, as we strive to make progress in our communities, organizations and families, we must seek to understand and build resilience. With her new book, *The Resilience Dividend*, Judith Rodin provides valuable insights into the growing importance and transformative potential of resilience. Highly recommended for all those seeking to create lasting positive change in the world."

—**Muhtar Kent, chairman and CEO, The Coca-Cola Company**

"*The Resilience Dividend* delivers powerful proof that building resilience helps individuals, communities, and cities better recover from disasters and disruptions. Judith Rodin details connections between human, environmental, and economic systems, and offers a strategy to proactively address the threats they face. This very important book will help tackle complex challenges today and well into the future."

—**Mark R. Tercek, president and CEO, The Nature Conservancy,**
and author of *Nature's Fortune*

the

RESILIENCE
DIVIDEND

Managing disruption, avoiding disaster, and growing stronger in an unpredictable world

JUDITH RODIN

P

PROFILE BOOKS

First published in Great Britain in 2015 by
PROFILE BOOKS LTD
3A Exmouth House
Pine Street
London EC1R 0JH
www.profilebooks.com

First published in the United States of America in 2014 by
PublicAffairs, a Member of the Perseus Books Group

1 3 5 7 9 10 8 6 4 2

Book design by Cynthia Young

Printed and bound in Great Britain by
Clays, Bungay, Suffolk

A CIP catalogue record for this book is available from the British Library.

ISBN 978 1 78125 358 8
Export ISBN 978 1 78125 363 2
eISBN 978 1 78283 111 2

The paper this book is printed on is certified by the © 1996 Forest Stewardship
Council A.C. (FSC). It is ancient-forest friendly. The printer
holds FSC chain of custody SGS-COC-2061

FSC
www.fsc.org
MIX
Paper from
responsible sources
FSC® C018072

For Paul and Alex

Contents

INTRODUCTION
Why Resilience Matters

I was in Beijing speaking at a conference on global health when Superstorm Sandy struck New York City with incredible force on October 29, 2012. When I understood just how catastrophic the storm was, I frantically tried to reach my chief of staff, who lives in Brooklyn, but the phone lines were completely jammed. I was worried. Our headquarters are in Manhattan. Many of my colleagues and staff members live in the New York area. I had no idea whether they were OK or what the status of our work was. As I watched the flood waters surging through Wall Street on TV, I urgently kept texting my executive assistant, who lives in New Jersey. No response. As I learned later, communication channels throughout the region had either been taken down or were overwhelmed. Not even emergency personnel could get through. People and places I cared about were in danger, and there was nothing I could do.

In the end, we were lucky. None of our staff members suffered injury, although several had to abandon their flooded homes, and many could not return to them for months. I managed to get a flight back, but only days later. Our New York offices were closed for a week

1

because the area of Manhattan where we are located was without power, but we were able to keep some operations going and to help one another by communicating via our personal e-mail addresses. We were disrupted, for sure, but we continued to function, and the foundation was back to almost normal within a week.

That was not the case for many throughout the region. Superstorm Sandy brought damage beyond what we had ever seen in this area and even greater than we had imagined, though I was well aware of the devastation that a storm of this magnitude could wreak on New York City. Indeed, The Rockefeller Foundation had helped to support the development of a report by the New York City Panel on Climate Change that explored the potential effects of intense hurricanes, extreme wind, coastal flooding, and storm surge on the city's infrastructure. We had also funded groups of architects, engineers, and planners to collaborate on innovative design solutions for the city's response to rising sea levels, which were exhibited at the Museum of Modern Art.

In other words, our region knew a great deal about the worst-case scenarios related to storms and sea rise, but until Superstorm Sandy hit, it had all been hypothetical. Now the nightmare had been realized, and we could see that New York should have been better prepared and could have responded more effectively than it did. It was a wake-up call we could not ignore.

Only weeks after the storm, Andrew Cuomo, governor of New York, convened the NYS2100 Commission, a group of skilled and knowledgeable people whose task was to study the effects of the storm and make recommendations for what we should do to better prepare and rebound more quickly when the next shock hit. The commission had a broad and sweeping charge to make New York more resilient. Governor Cuomo asked me to act as cochair of the commission, and I jumped at the opportunity because I knew The Rockefeller Foundation had a lot to offer. For years, we had been working on issues of resilience, many of them related to climate change and weather disruptions, through our offices, partners, grantees, projects, and endeavors in countries throughout the developed and developing world. Participants in our 100 Resilient Cities initiative include places as diverse as Rome and Mandalay, Glasgow and Medellin, Melbourne and Rotterdam, Da Nang and Vejle.

I knew, therefore, that we had a lot to contribute, and I knew the work of the commission was vitally important, but when I visited some of the areas most devastated by Sandy, I realized how truly essential it was. I saw homes destroyed, neighborhoods disrupted, people's lives in disarray. In Breezy Point, where more than a hundred houses had burned to the ground, we talked with a firefighter who was digging through the rubble of what had been his home. He was trying to find his father's World War II medals.

In Bay Ridge, I walked to the end of a pier and looked across New York Harbor. From that vantage point, the vulnerabilities of the area were dramatically obvious. There were the low-lying neighborhoods of Staten Island exposed to sea rise, flooding, and storm surge, where people had died in the storm. I saw damaged dunes and other soft, natural infrastructure that had been washed away, leaving neighborhoods completely unprotected. Sited at the margin of the upper bay was Owl's Head Wastewater Treatment Plant, which had failed during the storm, allowing raw sewage to flow into the waters. In other words, I was looking at threats to the three interconnected elements that make up our world: human beings and their communities, the natural systems we share and depend upon, and the built environment that reflects our shelter, our commerce, and our aspirations.

Although I had always believed our resilience work at The Rockefeller Foundation was critical, it was in that moment I realized it was the most important work that we could do. Since then, my conviction has only grown stronger. In a time as turbulent as ours, we have no choice: we must all work to build greater resilience.

WHAT IS RESILIENCE? Resilience is the capacity of any entity—an individual, a community, an organization, or a natural system—to prepare for disruptions, to recover from shocks and stresses, and to adapt and grow from a disruptive experience. As you build resilience, therefore, you become more able to prevent or mitigate stresses and shocks you can identify and better able to respond to those you can't predict or avoid. You also develop greater capacity to bounce back from a crisis, learn from it, and achieve revitalization. Ideally, as you become more adept at managing disruption and skilled at resilience building, you are able to create and take advantage of new opportunities in good times and bad. That is the resilience dividend. It means more than effectively returning to normal functioning after a disruption, although that is critical. It is about achieving significant transformation that yields benefits even when disruptions are not occurring.

In the twenty-first century, building resilience is one of our most urgent social and economic issues because we live in a world that is defined by disruption. Not a month goes by that we don't see some kind of disturbance to the normal flow of life somewhere: a cyberattack, a new strain of virus, a structural failure, a violent storm, a civil disturbance, an economic blow, a natural system threatened. Yes, the world has always known disruption, but there are three disruptive phenomena that are distinctly modern: urbanization, climate change, and globalization.

The world's population is more rapidly urbanizing than at any time in human history, forming into highly concentrated urban and metropolitan areas, some of truly astonishing proportion both in terms of population and geographic size. Cities are extraordinary and wonderful places, yet their growing populations and increased density make them newly vulnerable to disruption, crisis, and disaster in many ways. They are more susceptible to weather and climate-change threats, because, as they grow, buildings and structures are often developed in areas that are more vulnerable to hazards. They are more in danger of systems dysfunction because infrastructure is inadequate, nonexistent, or poorly maintained. They are more likely to experience rapidly spreading disease outbreaks because of the close contact of shifting populations and insufficient health-care facilities. Economic systems are burdened, governance structures are strained, and social cohesion comes under stress. What's more, the expansion and further development of urban areas typically affect ecosystems, the natural systems that are fundamental to human resilience, so the impact of urbanization is almost always a social-ecological one.

The second twenty-first-century problem is climate change, which, in the last decade, has emerged as an undeniable contributor to the severity and extent of the disruptions we must deal with. We face threats from weather- and environment-related issues as never before: shifts in the carbon-nitrogen-oxygen cycle, global warming, sea-level rise, dramatic fluctuations in rainfall, increase in storm intensity, longer periods of more intense heat, land loss and subsidence (the subsiding, or sinking, of land), and the disturbance of natural ecosystems. Extreme weather events are increasing in frequency and severity. Many communities face flooding that destroys infrastructure, threatens economic activity, and tears at social cohesion. Other areas undergo constant stress due to lack of water and become so afflicted with chronic drought that people become "climate refugees," leaving their homes to join the urbanizing waves.

The third factor of the twenty-first century is globalization. We are well aware of this phenomenon and have seen its effects in all aspects of our lives—from the sprawling supply chains of global business operations to the increasingly multicultural populations of our institutions to the extraordinary mobility we have across geographic borders, time zones, and social networks. Globalization has accelerated the pace of change, introduced new and unaccustomed risks, added complexity to our systems, and increased the amount of volatility we face—particularly economic volatility. Our globalized commerce is unpredictable and puts strains on individuals, families, enterprises, economies, and governments. In a globalized world, disruption is such a regular occurrence and fundamental feature that change management has become a recognized field of study and practice.

These three factors are intertwined and affect one another in a social-ecological-economic nexus. Because everything is interconnected—a massive system of systems—a single disruption often triggers another, which exacerbates the effects of the first, so that the original shock becomes a cascade of crises. A weather disturbance, for example, can cause infrastructural damage that leads to a public health problem that, in turn, disturbs livelihoods and creates widespread economic turmoil, which can lead to a further degrading of basic services, additional health problems, and even political conflict or civil unrest. In this way, a discrete disruption can quickly devolve into a full-on disaster. People are injured and die, often in shocking numbers. Survivors suffer trauma and hardship. Livelihoods are threatened or destroyed. Institutions are crippled, businesses fail. Infrastructure is overwhelmed. Communities are weakened and sometimes wiped out. Precious assets—from life-giving forests to cherished works of art—are ruined. Financial resources are depleted.

The losses from disruption are so extensive they are impossible to accurately calculate. We can get a sense of their scope, however, from the World Bank's estimate that, between 1980 and 2012, nearly $4 trillion has gone into relief and recovery efforts worldwide for natural disasters alone. But that figure includes only quantifiable damage, and only from one kind of disruption, and says nothing about the greater toll on people, the environment, and economies exacted by the interruption of activity, loss of opportunity, and all the rest. Disruption comes in much smaller increments, too: local shocks, organizational disturbances, individual setbacks. The damage done by these may not be as costly, but can be devastating.

There is no question that building resilience must become a priority for us all. As we learned during Superstorm Sandy, and as people and organizations throughout the world have learned from disturbances of many kinds, we need a keener awareness of the threats we face, greater ability to withstand and survive the disruptions we can't avoid, and a deeper commitment and broader capacity to resume functioning so we don't suffer debilitating loss or even collapse. We can no longer accept our vulnerabilities or ignore the threats we live with. Nor can we devote such great amounts of resources to recovering from disasters that could have been prevented or responded to more effectively. Nor can we continue to delude ourselves that things will get back to normal one of these days. They won't.

The good news is that resilience building is a concept that can be learned and a practice that can developed; resilience is not an inborn individual trait or an inherent characteristic of a company or community. Any entity can build resilience. Too often, however, resilience thinking does not really take hold until a galvanizing event or a major shock—such as Superstorm Sandy—brings the need into high relief. But we should not need things to go terribly wrong for us to work to make them more right. We need to take action, and we need to do so in anticipation of disruption, in advance of shocks, in preparation for stresses—not after they have started to wear us down.

The goal of this book is to help frame and contribute to the process of building resilience by providing a template for thinking about resilience and by describing methods for putting that thinking into practice. I begin by defining the five characteristics of resilience (aware, diverse, integrated, self-regulating, adaptive) and then step back for a look at the roots of resilience thinking in ecology, engineering, and psychology and describe how systems theory and the concept of the adaptive cycle have come to be relevant in many disciplines today. I then explore the three phases of resilience building—readiness, responsiveness, and revitalization—and conclude with a discussion of the fundamental concept that gives this book its title: the resilience dividend. Throughout, I tell stories and draw on examples of individuals, organizations, and communities around the world.

I stress that resilience building must move forward on three fronts: structural, social, and natural. In all three, we need to seek both "hard" and "soft" solutions. We need to develop technologies, systems, mechanisms, and products that will prevent or protect us from the threats we can identify or predict. Just as important, we need to strengthen and improve our approaches to governance and leadership, knowledge creation, communication, community development, and social cohesion. As we'll see in almost every instance, resilience is increased where there is an optimal combination of hard and soft solutions. Superior infrastructure alone cannot ensure resilience, nor can resilience be maximized with only human effort.

If we build resilience as I know it can be built—because I have seen individuals, organizations, and communities around the world do it successfully—we can not only survive whatever crises come our way and emerge from them stronger; we have the chance of realizing the higher benefit: the resilience dividend. We will have the capacity to create and take advantage of *new* personal, social, and economic opportunities: endeavors we might never have imagined possible and achievements that seemed out of reach. When we do that, we can create and lead lives less shadowed by threat, develop communities and organizations that are more productive and innovative, and strengthen societies such that they are brimming with greater opportunity and prosperity.

1

THE RESILIENCE FRAMEWORK
Five Characteristics

Let me begin our exploration of resilience in what might seem like an unlikely place: Medellin, Colombia. What happened in Medellin—and is still happening there—is a vivid illustration of the dynamic and constantly changing nature of resilience building and how it almost always involves structural, social, and natural factors. It also demonstrates two simple truths: that resilience is not (and never reaches) an end state and that building resilience brings with it benefits that are sometimes beyond what you can imagine. Medellin, although still struggling with vulnerabilities, has so built its resilience that it is now beginning to realize the resilience dividend—of opportunities and possibilities it had never before considered possible.

Depending on your age, where you live, and your global experience, you probably think of the city of Medellin, Colombia, in one of two ways. You may have a lingering impression of the place as it was in the 1980s—the drug and murder capital of South America, home to the infamous Pablo Escobar and his Medellin cartel. Or you may think of it in a very different way, as it has emerged in the last decade or so—a dynamic and exciting place, an emerging travel destination, a city chosen from among two hundred contenders around the world as Innovative City of the Year 2013[1] and host, in 2014, to the seventh annual World Urban Forum, a global conference organized by UN-HABITAT. If, in 1985, you had said the city might be a good place to host a major international conference or that you were planning to vacation in Medellin, the response would have been disbelief.

In Medellin's worst days—the early 1990s—it was a city trapped in a downward spiral of violence, poverty, citizen flight, and drug crime. It was not unusual for there to be upward of 5,500 murders per year and more than 15 murders in the city per day. At its peak in 1991, there were 381 murders per 100,000 people.[2] In New York City that rate would translate to 32,000 homicides each year.[3]

When a bad thing happened—another murder, a gang fight over turf, a community dispute over sanitation or water, the failure of a business, the destruction of homes by a landslide on one of the steep slopes surrounding the downtown—the city took the punch and fell back on the ropes. Every disruption seemed to link to another disruption. People did not bounce back so much as hang on, cope as best they could, and absorb the blows that kept coming.

For people like Adriana Restrepo, who has lived for years in a hillside barrio called San Javier, Medellin was a scary place to be. When she was a teenager, there was often nothing to do but stay inside her family's small house for days on end until the shooting subsided. Neither she nor the city had the capacity to overcome the constant shocks, relieve the grinding stress, or find a path to something new. Restrepo says she was "ashamed" to live there.

With all its troubles, Medellin has always had plenty of assets, however, starting with its beautiful environment. It lies in the verdant Aburra Valley, with the pleasant Medellin River flowing through the heart of the city, and enjoys a spring-like climate with an average annual temperature of seventy-two degrees Fahrenheit, or about twenty-two degrees Celsius. It is surrounded by beautiful hills rising toward the snow-strewn Andes mountain range. Not everyone is ashamed to live there, and even those who rue its faults still want the city to succeed.

But for decades these assets were overshadowed by Medellin's vulnerabilities. Economically, the city was plagued by the suffocating presence of two illegal "industries"—drug trafficking and human trade. Socially, there was a big divide between rich and poor and physical isolation of one neighborhood from another. Extremely poor neighborhoods perched on the steepest hillsides, where residents could gaze over the buildings of the downtown and across the valley to where the wealthy (many of them drug lords) lived in gated communities and minipalaces on the hills across the city. The educational system was lacking. The public transportation system was poor. Prisons were overcrowded, but incarceration did little to restrict the drug trade—illegal business could easily be conducted from behind bars. International companies steered clear of Medellin. Tourists did not come.

The city population was growing, however, not just because people came in seeking some kind of opportunity but because many were escaping the violence, illegal activity, and guerilla warfare in the countryside. Many people had few choices but to live in shacks and tiny structures erected in the least desirable areas of the city. As crime grew worse and the city swelled with newcomers, there was an exodus of educated and capable residents who saw no alternative but to escape what seemed like a dying place. They took up residence in other parts of the country, in other countries in South America, in the United States, or elsewhere abroad.

Finally, in the 1990s, the city hit bottom. Then at last it began to face its threats, overcome its vulnerabilities, and build resilience. It set off on a multifaceted effort that involved numerous initiatives and groups, including the national government, departments of city government, businesses, community groups, nongovernmental organizations (NGOs), and individuals, including the mayor, business and community leaders, as well as—and this is very important—ordinary citizens. There were mothers' groups, volunteer street monitors, neighborhood watch associations. The city found many ways to chip away at its issues and reduce the threats and incidences of violence, while taking action to become more resilient as well, although the way was hardly smooth or the going easy.

By 2014, Medellin was on a new path. It had built its resilience through concerted efforts to increase accessibility and mobility. An innovative and integrated transportation system connects many of the most isolated neighborhoods of the city to economic opportunities never before available. The most stark and dramatic evidence of Medellin's successful approach to building resilience thus far is the reduction in violence. The city reported that its homicide rate had fallen from a high of 381 homicides per 100,000 inhabitants in 1991 to an average of 38 per 100,000 residents in 2013.[4] That's a dramatic change from the time when people were being murdered nearly every hour of the day.

There is now a palpable sense of excitement in Medellin. People are energized. Most neighborhoods are no longer dominated by gangs. Adriana Restrepo and her daughter, Stefania, thirteen, walk to school, work, and community meetings. Many who left the city in its worst days are returning. The population has grown to 2.5 million, making Medellin second only in size to Colombia's capital, Bogota. Twentysomething Martin Zapata, for example, is working along with his girlfriend to build an online home décor business. He returned to Medellin after spending several years living in California with his parents. "California was nice," he said. "But here it is exciting. We have a lot of work to do."[5]

That is true. I will not assert that Medellin is a perfect place, that drugs and corruption are now unknown there, or that the city does not have significant vulnerabilities and threats to its well-being. I will say that the people and organizations of Medellin are intensely aware of the fragile nature of their success and of the great deal of work that must be done to further build the city's capacity to reduce its vulnerabilities, deal with shocks, and find ways to adapt and improve more quickly than in the past—and they are confident of their ability to further improve their city. Adriana Restrepo now says she is proud to live in San Javier.

In 2013, Medellin was selected for the 100 Resilient Cities, an initiative pioneered and funded by The Rockefeller Foundation (and joined by several partners, including the Clinton Global Initiative), the goal of which is to enable one hundred cities around the world to build resilience in order to better address the increasing shocks and stresses of the twenty-first century. In their application for consideration in the program, the city's leaders wrote that Medellin "is a good candidate because in spite of its numerous and continued efforts it is still rated as the most inequitable city in Colombia, and Colombia, in turn, is one of the most inequitable countries in Latin America."[6] That is a bold and difficult admission for a city to make about itself.

This awareness of and commitment to place, a sense that obstacles can be overcome, and the availability of sufficient assets—infrastructure, institutions, and leadership—to fix things that go wrong and improve things when possible—these are telling signs of greater resilience.

THERE ARE FIVE MAIN characteristics of resilience and they can be developed, to a greater or lesser degree, by any individual, community, or organization. To be resilient is to be aware, adaptive, diverse, integrated, and self-regulating. These characteristics are all present, to different degrees and in different manifestations, in all resilient entities.

AWARE

Being aware is an essential aspect of resilience building because you must know what your strengths and assets are, what liabilities and vulnerabilities you have, and what threats and risks you face, to be able to effectively prepare for disruptions, respond to them, and bounce back from them. What's more, you need to be aware, as much as possible, of all aspects of a situation—the infrastructural elements, human dynamics, and natural systems—and how they interconnect.

Of course, the nature of disruption in the twenty-first century (and, indeed, for all human history) is such that it's impossible to predict, plan, or completely prepare for every possible stress and shock. Totally unexpected things happen. Circumstances change rapidly. Secondary effects proliferate. So being aware is not a static condition. There are fundamental unchanging factors to be aware of (such as a river running through your city) and there is also the need for

TABLE 1.1. THE FIVE CHARACTERISTICS OF RESILIENCE

AWARE	The entity has knowledge of its strengths and assets, liabilities and vulnerabilities, and the threats and risks it faces. Being aware includes situational awareness: the ability and willingness to constantly assess, take in new information, and adjust understanding in real time.
DIVERSE	The entity has different sources of capacity so it can successfully operate even when elements of that capacity are challenged: there are redundant elements or assets. The entity possesses or can draw upon a range of capabilities, ideas, information sources, technical elements, people, or groups.
INTEGRATED	The entity has coordination of functions and actions across systems, including the ability to bring together disparate ideas and elements, work collaboratively across elements, develop cohesive solutions, and coordinate actions. Information is shared and communication is transparent.
SELF-REGULATING	The entity can regulate itself in ways that enable it to deal with anomalous situations and disruptions without extreme malfunction or catastrophic collapse. Cascading disruptions do not result when the entity suffers a severe dysfunction; it can fail safely.
ADAPTIVE	The entity has the capacity to adjust to changing circumstances by developing new plans, taking new actions, or modifying behaviors. The entity is flexible: it has the ability to apply existing resources to new purposes or for one element to take on multiple roles.

"situational awareness"—an ability and willingness to constantly assess, take in new information, reassess and adjust our understanding of the most critical and relevant strengths and weaknesses and other factors as they change and develop.

You can develop situational awareness through many methods of sensing and information gathering, especially robust feedback loops. These can be as simple as a regular meeting of multiple stakeholders in a community or company or as complex as a monitoring system for a global telecommunications network. For us as individuals, there are many techniques for developing and increasing what psychologists call mindfulness. Ellen Langer, professor of psychology at Harvard and a former collaborator of mine, describes mindfulness as "a flexible cognitive state that results from drawing novel distinctions about the situation and the environment."[7] To be mindful, according to Langer, is to be able to develop new mental categories, be open-minded, receptive to different and new perspectives and new information, and to focus on processes rather than on outcomes.[8] In other words, when you are mindful you are more able to understand situations as they actually are, not as you assume they should be or always have been ("This can't really be happening, can it? . . .") and thus to respond more quickly and appropriately.

IN THIS AGE OF COMPLEX SYSTEMS and sprawling cities—and in which human, natural, and infrastructural systems always affect one another—an effective method of developing situational awareness (and, for individuals, to help increase mindfulness) is often overlooked or undervalued: going out into the field and taking a look. Tom Peters and Robert H. Waterman, in their classic management book, *In Search of Excellence,* popularized the principle known as "management by walking around," which was purportedly first practiced at Hewlett-Packard—and the method applies to information gathering in a disruption as well. Walk from house to house. Make an inspection. Go into the field. Too often today, we rely only on information displayed on one or more screens.

Daniel Homsey, director of neighborhood resilience for the city of San Francisco, has plenty of screen-based information at his fingertips, but he also knows the value of walking around. He learned it emphatically one day in January 2004, when the city experienced a particularly heavy rainfall—of the "hundred year" variety.

On that day, rain pelted down on San Francisco's seventy-three hills, and within minutes San Francisco's gravity-fed, "combined" sewer system—it carries both rain water and sewage—was filled with millions of gallons of drainage. Although the system is designed to handle huge quantities of water, certain variables—such as isolated storm cells concentrated over a watershed, the accumulation of debris in the system during the dry season, or storms of increased intensity and unusually heavy rainfall—can exacerbate the strain on the system. As a result, pressure at the bottom of the system built until water was forced up and out of manholes in the Mission and Excelsior neighborhoods. Residents found their streets and homes flooded with up to four feet of blackwater—"rain and poop," as Homsey describes it.[9]

Later it was determined that although the flooding was severe, it was of short duration. Once the blockage in the pipes cleared, water flowed back into the system as quickly as it had appeared. This kind of flooding tends to be confined to small areas, and it can go undetected unless a city staffer or official happens to be at the scene in the moment of the event—thus the importance of walking around. When Homsey visited homes along Shotwell Street in the Mission District and Cayuga Street in the Excelsior, he was in disbelief—one resident showed him the brown high-water mark, halfway up her wall.

This was a cascading disruption—the intense rainfall led to an infrastructural dysfunction and also revealed some "interesting economic and social justice problems," as Homsey puts it. San Francisco is one of the most expensive cities to live in and is short on affordable housing. In one of the flooded neighborhoods, many residents were undocumented people who lived, uncounted, with relatives. They were apprehensive about seeking help from traditional response professionals because they feared deportation, so they undertook recovery efforts on their own. Many dragged household items—mattresses,

rugs, couches—into the streets so they could dry. But these possessions were soaked with blackwater and posed a potential health threat.

At the direction of the mayor, Homsey rapidly organized a multi-
agency working group representing the city and nonprofits to deal
with the immediate situation. Given the reluctance of some residents
to engage with the government, it was decided that the San Francisco
Department of Health would dispatch restaurant inspectors into the
area to lead the outreach process. Why? They had competence in engaging these communities in a culturally sensitive way and spoke the
necessary languages.

Longer-term, the city took steps to ensure such a scenario would
not be repeated. When storms were in the offing, they mobilized
maintenance workers to clear sewers of debris. The San Francisco
Public Utilities Commission also continued to build the capacity of
the system, a multibillion dollar investment. They also pursued some
innovative solutions. With the help of a grant, the Mission neighborhood—which took the brunt of the flooding—tore up its old sidewalks and replaced them with permeable pavement and landscaping.
Now, when water enters the neighborhood it will not flood homes
but sink into the ground and, eventually, back into the system.

The storm, and Homsey's onsite visits, increased the city's awareness of specific infrastructural and social vulnerabilities—linked to
urbanization and climate change. Today, Homsey manages a program
called the Neighborhood Empowerment Network. It works with
communities to build awareness of potential threats and then offers
the necessary technical support to create and implement resilience action plans, customized by the community, allowing for consideration
of their unique threats, needs, and culture.

IT ISN'T ALWAYS EASY TO DEVELOP situational awareness, especially
when a disruption is very severe, long-lasting, or widespread and
when conditions change rapidly, reliable information is not readily
available, and feedback loops are cut off or do not exist. This was the
case in Kenya in 2007, when the country was thrown into a six-week
period of political and social upheaval and violence after the results

of the presidential election were announced. While events were unfolding, people had little awareness of what was going on and did
not trust the sources they could tap into, and there was a blackout
of established media that lasted several days. The dangers were great
and the violence widespread—all told, some 1,200 people died and
600,000 were displaced—and it was difficult to make basic decisions
that might turn out to be matters of life or death.[10] *Is it safe to go to the
market? Where are the attacks taking place?*

The need for situational awareness was so acute that, just a few
days after the election results were made public, four Kenyans—Ory
Okolloh, Erik Hersman, David Kobia, and Juliana Rotich—formed a
nonprofit technology company called Ushahidi ("testimony" in Swahili). They developed an online crisis mapping platform and had it up
and running within a few days. Citizens texted or e-mailed information about incidents of attacks, murders, protests, property destruction, and confrontations. The system synthesized and displayed the
information on a map in near real time so people could make better
decisions about their actions.

Given its success, the Ushahidi team adapted the platform for use
in a wide variety of crisis situations. Since 2008, it has been deployed
in the earthquake disasters that struck Haiti, Chile, and Christchurch,
New Zealand, and used to monitor unrest in the Democratic Republic of Congo. It was even relied upon in Washington, DC, to track
road conditions during the major snowstorm in 2010 that buried
the mid-Atlantic coast under two to three feet of snow and became
known as the Snowpocalypse.[11] The system was further refined for use
in election situations (and called Uchaguzi, "election" in Swahili).[12]
When the next Kenyan presidential election took place, in 2013,
Uchaguzi served as an awareness builder and an early warning system
that helped prevent incidents from escalating into full-blown crises.[13]

AWARENESS IS JUST AS IMPORTANT in times of relative normalcy
as it is in times of disruption. Large office buildings and residence
towers, for example, are complex systems with many elements, all

of which affect the capacity of the building to function normally and operate without critical failure if something goes wrong. Typically, these buildings have separate sensing, management, and control mechanisms—power, central heating and cooling, lighting, fire systems, security, elevators—and generally the subsystems function independently of one another. It's difficult for building operators, management company executives, and tenants to get the information they need to manage their operations as efficiently as they would like to—or to act as quickly and effectively as possible during a disruption.

Rudin Management, a developer and manager of commercial and residential properties in New York City, worked with partners to develop a building management system that brings all this information together. It's called Di-BOSS, the Digital Building Operating System Solution, and it enables what John Gilbert, Rudin's chief operating officer, calls "real-time commissioning." By pulling together and analyzing the data streams produced by subsystems, Di-BOSS provides operators with a full understanding of a building's state so they can make precise adjustments to systems. It also uses machine learning technology to predict future conditions. That means minor failings can be caught and corrected before they become major problems.

The development of the system began at Columbia University's Center for Computational Learning Systems where Roger Anderson was conducting research into the smart electric grid in collaboration with Consolidated Edison of New York (ConEd). Anderson wanted to get a commercial perspective on the issue and got in touch with Rudin. Anderson started off by asking John Gilbert about the East Coast blackout of 2003 that eventually affected 50 million people in eight states.[14] Anderson explained that his research showed there had been about a forty-second gap between the time ConEd knew there was a problem and the moment the lights actually went out. Anderson asked Gilbert whether a forty-second warning would have made a difference to Rudin's actions. Gilbert answered yes: "It would have prevented hundreds of people from getting stuck in elevators in our 10 million square feet of office space."[15]

They decided to collaborate and developed a technology to feed information directly from ConEd to a building's elevator system. Today's elevators are highly sensitive to electricity fluctuations and are designed to shut down when power falls below a certain level. When that happens, of course, it may cause an "entrapment"—people stuck in the elevator. With the new system, when elevators receive a warning, they are programmed to stop at the nearest floor, let people out, and then shut down until the problem is resolved.

That system led to the development of Di-BOSS. The awareness it provides also fuels larger and longer-term improvements. "From a resiliency standpoint," Gilbert says, "it's not only about how you get the building back up, but once it's tuned, how you keep it tuned. And then, if it starts to get out of tune, how do you figure out that it's out of tune and take the steps necessary to fix it?" After installing Di-BOSS, Rudin Management saved $500,000 in a single building over the winter of 2012–2013.[16] Gilbert thinks of this as resilience with a small "r"—"bouncing back every day, and doing what you need to do every day, better than you did it the prior day."

DIVERSE

The second characteristic of resilience is diverse, which implies that the person, organization, or community has enough different sources of capacity such that it can successfully function even when elements of the capacity are unavailable or compromised. Diversity provides the ability to withstand some amount of unaccustomed stress or even continue functioning during a shock or crisis. Being diverse means that the individual, organization, or community does not rely completely on any one element for a critical function. It has redundant elements, a number of alternatives or backups, so it can call up reserves during a disruption or switch over to an alternative functioning mode. Critical, core components or activities can be replaced by others. Being diverse also means that the system possesses or can draw upon a range of capabilities, information sources, technical elements, people, or groups.

MANY KINDS OF DIVERSITY come into play in the resilience of both hard elements, such as infrastructure and systems, and of soft elements, such as people and ideas. When disruptions occur, especially unexpected or complex ones, it is always valuable to have a range of types of knowledge and perspectives available to bring to bear on the problem.

We can see this through a negative example: the disaster at the Fukushima nuclear power plant after the earthquake and tsunami of 2011 in Japan. William Saito served as chief technology officer of the National Diet's Fukushima Nuclear Accident Independent Investigation Commission (NAIIC) and was deeply involved in the development of the commission's report about the Fukushima plant disaster. The report argues that one of the causes was a distressing lack of diversity of views. It was "groupthink," Saito maintains, that made it possible for a group of highly skilled and experienced engineers and administrators to ignore threats and warning signs and make such basic mistakes as siting backup generators in the basement, making them susceptible to water intrusion.

"In groups, we actively work to eliminate the diversity needed to broaden our perspective," Saito writes. "And we deliberately inhibit the free flow of information from the extremities to the brain." This makes it difficult for groups to perceive important signals, especially about vulnerabilities, that could be addressed. "We need to embrace diversity: diverse perspectives and diverse identities, in terms of gender, ethnicity, age, and education," Saito writes. "And we need to evolve better protocols to transmit information throughout our organizations; a resilient dynamism; especially in an increasingly complex and interconnected, multi stakeholder world."[17] Saito argues that it was this lack of diversity of opinion that made it possible for the operators of the Fukushima nuclear plant to miss signals about the facility's vulnerabilities both before the tsunami struck and as the crisis turned into a disaster.

Although Saito is critical of certain traits of Japanese culture that underlie the problems related to the Fukushima disaster, he believes the tendency to want to shut out diversity is universal. We can see it in the city of Lewiston, Maine, for example, an old mill city about an hour north of Portland. Fortunately, they discovered the positive effects of being diverse—in this case, having a diversity of population—and have become more resilient as a result.

In 2000, Lewiston had a population of about 36,000, nearly 96 percent of which was white.[18] Then came an influx of new residents: immigrants from Somalia who had been displaced during the Somali civil war and had come to the United States in a resettlement program. Most of the 12,000 refugees took up residence in the Atlanta area, but some migrants found their way to Lewiston, which, despite its unfamiliar cold climate, was small and quiet and seemed to offer opportunity. Other Somalis followed.

At first, the small city responded with concern. The mayor at the time, Laurier Raymond, wrote an open letter that tried to discourage further Somali settlement, and it gained national negative attention. There followed several years of tension and conflict, through which the Somalis persevered. They took jobs, founded a variety of businesses, and sent their kids to school.

Gradually, the diversification of the population began to have a positive effect on the city. New businesses moved in and, in 2004 *Inc.* magazine named Lewiston one of the best places to do business in the United States. In 2007, the National Civic League named Lewiston an All-America City.[19] In 2009, an article in *Newsweek* declared that "the place has been transformed. Per capita income has soared, and crime rates have dropped."[20] By 2010, it was becoming obvious that the Somalis were making a major and positive contribution to the revitalization of the city of Lewiston, particularly its formerly defunct downtown area.

The presence of Somalis does not fully account for the revitalization of Lewiston. But they offered new alternatives and different viewpoints. They opened different kinds of businesses, including clothing and grocery stores that catered to their dress and dietary habits (but in no way excluded patronage from local residents), as well as other entrepreneurial ventures such as restaurants, language and translation services, tax preparation services, and a business consultancy. They brought new income streams and a broader tax base: greater and more diverse assets available to the city in case of disruption.

At a hearing of the US Senate Judiciary Committee on immigration reform in 2011, then-mayor of Lewiston Larry Gilbert credited the Somalis for bringing "new life and energy" to the city.[21] Apartments once inhabited by long-gone mill workers became home to these new families. The immigrant population also brought much-needed youth. Enrollment of Somali children in public schools—in a city and state with an aging population and low birthrate—brought federal and state money to Lewiston.[22] And the presence of young people makes it more likely that Lewiston will have a workforce for the future—which is important because the state of Maine may only have two workers per retiree by 2030.[23]Paul Badeau, former director of marketing at the Lewiston-Auburn Economic Growth Council, described the arrival of Somalis as "an absolute blessing."[24]

This diversity has helped Lewiston achieve a resilience dividend because it has improved the city's ability to work through conflict and solve problems. According to the National Civic League, "local, state, and non-profit organizations have worked closely with city and public school staff to educate themselves about our new residents and to ensure that limited resources are focused on addressing specific needs minimizing needless, redundant, or ineffective programming."[25] The league also recognizes that, though significant gains have been made, still more needs to be done.

Lewiston—once an isolated monocultural city—experienced a disruption and learned what it needed to do to improve and benefit from its diversity, so that it could be more prepared to manage the next disturbance, minimize the attendant crisis, and reap the benefits more quickly.

DIVERSITY OFTEN INVOLVES systems redundancy; even something as simple as a backup generator located in a nonvulnerable place, which may be the key to avoiding cascading failure or dysfunctionality during a crisis. The need for organizations and institutions to have emergency backup power sounds obvious, but it is striking how often the lack of a generator, or its precarious installation, causes problems.

During Superstorm Sandy, for example, two New York City hospitals lost power when the local utility went out and the hospitals' backup generators, located in basements that experienced heavy flooding, were disabled. Patients were put at risk. Although New York University (NYU) had a similar problem with the generator at its Langone Medical Center, NYU had developed a small cogeneration system that operated independently. The gas-fired unit not only created electricity, it harnessed the heat created in the generation process to run the heating and cooling system. So, while much of Lower Manhattan was blacked out, many of NYU's main buildings were lights-on. Classes were soon back in session.[26]

During an earthquake in Chile, it was the presence of an emergency generator and continuity planning and procedures at a radio station that kept lines of communication open when official channels were knocked out. On Saturday, February 27, 2010, an 8.8 magnitude earthquake shuddered the coast of central Chile, not far from Concepción, the capital city of Concepción Province and the Bio Bio region. The quake cut off electricity and nearly all communications—landlines, cell phone networks, and computer systems, of both the government and private providers—were out. To make matters worse, Chile does not have an emergency broadcast network of the kind that is common in many other countries.

On the positive side, people in the region were accustomed to such events. Chile has experienced many earthquakes. Building codes were introduced in the 1960s, and homes and infrastructural elements have been rebuilt such that they are less vulnerable to damage. This is largely why the 2010 earthquake, although more powerful than the one that devastated Haiti in January of that year, did not cause nearly as much damage.

Still, it was bad. Desperate for news and information about what was happening and what services were available, people turned to their battery-powered radios, which had been popular during the years of the previous political regime, a dictatorship, when power was frequently cut off without warning. People searched the dial for a signal and found nothing until, not more than fifteen minutes after the earth had stopped shaking, they heard the voice of Mauro Mosciatti of Radio Bio Bio, 99.7 FM, one of the largest stations in the area. Mosciatti said he didn't have any news or information to offer but promised the station would continue broadcasting and would deliver updates as soon as they arrived. This was possible because Radio Bio Bio had a contingency plan and was equipped with an emergency generator. As soon as the electricity failed, Mosciatti and his colleagues had fired up the generator, switched over, and were back in business.[27]

The region suffered grievous damage—hundreds of people died, hundreds of buildings were damaged, and there was considerable looting—but Radio Bio Bio was able to play a valuable role by broadcasting information about casualties, damage, and available services. Thanks to its backup plan and the redundancy in its system, Radio Bio Bio was able to continue functioning.[28]

IN TODAY'S GLOBALIZED business environment, diversity has become a critical issue for companies, like the fitness apparel company Lululemon, that depend on the global supply chain. In March 2013, Lululemon made headlines for all the wrong reasons: customers were complaining that the fabric in their highly popular black yoga pants—a proprietary material called "luon"—was too sheer. (That is, thin.) Wearers found themselves showing off more of themselves than they had expected. The company issued a recall that affected nearly 20 percent of women's bottoms and wound up costing the company approximately $2 billion in market value.[29]

Although the problem for Lululemon was, on the surface, the sheerness of its pants, the real vulnerability lay much deeper—a lack of redundancy in its supply chain. Luon, essential in producing the stretchy yoga pants, came from a single source: Eclat Textile Company, a Taiwanese supplier the company had worked closely with since 2004. Eclat, in turn, also relied on a single source for the fibers necessary to manufacture luon: a glaring lack of diversity without any redundant options all the way from the source to the store.

What's more, Lululemon was perfectly aware of the weakness in its supply chain. In its 2012 annual report, the company flagged its dependence on a limited number of suppliers as a potential risk, concluding, "We have limited control over [our third-party suppliers] and may not be able to obtain quality products on a timely basis or in sufficient quantity."[30]

The brand's reputation for high-quality garments—which had helped Lululemon's share price soar 500 percent since its initial public offering in 2007—was tarnished.[31] Investors filed a lawsuit. Customers took their business elsewhere. A company that was on the rise and cornering its market stubbed a toe and stumbled over a too-well-known vulnerability. It had simply failed to take any action that would increase its readiness for a disruption to the supply chain.

In 2014, 80 percent of retailers identified their international operations as a potential risk—up from 47 percent in 2009.[32] As companies increasingly base their business on globe-spanning supply chains, resilient systems become even more essential—and that resiliency depends in no small part on having diverse, redundant options to call on when one part of the system is spread too thin.

INTEGRATED

Being integrated, a third characteristic of resilience, means that the elements of the system are effectively coordinated. Individuals, groups, organizations, and other entities have the ability to bring together disparate ideas and elements into cohesive solutions and actions. Integration involves the sharing of information across entities, the collaborative development of ideas and solutions, and transparent communication with the people and entities that are involved or affected. It also refers to the coordination of people, groups, and activities.

It's important to note that resilience is characterized by *both* diversity and integration. Diversity brings a wide range of ideas and opinions, alternatives and options. But too many choices and elements without integration can lead to chaos and an inability to take any action at all—as is sometimes the case in a postdisaster situation. This was the scene after the earthquake in Haiti in 2010, when multiple groups and entities appeared on site with very little collaboration in decision making or coordination of actions. The result was a response that has been widely criticized as disjointed, ineffective, slow, and even harmful. However, a great deal of integration without much diversity can also lead to inability to take effective action, as we saw with William Saito's analysis of the Fukushima response.

To integrate ideas, people, institutions, and actions into an effective, resilient system requires the presence of feedback loops. Technological systems depend on feedback loops for successful functioning—such as the simple home thermostat, which measures the air temperature and sends signals to the heating and cooling unit to adjust its function. Natural systems, too, including human beings, depend on feedback loops for the integration of all the elements within the system. Your brain and skin maintain a feedback loop and send signals to regulate body functions, such as sweating.

Feedback loops can take many forms but always involve a method of sensing or gathering data, the ability to understand and analyze the data, and the capacity to then respond "back" in some way that is meant to keep the system functioning. We know how incredibly important feedback loops can be in disease control, for example, because data on the incidence of cases can enable authorities to issue early warnings and rapidly provide care. This is particularly critical in areas that are susceptible to epidemics, such as water- or vector-borne diseases (those passed along by blood-sucking arthropods, such as mosquitoes), where populations have a limited understanding of how disease spreads, and where there are relatively unsophisticated systems of communication.

Integrated medical systems rely on feedback loops. Dr. Tom Frieden, who is director of the US Centers for Disease Control and Prevention (CDC), served as New York City's health commissioner from 2002 to 2009. In 2002, two cases of plague occurred in New York City. Plague is highly infectious, can spread quickly, and has a high fatality rate. Even a single case cannot be ignored.

Frieden and his team needed to find out how the patients had come in contact with the bacteria that had caused the illness. "We had no idea whether those people had a good story of why they had the plague," Frieden says.[33] "Who knows, maybe they were terrorists who had released the plague and gotten infected themselves by mistake." All possibilities had to be considered.

To get a handle on the situation, Frieden and his team relied on a feedback loop: an in-place information system that monitored and tracked about 90 percent of all emergency department incidents in the city. By analyzing the data from these many different facilities, staff were quickly able to determine that there was no increase in fever or cough in the city—in other words, no outbreak. No warning was needed. No epidemic ensued.

It sounds like an obvious solution: use an in-place information system to gather and analyze vital information in a slightly different manner than it is usually deployed. But, as we'll see, many systems do not have such a feedback loop available to them. In Surat, India, for example, there was an outbreak of plague but no centralized information system. As a result, the health authorities could not gauge the extent of the problem, people relied on word of mouth to gain information, false rumors spread, and the situation rapidly got out of hand.

As you settle into your premium seat aboard the high-speed Thalys train, preparing for the eighty-five-minute journey from Paris to Brussels, you may feel, without thinking too much about it, that the future of rail has already arrived—certainly, systems integration is not on your mind. After all, you have phone connectivity, can recharge your battery-operated devices, and will have a decent range of lunch selections (vegetarian options available) as you speed along at around three hundred kph. None of the hassles of airline travel. A sense of safety.

Given such relative comforts and convenience, you may not be aware of the vulnerabilities of rail travel throughout the EU and, indeed, around the world. Rail, in all its forms—including high-speed, freight, metro systems, light rail—is such a part of our daily existence that we do not think much about how the major factors of change that I have outlined—urbanization, climate change, and globalization—have stressed the railway system. (In some areas, rail is also feeling the stress of its own success. Increased traffic strains capacity, exposes infrastructure to greater wear and tear, and reduces the time available for maintenance.)

The three forces of change are revealing as never before the extent of one of railway's most serious vulnerabilities—the lack of integration among companies, systems, technologies, protocols, and governance, which reduces the system's resilience in the face of shocks and stresses. Although the European Union has erased many of the barriers and delays once associated with national borders, the European rail system as a whole is hardly an integrated transport entity. A train traveling across Europe still may encounter a number of barriers—even some surprisingly basic ones, such as differences in voltages, signaling systems,[34] sizes of tunnels, and track gauge.[35] Some trains must be equipped with several different kinds of train control systems[36] in order to complete their journeys, and proficiency requirements and licensing for train engineers can vary from country to country.[37]

Just as significant as the weak integration that is evident in this crazy quilt of technical considerations are the institutional issues involved: inadequate integration of ownership, governance, safety, and innovation efforts. This is largely due to the many changes in the railway environment over the past several decades: shifts from state-run to private entities, increased competition from alternative forms of transport, changes in demand, reduction in capacity, technological advances such as high-speed rail, and significant political realignments.

These changes have resulted in a railway system that is complex and difficult to negotiate. The experience of the ride, as well as ticketing, timetables, and fare prices, varies from company to company. According to Tim Armitage, an expert on rail transport and an associate director at Arup, a global design and engineering firm, that's largely because railways in Europe "are now bound by European regulations, by EU law, and EU mandates. But member states are still able to interpret what that means for their own ends." As a result, there is no "uniform interpretation of the edicts that come out of the European Commission."[38]

Given the complexity and size of the railway network, this lack of integration has played a role in a wide variety of disruptions of railway service throughout Europe, and even in accidents. According to the European Railway Agency, in 2014, "on average a derailment or a collision is reported at least every second day in the EU, causing significant disruptions to railway operations."[39] (This likely makes matters sound worse than they are, because many of these incidents are minor and not disruptive to the entire system.)

Other disruptions are due to extreme weather events. Railways need to run on a level grade, which means they are often constructed in locations—such as along a coast or in a valley formed by a river bed—that make them vulnerable to the effects of storms and flooding. In the summer of 2013, for example, a powerful storm caused extensive tidal flooding in the United Kingdom, Central Europe, and Scandinavia, displacing tens of thousands of people, killing twenty-five,[40] and causing service outages in many parts of the railway systems in Germany, the Czech Republic, and Austria.[41] The lengthy interruptions to passenger traffic and commercial freight adversely affected the economies involved and repairs to infrastructure will be costly—as much as €100 million in Germany alone.[42] In 2014, a "perfect storm of storms," as Tim Armitage calls it, collapsed parts of the sea wall that protected the tracks in the town of Dawlish, on England's southwest coast. The line was out of service for three months and, largely due to the geography of the region, there were no alternative railway options available to passengers. A report issued by the UK Department of Transport concluded that the resilience of the railways would be further tested because "we will see an increasing incidence of extreme weather events in the future because of climate change."[43]

How can European rail create a seamless, highly efficient, and more resilient system? Changes in governance will help. In England, a fatal train derailment in Hatfield in 2000 caused a national uproar.

The underlying cause of the crash, according to Armitage, was determined to be a lack of systemic integration—a "problem with interfaces." A failure of knowledge-sharing and knowledge management among operating entities led to maintenance lapses that caused tracks to crack excessively without detection. These revelations led to the formation of Systems Interface Committees which try to put aside individual commercial considerations and work for the benefit of the industry and, says Armitage, "provide the glue between all the different commercial organizations."

Integration of human systems, in conjunction with the integration of technology advances, can lead to a bright future for rail. Arup—which has a specialty in railway design and development—imagines a system characterized by "integrated journey information and seamless connections to other transport modes" so that train travel will be a "hassle-free, holistic travel experience."[44] There are already systems in operation that give a sense of this future. For example, the London Oyster Card is a smartcard that can be used for travel on all forms of transport in London, including riverboats, and the Paris Metro system offers seamless ticketing between metropolitan and suburban systems. Colin Stewart, Arup's global rail business leader, headed up a team that produced a report called *Future of Rail 2050*, which looks at how rail could and should be further developed over the next several decades. For an industry that has been slow to adapt to change in the past, Stewart says, there has been a good deal of forward-thinking and planning in the past few years.[45]

For example, The European Rail Traffic Management System (ERTMS) is an initiative designed to implement a single standard for command systems and train controls across Europe so that trains won't have to switch systems as they traverse borders.[46] A Europe-wide automatic train protection system (ATP) will provide integrated, real-time data streams between the tracks, a control center, and the train itself in order to monitor speed and route status. If there is danger, the system can instigate automatic braking.[47] This "continuous, communication-based signaling system" will minimize accidents and permit even higher speeds, while also significantly increasing traffic capacity.[48]

The cost of investing in the right improvements in the European rail system will likely be less than the cost of doing nothing or not doing enough. When you factor in the social and economic impact of disruptions—of shutting down businesses, making it difficult for people to get to work, and interrupting the flow of freight around the world—a more resilient railway system will pay off now and for decades to come.

THE IMPORTANCE OF INTEGRATION to resilience manifests itself in many ways—in infrastructure systems such as the railways, and in human systems, as well. Cristina Rumbaitis del Rio, an expert at The Rockefeller Foundation who works with poor and vulnerable people affected by climate change, saw how integration made a big difference for two communities hit hard by the Indian Ocean tsunami in Sri Lanka in 2004. The tsunami was caused by one of the most powerful earthquakes ever—the earth vibrated one centimeter on its axis—and produced one of the deadliest disasters of all time, killing between 230,000 and 280,000 people, affecting millions more, and causing billions of dollars in damage.[49]

Rumbaitis del Rio has a particular focus on oceans and fisheries and worked closely with a community of fishermen who lived and worked on the southern tip of Sri Lanka. Most of their tangible assets, including boats and nets, were destroyed in the tsunami. The fish stocks, too, were disrupted. Even when the fishermen received aid and were able to buy fishing equipment and get back to work, they did not recover quickly. "It was largely because the fishermen were very disconnected," says Rumbaitis del Rio. "They weren't working collaboratively or in associations."[50] They were not, in short, integrated into any larger community or system that would enable them to find alternate sources of income or share resources.

Rumbaitis del Rio worked with another group in the same area, a women's collaborative that made handicrafts from coconut fiber. The coconut trees had been destroyed by the storm and the stock of their business was gone. The tourist trade evaporated and so they had no customers. "But they were organized with each other in a collaborative," says Rumbaitis del Rio. They put their heads together to solve the problem and found a source of coconuts in an interior lagoon that had not been harmed by the tsunami. They also had connections with other organizations, including an NGO in Germany, who helped them organize shipments of their products there. "They were able to bounce back much more quickly than the fishermen," says Rumbaitis del Rio. "They were connected."

LARGE COMPANIES CONSTANTLY wrestle with the problem of integration, or lack thereof. Mahindra and Mahindra (M&M)—a $16 billion Indian conglomerate—began as a small domestic manufacturer. In 1991, Anand Mahindra, grandson of founder J. C. Mahindra and now M&M's chair and managing director, left the company's steel-producing unit and took over as head of the company's vehicle business. That year, M&M was experiencing a triple whammy: an operating loss, a takeover attempt, and an influx of foreign competition as India liberalized its economic policies and opened its doors to foreign companies. "All of a sudden," Mahindra says, "you are looking at a future which was going to be potentially flooded—inundated—with competition, both locally and abroad." Many people told Mahindra they doubted his company would survive "more than a couple of years."[51]

What Mahindra found at M&M's vehicle manufacture unit shocked him: an almost complete lack of integration among the departments. Manufacturing ran the show. It decided what products would be produced and, therefore, determined what revenue and profit would be. Sales and marketing had little power or influence. The needs of the customer were almost completely ignored. General management skills were weak because there had been virtually no competition and, thus, little need for strategy. Productivity, work discipline, and quality were, according to Mahindra, "abysmal."

Mahindra knew the situation required more than change—it demanded transformation. He turned to the management practice known as business process reengineering to improve the workings of the company, in part by breaking down the barriers between the disciplinary "silos" of manufacturing operations, marketing and sales, and finance.

These structural initiatives had a social effect that such changes in organizations usually have: they disrupted the company's culture—its ways of doing things. It took a dramatic moment for this disconnect to become evident. One day not long before Diwali (a major Hindu festival), Mahindra made an announcement to the workers on the factory floor that the traditional holiday bonus would be awarded differently than it had in the past. For the first time, it would be linked to the achievement of performance targets and negotiated through the labor unions. In retrospect, Mahindra readily admits that neither his timing—with the holiday approaching—nor his method—of an announcement rather than a discussion—were ideal.

Not long after making the announcement, Mahindra looked out his office window and saw a line of angry workers making their way toward him from the factory floor, highly emotional and angrily pointing at him. Mahindra and a group of union leaders he was with scrambled into Mahindra's inner office and locked the door. A four-hour standoff ensued. The union leaders advised Mahindra to stay put until the workers left, but Mahindra at last decided it would be best to have a direct conversation. He walked out and asked everyone to sit down. "If you want to throw me over the railing," he said, "you can do it. But that won't change anything. The world is changing and there's not going to be a free lunch anymore."

The workers did not throw Mahindra over the railing. They calmed down and waited to hear what he had to say. He offered to meet them the next day, if they wished, and talk at length. One of them, a self-appointed leader, agreed. The mood completely changed. "They all came up and shook my hand," Mahindra says. "One of them even asked for my autograph." The incident came as a "huge culture lesson" for Mahindra. He saw the company had a "we're-all-in-this-together mentality." People were proud of M&M and its efforts.

That meeting marked the beginning of a five-year process that integrated and streamlined the efforts of finance, marketing, and manufacturing. Although other disruptions—including a labor strike—followed, M&M has proved to be highly adaptive and agile, in part because it made itself more resilient by integrating business processes with one another and, importantly, by bringing people together around goals and a vision. Today it's one of India's—and the world's—leading companies.

SELF-REGULATING

Self-regulating, the fourth characteristic of resilience, means that a system, or elements within a system, can regulate itself in ways that enable it to deal with anomalous situations and disruptions without extreme malfunction or catastrophic collapse. A self-regulating nuclear power plant, for example, would neither explode nor experience a meltdown that would affect the surroundings beyond the facility. It might cease to function but would not cause other disruptions. The Chernobyl nuclear facility was an extreme case of a system that was *not* self-regulating. There were insufficient mechanisms in place to control the lethal radiation, the failure caused damage for miles around, and the effects of the collapse are still being felt almost thirty years after the disaster. A self-regulating system does not cause cascading disruptions when it suffers a severe dysfunction. This is sometimes called "failing safely" and is often produced by the capacity to "island" or "de-network"—all of which mean that the failure is discrete and contained. A self-regulating system is more likely to withstand a disruption, less likely to exacerbate the effects of a crisis if it fails, and more likely to return to function (or be replaced) more quickly once the crisis has passed.

SELF-REGULATING DOES NOT mean that the system must rely on brute strength or rigidity to withstand disruption, as we can see in the example of two buildings—the Mediatheque in Sendai, Japan, and the Imperial Hotel in Tokyo.

Located on the northeast coast of Japan, Sendai was devastated by the 2011 earthquake and tsunami. The Mediatheque, a multipurpose arts facility, was designed in such a way that it not only survived without significant damage, it did not lose function during the massive disruption, which leveled entire buildings nearby and caused the meltdown of the Fukushima nuclear plant. Moreover, it returned to full operation within three months. It may take three decades for the Fukushima plant situation to be stabilized and self-regulating.

The Mediatheque, which opened in 2010, contains multiple flexible spaces that can be configured for studios, art exhibitions, film screenings, and large and small performances of various kinds. It was created in a collaboration between an architect—Toyo Ito, founder of Toyo Ito and Associates Architects—and Mutsuro Sasaki, a structural engineer. Ito imagined the Mediatheque as an open, fluid, free-floating framework uninterrupted by walls, columns, girders, and other elements that usually keep buildings upright and intact. Sasaki's task was to make Ito's free-floating space a safe and durable structure.

He succeeded. The seven-story Mediatheque has an all-glass façade through which you can see thirteen internal columns—ranging from twenty to thirty feet in diameter—that are composed of slender steel tubes extending from the ground floor all the way to the roof, interspersed throughout the building like leafless trees on a plot of land.[52] The columns, the four biggest of which are located in the building's corners, provide the foundational support that would typically be given by exterior walls. The columns connect to an underground framework of beams that conform to the most basic definition of engineering resilience—they "can bend and deform without breaking"—and it is these columns that absorb 60–70 percent of the energy generated during a seismic event, for example, an earthquake.[53] The floors themselves, which might also have been constructed of concrete and supported by posts and beams, are, in the Mediatheque, composed of steel plates "strengthened internally by a network of steel ribs."[54] This makes the floors light enough to be supported by the tubular columns, and thus they appear—because they are unattached to the façade and unbraced by interior walls, because, of course, there are no interior walls to brace them—to float within the space.

The Mediatheque proved that it was not only attractive and utilitarian but that its self-regulating features made it able to withstand a disruption without catastrophic collapse or cascading disruption when the 9.0 magnitude earthquake shook the island of Japan on the afternoon of March 11, 2011. A video of the building taken during the earthquake shows it shaking, its floors swaying, and its lights flickering off. But nothing cracks, crumbles, or collapses. As soon as the quake is over, the building is stable again. There was only superficial damage. Everyone who was inside during the quake stayed safe. That was not the case elsewhere. Throughout the affected area, more than 400,000 buildings collapsed or "half collapsed" to the point of dysfunction, and approximately 740,000 more were partially damaged.[55]

It's tempting to assume that this self-regulating element of resilience created flexibility and lightness and an independence of components that was only possible thanks to modern technologies and materials. But the basic concept is not new. An earlier and famous example is that of the Imperial Hotel in Tokyo, opened in 1922, which was designed by renowned architect Frank Lloyd Wright, who vowed to create a structure that would withstand the earthquakes that have long been common in that area.

Just as Ito and Sasaki collaborated to create a feat of architectural and engineering innovation, Wright brought in his trusted engineer, Paul Mueller, to do the structural work on the hotel. The two men, whose practices were based in Chicago, included many features designed to make the hotel more able to withstand seismic shock. These included an exterior reflecting pool, which looked like a design feature but doubled as a source of water for firefighting (this is an ancient method that you can also see outside the buildings of the Forbidden City in Beijing), special wall joints that could absorb seismic energy, and plumbing and electrical components that—like the floors of the Mediatheque—were exposed and suspended, instead of encased within walls where they could be damaged if the walls buckled or collapsed.

Wright and Mueller also picked up on a technique that had been used in Chicago to create flexible foundations for high-rise buildings built on unstable ground. The main structure of the Imperial Hotel appeared to be constructed in a traditional way, of brick and locally sourced stone, but was actually a series of independent structures—not unlike the independent modules and floating floors of the Mediatheque—that rest on separate foundation pads of concrete. This construction allowed the foundation to absorb seismic energy without transmitting it to the entire building and also enabled the untethered building segments to shift without ripping away from the foundation or damaging other segments.

The Imperial Hotel opened in 1922, and within a year its earthquake readiness was put to the test by the great Kanto earthquake of 1923. It did not escape without damage, but, like the Mediatheque, its self-regulating components allowed it to perform well in comparison to most of the buildings around it.

ADAPTIVE

The final defining characteristic of resilience is being adaptive: the capacity to adjust to changing circumstances during a disruption by developing new plans, taking new actions, or modifying behaviors so that you are better able to withstand and recover, particularly when it is not possible or wise to go back to the way things were before. Adaptiveness suggests flexibility—the ability to apply existing resources to new purposes or for one thing to take on multiple roles.

Being adaptive means you can also change in *advance* of a disruption, to avoid or mitigate its effects. And, in the wake of a disruption, being adaptive means making improvements and transformations to prevent the disruption from happening again.

IN 1981, A TORNADO STRUCK and demolished one of the two stores of a boutique electronics retailer called Sound of Music, based in

Minneapolis–St. Paul, Minnesota. Founded in 1966, Sound of Music had been losing business to big box stores such as Circuit City throughout the 1970s, had faced (and narrowly escaped) bankruptcy only two years before the tornado hit, and desperately needed to find a new way forward. Adapt or die. Some of the merchandise was destroyed at the store, but the company still had plenty of inventory— some of it slightly damaged—that could be sold, although not at standard retail prices. The company's founder and CEO, Richard M. Schulze, along with his management team, came up with a solution. Forget about the old business model: counters, high-pressure sales, inventory stored in the basement, home delivery. Instead, they would hold a tent sale. Stack all the boxes out in the open. Mark prices down to rock bottom. Let customers pick out what they wanted, negotiate a price, and carry it to their cars themselves.

The response was fantastic. People came from miles around. When all the inventory from the demolished store was gone, Schulze brought in more from the warehouse. Two years later, in 1983, Schulze rebranded Sound of Music and opened a store based on this tent sale idea—"a bigger store, better pricing, more selection," says Schulze—and called it Best Buy.[56] Thirty years later, Best Buy is the largest electronics retailer in the world.

Schulze will be the first to say that growth was hardly smooth sailing. The company has had to weather countless disruptions—supply chain debacles, aggressive attacks by market competitors, economic crises, overseas expansion. But where some 576 electronics retailers were unable to adapt—which forced them sell, liquidate assets, or declare bankruptcy—Best Buy relied on its market awareness and ability to adapt to new customer needs and new market conditions to prosper.

In the past several years, Best Buy has faced new types of market disruption. The most significant one has come from the online retailers—particularly Amazon—that have eaten into Best Buy's market share. In 2012, Best Buy experienced a different kind of shock: a management scandal. There followed a year of turmoil during which Schulze left the board of directors to explore the possibility of taking the company private. While he considered the options, it seemed that Best Buy—like its former competitors—might be sold or, as Schulze describes it, suffer a "disaggregation"—a breakup, sell-off of assets, or shrinking of the enterprise.

But in August 2012 Best Buy brought on board a new CEO, Hubert Joly. Schulze—who has been the heart and soul of Best Buy since its founding—decided that a private equity purchase was not viable, returned to the board as chair emeritus, and worked closely with Joly. The company began to deal with its vulnerabilities, which included a lack of new technology products (the lifeblood of the stores), online competitors, an aging customer base, and a high cost structure, and it quickly began to turn itself around. In 2013, Best Buy was number 2 on the *Forbes* list of best-performing companies.[57] The company's adaptive capacity was paying the resilience dividend.

"We still have a long way to go in addressing our vulnerabilities," Schulze says. He recognizes that the qualities of resilience are essential to Best Buy's future. They must further adapt to the online environment to grow the company's percentage of online sales and be more aware of the needs of two important customer segments—women and millennials. Best Buy must also add greater diversity to its product offering, and is looking into new areas such as personal medical electronics and home security to do just that. Without constant innovation and adaptation, Schulze says, it is impossible to survive in the current business environment, which is one of constant ups and downs or, as he puts it, "volatility all the time."

COMMUNITIES MUST ADAPT, just as businesses do. The people of Village de l'Est, a community of Vietnamese Americans living in a council district of New Orleans East, showed a remarkable capacity to adapt after Hurricane Katrina struck the Gulf Coast in August 2005. This flexibility enabled them to better recover and revitalize in the aftermath of the storm.

The group's adaptive skills were developed long before Katrina hit. Many members of the community had come from Vietnam in the years after the war ended in 1975. With the help of the Associated Catholic Charities of New Orleans, about a thousand settled in the Versailles Arms Apartments, a public housing project in New Orleans East (also called "Village Versailles"). By 1990, with continuing migration and generational entrenchment, the population of the community had swelled to nearly 5,000 people.[58] They had a shared history of displacement as well as their shared faith—roughly 80 percent of the community identified as Roman Catholic.[59]

As Katrina raged, residents of New Orleans were evacuated and sheltered in National Guard emergency shelters, the Superdome, and cruise ships docked at the Port of New Orleans, and they were also evacuated and resettled in cities in Louisiana, Texas, Alabama, and Georgia. But, to a large extent, the Vietnamese of New Orleans East were insulated from many of the complications and traumas of relocation and evacuation thanks to the community and social networks already in place.

The Vietnamese community evacuated early; nearly 80 percent had left the city when Katrina hit.[60] About half of them went to Houston, Texas, which had, at the time, the second-largest Vietnamese population in the country.[61] Most of the evacuees stayed with family or friends, many of whom had also settled there after the war. Less than a quarter stayed in shelters.[62]

In Houston, the people of Village Versailles swiftly adapted to their new location and lifestyle. In addition to their familiarity with disruption, another important factor in their ability to adapt was that the church effectively traveled with the community. The minidiaspora of displaced Vietnamese from New Orleans was able to come together, maintain a link to the institution that symbolized its unity, and thus preserve the identity of the community, even in unfamiliar and uncertain circumstances. The experience of this Vietnamese community was very different from that of other displaced citizens of New Orleans who struggled to adapt, found themselves isolated from one another, and, in many cases, moved from a shelter to a motel to a friend's home to a trailer for a period of years. The last of some 23,000 trailers supplied by the Federal Emergency Management

Agency (FEMA) remained in New Orleans until February 2012, six and a half years later.[63]

Only a few weeks after the storm, the community made a bold move. Led by Father Vien The Nguyen, the pastor of Mary Queen of Vietnam Church in Village de l'Est, three hundred parishioners returned to New Orleans, despite objections from both state and federal authorities.[64] They negotiated with Entergy, the utilities provider, to get back on the grid, restoring power and water to the community by November 2005.[65]

As they rebuilt and resettled, the community not only revitalized; they transformed. Though sometimes referred to as "Little Vietnam," the Village de l'Est, prior to 2005, had a population that actually was only about half Vietnamese—the other 50 percent of the residents was African American.[66] However, despite living in the same section of New Orleans before the storm, the two groups had limited interaction. But in the first week of November 2005, as the church reopened, Father Vien made a point of extending a hand to religious leaders within the black community and invited them and their congregants to join the first mass in New Orleans East since Katrina struck.[67]

As Vietnamese and African American community members continued returning, rebuilding, and re-establishing themselves, they continued adapting by strengthening the alliance between them. Eventually, the influence and power of these two groups working together culminated in a recognition of the Lower Ninth Ward and "Viet Village" as cultural districts in New Orleans. The area of the city that, before Katrina, had been seen as a combination of a low-income Vietnamese enclave and a "black ghetto" emerged as a culturally important, rich district, worthy of recognition and attention—and one that was significantly more resilient than it was before the storm.[68]

2

A MINDSET
Roots of the Thinking

The stories of Medellin, San Francisco, New York, Village de l'Est, M&M, Best Buy, and others not only manifest the defining character-istics of resilience—being aware, diverse, integrated, self-regulating, and adaptive—they also provide a glimpse of the conceptual roots of resilience thinking and practice in a number of different fields, par-ticularly ecology and engineering, as well as psychology. When you talk with leaders in these fields—such as ecologist Brian Walker, en-gineer Jo da Silva, and psychologist George Bonanno—they naturally speak from the perspective of their original discipline, but they also accept that concepts from their fields, as well as others (such as busi-ness management and city planning), are coming together into an ap-proach to resilience building that can be broadly applied across many domains (disciplines and fields of endeavor) as well as many scales (individuals, groups, organizations, and communities).

Brian Walker, whose background is in plant ecology, has become an internationally recognized expert on resilience. "Resilience," Walker writes, "is the capacity of a system to absorb disturbance and still re-tain its basic function and structure."[1] This idea, which is common to all disciplines that deal with resilience, was memorably brought home to Walker in 1971, the year he spent as a research fellow living among and studying trees in the Harvard Forest—some 3,500 acres that are home to New England's dominant tree species—located in Petersham, Massachusetts. Established in 1907, the mission of the Harvard research site is to investigate the "ways in which physical, biological and human systems interact to change our earth."[2]

More than forty years later, Walker thinks fondly of that forest year, because it enabled him to get at the meaning of resilience from inside a natural system.[3] During his time in the Harvard Forest, he compared the forest to the savannas in Africa where he began his research, and he came to understand another aspect of the resilience concept, one that is central to ecology and to all resilience-related thinking: resilience is *not* about *not* changing. Forests and savannas change as they develop. They are constantly disrupted: by fire, drought, development, pestilence. Forests and savannas can survive disruptions, however, by adapting in various ways. From his beginnings in ecology, Walker has broadened his thinking to include human systems. He writes that the idea of retaining basic function through disruption may sound like a "relatively straightforward statement but when applied to systems of humans and nature it has far-reaching consequences."[4] One of these consequences is that the systems of nature and the systems of humans are very much intertwined, and the resilience characteristics of one affect the other.

The second discipline that has contributed a great deal to resilience thinking is engineering. Jo da Silva, director of international development at Arup, a global firm of designers, planners, engineers, consultants, and technical specialists, founded her thinking about resilience on knowledge of materials, structural behavior, and networked infrastructure.

In engineering, too, the concept of shock absorption without loss of basic function is central. Da Silva has spent a good deal of her career designing buildings, and, for many years, she thought of resilience largely in terms of structural matters such as load-bearing capacity, ductility, contortion, and controlled-collapse mechanisms.

"I was also heavily influenced by my experiences in postdisaster situations," says da Silva, "witnessing how communities recover from physical collapse, such as the Indian Ocean tsunami, or social breakdown, such as the Rwandan genocide."[5]

So, over the years, da Silva and her firm have broadened their thinking beyond the traditional paths of engineering to include human systems. They're now viewing skyscrapers as "part of a social system," da Silva says. A building is just one element of a community, and a community is just one element of a city. Da Silva now pushes engineers not just to think of design and engineering in terms of the physical but to consider the "human outcomes of what they're doing."

The concept of resilience is also to be found in the field of psychology, although it is not as deeply rooted there as it is in ecology and engineering. According to George Bonanno, professor of clinical psychology at Columbia Teachers College, that's largely because there has been a "paradigm shift" in the discipline only over the past two decades or so, away from its long-term concentration on "dysfunction and pathology" (mental illness) and toward its more recent focus on "resilience and health." The shift toward a more positive approach to human psychology is an important development, but it has also given rise to a notion that some people are "naturally" resilient and some people just aren't.[6]

Bonanno believes that humans have the capacity to endure bad things and recover from them without collapsing or falling into a debilitating or dysfunctional state. "When something bad happens that you just really didn't want to happen, you would think, 'I'll never get over this,'" Bonanno says. That's because the intensity of the emotions is so great. But even after a significant shock most people, Bonanno says, "are going to be OK pretty much right away or if not right away, within a few days, at the very most a couple weeks."

Still, there are degrees of resilience. It is not what Bonanno calls a "binary" state—100 percent resilient or 100 percent unable to cope. People can be more or less resilient because of a number of factors, including their particular vulnerabilities, the circumstances of their situations, and the type of disruption they have experienced. Some people will struggle more than others in certain types of disruptions. Some will need more help than others.

"When you monitor people in time and you map those trajectories," Bonanno says. "You see more than two paths," Bonanno says. "You see a group of people who are resilient—in other words, they are functioning really well—but then you see people who are struggling. They're not dysfunctional, but they're somewhere in between. And then you have delayed reactions. There are lots of different patterns you see over time."

Bonanno's thinking comports with that of my Penn colleague, Martin Seligman, who is widely considered the father of positive psychology—the branch of psychology oriented toward promoting individual flourishing rather than diagnosing and treating dysfunction or deviance. Seligman came to this divergent way of thinking after years of studying a phenomenon called "learned helplessness," a state in which people come to accept a given situation or environment (although it may contain certain noxious elements) without trying to change things. About a third of individuals, Seligman found, were able to avoid becoming helpless in these situations, and Seligman wondered why.

The answer, he found, was optimism. "People who don't give up," he writes, "have a habit of interpreting setbacks as temporary, local, and changeable."[7]

"How human beings react to extreme adversity is normally distributed," Seligman writes. "On one end are the people who fall apart. . . . In the middle are most people, who at first react with symptoms of depression and anxiety but within a month or so are, by physical and psychological measures, back where they were before the trauma. That is resilience. On the other end are people who show post-traumatic growth," or those people who revitalize and, very possibly, transform from disruption.[8]

Importantly, as I have said, resilience of this type can be taught, and Seligman and his colleagues have developed multiple programs—including the master of applied positive psychology degree at the University of Pennsylvania—to teach and build resilience. One program is aimed at those who arguably need it most—members of the military. The Comprehensive Soldier Fitness program in the US armed forces aims to make soldiers as psychologically fit as they are physically fit. The course is designed around what Seligman calls "the building blocks of resilience and growth . . . positive emotion, engagement, relationships, meaning, and accomplishment."[9]

Although the psychology of resilience has been further broadened by a number of psychologists, including Mihaly Csikszentmihalyi (best known for his book *Flow: The Psychology of Optimal Experience*) and Daniel Kahneman and Amos Tversky (whom I'll discuss later), there is much more research to be done, especially into the role of resilience in leadership as well as the relationship between individual resilience and group resilience.

Today, the ideas from these three contributory disciplines—ecology, engineering, and psychology—are gradually being integrated and adapted into other disciplines. Resilience building is now on the minds of people in a wide range of other fields, including economics, sociology, politics and governance, health care, education, theology, and the arts, and applied in the burgeoning industries of management consulting as well as personal growth and improvement.

SYSTEMS THINKING

Now let me take a step further in this discussion of the roots of the resilience concept and bring in systems thinking. All of the disciplines—ecology, engineering, and psychology—that form the core of the concept of resilience draw on systems thinking. A system is defined as a set of interrelated elements that interact with each other within some defined boundary and are organized to perform a function or follow some purpose. The human body is a system, as is a forest, a community, a computer network, a company, a city, a society.

Systems thinking has been developing over the past seventy-five years or so, and the best-known and most influential hotbed of activity in this area was in the 1960s at the Systems Dynamics Group at Massachusetts Institute of Technology (MIT), founded and led by the renowned Jay Forrester. At first, Forrester concentrated on "industrial dynamics," which he, in collaboration with the former mayor of Boston, John Collins, then expanded to the study of urban areas—which

Forrester defines as a "system of interacting industries, housing and people"—with the goal of understanding why it was that efforts to solve the problems of cities (poverty, crime) often made them worse.[10]

A system of any kind, whether a city or an ecology, is made up of many elements, and an element, in systems theory, is often referred to as a "stock." Donella Meadows—who worked with Forrester at MIT along with her husband Dennis Meadows, and was the lead author of *Limits to Growth,* the 1972 book that first sounded the alarm about planetary limits and resource depletion—has written that "stocks are the elements of the system that you can see, feel, count, or measure at any given time. A system stock is just what it sounds like: a store, a quantity, an accumulation of material or information that has built up over time. It may be the water in a bathtub, a population, the books in a bookstore, the wood in a tree, the money in a bank, your own self-confidence. A stock does not have to be physical. Your reserve of good will toward others or your supply of hope that the world can be better are both stocks."[11]

Stocks change, increase, and decrease over time because of a wide variety of factors in what systems thinkers refer to as "flows." Meadows uses the example of a forest. The wood in the trees is a stock. It can be depleted by outflows, such as trees dying or being cut down. It can increase as new trees grow. As we'll see, understanding the stocks (we can also call them resources and assets) and knowing their status (by being aware and having feedback loops in place) are extremely important in resilience building.

To take a simple example, emergency management experts recommend that you have a stock of food and supplies to keep you going, without outside assistance, for seventy-two hours during an emergency. If that stock is low or nonexistent, you'll be more vulnerable to the effects of a disruption, such as a storm. A business without sufficient stock of capital will find it difficult to keep functioning during a period of financial stress or an acute disruptive event such as the collapse of a facility or a supply chain interruption. We saw this very clearly after the 2010 Gulf Coast oil spill, as fishermen without sufficient capital reserves or the ability to borrow went out of business, had to find new work, or were compelled to rely on compensation from BP.

THE FEEDBACK LOOP is an essential element of systems and of resilience building. Systems are self-regulating, meaning the elements behave and interact in such a way as to continue functioning to the system's purpose, and for this the system relies on feedback loops. Forrester writes, "Systems of information-feedback control are fundamental to all life and human endeavor, from the slow pace of biological evolution to the launching of the latest space satellite. . . . Everything we do as individuals, as an industry, or as a society is done in the context of an information-feedback system."[12] Forrester describes the simple feedback loop that comes into play when warming your hands at a stove. The key variable is distance, and the amount of heat you feel controls where you position your hands. The "intuitive lesson," Forrester writes, "is that cause and effect are closely related in time and space."[13]

But in complex systems, such as a city or a community or an organization, "cause and effect are not closely related in either time or space," Forrester explains.[14] "In the complex system the cause of a difficulty may lie far back in time from the symptoms, or in a completely different and remote part of the system. In fact, causes are usually found, not in prior events, but in the structure and policies of the system."[15] He goes on to say that complex systems, such as cities, present to us things that look like causes but are, in fact, "coincident symptoms." But because we are so much more attuned to simple cause-and-effect situations, such as hand warming by the stove, we apply the same thinking to complex systems and, as a result, "treat symptoms, not causes." Forrester concludes, drily, that the outcome of doing this usually "lies between ineffective and detrimental."[16] This is why, for so many years, the city of Medellin could not break out of its cycle of violence and poverty. It attempted to treat the symptoms, by shooting or arresting (or too often colluding with) drug dealers and street criminals, without addressing neighborhood cohesion, transportation, education, access to basic needs, and other elements of the city system. Keep this in mind as we look at specific stories of resilience building in this book, because frequently weaknesses and vulnerabilities in a system result from underlying structures and policies and not from the simple events that often bring them to the surface.

THE CONCEPT OF RESILIENCE did not directly arise from systems thinking but rather gradually emerged along with it. C. S. Holling, a Canadian ecologist, has provided important thinking in the development of resilience as a distinct and defined concept. Holling argues there are two different ways to look at natural systems—as either *stable* or as *resilient*. Stability, Holling writes, "represents the ability of a system to return to an equilibrium state after a temporary disturbance; the more rapidly it returns and the less it fluctuates, the more stable it would be."[17] (You'll notice that Walker's definition is essentially the same.) We generally think of stability as a positive condition, a good thing to have or be—and it is, as Holling agrees. Stability is particularly desirable in certain circumstances, such as those involving engineering. "If we are examining a particular device designed by the engineer to perform specific tasks under a rather narrow range of predictable external conditions, we are likely to be concerned with consistent non-variable performance in which slight departures from the performance goal are immediately counteracted."[18] This is the traditional engineering world that Jo da Silva describes.

But, Holling goes on, there is a second view of systems, and that concerns "another property, termed resilience, that is a measure of the persistence of systems and of their ability to absorb change and disturbance and still maintain the same relationships between populations or state variables."[19] Resilience, therefore, is not about achieving permanent stability of some standard state but rather about "absorbing" change and disruption without the system collapsing or being totally thrown out of whack—especially in systems that exist within environments subject to a lot of change—and achieving some new state of stability. "If we are dealing with a system profoundly affected by changes external to it and continually confronted by the unexpected,"

Holling says, "the constancy of its behavior becomes less important than the persistence of the relationships."[20]

These ideas are fundamental to understanding resilience and how to build and strengthen it. It is the capacity to absorb change, *especially in environments subject to a lot of change*—which accurately describes our world today. It is what Walker saw in the Harvard Forest, what Jo da Silva sees in communities and cities, and what Bonanno and Seligman see in people.

THE ADAPTIVE CYCLE

A final concept to understand about resilience is the adaptive cycle, which is the process by which a system absorbs change and disruption from external forces and how it adapts or changes in response. Holling was instrumental in developing this concept, and Brian Walker and many others have contributed to and refined the thinking over the years.

The adaptive cycle has four phases and is often depicted as a loop: rapid growth, conservation, a "release" of some kind—which can be caused by a disruption or the reaching of some threshold (more on thresholds later)—followed by a period of reorganization.

An example of the adaptive cycle is what happens in a forest. Trees grow rapidly at first, they get bigger, more trees grow, and the forest expands. Gradually, as the trees become large and certain species come to dominate and crowd out new growth, the expansion of the forest slows. Then comes some kind of release. A wildfire, perhaps, or a logging initiative or a massive ice storm that fells a large quantity of trees. The disruption can be seen as a threat to the stability of the forest or as a source of new energy and revitalization. If the forest can adapt, change character, continue to function, and still grow—even if with different species and in new directions—it shows resilience.

These four phases are not as sequential or as well defined as they might seem. Phases overlap and repeat, but this understanding that systems are dynamic, never static or stable for long, and that disruptions are an essential "natural" part of the never-ending cycle of adaptation

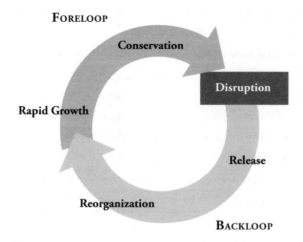

Figure 2.1. The Adaptive Cycle

and change is fundamental to resilience building. We should not want to make ourselves, our communities, businesses, and cities rigid and unchanging and forever fixed, but rather flexible, adaptable, and capable of absorbing disruptions and converting them into change that contributes to the system's overall functioning and purpose.

THE CONCEPT OF THRESHOLDS, popularly known as "tipping points," provides another way to approach the understanding of resilience in a system. "Thresholds are levels in controlling variables where feedbacks to the rest of the system change—crossing points that have the potential to alter the future of many of the systems that we depend upon," Brian Walker writes.[21]

A threshold is reached when a chronic stress or a known vulnerability—such as a financial downturn, a disease, or a storm—reaches a point such that it becomes an acute event and results in an emergency that compels us to take extraordinary actions and, eventually, rethink our relationship with our vulnerabilities. People get used to chronic stresses and come to consider them "natural," and it can often require a spike in the stress, an acute event, a tipping point, a crossing of a threshold, for the stress to become an emergency or crisis to which we'll respond.

Thresholds and tipping points are quite easy to see (at least in retrospect) and are often identified as the cause of a disruption or seen as the whole of the disruption, when they more often mark the culmination of an extended period of intensification of stress and, very often, the beginning of a long period of the further stress involved in recovery and revitalization. Even an earthquake, which can be over in seconds, is really a tipping point—the stress caused by the friction of earth's tectonic plates grinding against each other suddenly releases, becomes unstuck, and snaps with a great shudder to an unstressed state. The earthquake that caused extensive damage in Christchurch, New Zealand, in 2011 was not actually the first quake, rather it was just one of the earliest of a total of 12,000 shocks of varying intensity.[22]

Disruptions are almost always marked by such thresholds, or tipping points, although they take different forms. The collapse of the global financial services firm Lehman Brothers, for example, came in September 2008 after a long period of stress on the US financial system and led to a full-fledged financial panic that catalyzed the Great Recession.

THE CONCEPT OF THE ADAPTIVE CYCLE is familiar to us in many fields beyond ecology, particularly in economics and business, although it is often described using different terms. The economist Joseph Schumpeter famously coined the phrase "creative destruction," which is still very much in use and pertains to the resilience of an industry or economy and the entities within it.[23] In business, for example, a company starts small, grows fast, gets big, and begins to consolidate and routinize its success. A small competitor creates a rival product, service, technology, or business model that disrupts the industry and its conservative leaders—as Amazon's online retailing did with brick-and-mortar booksellers like Borders and Barnes & Noble. This releases new energy that causes a shift within the system and can lead to further innovation—just as changes in the publishing model fueled the rise of e-books and self-publishing.

There is more to be said about systems, feedback loops, and the adaptive cycle, of course, but I'll conclude this section with a comment from Peter Senge, another of Forrester's disciples, a longtime contributor to systems thinking and the author of the popular and influential book *The Fifth Discipline*. Senge writes that businesses and other human endeavors are "bound by invisible fabrics of interrelated actions, which often take years to fully play out their effects on each other." In other words, although the elements or stocks of a system may be relatively easy to identify, it's the interplay among them that is elusive, although terribly important. Senge cautions that, because "we are part of the lacework ourselves, it's doubly hard to see the whole pattern of change."[24]

This is why it can be so difficult for a system—such as a business or a community or a city—to adapt and change. Systems want to remain stable, to continue on as they always have. They often need some outside disruption, or outside stimulus and help, to improve and grow—if not in size, then in some other measure, such as quality or productivity, effectiveness or knowledge. Building resilience requires overcoming that desire of systems to continue as they always have, and ideally to do so without having to experience a cataclysmic shock to spur action.

3

~

A PRACTICE
Readiness, Responsiveness, Revitalization

Resilience is a concept with roots in the sciences that has today evolved into a practice, a real-world, hands-on, multifaceted process of *resilience building* that we all can learn and master. Resilience building takes place in three phases—readiness, responsiveness, and revitalization—but the phases are not quite as distinct or as sequential as that might sound. Indeed, resilience building must be approached in a holistic, integrated, inclusive, and iterative way.

READINESS

The city of Boston proved it had developed an exceptional state of readiness for a citywide disruption when, on the afternoon of April 15, 2013—Marathon Monday, as it's known there—two improvised explosive devices detonated on Boylston Street. Although the attack was unanticipated and unpredictable, Boston had been getting ready for just such an event for more than a decade—through network building and streamlining communications to improve awareness, undertaking situational drills and exercises to fine-tune integration, and finding and adapting best practices from colleagues worldwide to bring in a broad range of ideas and solutions.

Boston has participated, for example, in Urban Shield exercises, conducted by the Metro Boston Homeland Security Region. Urban Shield is a twenty-four-hour emergency situation simulation, meant to test the capabilities and capacities of first responders, emergency managers, and other public safety personnel. The cast of characters and agencies involved in these exercises is huge and diverse, including personnel from the police and fire departments, emergency medical services (EMS), the transportation authority, local health-care facilities and educational institutions, state government, and the Coast Guard, and it has support from the US Department of Homeland Security and other federal agencies. The exercise is under the supervision of a governance body called the Unified Area Command, which reviews policies and procedures, equipment and communication systems, and emergency operation centers.[1]

These drills are meant to replicate both the physical and emotional realities of responding to a crisis. The intended real-life effect was enough that Boston mayor Thomas Menino, in advance of the first day-long drill, released a statement to the public that they should not be alarmed by "simulated gunfire" or "officers responding to simulated emergencies."[2] Eight hospitals in the Boston area hosted segments of the exercise, including a simulated activation of the Medical Intelligence Center, which proved integral in alerting area hospitals to the potential influx of victims on the day of the bombings. The exercise held in November 2012 also exposed weaknesses in communication between the city's police and fire departments, which would hamper their ability to collaborate on solutions and coordinate their activities. Having discovered this vulnerability, the interoperability of the radio channels was improved after the exercise, which, according to Boston police commissioner Ed Davis, ultimately increased Boston's capacity to respond effectively to the marathon bombings.[3]

Boston's readiness on the day of the marathon was also a matter of a keen awareness of the exigencies and complications of the particular event itself—the marathon draws hundreds of thousands of spectators and creates a citywide disruption all its own, albeit a positive one. So, in January 2013, the Massachusetts Emergency Management

Agency "convened a multi-agency, multidisciplinary team to develop all the plans for the 117th Boston Marathon" that worked for three months to create "operational and coordination" plans for the event.[4]

With this plan in place, in March 2013 the Massachusetts State Emergency Operations Center hosted its annual premarathon Tabletop Exercise, which brings together members of the communities through which the marathon runs (Framingham, Ashland, Newton, Brookline, and Boston, to name a few) and federal and state officials, health and safety experts, communications teams, transportation authorities, hospitals, and volunteer organizations. One scenario they discussed involved the detonation of an improvised explosive device.[5]

In addition to these exercises and drills, the city of Boston treats all mass-attended civic and public gatherings, such as its July 4th celebration, its First Night festivities, and championship parades (Boston has been fortunate to win eight major league sports championships since 2001) as opportunities to drill, to better learn the weaknesses and vulnerabilities in operational plans, such as gaps in communications and methods for the distribution of resources.

On the morning of the marathon, the many organizations and agencies were at full readiness and on high alert as they normally would be. A multiagency coordination center was set up, and in it were stationed personnel from most of the groups that had participated in Urban Shield exercises—Boston police, firefighters, and emergency medical, Massachusetts state police, the National Guard, and the Coast Guard, and the Federal Bureau of Investigation (FBI), as well as the Boston Athletic Association, which organizes the race. During the marathon, staff at the coordination center maintained communications with the eight towns and cities along the marathon route (through their emergency operation centers) as well as with a host of other groups, particularly health-care facilities, to constantly add to and fine-tune their situational awareness: what was happening in real time.[6] The effort, in short, was well integrated, and there were ample alternatives, backups, and options that could be called into action if needed.

Outside the center, the marathon organizers had brought a highly diverse set of assets to bear on the event as well. Some eight hundred volunteers were standing by to help runners and bystanders, according to the Department of Homeland Security.[7] They tended first-aid and hydration stations, and emergency medical personnel were deployed along the race route—some on bicycles and in golf carts—all carrying "jump bags," which contain a variety of medical and emergency supplies including defibrillators, tourniquets, and oxygen.

Boston's readiness could not, of course, prevent the bombings from happening, but, when they did take place, the city and its people were able to respond effectively—even though the event was a shock and caused significant disruption. The high level of interagency and interdepartmental integration that had been developed during drills like Urban Shield and maintained from the coordination center during the marathon, as well as the high level of preparedness of medical personnel and staff, facilitated a response when the bombs went off that has been widely praised.

RESPONSIVENESS

Although it's impossible to remove all vulnerabilities, anticipate every threat, or prepare for all potential disruptions, resilient entities can continue to function effectively through both chronic stresses and acute events and regain function more rapidly once a crisis has passed. Although those officially in charge of keeping us safe and getting us through crisis—such as the many agencies that were so well prepared for the Boston Marathon—play important roles, they do not always function exactly as planned, and they are also not the only ones who respond in a crisis. We must be adaptive in our approaches and flexible in how we respond, including anticipating and leveraging the efforts of bystanders.

When the bombs detonated in Boston, for example, Massachusetts governor Deval Patrick was taking a few hours off and was on his way home to relax in his garden.[8] The explosions, thirteen seconds apart and two hundred yards away from one another, sent nails, ball bearings, and blazing-hot bits of exploded pressure cooker into the crowd of hundreds of people lining the sidewalks and cheering on family members, friends, and the field of runners in general as they concluded their feat of endurance. Patrick learned that something had happened not from any member of the multiagency coordination group but from his daughter, who called him from near the blast sites, wondering whether he knew what was going on. Mayor Menino was in the hospital after surgery to mend a broken leg and couldn't get to the scene right away.

In the event, no one required an official voice of authority—the governor or the mayor—to tell them what to do; they put their training to work, adapting their knowledge of how other mass events unfolded to the particular circumstances of the bombings. Across the city, first responders, emergency managers, surgeons and nurses, public officials, and lots of ordinary citizens determined what needed to be done, and they did it. Within a matter of minutes, communication between EMS personnel responding at the blast sites and staff in Medical Tent A, a half block past the finish line, established the need for a triage and trauma unit. That was not what the staff at the tent had been expecting; personnel there were accustomed to dealing with fatigue, heat stroke, dehydration, diarrhea, and heart attack, but not shrapnel wounds, massive bleeding, and severed limbs. However, thanks to the advance warning, by the time victims started to arrive at the tent, staff on hand were aware of what to expect and were preparing for the worst.

They quickly applied their standard trauma-ranking protocol. Victims were tagged: red meant a critical, life-threatening injury; yellow signified an injury that was not life-threatening; and green was for a person with a minor injury or no injury. Red-tagged patients were rushed to the rear of the medical tent, closest to the access for ambulances.[9] Stocked with IV bags, tourniquets, blood-pressure monitors, and oxygen, staff in the tent were able to stabilize victims with even the most gruesome injuries.[10] Just eighteen minutes after the explosion, Boston EMS had transported thirty red-tag patients to more than half a dozen Boston area hospitals, including Massachusetts General, Brigham and Women's, and Boston Children's Hospital— some of the highest-quality medical facilities in the world.[11] They, too, had been notified about the situation. Medical staff have a shift change at 3:00 pm, so there were lots of people on hand at the time of the bombings—personnel arriving for their shift and those getting ready to leave. Many of those who were at the end of their shift stayed on to help.[12]

The blasts killed 3 people and wounded another 260, many of whom lost limbs and had their lives permanently altered—but nobody who made it to a hospital died. Although that is impressive, remarkable, perhaps even staggering, it is not miraculous; and although first responders undoubtedly saved countless lives and acted stoically in a situation of chaos and distress, they did not see themselves as heroes. They, like Boston's hospitals, were ready. They were as aware of what was going on as they could be. They integrated their activities among individuals, agencies, and facilities. They understood the importance of rapid response and did what they had to do quickly enough to make a difference. As terrible as the circumstances were, the situation—at least as it pertained to the wounded (the search for the perpetrators was just getting under way)—had been stabilized in less than an hour.

Being prepared is not a matter of luck, unless you believe, as Branch Rickey is reputed to have said, that "luck is the residue of design."[13] Boston's response to the marathon bombings—which saved lives, maintained order, eventually captured the lone surviving suspect, and brought a community together to heal, all in less than a week's time—was hardly a matter of good fortune. It was, indeed, a matter of carefully and methodically attending to building the characteristics of resilience that enable an effective response to crisis.

REVITALIZATION

Resilience is not only about responding to shock and stress but also about learning and continuing to adapt and grow because of the experience. As a result, you can further increase your readiness for subsequent disruptions, find opportunities that emerge from what you have learned, effect positive changes, and build even greater resilience.

This is revitalization, and it can even lead to the opening of new opportunities that take you to a whole new level of success and performance, which means you've achieved the resilience dividend.

The city of Boston, postbombings, achieved a remarkably speedy revitalization. Although we know that the individuals and families affected—emotionally and psychologically, as well as physically—continue to deal with the effects of what they experienced, the city itself regained full function by the end of the workweek, when the second of the two suspects was captured. The streets were reopened, businesses continued their operations, tourism did not decline—in fact, it increased.[14]

Many factors contributed to this quick revitalization of the community, and one of the most important was that the city's agencies and institutions purposefully brought diverse groups of people together in an integrated way. Governor Patrick was concerned that the bombings might cause cultural groups to come in conflict with one another, placing blame and pointing fingers. To help avert such a reaction, Patrick helped organize an interfaith memorial service that was held Thursday, April 18—three days after the attacks. President Obama attended and spoke, as did Nancy Taylor, senior minister and CEO of the Old South Church in Boston—located on Boylston Street and often referred to as the "Church of the Finish Line" because of its location at the end of the marathon's 26.2-mile course. At the interfaith service, Taylor reinforced the need for the community to come together, not to split apart. "Another's hate will not make of us haters," she said that day. "Another's cruelty will only redouble our mercy."[15]

Institutions of all kinds can play an important role in response to severe disruption and in the revitalization needed afterward if they are aware of the issues involved and are flexible enough to put their institution in service as the situation demands. Taylor says that religious institutions can be especially helpful when unpredictable events strike, particularly those that involve terrible loss. "We have a lot of experience with this," Taylor says. "We handle these mysteries of life and death, of good and evil, of mercy and justice. The peculiar vocation of the church in such a time is to create an opportunity for gathering, for rebuilding of the community that's been literally shattered by the bombs. And as people run in different directions, we create opportunities for re-gathering."[16]

Regathering, especially in a location as steeped in community as a house of faith, is essential for a community's restabilization, as people come together to mourn, reflect, commiserate, comfort one another, and, as Governor Patrick put it, to commit to rebuilding and restoring what was lost.

Another self-regulating element that contributed to Boston's revitalization was the robust reaffirmation of the city's identity and sense of place. For that, the city got a big boost from another of its venerable institutions: the Boston Red Sox, the city's beloved baseball team. Just over a mile away from the Church of the Finish Line stands a landmark that is known to Bostonians as the "Cathedral"—I refer, of course, to Fenway Park, the oldest baseball stadium in America, opened in 1912.

It was there that an event was held on Saturday, April 20—less than a week after the bombings—that proved to be every bit as emotionally intense as the interfaith service. The Red Sox, before a park filled with Bostonians and baseball fans, led a ceremony during which they paid tribute to first responders, police officers, runners, victims and their families, and all those who had been affected by the event. Their purpose, they said, was to reaffirm Boston's strength as a city. The remarks of David Ortiz, the long-serving Red Sox slugger, were the highlight of the event. "This jersey that we wear today," he boomed into the microphone, "doesn't say 'Red Sox.' It says 'Boston.' This is our fucking city, and nobody is going to dictate our freedom!"[17] The crowd roared.

Six months later, as if to prove that assertion to the world, the Red Sox—who had finished the previous season in last place in the American League East—beat the St. Louis Cardinals to win the World Series. In early November, the team paraded through Boston in celebration along a route that took them to Boylston Street. When they reached the marathon finish line, the caravan came to a halt. A large crowd had gathered there. A player placed the World Series trophy on the yellow-painted concrete of the finish line and draped over it a jersey with the numbers "617"—Boston's area code—and the words "Boston strong," the same words that echoed on the street, chanted by the crowd.[18]

In April, the site had been a scene of tragedy. In November, it was one of reaffirmation. The City of Boston was celebrating its awareness of its strength and unity as a community and its ability to respond to disruption successfully—in short, its resilience. At the running of the marathon a year later, amid heightened security (including the use of a new, citywide surveillance system that is able to pick up on and analyze suspicious behaviors or abnormal activities[19]) and preceded by a week-long memorialization of the prior year's events, as many as a million people turned out to watch, cheer, and demonstrate that Boston had not only bounced back from the bombings but was stronger than ever.[20]

SOCIAL COHESION

As we see in the Boston story—and as we'll see in many other stories in this book—resilience building typically involves technological and infrastructure solutions. In Boston, communications and surveillance systems played a major role, as did medical procedures and devices. There are many tried-and-true approaches and innovations in technologies and infrastructure that help increase the resilience of our families and neighborhoods, businesses and organizations, cities and nations. However, although technology and physical infrastructure can increase resilience, by itself it is not enough. As Garret Hardin, author of the influential paper *Tragedy of the Commons*, writes, "There is no technical solution" that, by itself, can meet the challenges involved in sharing resources.[21] There is also a set of "softer" features—such as policies, norms, and behaviors. And all the characteristics of resilience contribute to and are affected by *social cohesion*. This is the glue that bonds people to one another, in families, groups, organizations, and communities. It consists of genuine commitment and caring, shared values and beliefs, engagement, common purpose, and sense of identity, and it makes all the difference in building resilience.

THAT IS JUST WHAT Rob Dudgeon discovered early in his career. Dudgeon is deputy director of San Francisco's Department of Emergency Management (SF DEM) and possesses a highly evolved and sophisticated view not only of what resilience looks like but how it can be built, and he came to that understanding in a very personal way.

Dudgeon moved to the Bay Area in 1989. San Francisco, unlike Medellin, has long been one of the world's favorite travel destinations. Like Medellin, it has lived for decades with a chronic stress, although quite a different one than that of crime and violence: the expectation of earthquakes. It's not surprising, therefore, that Dudgeon's path to resilience thinking started with the quake now known as Loma Prieta.

Dudgeon was nineteen years old and working as an emergency medical technician (EMT), when the worst earthquake since the big one in 1906 struck. It was Tuesday, October 17, 1989, and evening rush-hour traffic was building on the Nimitz Freeway (I-880) that threads through West Oakland to the San Francisco–Oakland Bay Bridge connecting the eastern suburbs to downtown San Francisco. *Boom*, the world began to shake.

Dudgeon had recently started working in Oakland. He had been brought up and lived in a working-class town in central California. Although the Central Valley area was predominantly white in the 1970s and 1980s, he had plenty of exposure to poverty throughout his childhood. But Oakland was different. It was tough, the inner city, and whenever Dudgeon answered a call there, he felt a certain amount of "trepidation" going in.

"The urban toughness was new to me," says Dudgeon. "The obvious racial tension that existed was kind of shocking. People hated me because I was a white kid in their neighborhood. We had racial tension in the valley, but it was different. You really only saw it overtly with gangs, and even then it was more about drugs and money than race."[22]

On emergency calls in Oakland, things would sometimes get dicey. A punch would be thrown, and "somebody would shoot at you from time to time," as Dudgeon puts it. Census data from 1990 reveal the economic differences between Oakland and its neighboring city. In 1989 in San Francisco, the per capita income was $27,000, with 12.5 percent of the population living below the poverty line. In Oakland, just across the bay, per capita income was $14,600, and 18.5 percent of the population lived in poverty.[23]

On a typical day in the ambulance, Dudgeon would travel the streets and highways of the city, often crossing the Cypress Street Viaduct, a utilitarian two-level structure that had been constructed in 1955–1957 to help relieve congestion on the Oakland streets that led onto the bridge. He would drive across the viaduct several times a day.

Dudgeon was on duty—but not on the bridge—when, just a few seconds after 5 pm, with both levels of the viaduct filled with the usual evening mixture of commuters headed home and commercial vehicles, the shaking started and continued for fifteen seconds. The upper roadway cracked, split, and collapsed onto the lower level—forty people were killed, crushed in their cars.[24]

Dudgeon worked calls through the night and ended up at a staging area that had been set up in an Oakland neighborhood, where the injured were attended to and dispatched to hospitals. It was one of the neighborhoods that Dudgeon had been careful about on earlier visits, but now ambulances lined the street, and he had plunged into the work. He and his fellow EMTs had worked all night, eaten nothing, and were nearing exhaustion.

Earthquakes are an accepted part of life in San Francisco. Most residents have felt a tremor at some point in their lives. People still tell family legends about how a great-grandfather or great-aunt fared during the quake of 1906. The 1989 seismic event—which received its name because the quake's epicenter was just a few miles from Loma Prieta, the highest peak in the Santa Cruz Mountains—was nowhere near as bad as the 1906 quake, which registered a 7.8 on the moment magnitude scale (MMS), leveled 490 city blocks, resulted in fires that caused 28,000 buildings to burn to the ground, and left more than half the city's population—400,000 at the time—homeless.[25] But it was the most destructive earthquake the San Francisco area had experienced in eighty-three years.

Rob Dudgeon was surprised that night, not so much by the power and devastation of the quake itself, but by what happened in the rough neighborhood where he found himself treating the quake's victims. "People who had next to nothing—living paycheck to paycheck is about as affluent as it gets—started coming out of the woodwork," Dudgeon said. The people he had been helping for more than a year now were helping the helpers. "They started bringing out tables and chairs," Dudgeon remembered, "and whatever they had in the fridge." He was stunned. "They were feeding us. It wasn't us feeding them—it was them taking care of us, because we were all just run ragged." Dudgeon's wife had heard the news that the viaduct had collapsed. She knew that was one of Dudgeon's frequent routes, but with the phone lines down "she didn't know whether I was dead or alive," Dudgeon says. Next, the neighborhood folks opened their houses. Some of them had gotten phone service back. "Come on in and use the phone," they said.

Dudgeon's experiences in 1989 taught him a lot about both disaster and resilience.

First, he saw that, in the wake of a serious disruption, the emergency services that are typically thought of as "first responders"—fire departments, police departments, EMTs, hospitals—may not be as invincible as we would like to think. They, too, may be affected by the disaster, whatever it is. They may be spread too thin and overwhelmed, as Dudgeon and his team were. They may be unable to reach the people in need. The firehouse may be underwater, the emergency vehicle destroyed, the phones out, the first responders themselves injured or killed. In the 1906 quake, for example, San Francisco's respected fire chief, Dennis T. Sullivan, fell through the floor of the firehouse when it gave way and later died of his injuries.

Second, Dudgeon realized that people are highly capable of helping themselves. "When you see what happens in an emergency, or just even on a bad day, people are really adept at solving problems,"

Dudgeon said. He also saw that what he had thought of as a rough neighborhood was a community. The people there knew each other. They had relationships. Even the least affluent still had valuable assets—food, tables, phones, goodwill—they were willing to share. They had suffered a shock—the collapse of a bridge, broken bodies, then the arrival of a stream of ambulances and EMTs—but they responded to help people they did not know to deal with a situation not of their own making. Dudgeon began to see that human relationships were just as important in dealing with a disruption as was the medical equipment and the training of the experts. He saw the rough neighborhood with fresh eyes.

Today, in his role at the department, that experience in 1989 informs how Dudgeon thinks about resilience. Although he is well versed in definitions and frameworks, he focuses mostly on practice. "In my mind, anything we do that makes a community better able to withstand any sort of turmoil, big or small, and recover from it just as fast as possible—that's resilience."

4

DISRUPTION
A World of Stresses and Shocks

"All life is a series of problems which we must try and solve," says Violet Crawley, better known as Lady Grantham, the fictional dowager countess on the television program *Downton Abbey*. One reason the show has proved so incredibly popular—not just in England where it originated and the United States where it soon migrated, but in some two hundred countries—is because the lives it follows are filled with disruption and stress.[1] The characters spend their episodes preparing for, managing, and trying to recover from one significant disturbance after another. The *Titanic* sinks. World War I erupts. Spanish flu breaks out. There are class conflicts, fatal accidents, political scandals, crimes, corruption, and economic crises. We can identify.

What's more, today's viewers connect with the show's larger context, a world in which fundamental societal shifts are taking place—class structures crumbling, gender roles being challenged, innovations cropping up in business management, technological advances inserting themselves into traditional tasks (toasters and sewing machines!), new approaches revolutionizing medical care, and destabilizing shakeups in political power. We recognize an era in which a sense of an established order is slipping away.

There is another factor in the popularity of *Downton Abbey,* the presence of an element we consider lacking in today's world: direct human engagement. The Downton characters work and play together, debate with and confront one another—across disciplines, classes, and social groups—trying to sort out situations, overcome vulnerabilities, and leverage resources to strengthen their communities, institutions (household, church, hospital, business), and society as a whole. They talk face to face. They touch. They share meals. They connect without electronic devices.

Today we face many of the same disruptions that previous generations were accustomed to—storms and earthquakes, disease and epidemics, systems failures and accidents, crime and social unrest—but there are additional factors that exacerbate the old disruptions and introduce new ones as well.

Twenty-first-century complications include complexity, congestion, and rapidity, but as I've said, the three factors that make our age so much different from that of the Crawleys—and that make resilience so essential—are urbanization, climate change, and globalization.

Now that we have explored the resilience framework—the characteristics, roots of the thinking, and the three phases of practice—let me step back for a moment to add some context about the nature of today's disruptions and why they demand that we focus more sharply on resilience.

URBANIZATION

The rapid growth of urban areas, especially in the developing world, and the resulting physical expansion of cities, along with an influx of migrants due to economic, climate, and civil reasons, lead to a rise in the risk of disruptions of all kinds—and increase the need for resilience for individuals, neighborhoods, and cities.

THERE ARE MANY ESTIMATES of the world's population, its growth rate, and the resulting population size at certain future milestones. In 2013, the world's population was around 7.2 billion, and experts estimate it will climb to more than 8 billion by 2025 and approach 10 billion by 2050.[2] This projected increase of 2 billion people in twenty-five years is staggering—in the thousand years preceding 1900, the global population did not grow by that many people.[3]

The greatest growth is expected to take place in the developing world.[4] Between 1995 and 2005, urban populations in developing countries increased by an average of about 165,000 new residents each day or 1.2 million people every week, according to the World Health Organization (WHO).[5] By 2050, Nigeria could be home to more people than the United States and by 2100 could be the second-most populous country on earth.[6] Are these countries capable of managing these populations? Is infrastructure adequate and safe? Can lives and livelihoods be secured? In far too many cases, the answer is no.

Although population growth continues to be of concern in terms of planetary limits, the rate of urbanization makes it an even more pressing issue—especially as it relates to resilience. Cities are dynamic places and the economic engines of the world: they occupy just 2 percent of the land, contain 50 percent of its population, yet account for 80 percent of the world's economic output (as measured by gross domestic product, or GDP).[7] Within the next several decades, the percentage of city dwellers is predicted to rise to 75 percent of the world's population, meaning the urban population will be in the range of 7 billion people. The lion's share of the urban increase, some 60 percent, is expected to take place in Asia.[8] Much of the growth will take place in smaller cities, those currently in the range of 100,000–500,000 people, creating dozens of new cities with populations in the millions.[9]

When cities expand in population, they must provide more housing, facilities, and infrastructure, and that usually means a great deal of construction and building. Arthur C. Nelson of the Brookings Institution posits that nearly "half of what will be the built environment of 2030 doesn't exist today."[10] That is an astonishing thought but not hard to believe when you travel in the growing cities of China, India, and South America and see bamboo scaffolding, swinging cranes, and streams of workers everywhere. The expansion also puts more pressure

TABLE 4.1. WORLD'S LARGEST CITIES[11]	
CITY	POPULATION
Tokyo, Japan	37,126,000
Jakarta, Indonesia	26,063,000
Seoul, South Korea	22,547,000
Delhi, India	22,242,000
Shanghai, China	20,860,000
Manila, Philippines	20,767,000
Karachi, Pakistan	20,711,000
New York, United States	20,464,000
Sao Paulo, Brazil	20,186,000
Mexico City, Mexico	19,463,000

on the natural environment, particularly those elements that provide what are called "ecosystems services" such as air and water, pollination, as well as disease and pest regulation.

The most concerning—and very common—way that cities expand to accommodate rising populations is by building and developing in vulnerable areas either within the city itself or surrounding it. This is not a recent phenomenon, and we see it everywhere. In the United States, as we'll see, cities including Tulsa, New York, Boston, San Francisco, and New Orleans have expanded into low-lying or coastal areas vulnerable to flooding or onto new, human-made areas. In our NYS2100 work, we learned that most of the areas of Lower Manhattan that flooded during Superstorm Sandy were human-made—landfilling began there as early as 1609.[12]

Cities have expanded into other types of vulnerable areas, in addition to those exposed to water incursion. In Medellin, the city has literally climbed the hillsides around the Aburra Valley as people poured in from the country. The residents of Medellin's San Javier barrio live on one of the city's steepest hillsides, with an incline of as much as 60 degrees.[13] (One of the steepest ski slopes in North America, Alf's High Rustler at Alta, is a mere 47 degrees.[14]) Most houses in San Javier have no foundations or pilings and are susceptible to damage or destruction in landslides, which are common.

Kibera, one of Nairobi's largest slums (with a population of more than 170,000[15]) and one of the largest informal settlements in the world, grew up on either side of the Uganda Railway Line's train tracks. The railway hauls freight between Kisumu, on the shore of Lake Victoria in western Kenya, through Nairobi, and on to Mombasa, Kenya's port city on the Indian Ocean. Kibera's residents use the railway bed as if it were a street—it supports constant foot and animal traffic and small shops are set up alongside—until a train comes through, which it does many times per day, and everybody clears the tracks. The hazards of having a train run through your community are many: air and noise pollution, business disruption, and the risk of injuries and deaths. A train derailed in 2013, collapsing onto its side and crushing flimsy homes and shops beneath its weight. No one was killed. But dozens, even hundreds, of people would have been harmed if circumstances had been different.

The most common type of area for development in growing cities that are short on space is in places where water reigns—riversides, floodplains, wetlands, beachfronts, and territory below sea-level—which are often most vulnerable in severe weather events. These water-proximate developments bring with them stresses and complications, including heightened demands on basic systems such as sanitation, health care, transportation, communications, education, and emergency services (police, fire, medical), as well as on the capacity of the city to support livelihoods through jobs or social safety nets.

When cities and populations are overburdened, chronic stressors grow and can reach a tipping or crisis point. In addition, they are more vulnerable when shocks occur. It is harder to escape a fire or earthquake from an overcrowded building. An overburdened sanitation system is more likely to back up into water supplies and spread disease. These systems do not "fail safely." When they are disrupted they often take other systems down with them.

BETWEEN 2011 AND 2012, the number of internal migrants (those who move within a single country) in the world was estimated at 381 million.[16] Although that is a small percentage of the world's population and rates of migration differ country to country, it is still a significant number and can mean that hundreds of thousands of people pour into a single city over a period of a few years. In Shanghai, China, for example, the inward flow of people currently "exceeds the natural growth rate by a factor of four."[17]

The dominant driver of migration into cities is most frequently what you would expect: economic opportunity and advancement. People move from one place to another to relocate with a company, take a new position, look for a job, start or expand a business.

Most economic migrants do not leave their own countries, and most move from a rural area to an urban one. This rural-urban economic migration is highly pronounced in China because it is a central feature of government policy. By 2025, China intends to move 70 percent of its population—or 900 million people—into cities.[18] As tens of millions of villagers migrate, a large percentage of them construct the buildings that make the urban area larger.[19]

Millions of people also move for reasons other than economic gain. These include voluntary migrants who move to a city in search of a different quality of life (such as greater acceptance of their cultural group), those who move to escape adverse climate change conditions, political refugees who move for fear of persecution or physical harm—such as those who fled Syria in 2013–2014—and those who are known as "displaced persons" for a variety of other reasons.

Civil migration is often driven by a combination of factors, such as the economic and political issues that created a massive migration of people from India's villages into its cities in the years after the country achieved independence in 1947. According to Aromar Revi, director of the Indian Institute for Human Settlements, at the time of independence about 45 percent of India's population lived in villages with populations of fewer than one thousand people. Then, encouraged by the country's new constitution, villagers began to move to the cities in search of economic opportunity and a new social identity.[20]

According to a report by the McKinsey Global Institute, India's urban population grew by 230 million people over a nearly forty-year period, 1971–2008, and could increase by 250 million more in the next twenty years. As of 2008, about 340 million people lived in India's cities, and that number could rise to 590 million by 2030, reaching 40 percent of India's total population. There could be as many as sixty-eight cities with populations of a million people or more, up from forty-two in 2010. The population increase will include an additional 270 million people of working age and an increase of 70 percent in net new employment—more workers and more jobs. The McKinsey Global Institute predicts that India's urbanization will involve a great deal of new development. As much as "700–900 million square meters of commercial and residential space needs to be built—or a new Chicago every year," according to the report, and transportation systems will have to be expanded and other infrastructural improvements made, as well. All of this will fuel and be fueled by economic growth. By 2030, the institute says, India's GDP will have multiplied five times.[21]

The influx of large numbers of newcomers into cities in any part of the world can affect the social cohesion of neighborhoods and communities. In some situations the new residents can, over time, play an important role in strengthening the resilience of a community or city. In Lewiston, Maine, as we have seen, Somali migrants brought robustness and diversity to the community and increased its vitality and strength. In India, the influx of villagers brought new energy and diversity to the cities, but it also led to the swelling of the slums and put stress on infrastructure. Migrant populations are often vulnerable because they have lost their livelihoods and have difficulty adapting to their new circumstances. This can make the community more vulnerable as a whole, especially when disruptions occur. Recently arrived members of a community may have lower awareness of threats and how to prepare for and respond to them and, because they have fewer assets, may require more help in recovery after a crisis.

CLIMATE UNCERTAINTY

As I described in the introduction, Superstorm Sandy was a major wake-up call for residents of the northeastern United States—a clear message that no place, no community, is immune to the effects of climate change and that we will be facing new and intense threats in the years to come. The same is true with extreme weather events in areas around the world.

Although volumes of data show the many ways in which our climate has changed and is changing further still, it's difficult to predict exactly when and how these environmental factors will affect and disrupt human populations and our organizations, systems, and activities. We live in an age that is characterized by climate uncertainty and unpredictability.

THE TEMPERATURE OF the land and ocean surfaces, averaged globally, increased by 0.85° Celsius between the years 1880 and 2012, according to the Intergovernmental Panel on Climate Change (IPCC)—a consortium of thousands of scientists and climate experts that acts under the auspices of the United Nations (UN).[22] The thirty-year span between 1983 and 2012 was, these scientists believe, the warmest period the earth has experienced in 1,400 years.[23] In the United States, according to the US Global Change Research Program, the "average temperature has increased by 1.3 to 1.9 degrees Fahrenheit since 1895 . . . and 2012 was the hottest year on record in the continental United States."[24] In 2014, we experienced the hottest month of May since the start of record keeping in 1880, according to the National Oceanic and Atmospheric Administration. "The combined average temperature over global land and ocean surfaces for May 2014," its statement reads, "was the record highest for the month, at 59.93°F (15.54°C) or 1.33°F (0.74°C) above the 20th century average."[25]

What does the warming of the planet have to do with resilience? Much more than you might imagine. For example, a 2014 report issued by the Center for Naval Analyses Military Advisory Board highlights the impact of climate change on fundamental social and political issues worldwide. "In many areas," the report reads, "the projected impacts of climate change will be more than threat multipliers; they will serve as catalysts for instability and conflict. In Africa, Asia, and the Middle East, we are already seeing how the impacts of extreme weather, such as prolonged drought and flooding—and resulting food shortages, desertification, population dislocation and mass migration, and sea level rise—are posing security challenges to these regions' governments." The report also warns that, in the United States, severe weather disruptions will have a negative effect on military installations, especially those along the coast.[26] In other words, the accelerating rate of climate change poses a severe risk to national security and has become a catalyst for global political conflict.

In addition, cities, communities, organizations, infrastructures, buildings, and systems will be affected because they have been developed for specific climate conditions that are now in flux. We are already witnessing, for example, the "Mediterraneanization" of northern Europe. Rising temperatures and more warm days will make cities like London and even Oslo feel more like areas much farther south. This has implications for city planning, public health management, and building design and construction.[27] As the environments of these cities change, people, organizations, and systems within them will have to adapt. Agriculture, trade, land and building development, infrastructure—all will be affected.

In San Francisco, for example, people have never worried too much about heat. Daniel Homsey, whom we have already met, says that city dwellers there have long relied on a simple, natural method of temperature control. "You open the window in the back room and the front room and the fog cools off your house," he says. But fog-conditioning will likely not be enough to keep San Francisco residents cool in the future, Homsey says, because one of the city's major threats from climate change will be heat waves.

Today, when Homsey works with neighborhoods to craft their resilience action plans, conversation veers toward worries about heat more than the traditional San Francisco threat, earthquakes. For Homsey, the issue is not only one of community resilience but one of personal loss. His aunt—who lived in the Mount Davidson area of the city, the highest geographic point in San Francisco and thus, theoretically anyway, one of its coolest—died in the heat wave of 1999.

A warming planet has other effects on people and communities equally direct and devastating as those they are finding in San Francisco. Hotter days, and more of them, can stress functional capacity and can be a drain on resources, such that it becomes harder to recover from a disruption of any kind when one occurs. The methods we use to keep ourselves and our buildings cool, such as air conditioning systems, often run on fossil fuels, emit greenhouse gases, and, in the long run, make the planet hotter still.

Prolonged episodes of extreme heat—heat waves—can have a devastating effect on human life and on many other species as well. According to a study by the Georgetown Climate Center, "Between 1979 and 2003, extreme heat caused more deaths in the United States than hurricanes, lightning, tornadoes, floods, and earthquakes combined."[28] Data suggest that both the duration and frequency of heat waves is increasing in many parts of the world, especially in large parts of Asia, Australia, and Europe.[29] Although heat waves have always occurred naturally, climatologists from the IPCC estimate that the probability of heat waves has doubled as the result of human activities, including the burning of fossil fuels.

Jane E. Brody, author and expert on science and nutrition, writes about the consequences of intensifying heat on the United States in particular:

> Hot weather kills more Americans than all other natural disasters combined.... With climate change, some experts predict ever-worsening summer heat waves and even more related illnesses and deaths. The Natural Resources Defense Council estimates that excessive heat caused by climate change could kill more than 150,000 Americans by the end of the century in the 40 largest cities. "As carbon pollution continues to rise, the number of dangerously hot days each summer will increase even further, leading to a dramatic increase in the number of lives lost," the council reported. Extreme heat claims an average of 117 lives each year,

but the real incidence is likely far higher. In addition, about 1,800 people die from illnesses made worse by heat, the council estimates. "Death rates from many causes rise during heat waves that are related to heat but not reported as such," said Dr. Christopher B. Colwell, director of emergency medicine at Denver Health Medical Center. "Lots of deaths that occur during heat waves are attributed to natural causes like heart attacks, kidney disease or respiratory disease."[30]

Despite the well-known phenomenon of earth's warming, we tend not to think of heat waves as major threats or as major disruptions when they occur, perhaps because there is rarely an acute event that brings them to our attention—no earthquake moment—or perhaps because their largest effect is on one of our most vulnerable and least visible populations, the elderly.

In 2003, Europe experienced a summer that some scientists believe could have been the hottest in centuries.[31] The temperature began to climb in June and the hot spell lasted through mid-August; temperatures reached highs as much as 30 percent above average. Across the continent that summer, 70,000 deaths could be attributed directly to the effects of heat.[32] The elderly suffered the most. In France, people aged sixty-five and over accounted for nearly four out of every five deaths during the heat wave.[33] Richard Keller, a professor at the University of Wisconsin–Madison, studied the heat wave and found that, in Paris, the majority of the victims were elderly women who lived by themselves, on the upper floors of apartments with no elevators or adequate ventilation. Keller argues that the death toll was "as much a social as a health and epidemiological disaster. There were social factors that made some people much more vulnerable."[34] These numbers are disturbing and do not pertain only to Parisian women. According to CDC figures, cited by the American Association of Retired People, people over sixty-five account for 40 percent of heat-related deaths, although, unlike in Paris, two-thirds of them are men.[35]

In addition to the cost in lives that summer, the heat wave was also a major economic loss. The European economies are estimated to have lost $11.6 billion, and there are likely to be continuing, prolonged economic impacts.[36] Caused by the heat wave's damaging effects on Europe's environment, more than 25,000 fires during the summer of 2003 destroyed nearly 650,000 hectares (2,500 square miles) of forest throughout Europe.[37] Forests are natural sinks for carbon dioxide, used by plants in the process of photosynthesis and thus removed from the atmosphere. The burning of the forests released massive amounts of CO_2 back into the atmosphere, which will inevitably have a warming effect in the future, increasing Europe's vulnerability and susceptibility to even hotter episodes and even greater losses.

OUR OCEANS ARE WARMING, too. The ocean's surface (to a depth of seventy-five meters) has warmed globally at an average rate of 0.11° Celsius each decade since the 1970s. The warming has affected the Greenland and Antarctic ice sheets, which lost ice at rates of 215 and 147 gigatons (a gigaton is one billion tons), respectively, every year between 2002 and 2011.[38] According to the US *National Climate Assessment,* the "dramatic decline of summer sea ice in the Arctic—a loss of ice cover roughly equal to half the area of the continental United States—exacerbates global warming by reducing the reflectivity of Earth's surface and increasing the amount of heat absorbed."[39]

The effects of both phenomena—warming and glacial melt—contribute to one of the most serious threats to human populations, primarily those along the coasts: sea-level rise. Glacial melt puts more water in our oceans, while warmer temperatures cause water to expand, thus raising sea levels. Between 1993 and 2010, the sea has risen at a global average rate of 3.2 millimeters per year, and since the middle of the nineteenth century, the IPCC reports, the rate of sea-level rise has been greater than the average rate over the previous two thousand years. As much as 75 percent of this rise, the IPCC estimates, is attributable to glacial loss and ocean warming.[40] In the United States alone, "global average sea level has risen by about 8 inches" in the last century and, by 2100, may rise another four feet.[41]

The effects of sea-level rise are exacerbated when combined with other environmental factors, such as subsidence. Although many factors contribute to subsidence, most of them are anthropogenic (related to human activity), including the draining of groundwater for purposes of agriculture or development. When underground water reserves are drawn off, sections of surface rock are left unsupported, and they slowly sink into the emptied space.

You need only look at European cities such as Rome, Venice, Amsterdam, and Hamburg to see the disruption that intrusive oceans can bring to a coastline, a city, its buildings, and its people. Guy Nordenson, a civil engineer and expert on coastal resilience and climate adaptation for cities, has studied and worked in such situations around the world.

In many cities beset by floods, Nordenson says, the mind-set has been to keep the water out, rather than to plan for the water to come in on occasion. In Rome, embankments were built to protect against floods from the river Tiber. In Hamburg, a whole new community was created in the former harbor warehouse district, and, to protect against flood, structures were raised by as much as nineteen feet.

But, increasingly, engineers and planners, as well as building owners and insurance companies, realize that walls and embankments and levees have their limitations, especially when it's clear the sea will continue to intrude farther into our built environment. The paradigm is now changing to design buildings, particularly the ground floors, so they can withstand some defined level of flooding that might be caused by the breaching or overwhelming of levees or other barriers. "It's the notion that there are reserve capacities and multiple lines of defense built into any resilient urban design that can deal with the possible failure of the first line of defense," says Nordenson. "This is new thinking in the flood world."[42]

The new thinking is generally known as "living with water" instead of trying to keep it out, and the concept (already well established in the Netherlands) is catching on in places around the world. Rather than create bigger barricades, you adapt your systems so they can continue to function even when water intrudes into areas where it is normally not expected. These solutions typically involve new takes on hard solutions—such as bulkheads, terraced edges, and deployable flood walls—combined with innovative soft approaches, such as parklands, wetlands, vegetation, and bioswales (landscape features that channel water runoff while absorbing harmful elements such as pollutants).

Although actions to mitigate further effects of climate change are urgent, and increasingly so, learning to adapt to sea-level rise and become innovative about ways to live more successfully with water will become an ever more important aspect of building resilience in the face of the climate change impacts that have already occurred. After Superstorm Sandy flooded downtown Manhattan in October 2012, the *New York Times* ran a story, "Rising Seas, Vanishing Coastlines," which imagined the effects of sea-level rise on three cities located along the eastern seaboard of the United States—Boston, New York, and Miami. The scenarios are highly discomfiting. In one scenario, an increase of twelve feet, which the *Times* article cites as possible as early as 2300, would submerge both of New York's airports (as well as Coney Island, the Rockaways, and parts of Jamaica Bay), turn downtown Boston into an island, and flood nearly 75 percent of downtown Miami. Another twelve feet would inundate large segments of all five of New York's boroughs, leave only Boston's most elevated neighborhood, Beacon Hill, and permanently flood Miami's entire metro area.[43]

It's striking to note that other computer models of sea-level rise for both Boston and New York show that, as the water reclaims low-lying land, the footprint of these cities will return to what they looked like originally—before groundwater drainage and landfilling took place.

INCREASED INCIDENCE OF flooding, caused by sea-level rise as well as by ever more intense storms and storm surges, will be experienced around the world. Many areas will also receive heavier rainfalls and greater amounts of precipitation from single-day events, which will also exacerbate flooding.

The effects of all this flooding will be made worse and more complicated as development and populations are increasingly present in coastal areas already vulnerable to flood. That cities have historically been established on coasts is no surprise or accident—water connects the world and its populations far and wide. And that cities have seen such dramatic growth is also not a matter of chance—cities are hubs of opportunity, growth, development, commerce, trade, entertainment, innovation, and other activities of all kinds.

Many cities were originally sited in locations where water intrusion was naturally a part of the environment and an accustomed aspect of life. Much of the area of the cities of the Netherlands—especially Rotterdam and Amsterdam—lies below sea level, where about 60 percent of the country's GDP is produced, thanks to their elaborate water management systems.[44] New Orleans and many other cities were founded and built on low-lying ground or gradually expanded into it. Cities such as Boston and New York grew by filling in marshy areas to make room for commercial and residential development. Boston's Back Bay neighborhood, with its elegant homes and tony shops, was once literally the back bay of Boston Harbor.

Cities regularly developed in floodplains, where land was cheap and new housing could often be erected without going through the elaborate permitting processes required in older or downtown areas. Many cities have both river and ocean frontages. Such places are vulnerable to flooding from both sea-level rise and river overflow, which can cause especially extensive flooding, spread of disease from sanitation overflow, crop destruction from salinity intrusion, and more.

But concern over flooding has done very little to slow the movement of people into coastal areas or to stem the growth of coastal cities. About 600 million people worldwide live on low-elevation areas along the coast, and the bulk of the world's twenty megacities (with 10 million people or more) are in zones at risk from sea-level rise and ocean surges, even those that do not lie right on the water's edge. Imagine: Beijing, Mumbai, Buenos Aires, Los Angeles, Mexico City, Moscow, Delhi, Rio de Janeiro, and New York—all are at risk of water intrusion of some kind.[45]

Coastal cities at risk of flooding are particularly vulnerable because of the density of people living in these places. In 2010, nearly

40 percent of the US population lived in coastal shoreline communities, although the shoreline (excluding Alaska) accounts for less than 10 percent of the land.[46] With large and growing populations exposed to increased risk of sea-level rise and flooding, the capacity of cities to respond to emergencies and catastrophes will be greatly tested in the years to come.

Climate change is also having an effect on storms. In the North Atlantic, hurricanes have increased in frequency, as well as in intensity and duration, and storms are stronger and more severe in all parts of the world.[47] Weather models show that warmer tropical oceans lead to both increased rainfall and stronger winds in cyclone systems, which produce hurricanes and typhoons.[48] By 2100, the intensity of these storms may increase in the range of 2–10 percent.[49]

The devastation of recent hurricanes in the United States, in Haiti, the Philippines, and Indonesia, was not due just to heavy rainfall but to high winds and storm surges—massive volumes of water that accumulate and are pushed onto the land, often intruding great distances, sometimes as far as thirty miles from the coast.[50] As sea levels rise and as storms get more severe, these surges and the high winds that precede them will be more capable of inundating and devastating cities and communities around the world.

DROUGHT OFTEN COMES along with high heat and heat waves, although it occurs in other ways, as well. Drought is not as simple as a lack of rainfall. According to the IPCC, "The term drought may refer to meteorological drought (precipitation well below average), hydrological drought (low river flows and water levels in rivers, lakes and groundwater), agricultural drought (low soil moisture), and environmental drought (a combination of the above). The socio-economic impacts of droughts may arise from the interaction between natural conditions and human factors, such as changes in land use and land cover, water demand and use."[51] So, drought has many causes, can be prolonged over years, and strikes certain areas of the world harder and more often than others, but according to the IPCC it is likely that drought has increased in both intensity and duration in parts of the world since 1970, and will continue to do so throughout this century.[52]

Drought has a significant impact on agricultural production and, subsequently, food security. In 2012, the United States experienced its worst and most extensive drought since the 1950s, affecting 80 percent of agricultural land throughout the country, causing the US Department of Agriculture to declare two thousand US counties as disaster areas.[53] The World Bank estimated that the drought in the United States, combined with a below-average farming season in Europe, caused a spike in global food prices of 10 percent between the months of June and July.[54] The worst droughts in the world are frequently in the Sahel, the central region of Africa that stretches from the Atlantic Ocean to the Red Sea. That area has experienced three major droughts in the past decade, the most recent of which destroyed most crops and led to widespread food insecurity and shortages.[55] There was widespread starvation and considerable loss of life.

Prolonged droughts have other far-reaching and potentially disruptive consequences. As farmers are unable to produce crops and are therefore unable to provide for themselves or their families, many will become climate refugees. This kind of population influx will undoubtedly test governments' ability to provide for their citizens and sustain functioning operations under an increased load, and the refugees will vie with existing residents in the contest to secure dwindling resources.

Thomas Friedman, the *New York Times* columnist, makes the connection between drought and political, as well as economic, outcomes, as manifested in the conflict in Syria. In 2006, Syria experienced a drought the UN would come to describe as the country's worst in forty years. In 2008, through its UN food and agriculture representative Abdullah bin Yehia, Syria requested more than $20 million to help some 15,000 farmers manage through the drought, which impacted over a million people.[56]

In a communication between the US Embassy in Damascus and the US State Department, discussing potential US involvement in contributing aid, one agent wrote, and Friedman quotes, "If UNFAO

[United Nations Food and Agriculture Organization] efforts fail, Yehia predicts mass migration from the northeast, which could act as a multiplier on social and economic pressures already at play and undermine stability." If this were to become true, a "system already burdened by a large Iraqi refugee population may not be able to absorb another influx of displaced persons, Yehia explained, particularly at this time of rising costs, growing dissatisfaction of the middle class, and a perceived weakening of the social fabric and security structures that Syrians have come to expect."[57]

A million farmers were affected, many of whom wound up looking for jobs and places to live in Syria's already strained and crowded cities, including Damascus and Homs, and when the Arab Spring began with protests and uprisings in Tunisia and Egypt, similarly dissatisfied Syrians had cause—and numbers—to stage a similar revolt. The resulting civil war—ongoing at the time of this writing—has caused more than 160,000 deaths.[58]

POLITICAL AND ENVIRONMENTAL issues related to climate change have caused various types of population displacements around the world, and they seriously test the resilience of the people affected and of the societies in which they live.

About a three-hour drive from Nairobi lies the newly established community of Lemolo A and Lemolo B, a collection of wood and cement buildings set in the rolling countryside of the Rift Valley. Leonard Korgoren, one of the two thousand Lemolo A residents, is a member of the Ogiek people, and, until 2009, he lived in the Mau Forest, approximately one hundred kilometers from Lemolo. There he followed a traditional livelihood that included a diverse set of activities, including beekeeping, collecting and selling firewood, hunting, foraging, and planting and harvesting small plots of maize.

The Ogiek had sustained themselves this way for decades in the Mau and might have continued to do so indefinitely. However, beginning in the 1980s, as the result of political and cultural disputes, native peoples in other areas of the country were disrupted and migrated to the great forest. They did not have the forest-dwellers' skills or attitude, however, and lived differently than did the Ogiek. They cleared trees to make room for their villages and cut down more to burn into charcoal and sell as fuel in the fast-growing nearby towns. In the past, Ogiek had picked up dead tree limbs and sold them as firewood, but now, with market competition, they began cutting down live trees, too.

Over a period of two decades, the Mau lost more than 25 percent of its 400,000-hectare forest, the result of cutting by forest inhabitants as well as by commercial loggers.[59] This deforestation became a serious problem for the entire Mau region, for Kenya, and even for neighboring countries. The Mau forest is the largest rain catchment area in the country, the origin of several rivers that feed lakes throughout Kenya and in Tanzania, and an essential source of water for the region. The rivers receded. Drought was prolonged. With this ecosystem service—water—threatened, downstream agriculture, cattle ranches, and tea plantations were affected, as was hydroelectric power generation.

The cause of the problem was deemed to be the presence of the 50,000 forest inhabitants, most of whom had no legal rights to the land. In 2004, the Kenyan government began a program of forced evacuations, and in 2008 the prime minister ordered that the forest be completely cleared of people.[60]

In 2009, Korgoren received his eviction notice. He had fourteen days to leave. "The forest policemen came and destroyed our houses so we couldn't return," Korgoren says. "They destroyed the fences. Animals got into the farms and destroyed our crops."[61] Korgoren and several hundred other Ogiek families were moved to a camp, where they stayed for three years, and then they moved to Lemolo. Each household was given a two-and-a-quarter-acre plot of land on which to farm maize, but gone were the beekeeping, firewood production, and hunting. To plant maize now they must buy seeds and fertilizer, which they can't afford. To grow enough crops to earn a living they must plant larger areas than they did in the forest, for which they need a tractor so they can plow, a piece of equipment that is completely beyond their means to buy or even rent.

The people of Lemolo are trying to build a community from scratch. They have erected homes and a schoolhouse, but they don't have enough teachers. There is no river nearby, and the rainfall is light and unpredictable in comparison to what they knew in the Mau. Clean water is hard to come by. But things are getting better, and Korgoren says he now feels "some hope that we are going to survive here." Still, the people of Lemolo are probably years away from being able to get beyond a subsistence existence. And it may take decades for the Mau Forest to come back to full functioning as a water resource.

The goal of the displacement may well have been to increase the resilience of the forest and to attempt to restore an important ecosystem service, but was it necessary to cause disruption to a large group of people to do so? Professor Alex Awiti, director of the East African Institute at the Aga Khan University, thinks not. "People and forests can coexist," he says.[62] Rather than being moved out, the indigenous peoples might have been given education and guidance, tools and practices, for living differently with the disrupted forest system so they could play a role in bringing it back. "We're missing an opportunity to work with communities to regenerate these forests," Awiti says. Their cottage industries, such as beekeeping, could have been supported and expanded into saleable products made from honey, wax, and the medicinal plants the Ogiek typically gather in the forest. There would also have to be stricter regulations regarding the cutting of trees. The Ogiek know the forest best and might be best positioned to help it recover—with help and partnership from the government and aid organizations.

The lesson: it's essential to deal with interrelated twenty-first-century problems through an integrated and inclusive process that builds resilience, rather than only through top-down solutions that deal with symptoms (new forest dwellers) rather than causes (climate change and economic stress).

GLOBALIZATION

The process of globalization, which has been going on for the past three decades and continues today, causes its own disruptions and also interconnects with and intensifies the other two twenty-first-century factors. Globalization involves industrial growth and a massive increase in demand for materials and ecosystem services (primarily water), both of which affect the environment and contribute to climate change. Globalization has created intricate networks of economic connections, especially among cities, that, along with technological advances that increase the speed of many kinds of activity, cause disruptions to cascade more quickly and with more devastating effect across geographic and political borders, cultural boundaries, and commercial supply chains and relationships.

Although globalization intensified in the latter half of the twentieth century and the world continues to globalize in the twenty-first, it has been a disruptive factor for centuries. Historian Alfred W. Crosby argues that it really began with Christopher Columbus and his voyage to the New World. "In 1491, the world was in many of its aspects and characteristics a minimum of two worlds—the New World, of the Americas, and the Old World, consisting of Eurasia and Africa," Crosby told an interviewer. "Columbus brought them together, and almost immediately and continually ever since, we have had an exchange of native plants, animals and diseases moving back and forth across the oceans between the two worlds. A great deal of the economic, social, political history of the world is involved in the exchange of living organisms between the two worlds."[63] Today, the post-Columbian exchange between the two worlds continues, has accelerated, and now involves almost every aspect of economic, social, political, and environmental activity.

IN 1857, THE AMERICAN AUTHOR NATHANIEL HAWTHORNE WROTE, "I am inclined to think that Glasgow is the stateliest city I ever beheld." [64] Indeed, throughout much of the eighteenth, nineteenth, and twentieth centuries, Glasgow was not only one of the stateliest cities in Europe—with its grand public architecture, impressive infrastructure, attractive city squares and green spaces, and a thriving arts scene—but also one of the most prosperous, in part thanks to its participation in the great global exchange of goods. Located on the banks of the river Clyde, which flows into the Atlantic, Glasgow blossomed as an international trade hub and industrial powerhouse, made wealthy by its commercial activities in tobacco trading, textiles, dyeing, steel working, engineering, locomotive manufacture, and, most famously, shipbuilding. Between 1870 and 1914, Glasgow's shipbuilders produced nearly twenty percent of the world's vessels.[65] In the 1930s, Glasgow shipyards produced two of the most iconic ocean liners ever built, the *Queen Mary* and the *Queen Elizabeth*.

But after World War II, as the world began to globalize, the nature of industry changed, and new types of commercial activity arose—particularly computing and other electronics businesses—Glasgow failed to change with the times. It clung to its shipbuilding enterprises even as other countries developed more efficient methods of manufacture and the big contracts went to companies in Korea and China and elsewhere. Glasgow's traditional strengths—in heavy manufacture and labor-intensive work—became liabilities. By the 1970s, the city had lost much of its industrial base and, with it, most of its jobs. With so many people made redundant and so little economic vitality, Glasgow went into a period of decline. The infrastructure, especially the public transportation system, suffered from lack of investment. Housing stock dwindled. Living conditions worsened. People struggled with poverty. Crime rates were higher than elsewhere in the UK. Alcoholism became a serious public health problem and the rate of heart disease soared to the point that Glasgow became known as the "heart attack capital of Europe." Some areas of the city, particularly the East End—once vibrant and teeming with activity—were hit particularly hard. Alastair Brown is a native Glaswegian and now the chief resilience officer for the city. "In the 1970s and early '80s," he says, "a lot of people looked upon Glasgow as an undesirable destination. It was seen as a grimy city, associated with crime and poverty. Glasgow had a poor image."

The city tried to respond, as so many other cities did, by developing social housing units. But they were on the outskirts of the city, not integrated into the urban fabric, and they became worlds unto themselves, cut off from the heart of Glasgow.[66] It seemed that the harder the city tried, the worse things became. "If you were to use a modern-day comparison," says Brown, "we were in danger of heading toward the way Detroit looks now." Glasgow's former stateliness was covered over with grime and obscured by pollution. As the tide of globalization raised the boats in distant harbors, Glasgow seemed to be sinking.

For decades, Glasgow suffered from the chronic stresses and constant disruptions brought about by its inability to find a new way in a changing world. It was not that the city was unaware of its vulnerabilities. Government officials, city planners, and residents knew something had to be done. But the city lacked leadership. Businesses and civic organizations were weak. There was little integration among social groups and no shared vision of what Glasgow could, or should, become. The city was deficient in the characteristics of resilience and did not know how to strengthen them. As a result, Glasgow faced the grim possibility of becoming a failed city. But, as we shall see, Glasgow—a city that had once prospered through the Columbian exchange and then suffered as its rules changed—found that globalization could become a boon once again.

GLOBALIZATION HAS INDEED BEEN A BOON and brought many benefits to people around the world. Illiteracy has been reduced—by as much as half in the last thirty years. Poverty, too, is loosening its grip. About 80 percent of the global population lives in countries where poverty is on the decline. People have access to advances in health and medicine, physical and social sciences, as never before. Yet globalization has not solved the world's problems—a billion people still live in poverty, without even basic services—and it has brought with it new disruptions, as well, just as Crosby asserts.[67]

In the field of health, for example, which is an essential asset and contributor to resilience, our global advances in medical treatment, and the sharing of knowledge worldwide, has also increased the incidence of iatrogenic disease—disease or illness caused by medical treatment, such as complications from surgery, hospital infections, or unintended harmful drug interactions, which killed approximately 225,000 Americans in 2000, making it the third-most likely cause of death after heart disease and cancer.[68] The so-called lifestyle diseases—including heart disease and obesity—can also be at least partly attributed to globalization, because they are largely a phenomenon of affluent societies and those where the middle class is expanding. These diseases are linked to such factors as smoking, diet, exercise, stress, and unhealthy body weight, which are, to a large degree, under our control and are affected by the type of work we do, our cultural behaviors, the foods available to us, and the amount of income we have to devote to nonessential goods and services.[69] According to the Centers for Disease Control and Prevention, nearly 70 percent of Americans over the age of twenty are classified as either overweight or obese, with 35 percent falling into the latter category.[70] In China, the percentage of the population identified as either overweight or obese jumped from 25 percent in 2002 to 38.5 percent in 2010. The WHO predicts that by 2015 more than half the Chinese population will be overweight or obese.[71] Today, obesity has become a greater global health threat than hunger or malnutrition.[72]

The Columbian exchange of infectious diseases also continues. Today, with our mobile and connected lives, an infected person can carry a disease around the world in less than a day. Diseases carried by mosquitos kill 750,000 people each year.[73] Even diseases that we thought had been conquered can return to trouble us. In 2014, the WHO issued a warning about the spread of the wild poliovirus and the rise of the incidence of polio in Syria, Israel, Pakistan, and several African countries. Sixty percent of all worldwide cases were the "result of international spread of wild poliovirus," the WHO statement reads, "and there was increasing evidence that adult travellers contributed to this spread."[74]

We would like to think that we have the medical defenses to protect us from both lifestyle and infectious disease. And of course we have developed an impressive array of antibiotics and other medications that can effectively prevent, treat, and manage the morbidity and mortality rate of these diseases. But our medical advances bring with them a new threat: the emergence of new antibiotic-resistant organisms. These could, according to Dr. Margaret Chan, director general of the WHO, put "an end to modern medicine as we know it. Things as common as strep throat or a child's scratched knee could once again kill."[75]

Our globalized economy is also contributing to a world where it can be dangerous just to breathe air or drink water. In late 2013, an eight-year-old girl living in the Jiangsu Province of China was diagnosed with lung cancer. The cause, said her doctor, was air pollution.[76] According to the WHO, one in eight global deaths in 2012—7 million in total—was caused by exposure to air pollution.[77] We face a problem with polluted water, too. A 2007 study by researchers at Cornell University concluded that contaminated drinking water affected 1.2 billion people around the world and led to 80 percent of all cases of infectious diseases.[78]

So, as much as we have globalized and improved the world, we have also introduced new vulnerabilities and threats. Urbanization and climate change will continue to be important factors for years to come, with the effects of heat, drought, and extreme weather events exacerbated for vulnerable urban populations. Globalization will not be reversed. And there are many other factors to consider as we assess our vulnerabilities to disruption, such as aging and inadequate infrastructure—from insecure power grids to failing gas pipes to bridges reaching the end of their lifespans—as well as political instability, wealth disparities, and threats to ecosystems.

Ecosystems are affected by all three twenty-first-century factors—climate change, urbanization, and globalization—just as human systems and built environments are, and it's important to consider the contribution that ecosystems make to building resilience. Ecosystems provide essential services that human beings rely on, including freshwater flows, pollination, disease and pest regulation, waste management, and climate change mitigation. As Fred Boltz, managing director for ecosystems at The Rockefeller Foundation puts it, "The ability of ecosystems to respond to changes in the biosphere in a manner that does not interrupt their provision of these services" is key to human resilience. "We have to recognize that ecosystems are an asset for human development and that their resilience—the resilience of the planetary system—underpins our own resilience."[79]

I DO NOT MEAN TO be alarmist about the state of the world—but I am alarmed. The threats we face to our personal health, to the health and stability of our communities and cities, to our natural systems, and even to our species, are formidable and growing in number and severity, affecting larger and more densely settled populations.

The very good news is that we have faced critical periods many times in the past, during which problems seemed insurmountable, but we have always found ways to meet the challenges. I have no doubt that with resilience building through innovation and collaboration, we can find solutions to prevent the problems of the world from accelerating toward planetary disaster—and take us instead toward a resilience dividend.

5

HOW CRISIS BECOMES DISASTER
The Human Factor

We face many threats in our twenty-first-century world, but not all the threats we can identify or imagine are likely to materialize, and, what's more, most disruptions—weather events or health incidents or financial losses—do not cause serious or long-lasting damage to the system.

After all, we can and do live with a rather steady, low-level series of disruptive incidents and chronic stresses that determine what kind of day we have or that affect, to a greater or lesser degree, how effective we are in our daily lives and how well our businesses and organizations function. Indeed, it takes a degree of resilience to manage even these everyday disruptions and continue functioning within a range of variation.

Sometimes, however, a disruption becomes a disaster. The disruptive event escalates into a crisis of great proportion, catalyzes other problems, cascades across domains and scales, spins things out of control, and disturbs human activity to an abnormal, unpredictable, and often unimaginable degree, causing injury and loss of life, destruction of property, damage to livelihoods, and upheavals in social, political, and economic endeavors.

What causes a disruption to become a disaster? *We do.* Disasters are almost always human made or, at least, intensified by how well people have prepared for, responded to, and recovered from a crisis. Disasters are the result of disruptions coinciding with vulnerabilities, our lack of awareness of the threats we face, our lack of diversity of options and choices to prevent disruptions or manage them when they occur, our inability to integrate our ideas and actions into effective solutions, and our instability and poor adaptiveness to new circumstances as they emerge.

These are the factors that make for disaster, as the people of Halifax, Nova Scotia, discovered in 1917.

THE GREATEST EXPLOSION IN THE HISTORY OF THE WORLD

Samuel Henry Prince was a pioneer in the field of disaster research, the first to talk about the complexity of disruptions and, most important, to describe how social factors always play a role in determining how disruptions play out and how they turn into disasters.

Prince's work began with a remarkable study of the explosion of the French munitions ship *Mont Blanc,* which occurred when it collided, while under way, with a second ship in the harbor of Halifax, Nova Scotia, on December 6, 1917. The cargo of the *Mont Blanc* contained trinitrotoluol, TNT, the most powerful explosive known at the time, and the collision caused "the greatest single explosion in the history of the world," as Prince describes it—a distinction it retained until the atom bomb blasts over Japan in 1945.[1]

Prince was in Halifax on the day of the explosion and narrowly escaped injury, perhaps death, himself. He saw firsthand how a single disruptive shock can unleash cascading shocks and disturbances. He saw how long-standing vulnerabilities can be unexpectedly exposed and also how people and institutions can respond with unpredictably great quantities of resilience.

The explosion was so colossal that Prince writes that the blast and its aftermath delivered "the combined horrors of war, earthquake, fire, flood, famine and storm—a combination seen for the first time in the records of human disaster." The city of Halifax shook as if it had "palsy." The sea "rushed forward in a giant tidal wave," drowning two hundred people. There was a "riot of fires" and a giant "death-cloud" hung overhead. A "tornado-like gas blast" tore trees from the ground, stopped trains on the tracks, slammed ships against the docks, catapulted people into the air, and rained down scalding iron fragments. War veterans said they had seen nothing so terrible in their worst battlefield experiences.

All told, some 2,000 people died; 6,000 more were injured. Property damage was estimated at $35 million and three hundred acres of land were left "a smoking waste"—with "churches, schools, factories blown down or burned."[2]

Prince realized that the effect of the disaster went well beyond death, damage, and disruption of ordinary functioning—indeed, he saw widespread social breakdown. There was "disintegration of the home and the family," the "government was in perplexity," the transportation system was dislocated, and "the wheels of industry ceased in their turning." It was so bad, he writes, that "the city ceased to be a city."[3] He compares Halifax to Pompeii—the ancient city buried alive by a volcano.

The disaster of the *Mont Blanc* was a socially constructed event, in that the conditions that escalate disruptions into disasters are created or caused by people. Crises become disasters when vulnerabilities are exposed, handling of the crisis is flawed, or other factors come into play. As the editors of the *Handbook of Disaster Research* put it, "The problems created by disasters are usually those that existed before: poor land use, unenforced building codes, lack of attention to mitigating community risks, poverty, inadequate medical care, substandard housing, among others. The best way to understand disaster effects is to know what the community was like prior to the disaster event."[4]

In the case of the Halifax explosion, the human contributions to the making of the disaster were numerous. The ship itself was just one of many moored in the capacious Halifax Harbour. Exactly how much risky cargo lay aboard the ships at any given time is not, according to Prince, publicly known. "Certainly there was too much to breed a sense of safety," he writes, "but no one gave the matter a second thought." This was no doubt partly because Halifax had long been a military place—"born as a military settlement," Halifax had been a "garrison city and naval station for more than a hundred and fifty years," Prince writes.

Times had changed, as had the nature and destructive power of munitions, but there was not sufficient awareness of the grave threat that faced the city of Halifax nor commitment to do anything about it. What's more, the *Mont Blanc,* 330 feet long, had been dangerously overloaded with munitions in New York, the port of departure, carrying 450,000 pounds of TNT, plus an additional 2,300 tons of another explosive substance, picric acid.[5] Although some alterations had been made to the ship to reduce the threat of fire and explosion, the cargo was still, in the judgment of author Rebecca Solnit, a "reckless" one.[6] (The 2014 sinking of the South Korean ferry that killed hundreds of passengers, most of them high school students, appears to have been loaded with cars and cargo in a similarly reckless fashion.[7])

The ship that collided with the *Mont Blanc,* the *Imo,* was an even larger vessel, more than 400 feet long, and it disregarded the basic rules of the sea as it steamed out of the harbor, which led to a confusion of signals, and the *Imo* plowed into the *Mont Blanc.* The collision sparked a fire in the hold. The crew, terrified of the inevitable result, abandoned ship and rowed away as fast as they could. When they reached shore, they ran, not trying to raise an alarm or warn the townspeople. Without a crew on board to try to steer the ship away from town, the burning ship drifted in toward shore. Having no knowledge of or warning about the explosives aboard, the fire department rushed to the scene intending to douse the flames, and citizens gathered to watch, instead of getting away from the area. The city of Halifax was neither ready nor prepared for such a threat. So, with the Halifax explosion, we see at least two of the factors identified by the *Handbook*: "unenforced" codes (in this case, disregarded shipping protocols) and "lack of attention to mitigating community risks."

TABLE 5.1. MOST EXPENSIVE NATURAL DISASTERS SINCE 1980[8]

DISASTER	YEAR	REGION	COST (US$)
Earthquake and tsunami	2011	Japan	$210,000,000,000
Hurricane Katrina and storm surge	2005	United States	125,000,000,000
Earthquake	1995	Japan	100,000,000,000
Earthquake	2008	China	85,000,000,000
Hurricane Sandy and storm surge	2012	Caribbean; United States	65,000,000,000
Earthquake	1994	United States	44,000,000,000
Floods	2011	Thailand	43,000,000,000
Hurricane Ike	2008	Caribbean; United States	38,000,000,000
Floods	1998	China	30,700,000,000
Earthquake and tsunami	2010	Chile	30,000,000,000

WE OFTEN CALCULATE THE LOSS of disasters in financial terms in order to try to understand their effect. The stated cost of a disruption is always an estimate and typically covers only those tangibles that can be priced—usually the cost of relief and of insured or replacement value of property—but these estimates, however inadequate, give us a sense of just how major a drain on our resources disaster can be.

As I've mentioned, the World Bank estimates that, between 1980 and 2012, global financial losses from physical damage brought about by disasters amounted to $3.8 trillion. Nearly three-quarters of that loss ($2.8 trillion)—and, indeed, more than 85 percent of all disasters—was caused by weather events and weather extremes: tsunamis, hurricanes, tornadoes, flooding, and drought.[9] The loss from the 2010 earthquake in Haiti was about $14 billion in reconstruction costs.[10] The losses from the global financial crisis that began in 2008 have been estimated as high as $25 trillion in the United States alone, or as much as 165 percent of the country's gross domestic product.[11] Obviously, we are spending huge sums recovering from these extreme and damaging events, more than we should afford and more than we need to. And, of course, there is no number that can be used to calculate the loss of life these disasters usually produce.

TULSA: FORMER FLOOD CITY

Tulsa, Oklahoma, has become a more resilient city and is cutting the amount of its losses from disruption, but it took a crisis moment—although hardly as bad as the one Halifax experienced—for it to finally come to terms with its long-standing issues of flooding, unregulated development, declining property values, and inadequate insurance. Today, the people of Tulsa are learning to live with water, have one of the most well-regarded flood protection programs in the country, and, as a result, they value the resilience-building process and know that it can help them face other changes in climate and population conditions.

You may not think of Tulsa, Oklahoma—or the midwestern United States, for that matter—as a place beset by the wicked problems of the twenty-first century. Urbanization in a city of 400,000 people? Climate change in a place that boasts of its location in the "heart of green country" and enjoys 221 days of sunshine a year, with an average daily temperature of 61° Fahrenheit?[12] Yes, images may come to mind of a tornado whipping through the rolling fields and tearing off roofs. (Oklahoma does lie in the heart of "Tornado Alley," the area of greatest tornado activity in the United States.) Or you might think that drought or heat would be the city's major threats. But the City of Tulsa, founded on the banks of the Arkansas River and officially incorporated in 1898, faced, for most of the twentieth century, the challenge shared with communities around the world: managing rapid urban development in a place of persistent flooding.

When, just after the turn of the twentieth century, two oil fields were discovered near Tulsa, population boomed. In 1910, the population was just under 35,000. By 1920 it had more than tripled, as almost 110,000 people called Tulsa home.[13]

From those earliest days, the threat of flood was evident. In 1908, flooding along the Arkansas River caused roughly $21 million in damages (in 2014 dollars).[14] A flood in 1923 resulted in losses of $19 million, and left 4,000 Tulsans homeless or displaced. This spurred citizens to action, devising the city's first-ever flood plan, which included moving the waterworks to higher ground and leaving lowland areas as parks and recreation areas.[15] It seemed as though Tulsa had begun to think in terms of resilience, making plans for long-term safety and adaptability.

But after World War II, when the United States was in the midst of an economic boom and the population of Tulsa continued to rise, new developments extended into the floodplains of the Arkansas River and its tributary creeks. Flooding of these newly urban areas in the 1950s eventually led to the construction of the Keystone Dam by the Army Corps of Engineers. One of its unintended secondary effects, in retrospect, was a false sense of security. The presence of the dam reduced the frequency of flooding, and therefore people were less worried about the problem of floodplain development and less inclined to take further action.

In the 1960s, Tulsa's population boomed again, growing another 25 percent. To accommodate this population, development continued in the floodplains and lowlands of the tributaries of the Arkansas, especially the Mingo Creek area to the east.[16] People had to live *somewhere,* and the cheap, flat land of the floodplains attracted developers and appealed to buyers. It was an easy, simple solution that addressed an immediate problem but without a focus on the long-term viability of those developments. Unchecked by municipal or federal regulations, builders built and people bought. And then they were flooded.

Throughout the 1960s and 1970s, Tulsa didn't go more than four years without a significant flood. Flooding in 1974 was particularly devastating: in April and May, flooding at Bird Creek resulted in losses of more than $3.4 million; June floods at Joe, Fry, Haikey and Mingo Creeks cost another $64.4 million; and, in September, some residents of Tulsa along Mingo Creek were flooded for the third time that year.

Ann Patton was a witness to the worst of the flooding—and to its solution. Today, at seventy-seven, she has retired to a life of personal writing (in 2012 she published *Dan's War on Poverty*, chronicling an antipoverty crusader's work in Tulsa, and in 2014 published *The Tulsa River* about the Arkansas River at Tulsa), but during the peak flooding years Patton worked as a reporter for the *Tulsa World*, Tulsa's main newspaper. She remembers the period that followed the 1974 floods well, as it marked what she calls Tulsa's "Great Drainage War."

"There was a huge citizen uprising," she says. "We had decades of civil war between the developers and the flooded housewives, and no one knew what to do."[17] Patton, as a reporter, did what she could— wrote story after story about Tulsa's flooding woes as well as issues of flood management, sometimes citing the work and theory of Gilbert White (1911–2006), often considered the father of floodplain management.

"Homebuilders in the development community believed that the floods we were having were freak floods," she says, "and that you couldn't organize your community around some bizarre, occasional occurrence." Patton disagreed and said so. "I was not at all objective. I sided with the people in the creeks, because it seemed to me that was no way to live. Why would you want a community where big swaths of people periodically wash away and die? Why would you live that way?"

In 1976, another flood struck. It killed three people, damaged more than 3,000 buildings, and caused damage of some $120 million.[18] By this point, unrest and outrage that nothing had been done to lessen the scope of Tulsa's flooding—and that developers were still being allowed to create new housing in the floodplains—boiled over. A protest at City Hall finally instigated governmental action, wide-reaching floodplain management directives, and development and institution of early warning systems.[19] Although this marked significant progress and reflected a turn of thinking to the long term, a necessary component of planning and building for resilience, it turned out not to be enough. The worst was yet to come.

Tulsa experienced its most devastating flood on record in 1984—an event that Patton refers to as the "Come to Jesus flood." In the middle of the night on Memorial Day, some fifteen inches of rainfall caused widespread water incursion. Come morning, 14 were dead, another 288 injured. Seven thousand buildings were damaged or destroyed. Relief and rebuilding efforts cost more than $400 million.[20]

Patton recalls an emergency meeting held in the basement of City Hall as the rain was still pouring down. "We knew almost nothing about what was happening," she says, "because the emergency communication system was so poor. Every so often somebody would run in and say, 'Well, they've found somebody else dead at this place and that place.' It was truly hell." Without feedback loops and diverse and redundant modes of communication, without capacity to generate situational awareness on a city level, Patton and others were, quite literally, in the dark.

Along with Patton in the basement was recently elected Mayor Terry Young, whom Patton describes as "young, remarkable, and brash." Young was adamant that no mayor should ever go through that experience again, and he was not the only convert to champion the cause. Equally concerned was the street commissioner, J. D. Metcalfe, and a small cadre of technical experts including engineer Charles L. Hardt, attorney Stan Williams, and planner Ron Flanagan. They pulled together a powerful team. One of the largest floodplain developers, Patton remembers, had a change of heart about his activity, but only after his sister survived the flood by standing on her kitchen table, holding her infant above the rising water. "He came to the city commission meeting after the flood and said, 'I will build no more in any floodplain in this community, and I will do whatever it takes to bring this community back.'"

The Come to Jesus flood of 1984 was a turning point, and Patton will be the first to tell you that. Further proof that it too often takes an acute, watershed event, a crossing of a threshold, to catalyze action that includes long-term planning for prevention and recovery. But it also required great technical skill, extraordinary political courage, and a cohesive, connected community, asserting its will to insist that changes be made, that lives and livelihoods be protected. "It was a grassroots movement. I don't think there's any other way to put it," says Patton. The community became aware of the fact that, not only was flooding a persistent threat, but their lives and livelihoods were, and would continue to be, at grave risk if significant changes were not made.

In 2014, with its comprehensive flood protection program in place, along with the new development regulations, the city has "no record of flooding in any structure built in accord with those regulations."[21] And, because Tulsans have a very different mind-set about water, Patton is more confident that the city is prepared to withstand the next hundred-year flood. "We learned how to pull ourselves together from the top floor of city hall to the bottom of a creek," she says, and "how to create a community consensus from the bottom up, with action and follow through to get results." Before the flood? "We did almost everything wrong," she says. "But we've done a lot right since." From establishing parks in floodplains to developing comprehensive building and drainage regulations, Tulsans have built their resilience and are now realizing the dividend: they enjoy the lowest flood insurance rates in the United States, which frees up resources for other endeavors, and national recognition as a community capable of successfully building resilience, which makes Tulsa an even more attractive place to work and live.[22] In earlier days, Tulsans knew they had a problem. Addressing that problem helped integrate groups within the community, produced diversity of opinions and options for improvements, and, most important, generated an awareness that "things" would not change—Tulsa would have to change itself. "We all have to take responsibility for our own salvation as best we can," says Patton, "with all the help we can get."

Still, for all Tulsa's progress, Patton knows that vulnerabilities remain. "The story of a resilient city is rewritten every day in countless small and large decisions by many people and requires, to use a cliché, eternal vigilance," she says. "In fact, as progress reduces the frequency of flood disasters, for example, apathy becomes a very real danger. As someone said, 'When the water dries out, so does the commitment.'"

As our planet's climate continues to change, as our population grows and increasingly flows into cities, and as those cities struggle to find ways to accommodate their growth, situations like the one in Tulsa will become more and more common, in the United States and around the world.

It will take commitment, action, and—I regret to say—many more existential moments for individuals, communities, and organizations to realize that climate disruptions, safety, community cohesion, and the built environment are all intimately connected and interrelated. The best time to effect change is *before* the threats, especially the known ones, take too great a toll.

"Resilience, in the classic meaning of the word," Patton says, "means the ability to bounce back." She believes the best defense against disaster is a strong community of people who are educated and informed about threats, who care about each other and the community, and who are willing to work together to be ready for whatever may come. They need to be able to identify what's wrong, determine what they're going to do about it, and then *do* it.

"And from those actions," Patton says, "I get a sense of peace, and I can live my life."

Utøya: Unaware and Unprepared

Sometimes a crisis escalates into a disaster that carries such impact and causes such damage that it can shake a community—even a whole society—to its core. This is particularly true when the disaster reveals a vulnerability the society had not been aware of or has not been compelled to confront fully. To do this, the disruption has to be on a scale that far exceeds other disruptions or seemingly be out of character for the society in which it takes place.

For Americans, 9/11 was such a disaster: there had been terrorist attacks before, even one on the World Trade Center, but this one was on such a scale that it forced people to come to grips with the fact that the United States was vulnerable to attack on its own soil.

For Norwegians, the date is July 22, the Friday afternoon in 2011 when Anders Breivik, an ethnic Norwegian citizen, murdered seventy-seven people—eight of them killed when a car bomb exploded at a government building in downtown Oslo and sixty-nine shot at a political youth camp on the tiny island of Utøya. The report of the 22 July Commission, the official group that investigated the Breivik shootings, calls the attacks the "most shocking and incomprehensible acts ever experienced in Norway."[23] The BBC goes further, calling it in a documentary program the "worst act of mass murder by a terrorist acting alone in the history of the world."[24] That's impossible to verify, but the assertion provides a sense of how people perceive the magnitude of this event.

Breivik's acts brought to the surface a long-simmering tension in Norwegian society regarding its multiculturalism, particularly its social attitudes and official policies regarding immigration and the acceptance of political refugees. Breivik, who saw the increasing presence of Muslims in Norway as detrimental to society, expressed the tension in public acts that forced the issue into the center of the national conversation. Norway became brutally aware that it was vulnerable to the kinds of disruption, including terrorist violence, that it believed could not happen in that country. Indeed, the 22 July report states that "hardly anyone could have imagined" such an attack taking place, especially at the youth camp. Norway is a peaceful country, after all, with only twenty-nine intentional homicides in 2010 in a country of some 5 million people.[25] "Sadly, however," the report goes on, "after repeated school massacres in other countries, an armed desperado who shoots adolescents is indeed conceivable—also in Norway."[26]

In the aftermath of the attacks, the conventional wisdom seemed to be that the attacks could have been prevented or, at the very least, handled more effectively, especially by the official first responders. The 22 July report came out in August of 2012 and presented, in five hundred pages, the many failings (and some successes) in detail.

There were repercussions. Norway's police chief, who had earlier apologized for the slow response of his force, resigned his position. In the elections of 2013, prime minister Jens Stoltenberg, a member of the Labor Party—which Breivik reviled for what he considered its liberal views—lost his bid for re-election and Erna Solberg, a member of the Conservative Party, came into power.

It's impossible to say if the July 22 attacks could have been prevented—although many claim they could have been—but it is clear that Norwegians, both citizens and authorities, were not fully aware of their vulnerability, nor were they prepared to deal with a disruption of this kind. To begin with, Breivik had been preparing for his attacks for many years and took actions that could, and did, raise red flags, which were largely ignored. For example, to construct his bomb, Breivik needed large quantities of fertilizer and an isolated place to work, so he took up residence in a farm to make the purchases look legitimate. He told people he was there to grow sugar beets, but did no farming.[27] He bought chemicals and other materials used in bomb-making, including a fifteen-meter fuse, from an online supplier based in Poland. Norwegian customs was alerted to the transactions and Breivik was placed on a watch list, but no investigation was conducted. He purchased a Ruger semi-automatic rifle, which he said he planned to use to hunt large game, although such rifles are not normally used for hunting, and Breivik did not hunt. In order to purchase a Glock pistol, he joined a shooting club and took lessons in the gun's use, but did not otherwise participate in club activities.

It's tempting, in hindsight, to say that Breivik could and should have been identified as a likely terrorist or mass murderer, but the same is often said of spree killers and terrorists, including some of the perpetrators of 9/11. There were many reasons Breivik was not suspected. He had no police record. He had not engaged in violent acts. He possessed the necessary licenses for his weapons. He had been brought up as a member of the middle class, lived with his mother in a well-to-do part of Oslo, had held jobs and started companies, although none had been particularly successful. In the United States, after a series of shootings that included three school attacks—Columbine, Virginia

Tech, and Sandy Hook—Americans are highly aware of the possibility that a potential killer might be "one of us"—which was the title of a popular book by Åsne Seierstad[28] about the massacre. But, before Breivik's attacks, that was not the Norwegian mindset. The 22 July Commission report considers this issue and concludes that, despite Breivik's suspicious actions, "the signals were not put in context with the intention and capacity building to carry out terrorist acts." The reason, the report suggests, is that Breivik did not fit the "prevailing view of who, what, and how someone could pose a threat to society." In other words, people might have paid more attention to similar actions of an outsider—perhaps a jihadist—but Breivik was an ethnic Norwegian, indeed, "one of us." Breivik's actions, the 22 July Commission report states, "exposed the fundamental vulnerabilities and lack of effective barriers against terrorism in Norwegian society."[29]

This mindset, low sense of awareness, and lack of preparedness for violence certainly contributed to the escalation of the July 22 crisis into a national disaster. As the day unfolded, it became clear that Norway's collective inability to connect the terrorist dots was baked into its systems. According to Aage Borchgrevink, a Norwegian author who wrote a book about July 22, it was the Norwegian tendency to trust one another, and society's institutions, that Breivik played upon. "He used trust as a weapon," says Borchgrevink.[30] Breivik was able to drive a rental van, with a 950 kilogram bomb inside, into a restricted parking lot at the front entrance to the government building which housed the office of the prime minister. The building had been identified years earlier as a potential terrorist target, and security upgrades were pending, but had not been implemented. Although a security guard took note of the van's arrival and checked to see if it was registered as a visitor, which it wasn't, that did not lead to an immediate or urgent response. Breivik had sufficient time to light the fuse to the bomb, step out of the car—wearing a police-style helmet with visor down and pistol drawn—lock the car, and hurry away.[31]

On the street, a pedestrian took note of Breivik, still with helmet and visor down, gun drawn, clad in an all-black outfit that did not look quite like any police uniform he had ever seen. The pedestrian watched as Breivik got into his Fiat, which he had parked earlier to serve as his getaway car, and proceeded to drive the wrong way up a one-way street. The pedestrian thought it was odd and had the presence of mind to take note of Breivik's license plate number. The bomb exploded a few minutes later, ripping the streetscape apart, damaging the government building, killing eight people, and wounding many more. Only then did the pedestrian call the police to report the license plate number, thinking the driver he had seen might have something to do with the bombing. The transcript of the call suggests that neither the caller nor the operator treated the information with sufficient urgency. This was compounded by inadequate protocols and communications systems, so the information did not reach the right ears in time to make a difference.

Breivik, therefore, was able to drive out of the city. (In other places, his license plate number might already have been transmitted to any number of agencies; the city might even have been in lockdown.) As he drove, Breivik heard the news on the radio that the bomb had successfully detonated. A bomb squad, fire and rescue services, and the elite emergency response team known as Delta were mobilizing toward the scene. All was confusion. Was it a bomb? A terrorist attack?

Breivik drove north for more than an hour, headed for his second pre-selected target: the island of Utøya, about forty kilometers from Oslo, a lake-bound speck of rock, woodlands, and open fields. The island is owned by the Workers' Youth League (the AUF), a unit of the Norwegian Labor Party, and each summer the AUF runs a summer camp for young people, a good number of them political activists. Many of Norway's political leaders, including then prime minister Stoltenberg, had spent time there. On July 22, several hundred people were on the island, a diverse group including campers from many countries, cultures, and faiths, including Muslims. The average age was around nineteen.[32] Breivik believed Utøya was an appropriate target, a symbol of what was wrong with Norway: a haven of liberal elites who wanted to open society to what he considered to be corrupting influences.

As Breivik drove, the camp members starting getting news of the Oslo bombing. At 4:30, camp leaders assembled an emergency information meeting in the Main Hall. There had been an explosion of some kind in Oslo, the camp members were told. Exactly what had happened no one really knew. But there should be no cause for alarm. Utøya was probably the safest place to be in all of Norway.

Around 5:00 pm, Breivik arrived at the quay where the ferry to Utøya docked. He said he had come to the island to check for bombs and requested passage over. Despite the homemade uniform, the semi-automatic rifle, and the fact that this strange figure was alone, Breivik was ferried to the island, and helped with his heavy case—which was packed with ammunition—to the main building. There, he met with the camp manager and the sole security person on the island. The security guard, a former policeman, began to ask questions. Breivik shot and killed him and two others. Breivik then walked to the café building where many campers were and opened fire. For the next seventy-five minutes, Breivik roamed the island, shooting camp members as they fled, tried to hide, or stood frozen in fear. In trial testimony, Breivik said he was amazed that no one confronted him.

Immediately after the first killings, campers began sending emails and texts and making desperate calls to each other, parents, friends, the police, and emergency numbers—112 for general emergency, 113 for medical. The system quickly broke down. Calls to Oslo that were not related to the bomb blast were ignored or diverted. The local call center near Utøya had only two phone lines and was immediately overwhelmed. Breivik himself twice reached an operator through 112 and offered to surrender, with no result.

In Oslo, the first responders already had their hands full at the bomb site. When it finally became clear that something terrible was happening on Utøya, it was decided to send members of the Delta force. They had to drive the forty kilometers in summer Friday afternoon traffic, because they did not have access to a suitable helicopter. Local policemen had been dispatched, however, and arrived at the ferry dock. But there was no emergency plan in place for an incident on Utøya. Lines of authority were unclear. The local police and Delta force did not have a common communications platform. The Delta force did not know exactly where Utøya was, because the island was too small to show up on their GPS system and they had a difficult time communicating with local police. The local police, possibly believing there was more than one gunman on the island, concluded they could not act on their own. The officers stood on the dock for a half hour, listening to gunfire and screams, as they waited for the Delta team to arrive.[33]

During that time, however, local residents as well as summer visitors to a campground at water's edge mobilized themselves. They heard the shots, saw people swimming away from the island, jumped in their boats, and began hauling swimmers aboard. The island is about six hundred meters from shore and the water is cold. Breivik had calculated that even those campers who tried to escape the island by swimming would likely drown, overtaken by exhaustion or hypothermia. In this calculation, Breivik did not figure on the resilience of the ordinary citizens who were on the scene. "They mounted a spontaneous rescue operation," says Borchgrevink. "Their boats were being shot at. They took personal risk. They were brave." These unofficial first responders are credited with saving dozens, perhaps hundreds, of lives that day.

When the Delta force arrived a little after 6:00 pm, the officers scrambled aboard an inflatable craft supplied by the local police, but there were too many of them. The engine swamped and they sat, dead in the water. The elite Delta force had to transfer into private boats which carried them to the island. Once there, it took them only minutes to locate Breivik and take him into custody.

The trial lasted some ten weeks, and the verdict was handed down in August 2012. Breivik was convicted of killing seventy-seven people, under that part of the penal code that covers terrorism and extreme acts of premeditated murder. His motives appeared to be an incredibly toxic mixture of political ideology and social bigotry, combined with deep emotional and psychological troubles, that had been brewing for many years, probably since childhood. Breivik was sentenced to Norway's maximum prison sentence of twenty-one years.

The term can be extended, however, in increments of five years and, as one Oslo resident put it, "Breivik will never be released in Norway. That would be impossible."[34]

How this national disaster could have occurred has been endlessly debated. Could the attacks have been anticipated and prevented? What did the acts mean for Norway, if anything? These questions were explored in television specials, articles and books, social media, and in the national conversation that continues to this day.

The Commission's report concluded that "22 July revealed serious shortfalls in society's emergency preparedness and ability to avert threats and to protect itself from threats."[35] Although the report details the lack of resources and technical shortcomings, it argues that the more important failings pertained to awareness, coordination, and leadership. Yes, it says, "the Storting (Norway's parliament) and the Government have had security and emergency preparedness high on their agendas for the past fifteen years."[36] But, "The ability to acknowledge risk and learn from exercises has not been sufficient" and "the ability to implement decisions that have been made, and to use the plans that have been developed, has been ineffectual." Coordination and interaction among groups—integration—was "deficient."[37] And, finally, "Leadership's willingness and ability to clarify responsibility, set goals and adopt measures to achieve results have been insufficient."[38]

One of the key conclusions of the report is that individuals play a "decisive role" in such crises particularly by "speaking up." I cite this passage because it addresses directly and eloquently the issue of responsibility: that we are all responsible for building the resilience of our societies:

It is widely known that many crises could have been averted or handled better if only individuals had expressed their concerns or got involved when they discovered shortcomings or faults. Instead of speaking up, they become passive bystanders, even though they often have valuable information and valuable perspectives that would improve the ability to prevent or manage a crisis. 22 July is, in fact, also a story about the many who knew that critical systems were not working the way they were supposed to, and that measures had not been implemented as planned. It is often the case that in situations in which many observe the same phenomenon, we fail to speak up. Where experts and authorities are involved, there is an extra tendency for many to become passive bystanders. The Commission is of the opinion that reporting risks in one's surroundings is an important part of an individual's responsibility to society. 22 July taught us with the utmost clarity that vigilance and engagement can be of the essence, and that it is important that apparently small and perhaps insignificant details or weak signals are given enough attention soon enough.[39]

What of recovery and revitalization? There is a general sense that the disaster of July 22 has had similar effects on Norway as the ship explosion did on Halifax. It affected attitudes, surfaced tensions, forced improvements, and—for all the horror that resulted and the pain that the affected must live with—it created change that many see as positive.

Following the release of the report, prime minister Stoltenberg promised that systems and security would be improved and, indeed, resources for security and police activities have increased. In 2013, a report by the Analysis of Civil Security in Europe (ANVIL) project concluded that Norway had achieved "a revision of the civil security system, culminating in inter alia an increased budget, initiatives to strengthen coordination, and knowledge production."[40] In July 2014, when there was the threat of a terrorist attack in Norway, the police expressed confidence they could handle whatever might come. Helicopters and bomb-sniffing dogs were on standby, police were watching airports, and the military was on alert. According to Odd Reidar Humlegard, the National Police Commissioner, the police were far more prepared to deal with a terrorist situation in 2014 than they had been before Breivik's attacks two years earlier.[41]

The 22 July commission noted that its own work contributes to the country's resilience as "one step in the efforts to improve society's ability to manage the next crisis—even though it will probably put society to entirely different tests."[42]

And, just as the Boston bombings led to declarations of "Boston Strong," prime minister Stoltenberg made it clear that the attack would not change the fundamental Norwegian nature or approach to life. "The Norwegian response to violence is more democracy, more openness, and greater political participation," he said.[43] Borchgrevink cites a study that evaluated the level of trust Norwegians feel toward each other and toward the country's institutions; it showed that trust had increased, not decreased, in the period after the Utøya attacks— with respondents in all groups expressing greater trust in minority segments of the population.[44] Indeed, many of the young survivors of that day say they are more resolved than ever to be involved in politics as a career.

On the third anniversary of the July 22 events in Norway, Borch-grevink characterized the national mood in an opinion piece that was posted on Aljazeera's website: "Breivik's stated aim was to spread conflict, but his acts brought Norwegians together."[45]

6

AWARENESS
Yes, It Can Happen Here

If it's possible to be ready for an earthquake, the city of San Francisco is, although it's more accurate to say the people and organizations there are in a constant state of *increasing* their readiness. That's a good thing because, as virtually everyone in the Bay Area is intensely aware, experts say there is a 63 percent probability that San Francisco will experience at least one major earthquake of magnitude 6.7 or greater before 2036.[1] The city is sitting, geologists warn, on a "tectonic time bomb."[2]

Increasing readiness is an important part of resilience building. The more ready you are, the less damage and dysfunction you are likely to experience when a disruption takes place. Although we cannot prepare ourselves completely for the specific circumstances of the *unpredictable* disruption, we can be ready for the predictable ones, and that general readiness contributes to our capacity to deal with whatever else comes along.

Increasing readiness involves developing awareness, reducing vulnerabilities, and preparing for disruption—in this chapter, I'll focus on awareness. We'll see how awareness helped the people of a Nairobi slum, the fish in an important ecosystem, and how it took decades of work for the people of San Francisco to become aware of their specific vulnerabilities to earthquakes.

WHAT SAN FRANCISCO IGNORED: 1906–1989

It can take a long time for people to gain awareness of their vulnerabilities such that they accept the importance of taking action to become more ready. San Francisco, for example, has been experiencing earthquake disruptions since the mid-eighteenth century, but it was only after a quake in 1989 that they got serious about reducing their vulnerabilities and increasing their readiness.

This is partly due to the limits of human memory. By the time the Great San Francisco Earthquake struck in 1906, who remembered there had already been a Great San Francisco Earthquake back in 1868? That one destroyed buildings throughout Oakland, San Francisco, Santa Rosa, and San Jose, killed thirty people, and still ranks as "one of the most destructive earthquakes in California's history."[3] Yes, engineers and building developers, among others, paid close attention to what had happened. New construction methods were widely discussed, and some designers took them on board. A few buildings went up—notably those on the Berkeley campus of the University of California, as well as a few downtown—that were more robust and designed to withstand a big shake. However, the new methods were mostly ignored, largely because there was no legal requirement to adhere to the proposed safety measures.[4] Plus there was a tremendous demand for new housing as people and businesses poured into the city, so more and more land was reclaimed from San Francisco Bay, and up went lots of new buildings, built without the known earthquake safety measures and sited on vulnerable ground that was most susceptible to quake.[5] We see the same thing happening today in rapidly growing cities in the developing world, with the result that buildings and neighborhoods are just as vulnerable to disruption there as the new neighborhoods of San Francisco were a hundred years ago.

So, when the second Great San Francisco Earthquake hit in the early morning of April 18, 1906, the damage was much worse than it had been thirty-eight years earlier, largely because the city was much more densely populated and built up but also because it was not significantly more ready than it had been—except for those few well-designed buildings that did, indeed, fare better than most others.

Jack London, the world-famous author of *The Call of the Wild*, lived on a ranch in Glen Ellen, California, about forty miles north of San Francisco. Around 5:15 on the morning of the quake, he was routed out of bed. A telegram had arrived from the editor of *Collier's* magazine requesting that London immediately ride to the city and write a report on what he saw. A half hour later, London and his wife, Charmian, were on horseback, and soon reached a spot where they could see the smoke rising from the burning buildings in Santa Rosa and San Francisco. Later, in his *Collier's* report, London wrote, "San Francisco is gone."[6]

Everyone knows something of the story of the Great San Francisco Earthquake of 1906. The US Geological Survey (USGS) tells us that it was "one of the most significant earthquakes of all time."[7] It was a gargantuan disruption, a 296-mile rupture of the San Andreas Fault that caused a 7.8 magnitude quake. Together, the earthquake and the fires it caused leveled roughly three-quarters of the city—490 city blocks and 2,830 acres of land—which was, at the time, the largest US metropolis west of the Mississippi River, with the country's fastest-growing economy.[8] "An enumeration of the buildings destroyed would be a directory of San Francisco," London wrote. "An enumeration of the buildings undestroyed would be a line and several addresses."[9]

We know that after the quake there came a cascade of related disruptions, the most terrible of which was the fires caused by rupturing gas mains and made worse by firefighters using dynamite to try to stop the flames by creating firebreaks of building rubble. They were forced into that technique because they had no water for their pumps and hoses—some 30,000 water pipes and three hundred water mains had burst in the quake.[10] The fires raged for two days and nights, and more than half the city's population—400,000 at the time—found themselves homeless, adding another disastrous social dimension to the event. "All the shrewd contrivances and safeguards of man," London wrote, "have been thrown out of gear by thirty seconds' twitching of the earth-crust."[11]

The San Francisco earthquake of 1906 was intensely studied and analyzed by observers and experts from the local area and around the world. A State Earthquake Investigation Commission was formed, chaired by A. C. Lawson, which issued a comprehensive report of its findings. One point that could have been predicted: "areas situated in sediment-filled valleys sustained stronger shaking than nearby bedrock sites, and the strongest shaking occurred in areas where ground reclaimed from San Francisco Bay failed in the earthquake."[12]

Another section of the report, on the "mechanics" of the earthquake, was written by Henry Fielding Reid, a geophysicist, in which he formulated the theory of "elastic rebound" which became the basis for seismic study for years to come.[13] "It is impossible for rock to rupture," Reid writes, "without being first subjected to elastic strains greater than it can endure." When that happens, "a rupture then takes place and the strained rock rebounds under its own elastic stresses, until the strain is wholly or largely relieved."[14] He described a geophysical form of resilience—a rapid bounce-back to an unstressed condition.

The event came to be considered one of the most significant disasters in the history of the United States, but, between 1906 and 1989, the memory of the big quake and its effects faded. Besides, San Francisco rebounded like the tectonic plates beneath it and was growing again. In 1915, less than a decade after the quake, San Francisco applied for and won the rights to host the Panama Pacific International Exposition to show itself off. In midcentury came an economic boom followed by decades of growth, during which San Francisco became a national hub of learning and commerce—an "imperial city" once again.

Over the years, there were many smaller tremors that rattled windows and caused some damage, but nothing like the early devastations. San Francisco continued to expand and kept right on reclaiming land for new development and erecting buildings vulnerable to earthquake.

So, when in 1989 the Loma Prieta earthquake killed 40 people, injured 3,700 more, caused $6 billion in property damage, and created massive disruption, San Franciscans could not quite believe it.[15] It seemed impossible that a bridge had fallen, that buildings had collapsed, that commuters had been crushed in their cars. These events were simply not supposed to happen in a modern city.

Was it possible San Franciscans were unaware of their vulnerability? Had they ignored the threat? Or had they forgotten the lessons of the past?

Patrick Otellini, the city's director of earthquake safety as well as its new chief resilience officer (as part of the 100 Resilient Cities initiative), explains that "people like to stick their head in the sand and forget about this stuff. Because it brings into question what you do in your normal, day-to-day life. And that means change, and a lot of times people don't want to change."[16]

However, the 1989 quake marked the beginning of a new period for the city. In the past twenty-five years, San Francisco has heightened its awareness of its vulnerabilities, taken steps to mitigate the threat, and improved its preparedness for an earthquake or any other disruption that might befall the city and its people. Along the way, San Francisco has become a hotbed—not just of venture capital activity, high-tech firms, gay rights, and tourism—but also of resilience thinking and action.

The city is well aware of its assets, its vulnerabilities, and the threats it faces and is committed to increasing its resilience. San Francisco was selected to participate in the 100 Resilient Cities initiative and, in its application, states, "San Franciscans have embraced our historical resilience, choosing the phoenix as the centerpiece of our City's Flag. It is this spirit that has carried us through ensuing challenges, as well as instilled in our residents a desire to invest resources so that when future times of stress occur we will once again bounce back and resume our place in the global economy."[17]

IDENTIFYING
VULNERABILITIES AND THREATS

Ann Patton, talking about Tulsa and the floods, defined awareness very simply and directly: you have to know what's wrong before you can fix it.[18] It may sound almost absurd to say that the first step in increasing readiness is to be aware of what's wrong in your community, organization, or city. Isn't it obvious? Shouldn't it be obvious?

The answer is no. Today, in particular, situations are complex and change quickly. With the climate and ecosystem changing so dramatically and cities growing and transforming radically, it can be very difficult to be aware of all the potential vulnerabilities and threats you may face. Just knowing what's going on can be challenging, especially in a city but also in our smaller towns and communities, and in the natural environment, as well.

Climate conditions are causing new threats that we are unaccustomed to and therefore unprepared for—like San Franciscans and the new threat of heat wave. As we've discussed, the population is growing worldwide and demographics are shifting. As a result, social conditions change rapidly and vulnerabilities look different to different people and groups. In New York, people who live in Lower Manhattan and areas of Brooklyn that have been built up along the East River in recent years are much more concerned about flood than uptown residents. In Miami, the population skews older, which means there are health vulnerabilities related to heatwaves and hurricanes. In Nairobi, the population skews younger—a large percentage of the population is under twenty-five—which could mean the city is vulnerable to economic and social disruption. Will there be jobs for all these young people? And in the oceans of Asia, overfishing is depleting the food supply, affecting the natural habitat, thus threatening the food security and ecosystems of billions of people.

Economic issues must be considered. San Francisco is blessed with the presence of large, wealthy businesses, but it has not yet confronted the problems it is creating with social cohesion. Great wealth disparities can make populations more vulnerable to disruption.

What's important to remember is that the vulnerabilities (and, as we'll see, the assets) you have before a disruption will largely determine what happens during a disruption. So, as Shaun Donovan, the US secretary of housing and urban development (HUD), who has thought long and hard about these issues, puts it, "The very first step in moving toward resilience is awareness."[19] (In 2014, Donovan was named to lead the Office of Management and Budget, where he will have an even greater capacity to influence government agencies with his resilience thinking.)

VULNERABILITIES CAN MEAN weaknesses, problem areas, and gaps that might be particularly susceptible to threats or that could cause problems to your community or organization—and they can be thought of in three broad categories: natural, structural, and social. However, vulnerabilities always overlap and intertwine, so the differentiation, although useful, is slightly artificial.

Our ecosystems, for instance, are deeply connected to our water sources, food supply, global health, industry, and economic vitality. Yet we have historically thought more about threats to the valued natural assets themselves, such as our clean water supply or fish stock, than about the complex ecosystems that produce those assets. As we consider the natural vulnerabilities we face, we must also consider how these assets are intertwined. How do these ecological systems converge with our social systems, supply chains, and issues of food security? As Fred Boltz explains, "There are values of ecosystems that we presently do not understand or appreciate."[20] Take, for instance, how the disappearance of a species might impact global health. A species of bird, insect, or bacteria could be "a key regulator of a disease," says Boltz, and if one of these regulators were to disappear, disease could occur in its absence. "We don't presently know about all these regulators or value them," he says—that is, until we experience a shock that belatedly reveals their function and demonstrates their critical role in the system. If we want to reduce our vulnerabilities and protect these assets, we need to revalue and better understand entire ecosystems. Their resilience underpins our own.

In addition to threats to natural systems, we need to consider the vulnerabilities of our structures: buildings and bridges, computer networks, and transportations systems. Which buildings are vulnerable, what are they vulnerable to, and what might happen if a threat became a disruption? Which structural elements need repair (in the United States, more than 65,000 bridges are "structurally deficient" and more than 20,000 are "fracture critical"—meaning a failure of one vital component could lead to collapse[21]) and might be a problem if floodwaters got too strong? What about the elements of the electrical distribution system—power generation plants, transformers, and transmission lines? What about the components of the cell phone networks in countries where there are few landlines? What's the condition of the water systems, transportation networks, databases, and computer networks? How could the disruption of one part of a system lead to cascading failures? What else might be disrupted by such failures? For example, the 2013 collapse of the Rana Plaza building in Bangladesh tragically killed more than a thousand people. It also disrupted business, sparked civil unrest and protests, and badly damaged the country's reputation.[22]

This emphasis on the structural is essential because the elements of the built environment as well as the physical elements of key systems— including transportation, communications, and utilities—are indeed highly susceptible to disruption of all kinds, from flood to terrorist attack, as we have seen during 9/11 and Superstorm Sandy.

Then, of course, there are the vulnerabilities that you aren't really aware of—or can't accept as such—until a disruption reveals them to you. These are everywhere: security holes in computer systems, unseen faults in gas lines.

It is possible, however, to focus too much on the structural and not take into full account the third category: people-related vulnerabilities that have to do with individuals, organizations, and institutions, networks, communities, and cities.

For example:

- Classes, factions, groups, or neighborhoods that are underserved, marginalized, underrepresented, or at odds with one another.

- Health issues and threats to well-being, such as infectious or lifestyle diseases or workplace dangers.

- Livelihoods that may be in danger or economic stresses that could become acute.

- Institutions that are absent or not strong enough to play necessary roles in the event of a disruption or disaster.

- The absence of key individual players or roles, or a shortage of those with necessary skills and commitment to the system.

- Weak social networks or networks that do not connect with one another.

- Poor institutional governance or a lack of leadership.

One of the reasons that people can be unaware of or unwilling to fully address vulnerabilities is because they are often chronic stresses. When chronic stresses develop slowly over time, they often come to be thought of as normal—just the ways things are. The people of New Orleans and flooding. The city of Medellin and crime. Nairobi and its huge slum population, underrepresented and underserved. Readiness begins with awareness but it does not end there. Once you become aware of a vulnerability, you need to gather enough knowledge about it so that you can consider what actions you might take to mitigate it, a process that often requires evaluations and measurements.

Assessments, Investigations
and Enumerations

But what to measure? For each of the five characteristics of resilience, there are indicators that fall into several categories of outcomes: the natural and built environment, health and well-being, the economy and society, leadership and governance. Under each category are specific indicators that you can choose to assess, evaluate, and track to determine the progress of factors that are involved in resilience building. For example, the homicide rate in Medellin; drug-related emergency room visits in towns with escalating drug-related health issues; in Surat, India, the number of kids who come down with infectious disease; in San Francisco, the number of buildings that are vulnerable to the threat of earthquake; in slum neighborhoods of Nairobi, the number of dwellings that have water and toilets; water and air quality in Beijing; the size of fish stocks in the sea; crop yields in sub-Saharan Africa; or the number of natural pollinators, such as bees in the United States.

SUCH INDICATORS ARE ESSENTIAL to assessing a vulnerability and creating widespread awareness of it so that you can eventually take action. In San Francisco, you could trace the speedup in readiness efforts to the careful assessment that was done of the buildings damaged by the1989 Loma Prieta quake. Some 16,000 residences were unlivable after the quake, another 30,000 damaged.[23] In a matter of moments, San Francisco and its residents became aware of just how vulnerable they were.

Laurence Kornfield, who was then chief building inspector and still serves San Francisco as a special assistant to the Earthquake Safety Implementation Program, led a team of inspectors, engineers, and contractors on a block-by-block investigation of the city, making handwritten notes, indexing and cataloging damage to various kinds of buildings in disparate city sections and neighborhoods. They followed what was then a new inspection procedure developed by the Applied Technology Council (ATC), a private consulting firm, known as Post-Earthquake Safety Evaluations of Buildings, or, in the industry, ATC-20. (Since 1989, the ATC-20 has become a national standard, and it is applicable in other situations—the same inspection was done on buildings around Ground Zero in New York City after 9/11.) Conducting such work is tedious, no doubt—it requires trudging from street to street, following a defined protocol, diligently making notes—but absolutely necessary.

Through this assessment of San Francisco's buildings—damaged, at risk, or safe—Kornfield and the group gained a foundational understanding of the city's structural vulnerabilities. The next step was to evaluate how different types of buildings would fare if another earthquake hit. To get that effort under way took some time and some funding, but, in the late 1990s—after much rebuilding and restoration had been completed following the 1989 quake—Kornfield secured $1 million from the city's Building Inspection Commission to make predictive assessments of how San Francisco would fare in the event of an earthquake on the scale of the 1906 event—a *third* Great San Francisco Earthquake.

Kornfield outsourced much of the investigation to ATC, experts on the effects of seismic activity on the built environment. Using the data collected in the wake of the 1989 quake, ATC forecast the consequences to San Francisco of four possible earthquakes: three of varying sizes and in different locations along the San Andreas Fault to the city's west and one along the Hayward Fault to the city's east.

Their projections were ominous, even grim. If a 7.2 magnitude earthquake ruptured sixty kilometers of the San Andreas Fault (one of the scenarios imagined) just off the coast of San Francisco, the structures would fare badly. Of San Francisco's 160,000 buildings, some 27,000 would become uninhabitable (3,600 would have to be demolished and rebuilt) and 73,000 more would be damaged.[24] Most of the damaged buildings, according to the ATC, would be of the type known as "soft-story." These are wood-frame structures whose ground floors could not, in an earthquake of that size, support the weight of the levels above them. They would buckle or collapse.

The human damage would also be high. As many as 300 people could die, another 7,000 would be injured and require medical care.

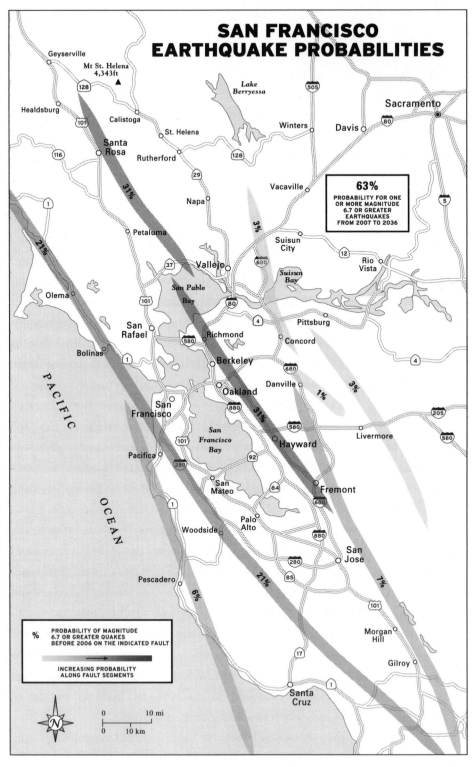

SAN FRANCISCO EARTHQUAKE PROBABILITIES

Geyserville

Mt St. Helena
4,343ft ▲

128

Healdsburg

Calistoga

101

St. Helena

Santa
Rosa

116

Rutherford

Napa

Lake
Berryessa

505

Winters

Davis

Sacramento

128

Vacaville

80

5

63%
PROBABILITY FOR ONE
OR MORE MAGNITUDE
6.7 OR GREATER
EARTHQUAKES
FROM 2007 TO 2036

Petaluma

31%

3%

Suisun
City

12

Rio
Vista

Vallejo

37

580

Suisun
Bay

21%

Olema

San Pablo
Bay

101

80

4

Pittsburg

San
Rafael

580

Richmond

Concord

4

Bolinas

1

Berkeley

680

PACIFIC

Oakland

Danville

1%

3%

205

San
Francisco

880

31%

San
Francisco
Bay

580

Livermore

580

Pacifica

101

Hayward

280

92

OCEAN

San
Mateo

84

Fremont

680

Woodside

Palo
Alto

880

San
Jose

Pescadero

6%

21%

280

85

7%

101

% PROBABILITY OF MAGNITUDE
6.7 OR GREATER QUAKES
BEFORE 2006 ON THE INDICATED FAULT

Morgan
Hill

INCREASING PROBABILITY
ALONG FAULT SEGMENTS

17

Gilroy

N

0   10 mi

0   10 km

Santa
Cruz

SOURCE: USGS

The cost for rebuilding—mostly uninsured structures—could climb to $30 billion.

Those losses are only from the quake. If you take into account subsequent fires—the ATC estimates that as many as seventy would spark simultaneously—another 2,700 buildings would be damaged, the fire department would be overwhelmed, and, depending on weather, wind, and other factors, fires could burn countless city blocks for hours.[25]

Thanks to the two-decade long period of assessment that began after the 1989 quake, there is no question that San Francisco has a much better awareness than ever before of its vulnerabilities and the potential consequences of its most probable and devastating disruption—and it is all spelled out in the *Community Action Plan for Seismic Safety* report, released in 2010.

A question from the preface of the report stands out: *Is it acceptable to have hundreds of people die, thousands injured, and thousands of housing units destroyed—when those impacts are largely preventable?*[26]

No, the city decided. And today San Francisco is in the midst of a thirty-year work plan to reduce its vulnerabilities, strengthen its defenses, and do whatever it can to prevent what is now a well-known and inevitable disruption from becoming a disaster.

GATHERING INFORMATION is incredibly important to our ability to be aware of our situations, especially our vulnerabilities, and it can be essential to a community's efforts to overcome them and to be readier to deal with the disruptions we cannot predict. In many cities of the developing world, for example, the most basic information—such as population data—can be hard to come by. In particular, people living in informal settlements are sometimes not counted, and it's nearly impossible to reduce vulnerabilities that are connected with the larger community if you're not officially recognized and thus lack any political clout. As Sheela Patel, founder of Shack/Slum Dwellers International (an organization that I'll discuss further), argues, the first step to being included in a community, and in determining its future, is to be *counted.*

This was the case with Kambi Moto, a neighborhood in the Huruma slum of Nairobi. Until 2001, Kambi Moto was literally not on the map—it was not marked on maps of the city. The government mostly ignored the settlement, utilities didn't serve the area, and people typically didn't know who their neighbors were.

Residents there lived with a myriad of chronic stressors. Though they had resided on the land for decades, they did not own it, so the threat of eviction was constant. Fires frequently ripped through the neighborhood, which accounts for its name—Kambi Moto translates as "Camp of Fire." Without clean water or a sewage system, disease could spread quickly. The streets and gutters were clogged with refuse, including the plastic bags filled with human waste commonly known as "flying toilets" because people tossed them out their windows onto the street. Good jobs were few and far between, so prostitution, muggings, and gang violence ran rampant. No wonder people mostly kept to themselves. "The settlement was having a lot of problems," says Michael Njuguna, a Kambi Moto resident. "No toilets. No water. Every day the shacks were burning."[27]

In 2000, ten women from Kambi Moto decided that things had to change, and, for that to happen, they knew they had to get the attention of the city. They would seek two things. First, tenure on their property. Second, provision of basic services, particularly water and sanitation. To gain access to the halls of power, however, they needed to prove that Kambi Moto had resources and commitment—as well as votes—and for that they needed data. But they had none. They did not have the most basic information: how many people lived in their community, how many houses there were, who held jobs. They needed to conduct a census, but in a community with so little social cohesion that could prove difficult. Who would manage the project? Would people cooperate?

The women started their work indirectly, by forming a community savings group. They gained the support of two organizations that serve Nairobi's urban poor—Pamoja Trust and the Kenya Federation of Slum Dwellers (known as Muungano wa Wanavijiji), successfully recruited members to the savings scheme and built up a cash reserve.

Although the primary purpose of the savings group was to reduce financial instability, it had other benefits that would be useful in the data-gathering effort—it fostered trust, strengthened social cohesion, and helped its members learn how to work with outside organizations. "We came together to solve our problems," said Njuguna, who became one of the community's key leaders.

Next they embarked on a data-gathering process known as "enumerations"—documenting the number of people, dwellings, and facilities in the slum areas. They hoped the information gathered through these surveys would enable them to paint a picture of their community as larger, more cohesive, and harder working than generally understood and that would force the city powers to pay attention, recognize them, and, ultimately, provide them with services and even grant them tenure on the land.

The enumerators, as they called themselves, were neighborhood volunteers. Even so, they encountered some problems at first. Slum residents were unaccustomed to receiving visitors. There is plenty of gang violence in these areas. What did these so-called enumerators really want? Some residents refused to let them in. Others were worried their landlords would not want them to answer questions about their dwellings and, if they did, there might be repercussions.

Gradually, however, the enumerators made progress. They would sit with the house dweller, talk a bit, explain the survey, and then bring out the multipage form and start asking questions. What is the name of your village? What is the name of your cluster? Who owns the structure? Where does the owner live? Who lives here? How long have you lived here? Is your roof made of *mabati* (iron sheets), *mbao* (wood), *plastiki* (plastic), *nyasi* (grass), *vyuma* (sheet metal), or *nyingine* (other)? Where do you get water? What type of toilet do you use? How do you dispose of solid waste? What kinds of transportation do you use? What is your household income and expenditure?

The enumerations, conducted through 2001, provided a wealth of information about Huruma and gave the community organizers the data they needed to get started with local planning and, according to Jane Weru, a leader of Muungano, it established a "process by which consensus was built and the inclusion of all residents negotiated."[28] Residents unanimously agreed their most pressing need was land tenure. Without it, any improvement efforts would be futile and they would have difficulty demanding the provision of services. The vision of a stable future, without fear of eviction, united them. In other words, the enumeration delivered more than crucial data—it built community cohesion.

To communicate what they had learned through the enumerations, the group created a map of the neighborhood which, through visuals, made a number of issues explicit, particularly its vulnerabilities and gaps and weaknesses: high-crime areas, blocks with no water sources, concentrations of prostitution. The community gained an understanding of itself it had never had before. For example, they learned that no household in Kambi Moto had its own toilet. People had use of a public toilet—a pit latrine and six stalls—provided by the Nairobi City Council, but it cost too much for them to use regularly. That's why they so often resorted to flying toilets, even though they recognized the health threats involved. The enumeration data also revealed that slum residents relied on forty-five privately owned water sources, which charged two shillings for twenty liters of water—much more expensive than Nairobi's market rate.[29] Indeed, the water fees amounted to as much as 30 percent of a resident's household income.[30] They could see that crime was higher in densely built areas on the very edge of the Huruma slum, where visibility was low and access was limited.

Huruma's formal assessment provided the community with the data it needed to go to the city council and begin a discussion about gaining tenure—essential to building resilience in the Huruma area. You cannot be ready for a disruption or effectively recover from one if you live with such a fundamental vulnerability as not knowing whether you will have a place to call home. When they explained the enumeration process and what they had learned, Michael Njuguna saw a shift in the government's perception of the group almost immediately. "They started listening," he says. Here was a group that had organized itself, built a governance structure, forged partnerships, and managed a project of significant size. What's more, by forming a community savings group and enabling microborrowing and microlending, the group had saved enough money to support its bold proposal: to self-finance and build new houses or upgrade existing ones. They would do it, they said, but only if the government would do its part and promise them tenure on the land. Indeed, with the data in hand and Muungano by their side, community leaders had already started hammering out a plan for Kambi Moto's transformation—which is now under way. Clearly, the group had found its voice and gained a degree of political power.

ASSESSMENTS AND KNOWLEDGE-GATHERING initiatives like these are crucial when addressing complex, systemic vulnerabilities such as the ones the residents of Kambi Moto faced—revitalization and political empowerment of an underrepresented human community—and they can also play an important role in understanding emerging vulnerabilities in ecosystems, such as the depletion of fish stocks.

Our oceans provide us with an abundance of resources—including food, carbon cycle regulation, livelihoods, and recreation.[31] The multibillion-dollar global fishing industry employs more than 200 million people worldwide and serves as the economic backbone for many communities, and it provides an essential source of protein and nutrients for billions of us.[32] Today, our oceans are vulnerable, their resilience threatened by overfishing, which often goes along with urbanization and globalization, and by the rising temperature that is part of climate change.

In the northeastern United States, for example, the stock of one of the area's staple fishes, cod, has been severely depleted in the Gulf of Maine. These iconic fish (which gave Cape Cod, the New England vacation area, its name) were once so plentiful that, as legend has it, you could walk across the water on the their backs.[33] Over the past several decades, however, their numbers have declined, even though catch quotas have been set, and it will take a concerted conservation effort to restore them and avert a significant economic loss for the region.[34]

To understand why the cod stock (and other species) was on the decline, scientists have done a sophisticated form of enumeration. By studying data from a nearly forty-year period, 1968–2007, they found one reason: fish were moving north or farther out to sea where the water was cooler, closer to the temperature they had been used to.[35]

The rising temperature of the Gulf of Maine caused other disruptions to marine life. In 2012, researchers noticed that hake and herring, a favorite food of baby puffins, had also moved farther north. The puffins tried to adapt by catching larger fish, but they were harder to swallow, and many of the puffins died as a result.[36] Record high temperatures also caused changes in the stock of phytoplankton, a building block of the marine food chain. Shrimp stocks declined, and certain whale species, such as the right whale, were recorded traveling greater distances than usual to find food.[37] In short, the data revealed that the ecosystem of the Gulf of Maine had experienced a series of cascading disruptions. The impact on the region's economy was so great that in 2014 Congress allocated $32.8 million for fishery disaster relief funds in the northeast.[38] Variations of similar stories can be found around the globe (though, in many cases, minus the relief funds).

"Science tells us we have about ten years to reverse the decline in fish stocks that we're seeing," says Cristina Rumbaitis del Rio of The Rockefeller Foundation, "otherwise we're going to get a collapse of those marine ecosystems."[39] The good news is that we have sufficient knowledge and awareness of the problem to take action. And Rumbaitis del Rio says the fishing industry has started to "take notice" because its "future business depends on it. Companies like Darden, which used to own Red Lobster, and other seafood chains in the United States are making commitments to source nearly 100 percent of their seafood from sustainably managed fisheries." So, "unless you super overdeplete them and really disrupt the ecosystem," says Del Rio, "most species can bounce back and bounce back pretty quickly."

It is through a better understanding of this critical vulnerability that the private sector, governments, environmental groups, and fishermen can all become stewards of our oceans—and take steps now to avoid even greater disruption to our oceans and their resources. But first we must be aware of the complex interdependencies of these systems (even if we don't understand every connection) and work to protect not only our fish stocks but the marine ecosystem that produces them.

7

READINESS
We're All Responsible

Now, with awareness turned into knowledge through the gathering and analysis of information, questions arise: Who will do something with the data about these assessments and important factors? Who will take responsibility for improving readiness in the face of the vulnerabilities? Who should decide which vulnerabilities are most important to address and determine how to do so? Should readiness be an individual responsibility or taken on by a group? Should it be the responsibility of official bodies, such as government agencies, business associations, or health-care institutions, or by neighborhood or community groups?

The answer is that the responsibility for resilience building can and must lie in many places and with everyone. We have seen resilience-focused agencies in cities, resilience functions in business organizations, and community organizers focused on resilience. Responsibility can be formally bestowed or informally shouldered. Whatever the resilience-building structure looks like, we know that resilient places *always* have strong individuals, groups, institutions, and networks that can come together to increase readiness.

GOVERNMENT: COORDINATING THE PLAYERS

Let me start with a look at the government's role and, to do so, I'll return to the city government of San Francisco. You remember Rob Dudgeon, who, as a young man, was working the ambulances during the 1989 Loma Prieta earthquake and bridge collapse. Today, he is deputy director of San Francisco's Department of Emergency Management.

Dudgeon separates authority for increasing the city's readiness into three main areas. First, there is the policy level, and the responsibility for that lies with the city's elected officials. It is their job, Dudgeon believes, to identify major vulnerabilities, choose which ones to address, oversee the allocation of resources, and to think in a meta way about how the city might manage and recover from a major disruption. "How do we deal with sea rise? How do we deal with the changes the weather will bring to our hillsides? To me those are all planning questions," Dudgeon says.

For the most part, Dudgeon's agency wants to keep San Francisco's elected officials "out of the weeds" of emergency preparedness and management so they can deal with crucial high-level, often difficult, planning choices. "Let's not talk about where you are going to park the fire engine," he says. "Let's talk about what parts of the city you're willing to let burn." Obviously, no city leader wants to let any part of the city burn, but thinking about such overarching issues—what happens if?—are matters of policy and, of course, politics.

The second area of readiness responsibility is tactical in nature and falls to the specific disciplines: fire, police, health, public works, and others. They work "within the yellow tape"—the "DO NOT CROSS" plastic ribbon that routinely surrounds the scene of a crime or disruption.

The third area of responsibility is one I mentioned earlier: coordination. That's the role of Dudgeon's group. It takes responsibility for a specific area of readiness-building activity—which Dudgeon dubs "beyond the yellow tape"—that is, between the emergency scene responders and the policy makers. "It's about getting people to work together more than it is about authority," he says. "We have to make sure everybody's at the table and work with the various constituencies." It is a form of solution crowdsourcing.

An example of San Francisco's readiness and resilience building can be seen in their Lifelines Council, a convening of city government and private sector players to facilitate self-regulation and rapid restoration of basic services: electricity and power, water, communications networks, sanitation, transportation, and others—a city's "lifelines" in the aftermath of a disruption or catastrophe.

These are services that are vital to a city's resilience, as their reestablishment allows for and facilitates the beginning of recovery and revitalization, and the city of San Francisco is keenly aware of the importance of securing these lifelines. In the 1906 earthquake, as we've seen, fighting the raging fires was nearly impossible after three hundred underground water mains burst during the crust's shaking.

The council, a working group composed of people involved in the accessibility, delivery, and maintenance of these essential services, includes representatives from city departments including emergency management, public works, real estate, and technology, and the Public Utilities Commission, as well as private partners such as Pacific Gas and Electric, AT&T, and Comcast, to name just a few.

The purpose of the group is to address "post-disaster reconstruction and recovery through local and regional collaboration" that will result in "a more clear understanding of inter-system dependencies necessary to enhance planning, restoration and reconstruction."[1] Fundamental to the Lifelines Council—and to resilience more broadly—is understanding how these various systems overlap and work with (and sometimes at odds with) each other, coming to terms with how a failure or breakdown in one system might or inevitably will affect others. Generating this awareness allows the Lifelines Council and the City of San Francisco to prioritize which services must be online and recovered first to ensure that services throughout the city will be operating as needed.

It's not the job of the council or of any one of its members to have every answer, says Dudgeon. Nor is any one player expected to have available every type of technology or system or supply that might be necessary to solve a problem. As Dudgeon sees it, the job of his department is "to work with federal and state partners and community groups so that we can plug into them as best we can," if and when a local emergency arises.

After all, says Dudgeon, "all emergencies are local."

HEALTH CARE: ## SCALING EVERYDAY SYSTEMS

The readiness of our health-care system to deal with health-related disruptions is essential to the resilience of a community or city. Being ready for medical emergencies—whether it be a disease outbreak that results from contamination due to flooding, the rapid global spread of an epidemic, or responding to an event such as an earthquake, a heat wave, or a terrorist attack—requires coordination and communication among many groups and individuals: EMS, EMTs, and hospitals (with their surgeons, physicians, nurses, staff), as well as, in some cases, government agencies at both the state and federal level, as we saw in the Boston Marathon bombing example.

Tom Frieden, director of the Centers for Disease Control and Prevention—the agency of the US government responsible for oversight of the country's health and well-being, from monitoring disease outbreaks to rolling out new vaccines—is working to build readiness into the everyday health-care system. "If you think you've got an emergency system that you can pull off the shelf or out of the closet and use it when there's an emergency," Frieden says, "forget about it. Not going to happen. What you need are everyday systems that can be scaled up."[2]

This is exactly what the CDC did when the H1N1 virus—or "swine flu"—spread across the United States in 2009 and 2010 in a large outbreak that constituted a grave public health threat. The CDC estimates that the incidence of cases was between 43 and 89 million from April 2009 through April 2010—a broad range, for sure, but a significant number even at the low-end estimate.[3] Some 12,000 people died from the disease in the United States, including more than a thousand children, and the death toll worldwide is estimated at between 151,700 and 575,400, another broad range but also a very high count. Not surprisingly, the CDC reports that "a disproportionate number of deaths occurred in Southeast Asia and Africa, where access to prevention and treatment resources are more likely to be limited."[4]

Fortunately, the CDC already had a structure in place that enabled it to rapidly distribute the H1N1 vaccine throughout the United States. They repurposed the Vaccines for Children program, originally developed to provide vaccines at no cost to kids who might not get vaccinated because their families did not have the ability to pay. The program was already reaching approximately 40,000 clinicians, and, in just a few weeks, the CDC was able to scale it up to more than 80,000 clinicians. The CDC was thus able to provide the flu vaccines to any doctor who requested them within that system and ended up making more than 300,000 deliveries, says Frieden.

By repurposing a program that is already in place, you avoid the problems, inefficiencies, and confusion that arise when people are asked to follow an emergency plan that is unfamiliar and possibly untested. The system remains unchanged, and individuals operating within it know what they have to do and how to do it—it's just that the situation and details are different. Maximizing output of an existing system and expanding its potential reach takes some doing, but it is usually easier and more effective than trying—on the fly and in an emergency—to implement an unfamiliar plan, especially when large numbers of people are involved.

But to scale up a system, and for any response to be effective, Frieden emphasizes that the existing infrastructure has to be robust, diverse, and have the capacity to be scaled. For the health and well-being infrastructure, that means including entities beyond hospitals and ambulances and their transportation and communications systems in the process. You have to make sure the infrastructure for water supply management and protection, sanitation quality management, and medical surge capacities are in place. By making small investments in building resilience every day, you steadily increase your ability to achieve a resilience dividend.

EDUCATION: LEARNING LEADERSHIP

Another essential part of developing awareness and improving readiness is education, and educational programs designed to teach readiness—and resilience in general—are cropping up everywhere.

Tulane University's Disaster Resilience Leadership Academy (DRLA), an interdisciplinary academic and research center focused on improving humanitarian leadership worldwide, launched a master of science in disaster resilience leadership in 2010. The focus is on the complexities associated with leadership in resilience—building community capacity that facilitates resilient outcomes—particularly the social, environmental, physical, and individual factors involved in resilience and resilience-building activity.

Ky Luu, DRLA's executive director, has been in the humanitarian community for more than two decades and reckons he's been involved, one way or another, in virtually every large-scale disaster response and recovery since the humanitarian crisis in Bosnia in 1991. He helped found the academy at Tulane after departing his post as director of the Office of US Foreign Disaster Assistance, where he oversaw response and recovery efforts on behalf of the US government and in his final year, 2009, led humanitarian assistance efforts in response to eighty-one disasters in fifty-six countries.

Luu has clearly learned the hard way what he now teaches and what we have discussed: that disruptions become disasters when leadership fails or other human-related factors exacerbate the problem. In one emergency situation after another, Luu saw that events were far worse than they had to be and that, in some cases, they might have been averted altogether. Time and again he saw there had been inadequate capacity-building to ready a community or country for threats and that inadequate mitigation measures had been taken to reduce the potential disruption from threats. When he left the Office of US Foreign Disaster Assistance, he wanted to do something that would help change that. He recognized, from his own experience and from discussions with colleagues around the world, there was no "systematic approach to strengthening resilience" for communities.[5] He strongly believed that individuals and communities have to develop the capacity to deal with risk—and that strong leaders play a fundamental role in that process.

Thus, Luu and colleagues built the academic program at the DRLA around four academic "pillars" that expose students to the complexities of building resilient communities: psychosocial and behavioral leadership, disaster operations leadership policy and management, leadership analysis, and environmental and hazards science. Although these branches cover topics ranging from water supply and sanitation to understanding how local environments might change in the years to come, Luu says that, at the end of the day, the program is fundamentally "about ourselves as part of the community."

In that sense, the state of Louisiana (Tulane is located in New Orleans) has been what Luu calls a "living laboratory" for the academy's students "in terms of how communities are coping and adapting to risk." An integral part of the program requires students to "adopt" a community in southeast Louisiana and conduct a formal risk assessment based on research, public records, and all manner of available data. They must also develop a survey tool to take into their community to make a more informal and qualitative assessment of what the risks and vulnerabilities are from the perspective of the people who live and work there. This helps change a student's habit of thinking about leadership in disaster as "an acute short-term response mechanism," as Luu puts it. What happens during a disruption, as we've discussed, is about what is in place and what has happened—or doesn't happen—*before* disruption occurs.

This community engagement can transform the students' thinking about vulnerabilities and the nature of disaster. They tend to start out by focusing on specific threats such as hurricanes or flood, but, after talking with the community members, they discover the social aspects where the deeper vulnerabilities lie. "Once they get into communities, they hear about things like crime, or that the community is really concerned about the roads," Luu says.

These two forms of assessment together give students a much more complete picture of what needs to be done in any given community to begin or continue resilience-building activities beyond emergency preparedness. "Only by understanding the perspective of the community," says Luu, "can students start thinking about ways to reduce risk and vulnerability." Resilient leaders, then, must have an awareness of both the chronic stressors within a community and the acute threats that may come and potentially create disaster. To do so, they must be proactively engaged with the community they are trying to strengthen.

Tulane's program can serve as a model for other institutions around the country and worldwide. As I experienced in my time as president of Penn, large universities, both public and private, are essential to the cities and communities in which they function as employers, contributors to well-being, and drivers of growth and improvement. It is not hard to conceive that programs like this one could be replicated in other educational institutions, such that students—with the leadership of professionals from the field—would conduct community-by-community risk assessments and analyses from the top down and the bottom up and begin creating comprehensive community resilience plans.

Indeed, just such a global network of resilience-building programs is under development. In January 2012, the Bill and Melinda Gates Foundation granted the DRLA $5 million to assist selected universities in Asia and Africa—carefully vetted by Luu and his colleagues—to develop programs modeled on the one at Tulane. By the end of 2013, twenty universities in eighteen countries were involved in the initiative, and Luu sees further expansion.

"This concept—addressing leadership and strengthening the capacity to be able to promote resilient outcomes and then doing the necessary research to really be able to provide the evidence base to do it—has caught on," Luu says. And, with the network expanding throughout the world, "we're able to really learn from others." It is, in effect, a feedback loop for sharing information and knowledge about a specific issue: leadership in resilience building.

There are many other resilience-building skills that can be taught, and that teaching need not take place in a formal academic setting. In places like Nairobi—where 60 percent of city residents live in informal settlements and hundreds of thousands of people depend for their livelihoods on day labor, seasonal jobs, or vulnerable one-person businesses such as street-side food stalls—individuals often need some help and a push to learn new skills that will increase their resilience.[6]

Linda Kamau, a software developer at Ushahidi, believed there was a great deal of potential, energy, and intelligence that could be tapped and leveraged in her city. She also knew that, although women compose 50 percent of the workforce in Kenya as a whole, only 15 percent work in technology.[7] The technology sector has tremendous potential to offer people of Nairobi a new source of livelihoods and more options for employment—in established companies or as entrepreneurs.

To help address these issues, Kamau cofounded AkiraChix, a community of female technologists that offers a one-year training program for women, most of whom are high school graduates from the Nairobi slums. The young women learn computing skills, including coding and webpage design. As part of the curriculum, each student develops a project to address a current problem in her community. Their background as slum dwellers, Kamau tells them, should not keep them from "coming up with ideas to fix their problems."[8] One AkiraChix student built a website that listed contact information for electricians, dress-makers, soap-makers, and other small businesses in her settlement—Nairobi's version of Angie's List. Others have started similar programs for the children, both boys and girls, in their communities.

BUSINESSES: AFFECTING DECISIONS

Businesses around the world have long understood the importance of readiness—particularly in financial controls, safety, and risk management—and have also embraced the concept of sustainability. Their thinking is now evolving toward resilience as an overarching theme, without abandoning many of the ideas that came before. The shift, however, can cause some conceptual conflicts to surface, particularly between the drive for efficiency and the resilience characteristics of diversity—especially surplus and redundancy. And when businesses think about readiness, it tends to be in a broad sense of the word: their organization is aware of the disruptions it might face and has plans for how it would deal with them.

At Shell, the global group of energy and petrochemical companies, Michiel Kool is executive vice president for safety, environment, and social performance, based at corporate headquarters in The Hague, the Netherlands. Kool joined Shell in 1984 and has served the company in various positions around the world. His training is in the physical sciences—he holds a master of science in mining engineering—so his thinking has gradually evolved, as it has for so many others who have come to resilience from one of the "hard" sciences. "There's a subtle but important difference between sustainability and resilience," Kool says. "With sustainability, the emphasis is on sustaining things and avoiding change. With resilience, it's more about accepting that change is inevitable."[9]

As a senior executive at a global company concerned about performance and profit, Kool has also had to adjust his thinking about interdependence. "Over the last few decades, the world has been driven by economic efficiency," he says. That compels a company to embrace such concepts as lean management and just-in-time supply chains. But those approaches can make a company vulnerable, as we saw with Lululemon. "A disruption in one part of the world can have immediate and long-term consequences in others." Kool cites the development and use of monocultures in agriculture—the growing of a single crop over a large area for long periods of time—which is a highly efficient method of growing crops but may not be resilient. If the crop is disrupted in some way, there is no fallback, no redundancy. "The trade-off between efficiency and resilience is one that we're having to think about," Kool says. "It will impact the way we build our facilities, how we connect supply chains, and how we connect with communities around us."

The origins of Shell's organizational focus on readiness lie in its foundational interest in safety. The oil and gas industry is a hazardous one, so the "notion of doing things well today to avoid problems later is very much at the heart of how we go about our business," Kool says. "A company like ours is all about managing risk and opportunity."

There are risks Shell is willing to take and, indeed, are essential to business growth and performance—on geology, oil price, markets, projects, technology—and that Shell well knows how to manage. But there is another category of risks, those the company is not prepared to take—including those that could lead to major incidents involving fire, explosions, and spills of the kind we have witnessed in the industry. "We take steps to reduce those risks to 'ALARP,' as low as reasonably practicable," Kool says. That means doing things pre-emptively, in terms of standards, procedures, competences, checks and balances, auditing, and other controls for design, operation, and maintenance to make sure that the oil and gas "stay in the pipe."

But Shell's resilience thinking has gone far beyond these essential issues of safety and risk management—for its products and systems and for those affected by them—to the consideration of the communities in which Shell works, engages, and serves. For example, Shell is working on two major projects in Iraq, and the company sees a long-term engagement there. But, Kool says, "it's inconceivable that we can have a long-term thriving business unless there is a thriving community and thriving society" around the projects. "That means that as we go about our business, we need to work with whomever we can work with—other companies, civil society, various levels of government, the United Nations—to make sure we achieve shared benefit." It is in everyone's interest that people who live and work in the areas where Shell operates have access to education and jobs, can build up their own businesses, and enjoy basic services such as safety, health, security, sanitation, and transportation.

This kind of initiative might be construed as just another effort on the part of a large company to build rapport with the community in which it operates—another program of social responsibility. But Kool sees it as essential to Shell's ability to mitigate the threat of disruption in the disparate areas of the world in which it has operations, precisely by improving social cohesion, building feedback loops that will enable the sharing of information during normal times and in times of crisis, and reducing the vulnerabilities of the people and institutions Shell engages with on a day-to-day basis.

Shell has developed its awareness of the importance of social cohesion through long experience in different parts of the world. The company has had experience in some places where they have found themselves working in communities that are completely disenfranchised or where there is a failure of government. That's why Shell is "very much prepared to do the upfront investment to get this right. Because we know that if we get it wrong it's going to be a very bad downside."

To emphasize the elements of resilience Shell is focusing on, Kool's group is called the safety, environment, and social performance group. "I don't think sustainable development is an activity," he says. "Sustainability is an outcome of doing a number of things really well. Do we find the right trade-offs between the short term and long term, and the right trade-offs between the social, environmental, and economic considerations in our decision making?"

WHEN THE DOW CHEMICAL COMPANY needed to reduce ground-level ozone (which the Environmental Protection Agency says "makes it harder to breathe"[10]) at their facility in Freeport, Texas—levels were over legal limits—they first considered buying a second smokestack scrubber to help filter and reduce harmful chemical emissions from their plant. But smokestack scrubbers have a certain lifespan, and, in twenty or so years, Dow would have to buy another. For a similar price, the Nature Conservancy (TNC)—the largest environmental nonprofit organization in the world—suggested Dow instead plant trees on a thousand acres of land, a mitigating action that will reduce pollutants in the atmosphere around the Freeport plant for much longer than twenty years, while improving the overall health of the ecosystem in the area.[11]

This is merely one example of collaborative solutions Dow and TNC have proposed to ensure Dow's long-term viability in Texas and in other locations, as well. "In Dow's case," says Mark Tercek, president and CEO of TNC since 2008, "TNC scientists and Dow engineers are trying to figure out how to solve problems together. And guess what? With Dow engineers and TNC scientists, one plus one is three. We come up with ideas and breakthroughs that neither side would by itself."[12]

Before taking the reins at TNC, Tercek spent twenty-four years at Goldman Sachs, where he served as managing director and partner. Given his background, he knows that to radically transform the relationship between business and the ecosystems and environments in which they're located or operate—to make them more resilient and viable long-term—requires cost-benefit analysis. "We live in a world of limited resources," he says. "If you want to ask society in any form—government, business, a household—to make difficult decisions about resource allocation, to do something that conventional wisdom would ask them not to do, it's folly not to think in terms of cost and benefits."

Tercek believes that businesses have a significant role to play when it comes to preserving, conserving, and protecting natural ecosystems, in part because "business can move faster than government." It is Tercek's mission to show commercial enterprises that these environments are not just landscapes where they operate but are an essential part of the businesses themselves—fundamental assets that can be strengthened and capitalized upon so as to make the endeavors more sustainable and to increase their long-term prosperity and growth.

A great deal of this work, says Tercek, is about raising awareness. "Business has to deal with reality," he says. "You can't be successful in business for very long if you deny reality." And the reality of the world today, as we've seen, is turbulence, change, volatility, and unpredictability. If you point out to business leaders vulnerabilities they have not been aware of, "they pay attention. And then, if you bring to their attention lower cost ways or better performing ways to address those vulnerabilities, of course they're interested. They'd be lousy businesspeople if they weren't."

Business and environmental resilience should not and must not be at odds. Partnerships such as that between Dow and TNC (as well as TNC and many other businesses around the world) are vital for seeking collaborative outcomes that are holistically beneficial to businesses, communities, and the environments in which they exist. "This collaboration and trust building, this joint problem solving is extraordinarily powerful," says Tercek. "It pays dividends."

Although Fred Boltz, The Rockefeller Foundation's ecosystems expert, agrees with Tercek that ecosystems should be understood as "assets to human industry," as he puts it, the practice of translating ecosystems issues into business terms can affect decision making in ways that are not always as well-considered as they might be.[13] "It can lead us to preserving iconic systems, charismatic species, and systems upon which the human footprint is very evident and which have an immediate cost to us," Boltz says. For example, people can easily see and understand the threat of a polluted river and be moved to take action about cleaning it up, but it is much harder for people to think about the upstream forest watershed area that delivers water into the river and needs preserving. But a transition in thinking is taking place within the business sector, especially in those industries that are highly dependent on natural resources, such as beverage making and agriculture. (As I will describe later, both SABMiller, the beer maker, and Coca-Cola, are involved in such conservation efforts.) Such companies are "increasingly active in trying to understand the contribution of ecosystems to their production," Boltz says. And, as they increase their awareness, they begin to make decisions that take into account the factors that build the resilience of ecosystems as well as the resilience of the company.

PARTNERSHIPS AND COLLABORATIONS: WORKING ACROSS BOUNDARIES

Increasing readiness often involves the engagement and collaboration of many players.

For decades, The Rockefeller Foundation has fostered partnerships and brought together disparate groups to address some of the world's most pressing problems, one of which is food security—an issue made all the more urgent as the world urbanizes and experiences climate change. As recently as the middle of the twentieth century, for example, famine and mass starvation were predicted by many. But, in the 1950s and 1960s, a concerted effort to address the problem of hunger changed the picture dramatically. A key figure in this extraordinary period was Norman Borlaug, a biologist and plant pathologist with The Rockefeller Foundation. From 1944 until his retirement from the foundation in 1983, Borlaug devoted himself to improving the state of food production, starting in Mexico and then in south Asia. Throughout, Borlaug collaborated with scientists, governments, academics, and civil society organizations, building global partnerships and focusing his research on agricultural techniques that could be transferred and taught around the world.

During that forty-year period, Borlaug, along with his colleagues and partners around the globe, bred new disease-resistant, high-yield wheat and rice varieties that could thrive in many different climates, developed new methods for soil and crop management, and improved almost every aspect of agricultural practice and food production.[14] (Today, we at The Rockefeller Foundation would describe this work as part of our resilience-building efforts.) The results were astonishing. Crop yields doubled in some areas, particularly in developing countries. Mexico, for instance, went from producing less than half the wheat its population needed to self-sufficiency in twelve years' time.

Building on the successes in Mexico, Borlaug and Haldore Hanson, a representative of the Ford Foundation, began developing new affiliations and partnerships—working with the Indian and Pakistani governments to determine which Mexican wheat varieties could thrive in Asia, where there was widespread starvation. The varieties and cropping techniques they identified led to the largest crop yield ever in Southeast Asia in 1966 and enormous seed purchases in subsequent years by India, Pakistan, and Turkey. In 1968, William Gaud, then the director of the US Agency for International Development, declared that a "green revolution" was under way, largely thanks to Borlaug's work.[15] (Borlaug, by the way, was awarded the Nobel Peace

Prize in 1970 and, after retiring from The Rockefeller Foundation in 1983 at age sixty-five, devoted twenty years of his "retirement" to improving agriculture in Africa. He died in 2009 at age ninety-five.)

Borlaug's work continues to be an inspiration for innovators in the world of agriculture and food security and continues to spark new collaborations. A new strain of rice, for example, was developed specifically to withstand the kinds of water issues I have described. This one can tolerate submergence for as long as two weeks, while conventional rice varieties can endure only a few days of water immersion.[16] This is a major advance for farmers whose lands are subject to flooding. The new rice has an intriguing provenance. In the 1990s, David Mackill, a specialist in rice genetics and breeding at the University of California–Davis, began experimenting with a rare variety of flood-tolerant rice he had obtained from the International Rice Research Institute, which The Rockefeller Foundation helped to found. This is a nonprofit organization that is home to the International Rice Genebank, which holds more than 117,000 rice accessions and will lend small quantities of rice to anyone for experimentation, research, or breeding.[17]

Mackill found that he could not cross the flood-immune rice with cultivated rice to produce the yields and agronomic attributes needed to make it commercially useful. However, by using a genetic rice map developed by other researchers, Mackill and his colleagues were able to develop a number of high-yielding, flood-immune rice varieties. Because these rice varieties can withstand long periods of time underwater, they were dubbed "scuba" rice.

This remarkable new rice variety will help build the resilience of rice farmers around the world by reducing their vulnerability to the sea-level rise and increased flooding that are predicted to cause a 15 percent drop in rice production in developing countries in the coming years. Scuba rice will also be an important asset to millions of the world's poor throughout India and Southeast Asia who depend on rice as a food staple.[18]

Another collaborative initiative that follows in the Borlaug tradition is the Alliance for a Green Revolution in Africa. It began in 2006 as a partnership between the Bill and Melinda Gates Foundation and The

Rockefeller Foundation, and it drew on our decades of agricultural experience and has been led by an experienced staff recruited from across Africa. The alliance set out to develop tools and solutions for Africa's small-scale farmers with the goal of catalyzing an African green revolution that would lead to greater food security and prosperity across the continent. To accomplish that, we knew we would have to examine opportunities for growth across the entire agricultural value chain—including farms, farmer organizations, research institutions, African seed companies, food processors, distributors, governments, and other partners—rather than focusing on a single domain or specific challenge. Crucial partnerships have developed, leading to a diversity of thinking and a range of innovative solutions in seventeen countries.

These investments have already begun to pay out the resilience dividend. An individual example is Janet Matemba, an entrepreneur and mother living in rural Malawi. For years, she ran her own microbusiness, selling biscuits, soda, cooking oil, and soap to farmers in her community. Then she decided to try her hand at selling agricultural products. With the support and partnership of the Rural Market Development Trust, an Alliance for a Green Revolution in Africa grantee, Matemba went back to school to get certified in agro dealing. With certificate in hand, she was able to secure credit to purchase fertilizer and seeds in bulk. She repackaged them in smaller quantities for sale to farmers and found that her new products were far more profitable than biscuits and soda had been. Her business grew so much that within a few years her shop had expanded to warehouse size, and, in one successful year, she sold $250,000 worth of seeds and fertilizer.[19] Matemba continues to build her business, hire more community members, help farmers improve their yields, and increase food security. She is, in short, building resilience in her community—an outcome sparked by her partnership with the Rural Market Development Trust.

PUBLIC-PRIVATE PARTNERSHIPS are those in which groups from the public sector ally with a private entity to develop and fund a project together. This was how, as part of an initiative called Project Impact, a disaster-resistant Boys and Girls Club shelter was created in Deerfield Beach, Florida.

Project Impact, launched in 1997, is really a hybrid, in that it was funded by the federal government and then engendered a number of public-private community-based partnerships. Project Impact was developed by the Federal Emergency Management Agency, and its purpose was to help communities assess their situation, identify vulnerabilities, increase awareness, and develop strategies to improve their defenses, reduce or remove their vulnerabilities, and mitigate threats so that when a disruption inevitably struck it would not become a disaster. FEMA, clearly understanding the importance of building resilience, hoped these efforts would significantly reduce costs for both the agency and the communities it worked with, by shifting attention—and spending—to readiness efforts and away from relief.

Seven communities were chosen to test the Project Impact approach, and each community was awarded a $1 million grant. A local person—a high school baseball coach, a town manager, a member of the chamber of commerce—was chosen to head the Project Impact initiative. To help them get started, Barry Scanlon, special assistant to FEMA director James Lee Witt, developed the *Project Impact Guidebook* that outlined four steps to building disaster resistance: partnerships, assessment, mitigation, and success. The initial partnership—between FEMA and the communities—provided a model for the intracommunity partnerships and collaborations to come. "We wanted to get away from government," Scanlon says. When talking to people in the communities, he would say, "This is your program. We're just here to help."[20]

Scanlon worked with the community leaders to identify and attract potential partners within the community, looking for the strongest and most engaged individuals and organizations who might be in a position to take on responsibility. In Deerfield Beach, Florida, for instance—Project Impact's first pilot community—the largest Toyota distributor in the United States stepped up to the responsibility. In Pascagoula, Mississippi, it was Ingalls Shipbuilding—one of the largest private employers in Mississippi and a major shipbuilder for the

US Navy. And although not every community has the "largest" one thing or another, they all have institutions and organizations of some kind—a Home Depot, a grocery store, a financial institution, a public library, a faith-based group—that are important entities as employers, resource providers, and, not insignificantly, as owners of physical facilities—particularly ones with public spaces where people in the community can interact to talk about readiness and could also shelter in case of an emergency. Partners could also be sources of education and training. A Home Depot in one Project Impact community, for example, offered classes in how to attach window shutters before a storm.

Scanlon and his Project Impact community leaders found that identifying potential partners was often easier than building partnerships with them. "The private sector does not see a lot of ROI in preparedness," Scanlon says. From a business perspective this may seem to make sense, as it can be difficult to quantify what the return on an investment in resilience might be. But we know there are returns—in the form of reduced cost of relief, fewer work days lost, and less money spent on health care and reconstruction, as well as in building stronger communities and workforces that will be more capable of sustaining long-term economic growth through ups and downs.

To help companies come around to the idea that readiness is a good investment, Scanlon would tell business leaders a story about General Electric. GE, he told them, operated a world-class facility in North Carolina, built to standards that exceeded those specified by applicable laws and regulations. In early September 1996, Hurricane Fran rammed into the East Coast of the United States, downing power lines and causing billions of dollars of damage. The GE plant came through with flying colors. Although the GE facility suffered no structural damage, there were significant social disruptions. The day after the hurricane, the plant was fully operational and ready to go, but nobody showed up for work. "All their houses were damaged," Scanlon says. "All the schools were closed." When Scanlon told the story to business leaders in Project Impact communities, he'd say, "If you want your employees at work, do something to make sure they're going to be at work."

In Deerfield Beach, the Moran family—owners of the Toyota distributor—got the message. They were already spearheading a drive to build a new Boys and Girls Club facility for the city. Scanlon and the Project Impact community leader went to the family and suggested they make an example of the new clubhouse. Why not build the club to standards higher than the south Florida building code, add features that would make it an excellent shelter, and then hold it up as a national model of a disaster-resistant Boys and Girls Club? The project went forward, and the $2 million construction project was funded in part with city donations, Project Impact support, and the Moran family and its Toyota dealership. It now qualifies as an emergency shelter for all of Broward County, where Deerfield Beach is located.[21]

These community partnerships are vital not only because they generate creative and collaborative solutions to vulnerabilities but also because they unite disparate groups in the community around a common cause of readiness. Everyone has their "everyday missions," as Scanlon calls them, which may not overlap or intersect. But pulling these resources together to build resilience strengthens community unity, identity, and communication—all of which inevitably increase a community's capacity to work together and problem-solve before, during, and after a disruption occurs. Scanlon believes that if you start to think of your community as disaster resistant, then you can apply that ethos to everything you do.

A postscript: Scanlon remembers having a casual dinner with friends at a house on the Delaware shore, not far from one of Project Impact's communities, the city of Lewes. He had vacationed with the same group earlier that year and had talked so much about Project Impact that his friends had been "bored to death." This time was different. When the pizza they had ordered arrived, it was impossible not to notice a pink sheet of paper taped to the box cover. It read: "Project Impact Hurricane Prevention Tips." Scanlon's friends could not help but be impressed.

"If a regional pizza chain can play its part," Scanlon says, "anybody can."

IF A SMALL BUSINESS LIKE A PIZZA CHAIN CAN PLAY ITS PART in increasing the resilience of its community, then certainly small organizations can play a similar role in a city like Glasgow.

As we've seen, the city was struggling to adapt to the post-industrial economy and rising globalization in the 1970s and 1980s, and it became acutely aware that adaptation would require fundamental change. However, big transformations often emerge from small resilience-building initiatives, and that is just what happened in Glasgow.

The resurgence began quietly in the late 1980s with a number of developments in what might seem like an unlikely area of renewal activity: the city's arts and culture scene. A new museum, the Burrell Collection, was opened in picturesque Pollok Country Park. The city came together with the private sector to sponsor an advertising campaign, called *Glasgow's Miles Better*, created to add luster to Glasgow's image and which proved highly popular. In 1988, the Garden Festival attracted hundreds of thousands of visitors to the city.

But it took a larger, more integrated push, with greater diversity of activities and voices, to lift Glasgow out of the resilience deficit it had slumped into during the previous decades. In the mid-1980s, the city council leadership decided to bid to become the European Capital of Culture. This is an initiative of the European Commission which "is designed to: highlight the richness and diversity of cultures in Europe; celebrate the cultural features Europeans share, increase European citizens' sense of belonging to a common cultural area;" and "foster the contribution of culture to the development of cities."[22]

Glasgow won the honor and decided to raise the bar. Rather than concentrate the activities into a few weeks of excitement, Glasgow elected to extend the run of the festival for an entire year. What's more, the organizers expanded the definition of culture to include more than the traditional arts—such as music and fine art and theater—so they could showcase all Glasgow had to offer, including its cultural history, its stunning architecture, its sports, and even the manufacturing arts associated with shipbuilding.[23] The *Queen Elizabeth*, after all, is a masterpiece of craftsmanship, a thing of beauty, and a global icon of European culture.

One benefit of taking on an initiative such as this is the phenomenon known as a deadline. It's one thing to feel a general urgency to create change and build resilience within a city; it's quite another to have to deliver under the watchful eyes of the European Commission, the previous winning cities, hundreds of thousands of visitors, and, indeed, the entire world. So, with only a short time to plan, Glasgow had no choice but to call on diverse groups from across the city and throughout Scotland—from national headliners to neighborhood arts organizations—to participate and contribute. Glasgow's arts institutions and cultural groups rose to the challenge and collectively staged a number and range of activities that was nothing short of staggering: 3,961 theater and concert hall performances, 429 exhibitions, more than 2,000 educational programs, and 2,212 community events.[24]

Not only did the individual groups and institutions perform, the private and public sectors came together to support them. The private sector invested some £6.1 million in the city's arts and culture[25] while public entities supported the £29.4 million opening of the Glasgow Royal Concert Hall and the restoration of arts venues such as the Tramway and the McLellan Galleries.[26]

What was particularly encouraging about Glasgow's response was that it generated terrific awareness of just how rich the city's assets actually were. Little by little, in small steps and isolated actions, the city's cultural base had been expanding and diversifying. "What we are doing in the year of culture," said Glasgow City Councilor Pat Lally in 1990, "is building on successful festivals and successful organisations that exist in the city already."[27] The assets were there, and the Capital of Culture year proved it.

As the year went on, Glasgow became more and more determined to capitalize on the long-term opportunity and began to see the Capital of Culture as part of a "bold, strategic decision to use the city's cultural infrastructure as a catalyst for regeneration" despite the "major economic obstacles."[28]

The success of the Capital of Culture year changed the city's narrative in a way that no advertising campaign could. Visitors from other parts of Scotland, from other countries in the EU, and from places around the world got a taste of the new Glasgow and they liked it. Nearly three out of every four domestic tourists reported they intended to return to the city,[29] and research showed that the year as Capital of Culture "substantially improved perceptions of the City at home and abroad," with nearly all Glaswegians agreeing that it "improved the public image of Glasgow."[30]

During and after the 1990 festival, Glasgow was possessed of a new pride, a more cohesive sense of identity, and the beginnings of a shared vision for itself. Alastair Brown saw firsthand how the Capital of Culture gave Glaswegians a new sense of themselves and their city. "We started to look upon ourselves not as a city that was full of unemployment and poor communities and high levels of deprivation," Brown says. "We had something positive to offer." They had demonstrated that the city could adapt and perhaps transform. Glaswegians use the old Scots word *gallus*—meaning self-confident, daring, and even cheeky—as an affectionate way of describing someone or something that punches above its weight. Certainly, gallus is an appropriate way of characterizing Glasgow's approach to resilience building in order to achieve a dividend.

However, not all of Glasgow's vulnerabilities were erased, nor were all of its challenges met during the Capital of Culture year. When the initiative came to an end, the city struggled to continue the momentum and find its way forward. It took another decade of work to bring together grassroots efforts, entrepreneurial initiatives, and government programs into a more intentional and strategic revitalization framework.[31]

Today, Scotland's largest city, with a population of 600,000, has regained its status as an important European urban player, although it looks very different from the industrial powerhouse of a century ago. The city continues to host world-class events, enjoys a thriving tourism and conference industry, and is the second biggest shopping destination in the UK, after London.[32] In the last five years it was named an IBM Smarter City and was selected for the 100 Resilient Cities network. And the arts community, which played such a key role at the dawn of the transformation, is thriving as never before. Glasgow is home to the National Theatre of Scotland, the Scottish Ballet, the Scottish Opera, the Royal Scottish National Orchestra, and the BBC Scottish Symphony Orchestra, as well as a myriad of smaller institutions and arts-related groups.

Glasgow is "a city in transformation," a place that is "recovering steadily from a post-industrial legacy of social, economic and environmental shock" and that aims to be "one of the most sustainable cities in Europe,"[33] as city officials wrote in their 100 RC application. "Glasgow isn't the shipbuilding, steel, coal town that it used to be," says the Scottish comedian Billy Connolly. "This is a place for life, writing, poetry, rock and roll, classical music, opera. It's buzzing, jumping, always will be. Always slightly ahead of the game...I love it. It sings and dances!"[34]

8

GETTING AHEAD OF THREATS
Addressing Vulnerabilities

Now, how do you go about addressing vulnerabilities? How can you increase readiness for future disruptions? What resilience-building actions can be taken to decrease the impact that disruptions will have?

What, for example, can you do to be more able to withstand an earthquake, less vulnerable to crime, better able to get through a drought, or avert a cyberattack?

Look to your assets. What strengths and resources can be brought to bear on the issue? Which individuals, groups, agencies, and institutions might generate ideas about reducing vulnerabilities and protecting against threats?

STRENGTHENING INFRASTRUCTURE:
SAN FRANCISCO'S 80,000 VULNERABLE BUILDINGS

We saw, in San Francisco, how a prolonged period of assessment made the extent of the area's vulnerability to the threat of earthquake unignorably clear. The next "big one" could be the city's most destructive ever. With the city's structures cataloged, the next step in the development of the *Community Action Plan for Seismic Safety*

(CAPSS) was to make recommendations for action. To do that, the leaders of the initiative engaged in a herculean effort of collaboration that took the better part of a decade to complete. They assembled a public advisory committee with more than a hundred individuals representing an impressive array of disparate organizations from throughout the city: the mayor's office, city agencies, the California Seismic Safety Commission, architects, engineers, real estate consultants, landlords, housing activists, property owners, as well as private citizens.

The advisory group came up with a list of seventeen recommended actions, based on the CAPSS findings, that would significantly reduce the city's seismic vulnerabilities and which were detailed in the city's Earthquake Safety Implementation Program. It was completed in 2011 and is exactly what it says it is: a detailed plan to put the CAPSS recommendations into place over a period of thirty years. It fell to Patrick Otellini—who was then the director of earthquake safety and, before that, had been a member of the CAPSS study advisory committee—to focus on its implementation.

The very first task: mandatory retrofits of soft-story buildings (wood-frame structures with large ground-floor openings), those structures identified as the most vulnerable and that account for more than half of San Francisco's 160,000 buildings. According to detailed construction cost estimates done as part of the CAPSS study, each soft-story retrofit can cost anywhere between $60,000 and $130,000.[1] But, in San Francisco's sky-high real estate market, the buildings themselves can be worth upward of $7 million. With these retrofits, Otellini says, "You get the most bang for your buck," protecting high-value property without displacing tenants, as the retrofits are typically limited to the ground floors, which often do not contain dwelling units.

The city now faced the same issue that businesses wrestle with: a cost-benefit analysis. How can we finance such a huge endeavor? Is the potential return really worth the investment? To finance the retrofits, the city proposed a $40 million general obligation bond—a collection of tax revenue—to fund low-interest loans for developers and property owners. A similar tactic was employed after the Loma Prieta quake, when a $360 million bond was approved—by the requisite two-thirds majority of the citizenry of San Francisco—to retrofit and rebuild the city's damaged or destroyed buildings. But times then were different—it was the 1990s, the United States was in an economic boom, and the threat of earthquake was fresh on San Francisco's (and California's) mind. In a staggering economy post-2008, more than a decade removed from a significant quake, the bond—which would have benefited a small percentage of Californians (and San Franciscans—some 60,000 out of 830,000)—failed to reach a two-thirds majority vote.

Otellini, however, was unfazed, in part because of what happened to the bond in the 1990s. "No one used it," he says. "People found that trying to qualify for public financing, jumping through so many hoops—it became very cumbersome." Instead, developers and property owners sought loans from the private sector, specifically from the banks with which they had already established working relationships and had some familiarity.

Otellini then made a bold move. He approached the banks directly. He knocked on the doors, he says, of "every financial institution in the city," explaining the retrofit ordinance, the size and rates of potential loans, inviting them—with the expectation of rejection—to come to the table and consider their options. To Otellini's surprise, they all accepted. "The overall message I heard was, we're San Francisco companies. We've chosen to invest here and have our operations here. We want to be a part of this." These financial institutions did not stand to gain large profits from the loans. Their agreement is at the heart of resilience: a community or city must be able to tap its own resources and make a commitment to strengthen itself, even if individual entities see only a small benefit. But, in the long-term, whatever strengthens a community or a city will likely strengthen the entire fabric of the network that holds it together and makes it run.

In 2013, Otellini organized a financing workshop, inviting representatives of the banks and some 6,000 property owners who had already been informed by the city of the retrofit ordinance. It was an opportunity for the two groups to meet, talk, establish relationships, and identify mutually beneficial outcomes. The workshop was such a success that it inspired another, held in 2014. At this one, engineers, contractors, manufacturers, insurance companies, and other related services were also invited, totaling more than 120 vendors. The goal, Otellini says, is to put together a long list of vendors so people have many choices of individuals and firms to work with, so they'll "be able to call fifty different architects and contractors and banks."

Mitigation—from deciding what to do, how to do it, and then motivating and encouraging citizens to do it—is not an easy or quick process. And, as Otellini says, "Most people are probably going to go with the path of least resistance." But, by corralling as many stakeholders as possible, from the CAPSS advisory committee to the financing and retrofitting fairs, Otellini and the City of San Francisco are making it easier for citizens to take action—mandated by the state and city—to reduce their seismic vulnerability.

Building resilience takes time. The ideas of rapid rebound and bouncing back from a disruption are valid, but rapidity and rebound time are relative. A structural element of a building (such as a beam) may, after deforming under load, return to its original form in a moment after the load is removed. Even those stressed tectonic plates of the earth experience elastic rebound within a minute or so after the tension is released. But human processes of change take longer. The catalyzing quake erupted in 1989, was over in a minute, but was followed by some two decades of awareness building, assessment, and development of an action plan. The Earthquake Safety Implementation Program, introduced in 2012, is scheduled for completion in 2042—more than fifty years after the Loma Prieta quake collapsed the Cypress Street Viaduct. The takeaway: you cannot, and should not, expect to build resilience overnight. "It's like exercise," Otellini says. "It's not something you do once and forget about. You have to do it every day, to be constantly doing it, constantly changing *how* you do it. That's how you get ready."

IMPROVING TRANSPORTATION:
THE MEDELLIN METRO

The process of getting a city like San Francisco ready for the known threat of earthquake seems quite different from getting a city like Medellin ready for the disruptions that come with urbanization and globalization—including crime and rapid growth—but, in fact, both involved structural actions.

Over the years, Medellin had tried to face its threats in many ways. To reduce the chronic stress of crime, they had staged military interventions against gangs. They had arrested and incarcerated drug traffickers and murderers until the jails were bulging, but the inmates kept right on doing business from behind bars.

Then Medellin focused on a single, specific vulnerability that, if addressed, might make the city more ready to manage further population growth and enable its citizens to pursue new livelihoods as businesses came in. The vulnerability was the lack of mobility, poor accessibility, and extreme isolation of the poorest and most vulnerable communities—the barrios—especially those that had sprung up on the steep hillsides. We know that fractured communities are vulnerable ones and that disruptions, such as violent crime, affect them more than others. Isolated people don't know one another and are less likely to share information about what is happening or generate ideas about actions to take. Disconnected communities can't pool resources and have a hard time coming together in groups and are thus more vulnerable to being threatened, bullied, terrorized, and taken over by gangs.

To address this vulnerability, Medellin's solution was to design and build its extensive public transportation system. The Metro, which began operating on November 30, 1995, has two rail lines, two bus rapid transit routes, and three cable car lines—small in comparison to the transportation systems of cities like London or Buenos Aires or Tokyo, but a major infrastructural development for Medellin.[2] Now the majority of residents have low-cost access to all areas of the city (one ticket, valid for ninety minutes, connects riders to all transport modes and costs around 1800 pesos, or ninety cents), so they can pursue opportunities that were previously out of reach.

The Medellin Metro is more than a transportation network, it's a striking example of what is known as "transit-oriented development"—an area that integrates transportation lines and stations with commercial enterprises, private residences and public housing, institutions, and public spaces. The idea is that mobility is fundamental to city life and that transportation infrastructure should be as much a part of the designed cityscape as are buildings and streets. The Medellin Metro connects a wonderful sprawl of community centers, health clinics, and training and youth-oriented facilities, as well as popular libraries located at the main transfer stations of the cable car network.

With the Metro system in place, Medellin did increase its readiness for growth and expansion. Indeed, the Metro is a shining example of the resilience dividend: it raises the level of city life above the baseline that residents were accustomed to even a few years earlier. The characteristics of resilience are there: the assertive presence of the Metro demonstrates the city's awareness of the importance of mobility. The elements of the system are diverse and integrated into the look and life of the place.

Yet, even these successful elements of the Medellin Metro system did not reduce the vulnerability of limited mobility and poor access in *all* the city's neighborhoods. The San Javier barrio, for example, was still isolated. Yes, the residents had much greater ability to get around the city than ever before—once they walked down the hillside to the rail stations and bus stops in the city below. But the barrio itself remained disconnected. It is a huddle of close-set one- to three-story brick houses that seem almost to perch one on top of the other, their corrugated metal roofs held in place with stones. The narrow streets peter out and become footpaths when the hill gets too steep. Climbing one of the byways into the barrio is more like a mountain hike than a city stroll.

Its isolation had made San Javier particularly vulnerable to the disruptions of drug trafficking, crime, and gang warfare. For decades, San Javier had been known as one of the most violent neighborhoods in a violent district in one of the most violent cities in the world. Because of its position, San Javier had become a favored route for drug traffickers in and out of the city. The neighborhood is so densely built, so easy to get lost in, and so difficult to navigate, gangs were able to divide the area into private turfs marked by invisible borders that residents simply had to be aware of—but that police and outsiders usually were not. If you entered the wrong zone at the wrong moment, even with the most in-nocent of purposes, gang members saw that as trespass. Shoot-outs and street killings were commonplace. And there was very little to stop them. Police and emergency vehicles could not easily negotiate the streets.

So, although the city of Medellin was building its resilience through actions such as building the Metro, neighborhoods like San Javier were still vulnerable. As Medellin became more aware of such vulnerabilities and the disruptions they could bring, it became more evident that the threat had to be faced. It could no longer be tolerated as "just the way things are." Something had to be done before the situation in San Javier exploded and affected the rest of the city's advancement.

As it turned out, the capacity was right there, waiting to be devel-oped. San Javier's geography made it nearly impossible to bring light rail or bus rapid transit to the neighborhood, but people were used to walking—it was just that the distances were too great. It could take a half hour to get off the hillside. If you held a job across the valley, it might take three hours by foot.

How can you still walk but cut your travel time, especially on a steep hill? *Escalators.* There are a number of versions of the story of how Medellin's escalators came to be—there are always many parents to a successful idea. The narrative, at various points along the way, involves the efforts of neighborhood residents, city officials, outside agencies, and others. Local mothers' groups and a team of engineers in the city's planning department—with nearly ten years of evidence demonstrating that public transit had improved the lives of people in many other parts of the city—figure prominently in the story, as does then Mayor Sergio Fajardo.

The idea seemed audacious. Build an escalator system into the hillside of San Javier that would turn a thirty-minute hike into a five-minute glide. Escalators would provide the hillside residents greater mobility, give official agencies much better access to the neighborhood, and better connect the community with the rest of the city, creating new opportunities, economic and otherwise. Like the other transportation solutions the city had built, it would reduce a persistent vulnerability.

The mayor, who had a penchant for expansive public architecture and infrastructure initiatives, agreed to an investment in the project that amounted to nearly $7 million.

The San Javier escalators, now considered the crown jewel of Medellin's transportation system (although not actually a part of the Metro system itself), opened in 2012 in a public ceremony that received international press coverage. Today the tangle of footpaths and lanes has been augmented by a series of six gleaming escalators of the kind you might find in any suburban mall, that climb 1,260 feet up the hillside.[3] They are open to the air on both sides, shielded from the elements by glass and orange-painted metal roofs.

The escalators, along with a network of elevated lateral walkways, have dramatically reduced the isolation of San Javier's residents and thus addressed an important vulnerability of the city as a whole. The barrio is now open to the rest of Medellin so people can easily get to jobs in the valley. The barrio is less vulnerable to gang activity and less attractive to drug traffickers who needed seclusion and counted on being several steps ahead of the authorities. Representatives of social programs are more regular visitors to San Javier now that access has improved. Community organizations, including the Red Cross, whose staffers and volunteers avoided such places, have been able to safely work with the people of Comuna 13. "Without the escalators, these groups and government agencies wouldn't come here to work because they had no way in," said one San Javier resident. "Now, with these institutions playing a role, we can organize and coordinate better social programs, which have been one of the main drivers of change in this neighborhood."[4]

OTHER FORMS OF INFRASTRUCTURE, such as online connection, can also improve access and lead to better integration within a neighborhood or among groups. It is hard to imagine a world without the Internet or to accept that our hyperconnected wireless network could fail so catastrophically as to completely disconnect large networks. But, as we have seen, inundative flooding (as well as other hazards) can knock out the electricity that powers our networks. What's more, cyber-breaches can disrupt the technologies involved in transmitting data around the Internet and sever our connections. (Sometimes the disruption is just an accident. In 2011, a woman digging for scrap copper severed a fiber-optic cable with her shovel and knocked out 90 percent of the connectivity for the entire country of Armenia for about five hours.[5])

We have become so reliant on the Internet as a method of communication, a source of information, and a way to create and maintain social connections that the loss of connectivity is hardly trivial in a crisis. What if we could achieve some degree of connectivity without relying on this global, distributed, open—and highly vulnerable—network? That is the intent of a "mesh network"—a local network of users connected by a series of routers and antennas installed on rooftops throughout a neighborhood, community, or even a small city. The network is driven by its own server and provides access to whatever information is stored there. A mesh network provided connectivity for residents in Red Hook—a neighborhood in Brooklyn—when Superstorm Sandy interrupted connectivity there.

The mesh platform also has the potential to be a powerful community-building and networking tool for areas in the developing world that lack connectivity or have limited or unreliable access. The routers (which cost between $50 and $80 each) are installed within view of each other throughout an area and automatically connect to one another and thus expand the network—so users can wirelessly access the mesh software and connect with one another.

Although in times of normalcy and in areas of good connectivity the mesh network has its particular advantages (it is a hyperlocal, private network, and thus avoids many of the security issues associated with connection to the World Wide Web), in times of crisis and disruption it could prove a vital lifeline—a backup communications and knowledge-sharing system—keeping community members in touch and facilitating communication that could help people marshal resources and direct first responders to community members most in need. Although it may not be feasible or beneficial to install mesh networks everywhere, those communities most vulnerable to systems breakdown and those with large gaps in connectivity (or those without access to the Internet at all) might consider such a network as an important element in improving readiness.[6]

RISK TRANSFER:
INSURANCE AND ASSET PROTECTION

Although the retrofits in San Francisco and the escalators in Medellin are physical solutions taken to reduce vulnerability to a specific threat in immediate and tangible ways, another medium through which entities can reduce their risk for when things go wrong is through the purchase of insurance.

We have already discussed the great and growing cost of disruptions around the world, but we have not yet fully explored the essential question: Who pays for the losses incurred in a disruption? How? The answers are not as clear cut as you might expect. The loss figures I cited earlier are for the total loss in a disaster, but, depending on the region and the event, insurance usually covers at least a portion of those amounts. However, insurance is a luxury that many in the developing world—or those living in the developed world but of modest means—cannot afford or do not have access to or forego because of underestimation of risk or the perception they are covered by government programs. The effect of this can be seen when comparing insured losses from disasters region to region. An interesting case exhibits itself when comparing two of the largest storms in recent memory: Superstorm Sandy, which caused significant disruption on the East Coast of the United States, and Supertyphoon Haiyan, which had catastrophic effects in the Philippines and Vietnam. Sandy caused $65 billion in losses, while Supertyphoon Haiyan caused $13 billion. Nearly half—$30 billion—of the losses incurred from

Sandy were covered by insurance, while insurance covered less than 10 percent of Haiyan's losses.[7]

There are two factors at play. The first is whose assets are affected and what types of assets they are. Supertyphoon Haiyan was the strongest tropical cyclone ever to make landfall and yet caused significantly less financial loss than did Sandy.[8] That is, of course, because Sandy did its damage to New York City, whose GDP is $1.3 trillion.[9] The GDP of the entire republic of the Philippines is a fifth of that, about $250 billion.[10] Where significant assets are at stake, more is likely to be lost—and more is likely to be insured. But, of course, such assets are mostly tangible ones and do not include lives lost or even livelihoods unrecoverable.

The second factor is the insurance market itself. "If you're in a well-developed market like Japan," says Martyn Parker, chair of global partnerships at Swiss Re, a global reinsurance and insurance provider that works with clients in both the public and private sectors, "you might see something like 40 percent coverage." But in countries like Pakistan or Bangladesh, Parker says, insurance might cover damage from earthquakes and floods only in single-digit percentages, "if it even reaches one percent."[11]

Overall, however, Swiss Re has found that insurance covers, on average over the last three decades, about 30 percent of total economic loss from these natural disasters, even in the most developed markets. The other 70 percent? "Of course," says Parker, "it falls to the citizens. It falls to the corporations. And it falls to government offices, both at the municipal and national level as governments often act as the insurer of last resort."

If weather events and natural catastrophes continue to cause $178 billion in annualized losses—and they very likely might cost more—and insurance companies cover an average of 30 percent of these losses, the price tag for citizens, companies, and governments will be almost $125 billion per year annualized.[12] And that is a best-case scenario. Becoming more resilient in a turbulent and unpredictable world will require that, when disruption inevitably strikes, insurance coverages have been secured, so that our cities, communities, and the people that inhabit them can recover more rapidly and to lessen the public expenditure in the aftermath of disaster that may be better applied to activities and initiatives that help us build resilience before disruption strikes.

Insuring against disruption is a complex process, and it involves a fair amount of psychology. As we've discussed, it is difficult to motivate people to spend now to avoid loss later on, especially when there is uncertainty about the likelihood of a threat actually occurring, as there almost always is. But insurance is a vital component to readiness, as payouts delivered when disruptions occur facilitate an entity's ability to respond to crisis in both the immediate and long-term phases of recovery and restoration.

Because the nature of disruption is changing and the potential for loss is growing, the insurance industry will face challenges and require changes in the years ahead. These changes, many of which are in process, will inevitably have wide-ranging consequences, which will have varying impacts country to country, city to city, person to person.

A startling example of these changes and their potential impact can be seen in New York City post-Sandy. After that storm, the Federal Emergency Management Agency was forced to reassess the city's floodplain map, which had been used to predict the extent of potential flooding as well as to calculate US National Flood Insurance Program premiums and payouts. Prior to Sandy, the map had not been significantly updated since 1983—the year it was first released. For New York, Sandy was an unprecedented storm: it brought the largest surge ever recorded in Battery Park, at the southern tip of Manhattan, of 13.88 feet—the previous high was 10.02 feet, set by Hurricane Donna in 1960. The surf in New York Harbor also reached record heights, with a buoy measuring a wave at 32.5 feet—the previous record, from Hurricane Irene in 2011, was 25 feet.[13] The flooding that resulted was greater than anyone expected, in part because of the outdated (and thus nearly irrelevant) floodplain map. Clearly, as we have seen, awareness is critical for readiness, and updating all floodplain mapping now, before the next emergency, is crucial in the United States and globally.

In June 2013, FEMA released an updated map, which nearly doubled the number of structures and residents deemed to be within New York City's high-risk areas. Some 90 percent of those structures had been constructed prior to their inclusion in the high-risk area mapping and therefore did not conform to floodplain building and development standards.[14] Cities and communities around the world will be forced to make similar dramatic reassessments of their risks and vulnerabilities, as unprecedented storms become the new global norm.

In light of these changes, New York City's Mayor's Office of Long-Term Planning and Sustainability engaged the RAND Corporation—a nonprofit research and analysis group with a focus on improving policy and decision making—to analyze how flood insurance coverage, the release of the updated map, and the new regulations would affect insurance coverage and rates.

They found that, for some people, the effect on insurance premiums will be minimal or, at least, tolerable. For residences built before 1983—when the first flood map was released—premiums would not change. In other cases, premiums may increase by $1,000 to $2,000. But for those whose buildings were previously outside high-risk areas for flooding but now fall within those zones in the updated map, the increase in premiums will be much steeper. According to the RAND Corporation, this includes nearly 30,000 one- to four-family buildings, and "a $429 annual premium . . . could well rise to $5,000 to $10,000 for the same amount of coverage."[15]

This could be an unbearable economic burden for those affected. Roughly 37 percent of households in owner-occupied units within the updated floodplain have an income of less than $75,000 a year. With an insurance premium of $5,000, these households would be paying more than 6.5 percent of their annual gross income on flood insurance. For comparison, census data indicate that the average household in an owner-occupied unit pays slightly less than 2 percent of its pretax income on housing expenses (such as insurance and repairs), excluding mortgages and property tax.[16]

Although these changes will dramatically affect the lives of individuals and families, it will also come at a cost to the city itself. Research from other regions of the country suggests that a $500 increase in insurance premiums could decrease a property's value by as much as $10,000.[17] Although this may not be the case for New York City, decreases in property value will lead to decreased property tax revenue—less money will be coming into a city's coffers.

The changing landscape of insurance makes obvious the range of inherent tensions and trade-offs that are inevitable when developing land use and building codes that foster resilience building. Some of these deliberations may even drive cities and communities to question their own identity, their essential qualities, when considering how environments—especially coastal areas—become potentially uninhabitable or even submerged. How and where will people live, and will everyone be able to (or should they be prevented from or encouraged to) insure their individual assets if where they live is a threat to them and makes their communities more vulnerable?

Of course, the insurance industry will play a role in how these policy decisions are made, and it is hardly blind to the coming challenges of our unpredictable, volatile world. There are pockets of resilience activity that provide alternative and novel ways of thinking about insuring cities, their assets, and their people—exactly the kind of innovation needed from businesses if we are to become a more resilient world.

Parametric insurance, also known as index insurance, can significantly contribute to the readiness of a country, city, community, organization, or person for dealing with disruption by guaranteeing rapid payout, facilitating a quick response and recovery. Such a system allows communities to "put a price" on their risk, says Parker of Swiss Re, and "helps drive the hazard mitigation implementation on a large community basis, as opposed to a citizen-by-citizen approach." Considering the ways that human populations tend to create developments on land with obvious vulnerabilities (although they vary from region to region), the purchase of parametric insurance could be a driving force in the resilience-building activities of many communities.

The unique feature of parametric insurance is that payout is based on a certain predefined metric—if that threshold is reached, payout is automatic. In many cases, no postevent assessment is required, no adjustors visit any sites, no haggling goes on over settlements, though a proof of loss is still required. So, for example, after an earthquake of a certain magnitude, at a certain depth, within a geographical region or after a storm produces certain wind speeds or certain storm surge, the insurance company cuts a check for the insured "within days, not weeks," says Parker of Swiss Re.

There may, of course, be some negotiation upfront, because the level of payment is also set in advance of any disruption. The benefit is that those insured (whether governments or institutions as well as individuals) know exactly how much money they will receive if the specified disruption exceeds an agreed-upon threshold. The payout can therefore be speedy. An added benefit is that the insured can calculate the level of insurance protection in comparison to the value of the assets at risk. If the fixed payout of the parametric insurance does not cover the full value of the assets, the insured might decide to seek additional coverage from a different source.

A downside of parametric insurances is that the payout could fall short of the total amount of the loss—just as there is the potential that the payout will exceed it. "We think the benefits outweigh the basis risk," says Parker. "Government has the freedom to spend that money however they wish. They can prioritize where the dollars go."

No city or community or individual is without risk, and the insurance industry, where it is available, can—indeed, must—be a useful tool by which entities can mitigate the potential costs of a known threat. For that to be the case, though, the industry itself—including public providers (such as the National Flood Insurance Program) as well as private ones—will have to continue to innovate, offering new products that are accessible, affordable, and allow the affected to decide how to overcome and recover from a disruption in a way that will best facilitate their revitalization and continued resilience-building efforts.

PARAMETRIC INSURANCE HAS SUCCESSFULLY INCREASED the resilience of farmers who make their livings tending tiny plots of land in drought-prone areas of Ethiopia. The Rockefeller Foundation, along with Swiss Re, is a funder of an experiment with parametric insurance run by the global nongovernmental organization, Oxfam. Originally called the Horn of Africa Risk Transfer for Adaptation initiative, or HARITA, it is now known as R4 Rural Resilience Initiative. Farmers who were previously deemed uninsurable can purchase weather-indexed insurance. When the rains don't come, or don't meet a certain threshold, growers know they'll quickly receive a predetermined payout or a percentage of the value of their insurance. Droughts that once forced farmers to sell their assets—including valuable oxen—to pay off small business loans no longer devastate livelihoods for years to come.

But it's not just the index insurance that's innovative—it's also HARITA's payment system and model for reducing risk. In many villages, farmers can purchase index insurance through an existing government program by working on projects that mitigate risk and improve resilience in their communities. No cash is required to purchase the insurance. (This model was proposed by one of the farmers.) They might, for example, improve local irrigation systems, create terraces, increase agroforestry, start composting and gardening, or build soil bunds, which are channels dug into the earth to direct water runoff so it doesn't pool around plants or create a destructive water surge on sloped fields. In this way, farmers buy insurance with their time and labor—which has the further benefit of reducing their community's vulnerability and the potential effects of the next disruption, whatever it might be.

Farmers can also apply for small loans from the insurance reserves at reasonable rates and use the money to invest in seeds and fertilizer or equipment, such as irrigation systems. More recently, HARITA has evolved to include a savings program as well. On average, "farmers insured through HARITA have increased their savings and the number of oxen—the most valuable animal and the main one used to plow the fields—relative to uninsured farmers."[18] The demand is clear: HARITA scaled from 200 households in 2009 to more than 20,365 farmers in eighty villages in 2013. Under its new name, the R4 Rural Resilience Initiative, the program has expanded from Ethiopia to Senegal as well.[19]

These measures—risk transfer through index insurance, risk mitigation through risk-reduction projects, smart risk taking through microcredit, and risk reserves through savings groups—improve the daily incomes of farmers in good times and increase their resilience so they bounce back more quickly, particularly when faced with predictable shocks, a great example of how people with minimal assets and few resources can realize the resilience dividend.

PRACTICING: WHAT COULD GO WRONG

No matter how diligent you are in reducing vulnerabilities or mitigating threats, you cannot predict or prevent any and every disruption, so you must also be prepared to fail more safely and rebound more quickly. Preparedness involves developing plans and protocols and practicing them. Microemergencies (minor disruptions) can serve as simulations of and practice for major shocks and threats.

THAT WAS THE THINKING behind Quantum Dawn, a financial catastrophe simulation, that Citi, the two-hundred-year-old global financial institution, participated in. The bank is attuned to the need for readiness and specific plans to manage disruptions. If banks go down, people can't access cash, business operations grind to a halt, and financial markets go haywire. If they are vulnerable to a threat, their dysfunction can create a devastating cascade of crises.

Over the past decade, Citi has shifted its approach from "perimeter-based" security (such as alerts and alarms) to a threat-driven model that predicts hazards, assesses risks, and implements interventions. Given the rapidly changing nature of the company's digital—and physical—environments, Citi employees spend a great deal of time understanding the business's current situation while also anticipating new threats and opportunities.

In July 2013, Citi and some fifty other banks, along with related institutions and agencies, including the Securities and Exchange Commission and the FBI—all of which are members of the Securities Industry and Financial Markets Association (SIFMA)—engaged in an exercise called Quantum Dawn 2 (a sequel to a previous exercise, Quantum Dawn, the original). The goal of the exercise was "to test incident response, resolution and coordination processes for the financial services sector and the individual member firms to a system-wide cyber attack."[20]

After Quantum Dawn 2 was complete, SIFMA issued an after-action report stating that the test "was completed successfully with robust engagement from all participants. The exercise successfully tested many of the industry's processes and protocols. It raised awareness among industry participants about working together in a coordinated manner to address systemic risk issues and verified the critical importance of information sharing both between firms and the government as vital to identifying attacks and mitigating the impacts."[21]

SIFMA came up with three findings and associated recommendations. First, the industry needed to "update its sector-wide response playbook" to ensure better integration among the "industry groups, market participants, and government agencies." Second, the industry needed to improve its guidelines and "decision frameworks"—decision-making processes—so they can better determine whether a cyber-incident is isolated to their institution or has gone systemic. (Much worse.) Third, communications needed to be improved—among industry players (Should we close markets?) and with the public (What does this mean to you?).[22]

With each imagined scenario and microemergency, Citi, and other like-minded institutions, re-evaluate their structures and systems to increase their readiness. What worked in the simulation? What were the stress points? What could be improved? Each finding becomes an opportunity to discover vulnerabilities and find ways to strengthen assets.

"The core to resiliency," says Don Callahan, Citi's head of technology and operations, "is understanding how bad things can actually get and then determining, is the system designed to take it? We've got to make sure—in the financial world—that we're anticipating what are the shocks we could get."[23]

ALTHOUGH IT IS CRITICAL to determine what disruptions are the most likely to occur and which ones would cause the most damage if they did, the best resilience plans also include building capacity to rebound from what cannot be as readily predicted. On a national level, in the United States, recovery and resilience planning is the job of FEMA. In early 2001, before 9/11 and before Katrina, FEMA named the three catastrophes that were most likely to befall the United States:

- A terrorist attack on New York City

- A major earthquake in San Francisco

- A hurricane that would overwhelm New Orleans[24]

Within four years, two of those scenarios were realized. There is plenty of debate and recrimination over why, if we were so aware of the urgency of these threats, we were not more ready for them.

In the case of New Orleans, it had been clear for years, decades even, that the city faced a grave threat of being overwhelmed by a storm—FEMA's ranking was not a big surprise. Indeed, when Katrina approached New Orleans in late August 2005, it seemed that almost everybody was well aware of just how devastating the effects of such a powerful storm might be—the authorities and governing bodies of the city, members of state and federal government, climatologists, ecologists, city planners, and countless others, including city residents.

Why, then, was the city not more ready to respond?

One reason is, as Barry Scanlon, formerly of Project Impact, puts it, "Mitigation isn't sexy."[25] In other words, it can be tough to get people to focus on developing readiness plans and conducting response exercises. But New Orleans had actually been working on readiness since 1999, after Louisiana narrowly escaped the powerful Hurricane Georges in September 1998. The City of New Orleans worked together with the Louisiana Office of Emergency Preparedness (LOEP), FEMA, and other organizations to assess the effect that Georges could have had on the city had it actually struck. They concluded that it might have been disastrous.[26]

Despite growing concern about the gravity of the situation, it took almost four years to create a proposal to develop a plan and to gain funding for it. Meanwhile, the magnitude of the threat was becoming more widely understood. According to a FEMA assessment in 2003, a storm in the area could become "a disaster of cataclysmic proportion" that would require "massive federal assistance" and first responders and their families could well become "victims" themselves.[27]

But it wasn't until May 2004 that FEMA finally contracted for the development of the plan. The approach was to conduct a live exercise, called Hurricane Pam, that would simulate the response to a catastrophic hurricane. The simulation scenario the group had proposed detailed a storm that was eerily close to the eventual reality of Katrina: an eighteen-foot storm surge overtopping and breaching levees; the city of New Orleans under fourteen to seventeen feet of water; as many as half a million residents stranded; thousands of people, without access to any form of private transportation, unable to "self-evacuate"; and "97 percent of all communications" dysfunctional.[28] FEMA, however, specified that the Hurricane Pam exercise should focus on "post-landfall and recovery issues" including search and rescue, sheltering, and temporary housing, rather than on evacuation.[29] They did not address the topics that we have seen are so important to a resilient response: leadership, continuity of government operations, and situational awareness through communications and feedback loops. The lessons from the exercise would be incorporated into a master plan.[30]

Starting in July 2004, more than three hundred federal, state, and local officials participated in a series of hurricane workshops, the last of which was held in August 2005, just days before Katrina made landfall. When Katrina did hit on August 29 there were many infrastructural failures, but, as bad as they were, the key weaknesses of response were in precisely the issues that did *not* get covered in the Hurricane Pam exercise. And the issue that was most clearly specified—the evacuation of people without access to private transportation—was the one that came to symbolize the inadequacy of the response. These were the ones who ended up stranded on rooftops, who drowned, or who endured the conditions of the temporary sheltering in the Superdome and eventually had to be rescued by the Coast Guard.

The response was such that the US House of Representatives was prompted to conduct an inquiry into what went wrong and why. It declared, in a report released in early 2006, that it was a "failure of initiative."[31] This story makes the point that planning—including the live execution of well-designed exercises—may not be sexy, but it can be a matter of life and death.

ALTHOUGH WE CAN SEE, in hindsight, the shortcomings of the Hurricane Pam exercise, there are many examples of practices and preparations with excellent outcomes. Some of the most interesting of these are ones that follow a basic resilience practice: they pick up on existing programs, organizations, and events that can be leveraged to teach and build resilience. San Francisco is a leader in this regard.

Each year during Columbus Day weekend, nearly one million people gather on the edge of San Francisco Bay to celebrate Fleet Week, a tradition that dates to 1908 and was revived in 1981. While members of the US Navy, Marine Corps, and Coast Guard display their skills and enjoy the city, residents take the opportunity to tour the docked ships, watch demonstrations, and marvel at intricately choreographed air shows.

With so many responders—both civilian and military—gathered in one spot, organizers recognized the opportunity Fleet Week presented and turned it into a large-scale preparedness event. Starting in 2010, joint humanitarian and disaster response exercises were undertaken by military officials, firefighters, police officers, EMTs, emergency managers (including the San Francisco Department of Emergency Management), and other local, state, and federal leaders. Through exercises, seminars, and demonstrations, they plan for the uncertain, under uncertain circumstances.

In 2011 officials conducted a tabletop exercise—a relaxed discussion analyzing an imagined emergency response scenario—during which responders assessed the medical response forty-eight to seventy-two hours following a hypothetical 7.9 magnitude earthquake along the San Andreas Fault. Using only existing knowledge and assets, the diverse group worked through the management, health, operations, transportation, and logistical issues they would encounter while setting up and operating a badly needed field hospital. In the process, they identified weak spots in their plan, including resource deficiencies, communications problems, knowledge gaps, and other vulnerabilities. They also began building the relationships that will be critical for supporting one another when crisis arrives.

The exercises, seminars, and discussions are not earthquake specific—others focus on urban search and rescue, medical exchanges, and the role of elected officials, social media, and the private sector in disaster response—nor are they limited to official responders. Fleet Week's curriculum also includes training programs designed to help the community improve logistical coordination, communication, operations, and leadership.

Resilience-building methods can be learned by anyone, and Fleet Week creatively takes advantage of this fact. Consider: are there programs in your community that might lend themselves to a bit of creative adaptation in the name of resilience education?

To close the loop on San Francisco and its preparedness activities, we need to take a brief look at its emergency web platform, SF72, and, in particular, how it was developed.

When the SF DEM began conversations about how to increase its citizens' readiness for disruptions—whether it be earthquake, heat waves, drought, or fire—they decided they didn't want to do it the "old way"—a one-off campaign about awareness or readiness to a specific threat or problem. Alicia Johnson, the city's resilience and recovery manager, remembers an early conversation she had with Rob Dudgeon and other members of the SF DEM team. "Forget this campaign thing," she said. "That's boring. We did that. It's not working. We should change the culture of preparedness."[32]

How does one go about changing—or even affecting—culture? Dudgeon knew that to do so SF DEM would need outside help. But he wanted to work with a partner skilled in communicating with the general public, rather than a firm expert at dealing with professionals in the disaster and emergency fields. Johnson looked no further than San Francisco and the design firm IDEO, globally recognized for its human-focused approach to design and innovation. After finalizing a contract between IDEO and the city—which required some work and persistence on Johnson's part, as these public-private agreements can be difficult to secure—the team went to work. "The most important thing we did," says Dudgeon in retrospect, "was *not* hire emergency managers."

IDEO began the process as it always does in its projects, with qualitative research—three weeks of in-depth interviewing and talking with people in many neighborhoods and communities in San Francisco, getting a sense of the city's current "culture of preparedness," asking questions such as: What does an emergency mean to you? What does it mean to be prepared? What or who is in your community?

From this assessment period, says Kate Lydon, IDEO's public sector portfolio director and lead on the SF72 initiative, came a set of insights. "The foundational insight," she says, "is that preparedness—and resilience—are about human connections. It isn't about one person having all the supplies they'll ever need for every possible circumstance; instead, it's about everyone having a few key items but, more importantly, having an active network of people that they can share with and get help from."[33]

"Preparedness," says the SF72 platform they eventually created, "is all about people."[34] So although the site does recommend a simple list of emergency supplies to have on hand—including water, nonperish-able foods, a fire extinguisher, and flashlight (and a bottle of wine!)—to last seventy-two hours (the time it might take to be reached by official aid or otherwise assisted by overburdened emergency services), its emphasis is on the connections and networks you already have in place, from social media platforms such as Facebook or Nextdoor—a neighborhood-by-neighborhood connectivity tool—to the members of your running club, your coworkers, and the friends and family you have on speed dial.

"In an emergency," says Dudgeon, "people do what they did yes-terday." SF72 wanted to break away from the fear-based messaging so often associated with preparedness activities, and it does it very point-edly by telling visitors to the site: *You're more prepared than you think.* You know your networks, your connections; you can fill in holes in your emergency supplies on your next errands run. Readiness, as SF72 knows, is about readiness to help each other and to receive help from others. A line on the site reads as follows: "actual emergencies look more like people coming together than cities falling apart."

9

～

RESPONSIVENESS
Social Cohesion Is the First Responder

No matter how aware and ready we may be, things still go wrong, and disruptions often confound all our plans and preparations. Our capacity to respond to a disruption, therefore, not only depends on how ready we are but also on the quality of our social cohesion, because it is usually friends, neighbors, colleagues—and often strangers—who respond first. In this chapter, we'll see what that meant after the Boston bombings, the explosion in Halifax, and in an unexpected cascade of disruptions in Surat, India.

AN UNEXPECTED CASCADE:
FLOOD THEN PLAGUE

Surat is an ancient city, settled in the eighth century on a bend near the mouth of the Tapi River, which flows west from central India and empties into the Arabian Sea. "This is a city of very great trade," wrote Duarte Barbosa, a Portuguese writer and explorer, in 1513.[1] For centuries, the river—and the streams and tidal creeks that feed into it—would swell during the rainy monsoon season (May through October) and often overflow its banks. The minor floods were an inconvenience. The major ones—which came every two to four years—caused damage, disruption, death, and disease. Malaria, carried by the mosquitoes that bred in the standing pools of water left by the flood, was commonplace.

Surtis have, therefore, long been aware of the threat of flood and have installed floodgates and other protections at various times in their history. They learned to recognize when conditions suggested a flood was likely, grew accustomed to moving to higher ground when the water began to rise, and became used to cleaning up after it had receded a day or two later.

But, in 1994, Surat was not so aware of new vulnerabilities to flood. (One of the reasons, as we shall see, was the presence of a new dam, the Ukai, which provided a sense of security that was not completely warranted. Just as we saw in Tulsa, dams, for all their infrastructural benefits, also cause considerable disturbance to the social and natural ecosystems they touch.) In August 1994, the monsoon rains were heavy in the state of Gujarat, where Surat is located. Toward the end of the month, the Tapi swelled, flooding fields and villages all along its course, and boiled up over its banks in Surat. A large area of the city was awash with river water, which ran as deep as eight feet.

The flood itself was not the worst Surat had seen—the crisis passed and the water subsided as it always did, but it left Surat's buildings and streets littered with mud and filth. The carcasses of drowned animals lay strewn and rotting in the summer sun, rats ran through the streets, and fleas and mosquitoes filled the air.[2]

As before, Surat might have dealt with the water, attended to the damage, accomplished the cleanup as it always had, and returned to business, but recovery was complicated by the outbreak of an unidentified illness. The first cases appeared in early September, in an area of the city largely populated by migrants and where water, sanitation, and drainage systems were in poor condition. Word of the disease spread quickly through the city. Victims were coughing up blood. They had trouble breathing. Some had already died.

Dr. Vikas Desai was on the faculty of the medical college in Surat at the time. She remembers receiving an urgent call from city

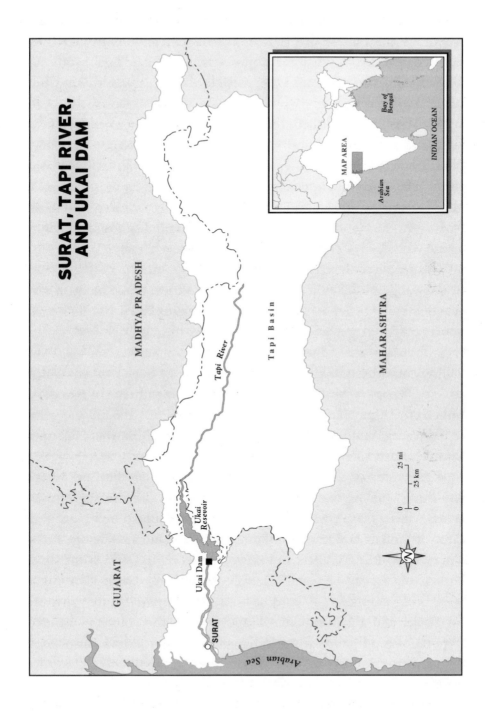

SURAT, TAPI RIVER, AND UKAI DAM

volunteers who were willing to go into affected areas and distribute antibiotics but needed advice on what precautions to take. Desai needed to know what the illness was, but public health officials weren't sure. Not malaria. One possible diagnosis was striking but unsettling—plague.

As more fell ill and died, that diagnosis became increasingly likely, and word spread that Surat was in the midst of a plague epidemic. Health officials and health experts engaged in a public debate about the problem. Yes, the infection appeared to be caused by the *Yersinia pestis* bacteria, which is transmitted to humans by fleas that have been feeding off the blood of infected rodents.[3] But no diagnosis was definitive or conclusive. The media followed the story closely.

The people of the city did not know what to think. They lost trust in the public health officials and city authorities. Many went to private doctors in search of help, but some private clinics, having no experience with plague and unable to address the high demand, closed their doors and refused treatment altogether.

The community began to fall apart. Many of Surat's migrants fled the city. "People were running away," Desai remembers.[4] In two days, some 200,000 residents fled the city of 1.6 million.[5] The life and work of the place ground to a halt. With few workers left in town, factories shut down, and some stayed closed as long as a month.

A few cases of the disease were reported in areas beyond Surat's city limits, fueling fears that all of India could became engulfed in crisis. Ashvin Dayal, who is The Rockefeller Foundation's managing director for Asia and leader of the Asian Cities Climate Change Resilience Network (ACCCRN) initiative, was living in Delhi at the time. "It was big news," he says. "Trains coming in to Delhi from Surat were being stopped."[6] According to a 2011 report by the Institute for Social and Environmental Transition, "Some countries banned imports of food grains from India, some foreign airlines suspended flights to the country and passengers from India to other countries were quarantined."[7]

After dithering over the diagnosis was done, Surat responded admirably. The city sprayed insecticides to kill the fleas, distributed penicillin and tetracycline (both antibiotics) throughout the city, un-clogged drains, and cleared streets. Two weeks after the flood came, the outbreak subsided, there were no more fatalities, and the crisis came to an end. The threat of a national epidemic did not materialize. With time, those successes became known, but the damage had been done—Surat was known as Plague City. "Our economy suffered," says Dr. Desai. "Our trade suffered. Health suffered. We got a bad name."

The plague awakened Surat to its vulnerabilities, particularly the stress of rapid urbanization and city growth. They found their response infrastructure—both social and physical—lacked integration and coordination. There were insufficient feedback loops. There was no clearly defined process for citizens to report cases of the illness. No agency established a central collection point for information about what was going on. Public officials were not connected to leaders of private medical facilities. As Desai puts it, "There was no owner-ship of the city." In the middle of their crisis response, no one was responsible.

CRISIS: THINGS GET OUT OF CONTROL

No matter how well you have assessed your vulnerabilities, no matter how much mitigation you have done, no matter how prepared you think you may be, things still can go wrong. Sometimes terribly so.

When Surat experienced the plague outbreak in 1994, the city was aware of its main vulnerability—flood—but it was hardly prepared for the cascading disruptions it experienced beyond the known threat: infrastructure collapse, inability to manage disease, government disar-ray, breakdown of social cohesion.

Those two weeks in Surat amounted to a crisis—the most acute period of a disruption. The scope, duration, and nature of a crisis period can vary dramatically, but it is easy to recognize. Normal functioning is shattered. People (and other living things) are in real and immediate danger. Systems are knocked out or overwhelmed or collapse. People are uncertain of what is happening and don't know exactly what to do. Fear rises and primal instincts kick in. The situation is unstable, uncertain, and not fully in control.

The crisis period is almost always marked by a well-defined moment—a few seconds or minutes when the disruption is at its worst, a signal event that evinces shouts and screams or eerie silence, causes a blizzard of tweets, overloads cell phone networks, makes headlines. People run or freeze.

Barry Dorn and Eric McNulty of the National Leadership Preparedness Initiative at Harvard refer to the acute, precipitating moment of a crisis as the "boom" event.[8] This is when the bomb explodes, the building topples, the shots are fired, the levee breaches, the fire erupts into a conflagration, when word comes through that a dozen disease victims have died. It is the time when the most basic questions may be difficult to answer. What is the problem? Who is at risk? What actions should be taken? How can we quickly return to normal function? Who will take responsibility for what?

To build resilience, you need to understand that response always involves many elements: the actions of individuals and communities, the deployment of tools and technologies, the work of unofficial or ad hoc groups that form in the thick of the crisis, and, of course, official first responders and agencies. All play important roles, all their contributions are most effective when well integrated, and their roles and responsibilities shift over time as the crisis worsens or abates.

When we think about emergency situations, we often think primarily about the role of the official emergency handlers, the agencies and services that are often called "first responders," and the tools and technologies they use. I will discuss both of those, but it's essential to recognize, just as Rob Dudgeon learned in the Loma Prieta quake, that "regular" people are just as important in responding to a crisis as are members of police, fire, and ambulance forces. In almost every case, your neighbors, fellow workers, family members, or passersby will be the very first people on the scene and the ones who will take the quickest, and sometimes most important, actions—and they may also be the ones who continue to respond to the needs of others long after the acute moment has passed.

INDIVIDUALS TAKE CARE OF EACH OTHER

In getting through a crisis, people rarely do or can act alone. They help each other in all kinds of ways—rescuing, sheltering, informing, tending, comforting. Such behavior rarely involves acts of heroism however much the media prefers such portrayals. People generally behave in a crisis as they have always behaved. During the Boston bombings, it was often noted that, in the seconds after the first blast, some bystanders rushed *toward* the wounded who lay near where the explosion had taken place, while others turned and ran away from the scene.

What was happening? Why did those people behave as they did? Such responses are affected by basic brain function as well as by readiness and people's learned capacity for dealing with crisis moments.

As Dorn and McNulty describe it, the brain operates using three networks of circuits. In the survival circuit, the "basement," our primal responses lie: fear, fight, or flight.[9] The well-known "fight-or-flight" response was first articulated in 1932 by Walter Cannon, the American physiologist. It is also known as the "acute stress response," and the basic idea is that "animals react to threats with a general discharge of the sympathetic nervous system"—a basic physiological reaction.[10] In the boom moment, for example, fear overrides everything. "You have no control of it," Dorn says.[11]

This age-old response helps protect us from danger, gets us out of bad situations, energizes us to take action. However, the basement of the brain is "a terrible place to make decisions," says Dorn. When in the grip of fear, key aspects of resilience—increasing awareness and gathering information, considering diverse options, developing integrated responses—are overridden.

We can't prevent the fear reaction after a boom moment, but we can develop ways to get ourselves out of it as quickly as possible. What's needed is some kind of protocol or behavior that kicks the mind out of the basement and activates the "routine" circuit network that Dorn and McNulty call the repository where you store "all your ways of doing things."

The routine circuits, in other words, are where you keep your preparedness, your knowledge of what to do in certain situations. You reach into the mind's metaphorical toolbox and grab something that is already there. Dorn, for example, is a physician. When faced with a situation that looks like a cardiac arrest, he is able to cut his fear moment short. He reaches into his toolbox for a well-known, five-step protocol and follows the steps methodically, without deviation. This enables him to respond almost immediately, gets him beyond fear and out of the basement. Aircraft pilots have a mantra—aviate, navigate, communicate—which keeps fear at bay when faced with a crisis situation in flight. Repeating the mantra gets them out of the basement and into the toolbox where they have access to a whole range of protocols and checklists they can follow to assess their situation and determine the best options for action.

An effective get-out-of-the-basement protocol might be something completely personal and even unrelated to the emergency. It could be a behavior, like rapidly tapping your knees. "It may be three deep breaths," McNulty says. "It doesn't matter what it is. But you should have something you can go to as a trigger script to reset your brain. Something that can get your brain out of survival mode and into thinking mode."

You need to already have the tools in the toolbox, of course, before the crisis arrives, and there are many protocols for emergency readiness and response available. People who have even the most basic protocols in mind fare better in a boom moment and the crisis that may follow, even if the event is not the one for which the protocol was developed. Research shows that something as simple as checking the location of the exits in an aircraft or hotel can cause you to respond faster and better if things go wrong. Indeed, as Alicia Johnson of SF DEM says, "The more complex your response plan is, the less likely you are to actually implement it."[12]

Once you have begun to respond to a crisis situation with a tool or protocol, your brain is much more able to rise to the third level, which Dorn and McNulty call the "laboratory"—the cortex, the most highly evolved part of the brain, which is responsible for complex thinking and problem solving. This is where the characteristics of resilience really come into play. You draw on your capacity to increase awareness, to gather and analyze information, to draw on diverse options and alternative actions, to adapt, to self-regulate, and to formulate integrated responses and take coordinated, inclusive action.

In crisis situations, we see how difficult it can be for people to get out of the basement and how important the protocols and tools can be for both official and unofficial responders.

THERE IS ANOTHER FORM of response to stress and shock that has been discussed in the past two decades known as "tend-and-befriend." This response is generally more associated with females than with males, although not unknown in men, and refers to the tendency to affiliate with other people in times of stress to come together rather than to fight or to run away. Shelley Taylor, the UCLA psychologist who is most closely associated with defining the response, writes, "Human female responses to stress (as well as those of some animal species) are not well characterized by fight-or-flight, but rather are more typically characterized by a pattern we term 'tend-and-befriend.'" Females respond to stress by "affiliating with social groups to reduce risk." This hormonal response is likely associated with the female's role as mother and caregiver of children. "The demands of pregnancy, nursing, and infant care render females extremely vulnerable to external threats," Taylor writes. "Should a threat present itself during this time, a mother's attack on a predator or flight could render offspring fatally unprotected."[13]

When this impulse comes into play in a crisis situation, it can be both helpful and may also lead to poor decision making or gaps in situational awareness. The brain basement of the "tend-and-befriend" response looks different from that of "fight-or-flight," but it is still not a place where all your tools and creative powers are available, as Jenny Chung found out on the day of the Boston Marathon bombings.

Jenny doesn't remember falling to the ground at the finish line of the Boston Marathon after the bomb went off, but that is where she was when her friend Rekha Drew found her just minutes after the first explosion rocked Boylston Street. Jenny, a thirty-six-year-old eighth-grade social studies teacher at the Putnam Avenue Upper School, a public middle school not far from the bombing site, had gone with a group of six companions to cheer on a friend who was running the race—her first marathon.

Rekha helped Jenny up. Both were dazed, confused, unsure of what had happened. Jenny made a quick self-assessment and decided she was OK, even though, as it turned out, she wasn't. She could walk, at least. Rekha looked around and saw that many others could not. Jenny's primary concern, however, was for Rekha who, at forty-three, was pregnant with her first child.

Now police officers were on the scene, following their protocols. "We were instructed to get out," Jenny says, but they had to find their friends first. They reunited with four of them, but one was still missing. The friends agreed that Jenny would walk with Rekha to Rekha's apartment in Boston's South End, about a mile away. The rest would search for their missing friend. (They eventually found him, injured but stable and OK, and got him to a hospital.)

As they walked toward the South End, Jenny began to realize that something was not right. "I definitely felt like something had hit me," she says.[14] Perhaps it was the action of walking that got her brain out of its primal mode or maybe it was focusing on a single, defined action: get Rekha to her house. As they walked, Jenny looked down and, for the first time, noticed a hole in the left sleeve of her North Face jacket. The down filling was spilling out. "Aw, this jacket is ruined," she said, not understanding why.

When they got close to the apartment, Jenny talked to her friend Matt, who was walking to meet them in the South End, on the phone. As soon as Jenny said hi, Matt knew something was wrong. "He said I sounded a little different," Jenny recalls, "a little bit off." Once together, all three went inside the apartment and Matt noticed the hole in Jenny's jacket. He unzipped it and lifted her shirt. "I saw the look on his face," Jenny says. There was a white area on her chest, indicating a deep wound. They had to get to a hospital right away.

Jenny may have gained access to the tools in her mental tool-box, but she was still not thinking on the highest level. She said she wanted to go to her regular hospital in Boston, Beth Israel Hospital, two miles away. No. Her friends convinced her to go to the nearest facility, Boston Medical Center. With traffic halted everywhere and Jenny still thinking she was OK, the three friends walked.

The emergency room at Boston Medical was packed with bombing victims. A nurse followed her standard protocol: she asked Jenny to rate her pain level on a scale of one to ten. Six. There were many other people in worse shape, so the nurse said Jenny would need to wait and sent her out of the emergency department to the urgent care unit. Matt figured they might wait hours to be seen and that Jenny could be in real danger. He convinced a nurse to take a look at Jenny's wound. When she did, Jenny was immediately sent to an exam room and then for a chest X-ray.

The X-ray showed that a piece of shrapnel—probably from the pressure cooker that had contained the bomb—had shot through Jenny's jacket and two layers of clothing, pierced the wiring of her bra, and lodged itself deep in her chest, two inches from her heart.

From that moment on, the official caregivers took over. That evening, a surgeon, who had already completed six operations that day, successfully removed the shrapnel from Jenny's chest, and she was soon on her way to a complete recovery. As much as Jenny is grateful and indebted to the medical team, she credits her friend Matt with "helping to save her life." But Jenny, too, might take some credit for tending to her friend, Rekha, who gave birth to a girl.

NEIGHBORHOODS ACT AS COMMUNITIES

Just as individuals respond to crisis by directly helping one another, communities respond in ways that go beyond the sum of the individual connections made. A community is a difficult phenomenon to define, as it speaks to a vast array of different kinds of groups and networks we build and include ourselves in—families, friends, cultural or religious groups, online social networks, book clubs, parent groups, sports teams, villages and cities, organizations and associations.

A community, by definition, implies some amount of social cohesion. The people within the community have a commitment to that entity. They care about the community and want it to thrive. They identify with its values and goals and ways of being and functioning. They have a sense of its purpose and its past and its place in the world. They feel a connection to other people who belong to the community.

The neighborhoods of a city or town are often thought of as communities. A neighborhood can be physically delineated and is usually aware of itself as such. When it comes to disruption—a flood, a terrorist attack, or a power outage—the people in your neighborhood will likely be experiencing similar setbacks and have needs and concerns similar to yours. And they may be the *only* people directly experiencing the state of disruption in the way that you are. For example, the people of the San Javier neighborhood, during the worst of the violence in Medellin, could be under siege while the folks in El Poblado, some ten kilometers away, were going about their everyday business. While elderly Parisians were dying in the heat wave of 2003, many of their countrymen were enjoying the summer sun on the Riviera.

However, when a crisis strikes, not all neighborhoods behave as communities. One of the most striking examples of this comes from the Chicago heat wave of 1995, in which 739 people died. After the event, social scientists studied the pattern of deaths and published some surprising results that author and New York University sociology professor Eric Klinenberg has written about extensively. Two Chicago neighborhoods, Auburn Gresham and Englewood, had similar demographics: 99 percent African American, nearly identical percentages of elderly and out-of-work residents, high rates of poverty and crime. But the death rates from the heat wave were dramatically different. Englewood suffered 33 deaths per 100,000 people while Auburn Gresham had just 3 deaths per 100,000.[15]

The reasons, in retrospect, were (or should have been) quite obvious. Although Auburn Gresham was a poor community, the people who lived there had strong social connections and a physical environment that facilitated those interactions. Neighbors knew each other. The streets were full of life. People belonged to and cared about community organizations. During the heat wave, community members checked on each other, especially those who were vulnerable in any way. Englewood, by contrast, had been in decline for decades, and its social fabric had been torn apart. The built environment discouraged participation in local life.

People fare better in crisis in strong communities because social cohesion provides an element of resilience that influences the type and degree of responsiveness under stress. Where people know each other, have worked or played together, belong to groups together, and have an understanding of who else is in their community, they are more likely to come together to respond quickly and effectively to a crisis. Friendship and direct personal connection can be a part of social cohesion, but it has much more to do with the strength and capacity of groups and networks that are already in place or that can quickly form when a crisis hits.

FOR A FAMOUS EXAMPLE of a neighborhood that demonstrated resilience in the face of a severe crisis, let me return to San Francisco and the 1906 earthquake. As we saw earlier, the earthquake itself was the boom moment for San Francisco, but then came the fires. In the two days of the worst burning, firefighters were hampered in their efforts by a lack of water, due to the burst water mains, and also a lack of leadership—they had lost their fire chief, Dennis T. Sullivan, who had spent significant time thinking about how to deal with fire in crisis situations. The firefighters were not getting the job done.

To deal with the situation, Mayor Eugene Schmitz reached into his mental toolbox and pulled out a ready-made solution: he called up the Army. In came troops from Fort Mason, located in San Francisco's Marina District at the northern tip of the city. Schmitz put them in charge of the firefighting effort and authorized them to use violent force as necessary to keep things under control. In effect, without any official declaration from the president or the governor, San Francisco came under martial law, with acting commander Brigadier General Frederick Funston its de facto leader.

Enlisting the services of the Army made sense, but the 1,700 troops that came in from Fort Mason came in as soldiers rather than as firefighters or, for that matter, as crisis managers—they had orders to shoot to kill if they came across looters. As we've seen, people behave in crisis as they do in normal times. They rely on tools from their mental toolboxes they already know and understand—which can work out well, as it often does for doctors and pilots, or not so well, as it did for these soldiers. Without access to water but equipped with plenty of explosives, they used dynamite to blow up buildings in an attempt to establish firebreaks that would halt the conflagration. But fires flared up where there was no fire before, and buildings were destroyed that need not have been. As neighborhood residents saw what was happening, they did what they could to save their homes. In some instances, when the Army ordered that a building be demolished, its residents protested but were forced, at gunpoint, to leave.

But even the Army could not cover the entire city and had to choose which areas to let burn, one of which was the working-class neighborhood of Telegraph Hill. There, according to the writer Henry Anderson Lafler, all the houses, along with all the possessions within them, "would not total in value a million dollars."[16]

What the residents of Telegraph Hill *did* have, however, was an unwillingness to watch their houses go up in smoke along with a willingness to take action. They did not run away nor did they wait for help. As Lafler writes in an unpublished account, the residents of the community came together to save their neighborhood. It was the "boys of the hill," Lafler writes, who fought the fires. It was "Toby Irwin, the prizefighter, and Tim O'Brien, who works in the warehouse," along with the washerwomen who lugged buckets of water up the hill for them. One man rolled out a barrel of wine, chopped it open, and doused the flames. "It was a great, brave, roistering fight of all the dwellers on the hill for their homes and their lives," Lafler writes, "and gloriously they won success."[17]

When the smoke cleared and an assessment of the fire damage was done, it became clear that regular people had been more successful at saving neighborhoods—with buckets of water and barrels of wine and collective action—than the Army had with dynamite and shaky leadership.

UNOFFICIAL GROUPS TAKE ON NECESSARY ROLES

All too often, official responders will *not* be available during the critical period of a crisis, for reasons over which they have no control. They, too, may have been affected by the disruption. Their facilities or equipment may have been damaged. Their people may have been incapacitated. They may not be able to get access to the crisis. Communication and control systems may be knocked out.

This is precisely what happened during the 9/11 terrorist attack in New York. "The attacks on 9/11 demonstrated that even the most robust emergency response capabilities can be overwhelmed if an attack is large enough," write the authors of the *9/11 Commission Report*.[18] Although New York may have had "robust emergency capabilities," they were not resilient because they lacked systems that were redundant, diverse, and self-regulating.

After the planes crashed into the Twin Towers, power and communications were cut off in the buildings (even the emergency lighting system didn't work), and for safety reasons the backup generators were shut off. Officials weren't able to effectively issue instructions to tenants, because parts of the public address system had been destroyed by the attack. Responders were hindered by other communications failures: the sheer size of the buildings impeded firefighters' radio signals, and Port Authority Police Department radio signals only worked when near the command center. Existing systems lacked the robustness and integration to deal with the sheer magnitude of the attack—reports of missing or injured officers overwhelmed the New York Police Department's radio channels, and calls to emergency operators flooded the 911 system, leading to disconnections and delays. And then there was the human toll: of the nearly 50,000 officials who responded, 343 firefighters and 60 police officers were killed, and thousands more were injured or incapacitated.[19]

Building in the requisite systems features of resilience is the first line of defense. But if official first responders and their systems are disrupted or disabled, other organized groups—although not in any way official—may take on the role of first responder.

That is what happened in Lower Manhattan on 9/11, where people found themselves trapped, unable to escape the smoke and mayhem by any of the usual exit routes. Streets, subways, tunnels, and bridges were all closed. People did what made the most sense to them: they fled to the water's edge, hoping for rescue, ready to swim if it came to that. The Coast Guard was quickly on hand but did not have time to bring up the necessary resources to evacuate everyone in need. So Coast Guard officials sent out a radio call for help to any and all available vessels to assist. The response was extraordinary. Commuter ferries, tugs, party boats, commercial vessels, private yachts—hundreds of watercraft of all varieties, most of them with private citizens at the helm—rushed to the scene. Over a nine-hour period, these unofficial responders ferried nearly a half million people to safety. It was the largest sea evacuation of all time.[20]

Another intriguing example of unofficial responders stepping into the breach comes from the Halifax explosion of 1917 that I described earlier. Both the Army and the fire brigade performed well in that crisis (not a surprise because the Army had long been a regular presence in the city), but the damage was so horrific and the number of people affected so great that the authorities could not possibly manage the entire situation, so other groups stepped in to help. One of the first vulnerabilities to be exposed was the inadequacy of Halifax's healthcare facilities. "Prior to the catastrophe," Samuel Henry Prince writes, "public health organization was not a matter for civic pride." The dispensary, for example, was underfunded and provided "indifferent service."[21] So it was not to the dispensary that victims of the blast were immediately taken. The first relief station, close to the site of the ship blast, was set up by a group of actors from the Academy Stock Company, a local theater group. Less than three hours after the explosion, the actors were providing shelter for the shocked, caring as best they could for the wounded, and dispensing whatever supplies they had or could muster.

The presence of established groups contributes to social cohesion and a sense of community that provides the capacity for them to respond in an emergency. The actors' group could just as well have been a garden society or a civic association. People who have organized themselves, learned to collectively solve problems and respond to microemergencies, who know each other and have a degree of trust in one another, can effectively apply themselves to other situations, such as crisis.

Yet the actors brought some particular assets to the situation. Prince argues that the members of the stock company had the capacity to respond to the emergency because they were, in effect, trained in resilience building. Actors, Prince writes, are skilled in "collective behavior"—working to mount theater productions, acting together on stage, and playing supporting roles behind the scenes. What's more, actors are "accustomed to think quickly, to live in restricted spaces, and to meet emergencies." Everything they do on stage unfolds in real time, and, although they are usually following a script, actors have a high degree of situational awareness.

That's why, as Prince puts it, the actors were able to leave behind "the school of Thespis" (the ancient Greek actor) and find a place in the school of Esculapius (the Greek god of medicine).[22] Prince gave a name to the group of official and ad hoc responders to the Halifax crisis: the "disaster protocracy."[23]

SOMETIMES PEOPLE WHO RESPOND to a crisis are not members of a particularly well-established or well-populated (if unofficial) group, as the Stock Academy in Halifax was, but assume a crucial role almost by accident.

There aren't many places to surf in New York City, but Rockaway Beach is one of them. This unique asset has drawn residents, tourists, and nonlocal New Yorkers to Rockaway throughout the years, and the beaches have gained in popularity as a surfer's haven. This has had a somewhat disorienting effect on the community—residents of the Rockaways weren't always supportive of the Brooklynites who were "robbing their waves." There was tension, sometimes animosity, between the locals and the surfers.

When you locate the neighborhood of the Rockaways on a map, it won't surprise you that it was hit hard when Superstorm Sandy blasted through the area: it is a narrow strip of land that juts out from the southern coast of Long Island, demarcating Jamaica Bay to the north and reaching toward the lower bay of New York Harbor. In Breezy Point alone—a community at the very tip of the Rockaways—more than two hundred homes were flooded to the point of requiring demolition.[24] Some areas of the Rockaways peninsula were under as much as four feet of water. Breezy Point residents found themselves without power, electricity, and heat—and isolated, too, with public transportation systems incapacitated. In addition to the damage caused by flooding, about 135 houses were burned to the ground when water intruded into one home, sparked out its electrical system, and started a fire which, with no firefighting authorities available, quickly spread.[25]

The Rockaway Beach Surf Club, located at Eighty-Seventh Street near the center of the Rockaway peninsula, suffered flooding and some damage but was not destroyed and could still function. Bradach Walsh and Brandon D'Leo, the club's founders, had originally established it as a place for surfers to hang out and gather.[26] On October 30, the day after Sandy hit, Walsh and D'Leo set about cleaning up the mud and clearing debris.

Soon enough, the Surf Club became a resource and distribution center of emergency relief supplies for the people of Rockaway who were in need. The club was in a convenient location, it had space, it was already known as a community meeting place, and the owners were committed to helping others. Word got out that supplies could be dropped off at the club and could be picked up there by residents or would be distributed throughout the area. Residents could make specific requests through the club's Facebook page. Supplies started coming in from people throughout the New York area. Just as important as supplies, however, were volunteers. Person power. Services and official organizations did not arrive to the Rockaways as quickly as another group: the surfers of Brooklyn. Eventually, some 5,000 volunteers—most of them surfers—got involved.[27]

These volunteers, who organized themselves from the Rockaway Beach Surf Club, did what they could to help the residents of the Rockaways: canvassing neighborhoods to see what supplies were needed and where, returning to the club with a list, and then heading out again to make deliveries; clearing rubble and debris from the streets to improve transportation; taking care of houses that had been flooded by water steeped with sewage. More than seven hundred houses in the Rockaways had to be cleaned or completely gutted, and surfers were there to do the wet and dirty work for and with their fellow surfers.[28] Sandy was a devastating wave they all rode out together.

Of course, after Sandy, the Rockaways have received a great deal of attention and resources from a wide variety of government, civic, and philanthropic entities. But the Rockaway Beach Surf Club, a community hangout, was the center of social cohesion during the height of the crisis.

The effort and coming together of community was not lost on Rockaway residents, and, despite lingering devastation from the storm as the Rockaways continue to recover and rebuild, the community is more cohesive—and more defined—than before. "We had so much help from the hipsters"—the local Rockaway term for Brooklyn surfers—"that now everyone is friends with each other. It doesn't matter if they're not from Rockaway now," said Alex Karinsky, founder of the Gotham Surf Club in Rockaway, speaking with a *New York Times* reporter. "They're here. There's a whole new level of social camaraderie that never existed. We're all in it together. It's a real positive thing."[29] After a disruption, sometimes a community redefines itself—making the postcrisis period that much easier to manage—just as they did in Village de l'Est in New Orleans.

THERE WERE MANY OTHER entities, along with the Rockaway Surf Club, that took on new roles during the Sandy crisis. Many came from what is being called "the sharing economy," a new force in building the social fabric of resilience.

Molly Turner is the director of public policy at Airbnb, the web-based bed-and-breakfast service that has more than 600,000 listings in 34,000 cities in 190 countries around the world.[30] As Sandy approached, she was concerned about how the storm would affect Airbnb's hosts and their expected guests, just as she had been when Hurricane Irene threatened a year before. As that storm approached in August 2011, Airbnb worked with guests and hosts to arrange rebookings for those affected by the storm. Although Irene caused a good deal of flooding and knocked out power for millions of area residents, it had not become the disaster that had been predicted.

Airbnb grew wildly in the following year. "By the time Sandy came around," Turner says, "our community had grown exponentially. Not only did that mean that the rebooking problem was a bigger issue for us; it meant that we had a massive community in that region that was impacted by the storm."[31]

Even before the storm had passed, it was clear to Turner—and many of Airbnb's hosts in New York City—that the extent of the damage was much greater than people had expected. Indeed, as many as 40,000 residents in New York and New Jersey were displaced.[32] (As of December 2013, more than a year after the storm's landfall, some 30,000 residents had still not returned to their homes.[33]) So Turner saw there was a far more urgent need to fill than just rebooking tourists who had planned to travel to the city. "We started getting calls from some of our most engaged hosts in New York City," Turner remembers. "They told us they were fine. They had extra space in their homes. They wanted to offer it up to displaced New Yorkers."

Good idea, but Airbnb was not set up to offer free accommodations. Then an Airbnb host, based in Brooklyn, called and pleaded. Wasn't there some way she could offer her accommodation for free to people displaced by the storm? Yes, there was. "Our engineers stayed up all night long, basically rebuilding the whole backend of the website to enable people to list their properties for $0," Turner says. The team also created a new landing page—www.airbnb.com/sandy—where hosts could click a button to automatically have their listing posted for free. "Within about a week," Turner says, "we had over 1,400 hosts offer up the extra space in their homes to displaced New Yorkers for free."

Airbnb's response to Superstorm Sandy is particularly interesting because it also demonstrates the important role of spare capacity—or as it is also called "latent surplus"—in response to crisis. "Even in a city where there is a huge housing shortage," Turner says, "there are still people living in houses that are too big for them or that they only use part time because maybe they travel a lot for work." Information about spare capacity is not always available or easy to access. Indeed, it may be invisible, at least "officially." Who knows exactly how many bedrooms there are in New York City (or any city) and how many of them are occupied at any given time? The ability of a city or community to identify latent resources and leverage spare capacity in a time of vital need is a characteristic of resilience that can go a long way in improving a city's ability to respond well to crisis. Through Airbnb's efforts, people found free accommodations, and the cost to official agencies of sheltering displaced residents was reduced.

What's more, Airbnb was able to provide storm victims with a much-needed sense of comfort, community, and social cohesion. In order for people to recover from a crisis, it's important for them to know there are people—whom they *don't* know—in their city or even in their neighborhood who are selflessly willing to help. One man, whose home was destroyed by Sandy, recalls being greeted at the door by his Airbnb host, her boyfriend, and their small dog. In a video montage of Sandy remembrances put together by Airbnb, he says the welcome "made me feel like I was visiting a family member."[34]

He was not a member of the family, of course, but he felt like a member of a community—the Airbnb community. "The more people that use Airbnb and the bigger community we have," says Turner, "the more helpful we are going to be." The larger the network of hosts and of guests, the more housing Airbnb will be able to provide to people displaced by disasters and catastrophic events. Just as almost any established community group can take on a new role during a crisis, a service like Airbnb is valuable because the members of its community already know how it works. Airbnb was able to quickly adapt its platform so that accommodations could be rented for free. Although this took a good deal of work on the part of Airbnb's engineers and designers, it was a breeze for its customers, primarily because the system—posting, searching for, and placing bookings online—was already in place. "We built the tools to enable our community to do what they wanted to do already," Turner says.

"You can't expect people or communities to start new habits during the disaster," she says. "What's going to be most effective is people relying on existing services they're familiar with." This is just what the CDC did when they distributed the swine flu vaccine through the established vaccine distribution program. And it is, as we'll see, why some aspects of the Katrina response went spectacularly well.

Tools and Technologies Support Action

All of these entities—individuals and organizations, official and unofficial responders—benefit from the use of tools and technologies that increase awareness, enable response, and limit damage.

The dynamite used by the Army in the response to the 1906 San Francisco proved not to be the best application of technology, but the assessment of the damage was greatly facilitated by a very different technology that was then in the process of development. A well-known photographer and inventor, George Lawrence, had been experimenting with aerial photography—the first to do so—for several years. After the quake, Lawrence rigged a large-format camera (its negative measured 18" × 48") to a multikite apparatus he dubbed "Captain Airship," flew it some two thousand feet above San Francisco, and captured images that enabled a block-by-block visual analysis of the city and the damage it had suffered.[35]

In the age of Google maps, we expect to be able to access an aerial view of almost any location on earth, but in 1906 such an understanding had to be pieced together from information gathered at street level. Lawrence's photo was a revelation about how important good information—especially information that provides perspective and facilitates new understanding that we cannot directly gain with our own senses—is to developing the best response to a crisis. Although Lawrence made his photograph three weeks after the quake hit, it was still highly useful in understanding what areas of the city were most in need of attention.[36]

The twenty-first-century version of Lawrence's kite-borne camera is the drone. The "unmanned aircraft system," as the Federal Aviation Administration classifies the drone, has the capability to fly high above a disruption, out of harm's way, and also to dip low for a closer view. There is no onboard operator, so the device can be deployed in situations that would be life threatening to a pilot, and drones can be activated more quickly and easily than can conventional aircraft.

A videographer, photojournalist, and storm chaser named Brian Emfinger demonstrated the value of the drone when a tornado struck the town of Mayflower, Arkansas, in April 2014. After the worst of the winds had subsided, he sent up a small drone equipped with a video camera. The drone traveled smoothly along the path of the tornado at an altitude of about 150 feet, sometimes hovering over a particular site, providing a great deal of useful information about conditions immediately after the storm. The video shows damage to buildings and infrastructure, the location of emergency response vehicles, traffic buildups, and downed power lines and trees.[37] The local TV station, KATV (where Emfinger worked at the time), picked up the footage.

Drones have tremendous potential value to improve responsiveness during a crisis, particularly for search and rescue. When communications systems are out and people are trapped or isolated, a drone could find them and transmit their locations to emergency responders. Drones could also be useful, just as the aerial photographs were

*Photograph of San Francisco after the 1906 earthquake, taken by a
kite-borne large-format camera (Library of Congress)*

in San Francisco, in creating images to enable the quick evaluation
of the condition of damaged sites. This would be particularly helpful
in situations where there is considerable danger even after the crisis
has largely subsided but the response is still going on—such as the
mudslides in Washington and Afghanistan in 2014 where the ground
was too unstable to allow individuals or vehicles to enter the area, in a
building collapse where elements are still unstable, or during an outbreak of violence.

Drones have limitations, in that they do not have the capacity to
provide a detailed view of a very large area, which is why they were
not an effective tool in the search for the missing Malaysian Airlines

flight 370 in 2014. The use of drones for such purposes is also currently in dispute. The Federal Aviation Administration bans them for commercial use, but whether such activities should be categorized as commercial is a matter of debate. Certainly, an effective response to a disruption is greatly aided by aerial imagery, whether it is gathered by drones, aircraft, imaging or radar satellites, cameras on kites, or other sensing devices.

TECHNOLOGIES FOR GATHERING and sharing information and, even more important, for establishing feedback loops (so that information can be gathered, analyzed, and then fed back to inform action) during a crisis are critical to a response effort. Without this situational awareness, governments, aid organizations, and individual responders cannot make well-informed decisions, efficiently allocate scarce resources, or adapt to rapidly changing conditions—actions necessary to prevent a crisis from spiraling out of control into disaster.

The effective use of big data is emerging as an important factor in improving crisis response, and Palantir Technologies, led by CEO Alex Karp, is a leader in this field. Palantir (named after the crystal-ball like "seeing stones" from Tolkien's fantasy series) has, since 2004, been developing software and technology solutions to help governments, financial institutions, and other large organizations (such as pharmaceuticals) organize, visualize, and analyze large amounts of data. The company's goal, says Brian Fishman, one of Palantir's lead engineers, is to transform complex data (such as clinical files, IP addresses, census figures) into easily readable displays—"a single format" that will help people "answer questions."

Palantir's big data–driven information-sharing platform, called Palantir Gotham, ingests huge quantities of data from a variety of sources—such as satellite imagery, crowdsourced maps, and publicly available information from the US government and the European Union—and supports a number of complex analytical applications, including mapping tools. In Palantir's disaster relief work, such as during Supertyphoon Haiyan, which hit the Philippines in early November of 2013, Palantir Gotham used Raven, a high-scale web-based mapping application, to help in the relief efforts.

Palantir is a paragon of readiness. Even before Haiyan made landfall, Palantir contacted two trusted partners—Team Rubicon, an organization of US veterans who apply their military experience to disaster relief efforts, and Direct Relief, a group that supports local health-care organizations after disasters—to help them adapt and deploy their technology platform for use by the many aid organizations that would be responding to the crisis in the Philippines—a crisis that devolved into a disaster. Haiyan's nearly two-hundred-mph winds and heavy rains washed away entire communities, killed more than 6,000 people, and disrupted critical lifeline systems. More than a million households were damaged or destroyed, leaving over 4 million people scrambling for temporary housing.[38]

In situations like this one, Palantir's applications provide responders with information that constantly updates so they can get a real-time understanding of what's going on and can also compare the current situation to earlier conditions. For example, you can see which areas have power and which do not, which areas are secure and which are not. That kind of information influences key decisions, such as where to set up a base of operations and where to concentrate relief activities.

With Palantir, Fishman says, the user can say, "'I want to know everything that's going on within this circle around this city.' You can pull up a bunch of information, put a timeline on it, and then ask, 'What's going on today? What was going on three days ago? Show me all of the aid shipments, for example.'" A tool like Palantir "can give folks that are coming from the outside the ability to execute a lot better than they would otherwise," Fishman says.[39]

In addition to the big-picture knowledge provided by Palantir and the Raven map application, the responders in the Philippines also needed more close-up information. That could only be supplied by on-the-ground personnel, many of them Direct Relief and Team Rubicon volunteers. They used a two-way satellite communications device that looks like a cross between a two-way radio, a smartphone, and a game controller and communicates with texts, not voice. It operates wirelessly via the Iridium satellite constellation, a global network of satellites that, Iridium claims, offers communications coverage for "every inch of the earth's surface."[40] That is essential in crisis situations, where landlines are often down and cell phone systems out of commission. The device is equipped with GPS and sends out a personal locator signal so the user's location can be pinpointed, even if he or she is incapacitated.

In the Philippines, Direct Relief volunteers used the device to gather knowledge for a number of health-care providers, including the Red Cross, about the status of clinics, hospitals, and other health facilities. They sent messages about which facilities were operating, how many patients were being treated, and what medicines or supplies were needed. The information was fed into Palantir and displayed, so responders could see both the big picture and get more granular detail as well.

Not only was the information valuable during the Philippines crisis, it can be used to improve other health facilities that might be vulnerable to similar threats. What kinds of physical structures fare best in which conditions? Which supplies should be stocked? What medicines can't be stocked (because of a short shelf life, for example) but might be needed?

Fishman says the knowledge could also be used to develop a common reporting procedure for health facilities during crisis periods, so they would gather clearly defined pieces of data (e.g., number of patients and supply inventories) and communicate them in a standard way, so the process could be much more efficient. Perhaps the most critical and valuable element of the satellite capability is that you can collect and share information anywhere in the world at any time regardless of the availability of cellular service. In situations like the postearthquake period in Chile, for example, authorities and responders would not have had to rely only on Radio Bio Bio for information.

GOOGLE IS ALSO BRINGING its considerable resources to bear on the application of data to improving responsiveness in a disruption. The Google Crisis Response Team—an initiative started at Google .org, the company's philanthropic unit—is developing technology to provide answers to response-related questions as a crisis unfolds. Google's Person Finder tool is an open-source, public record that is designed to help first responders, volunteers, and family members locate missing persons. It works by checking a search query about a specific missing person against lists of people who are known to be in shelters, hospitals, and other such facilities. Person Finder was developed to help locate people missing after the Haiti earthquake in 2010 and has since been used in many other crisis situations, including the earthquake in Christchurch and the tsunami in Japan in 2011, the Boston bombings, and Supertyphoon Haiyan.

Public Alerts, another Google.org tool, is an online product to help visualize and distribute any number of existing alerts, watches, warnings, and bulletins in regions around the world. On my office computer in New York, for example, I can track flood warnings in the Midwest, earthquake status off the coast of Papua New Guinea, and the incidence of fires on the western coast of Australia.

This information can be vital to people who may be personally at risk from a disruption and also to organizations whose operations could be affected—such as executives concerned about their global supply chains or disaster response teams that need to summon and deploy volunteers.

Google wants to make these alert tools even more useful through localization. You can already receive relevant weather warnings—provided by the National Weather Service, the US Geological Survey, and other agencies—through Google Now, Google Search, or Google Maps. Next steps for the Crisis Response Team include expanding into other geographies, ensuring that affected (or potentially affected) individuals are receiving alerts, and adding layers of relevant content to the alerts they see.

Yes, Google wants people to know what's happening but, even more important, to understand "how it impacts me," says Meryl Stone, partnerships manager for Google.org's Crisis Response Team. They need to know "what I can do to better respond for myself, and my family, and my community." The goal is to provide "contextual information" around an alert, such as "where to go to seek shelter, where to get clean water and other supplies, where neighbors are actually sharing supplies, where hospitals have open beds."[41]

To achieve that level of contextualization, Google will require access to much more data from many more sources than it now has, and that raises issues of privacy and security. But the difficulty is not necessarily or simply a matter of gathering more data but of enabling organizations, governments, and individuals to publish and host data in formats that are readily accessible, and thus more easily integrated into Google's—as well as the Internet's—suite of new and planned tools. If Google can establish relationships with more data sources, including individuals, Stone believes the company "can create a really beautiful and helpful story around how to respond and protect yourself from an event. And how to prepare for the next one."

10

Ꮆ

LEADERSHIP EMERGES
Institutions and Individuals Step Up

Although the most immediate responders in a crisis are typically individuals, community members, and established groups that may shoulder emergency tasks they never expected to be part of their charter, the role of authorities and official agencies is no less essential. The response of individuals and ad hoc groups can be random and localized, and their energies may flag. What's more, deep expertise, knowledge, and specialized systems or tools may be required that regular folks cannot be expected to have.

When disruption strikes, we need coordinated and effective response from official agencies, emergency services, and trained experts but, especially in cascading crises, it may not always be clear which entities or individuals should be responding, to what, and how. Samuel Prince brought his level-headed view to this issue. He writes, "That part of the social sensorium which is most closely organized in normal hours first recovers consciousness in disaster." In other words, the authorities or agencies, bodies or organizations, that are most aware, readiest, and best organized will have the greatest ability to get out of the basement, reach into the toolbox, adapt, and deliver the most effective and rapidest response to a crisis. In Halifax, that organization was the Army. "The army has the intensive concentration, the discipline, the organization and often the resource of supplies instantly available," Prince writes. "Its training is of the kind for the endurance of shock."[1] They also had luck on their side: soldiers were stationed close to the blast site and could get to the scene. It's important to note how differently the Army responded in Halifax and in San Francisco, and at least one important difference was governance. The Army in Halifax did not have authority to manage the entire crisis, nor were they given instructions to shoot to kill; in San Francisco, the mayor essentially ceded leadership to Brigadier General Funston, and individual soldiers had a high degree of autonomy. There was insufficient awareness of the problems and not enough integration of plans and coordination of action.

In Halifax, the firefighters were another trained group that largely remained organized and responded to the general alarm soon after the explosion. The fire chief and deputy fire chief were killed in the blast, so the men were temporarily "leaderless," but a city controller took command and, despite the chaos and mayhem and exodus of people unfolding around them, the firefighters "remained at their posts."[2] The firefighting organization, in other words, was self-regulating largely because of built-in redundancies. Despite the loss of a key element, it did not collapse, require outside propping up, or cause damage to any other organization because of its loss—unlike what had happened in San Francisco in 1906.

WELL-TRAINED BOOTS ON THE (SOGGY) GROUND

When authorities, agencies, or official first responders are ready, really know what they are doing—and *do* it—their ability to deal with a crisis, even one of a scope far beyond what they have trained for or even imagined—can be amazing to behold. When Hurricane Katrina hit the Gulf Coast in 2005 and caused a series of cascading disruptions—flood, collapse, loss of essential services including utilities, sanitation, communication—the US Coast Guard (USCG) was ready.

It was one of the Coast Guard's largest search and rescue missions ever. More than 5,600 personnel participated, some 50 percent of whom responded from other parts of the United States.[3] The mission involved more than 150 marine craft, a hundred surveillance and communication aircraft, and rescue teams. The Coast Guard's certified rescue swimmers battled floodwaters muddled with oil, pollutants, and waste (from ruptured or flooded sewage lines) as well as debris from damaged homes, some of it torn away by the downdraft of Coast Guard helicopters hovering overhead.

Of the 60,000 people who were unable to escape the floodwaters—they fled to their rooftops or were stranded on isolated patches of high ground—the Coast Guard rescued more than 33,500, including 24,135 who were considered in peril and another 9,409 who were patients in medical facilities.[4] The mission was conducted and completed without any loss of life and without any damage to the Coast Guard's physical assets. When the response to Katrina was over, all assets—aircraft, vessels, personnel—returned to their home ports and bases capable of normal functioning.[5]

The Coast Guard was able to conduct such a successful response for many reasons, among them preparedness and effective governance. Before the storm made landfall, the Coast Guard moved its command and control posts away from the hurricane's path, so they would not be rendered dysfunctional. Headquarters for USCG District 8—which serves twenty-six states in the Midwest and along the Gulf Coast—was relocated from New Orleans to St. Louis, 600 miles north. Air assets—such as rescue helicopters and surveillance planes—were restationed to Shreveport, Louisiana (roughly 300 miles northwest of New Orleans), and Jacksonville, Florida (550 miles to the east).[6]

On August 28, the day before Katrina made landfall, the Coast Guard readied crews, aircraft, and other assets located outside the gulf region—in New Jersey, Massachusetts, North Carolina, and Georgia—to assist with search and rescue operations. On August 29, as the storm grew closer, USCG Disaster Assistance Teams readied themselves in Ohio, Kentucky, St. Louis, Pittsburgh, and Miami—ready to parachute in once the worst of the storm had passed.

A report issued by the US Government Accountability Office, which conducted a review of the Coast Guard's documentation of the incident and interviewed members of the Coast Guard throughout the gulf region to assess the USCG's response, cites this as an important factor in the Coast Guard's ability to "confront the hurricane." It did so by "first preserving Coast Guard personnel and resources and then quickly responding with search and rescue assistance."[7] In other words, the Coast Guard was highly aware of the danger that official responders face in a crisis and of the fact that they cannot offer an effective response if they have been made dysfunctional themselves. Once again, the airline industry offers a useful protocol: *In case of an emergency, put on your own oxygen mask first. Then help others.*

The actions taken by the Coast Guard before the storm became a crisis were planned and practiced with such regularity that, when it came time to respond, service members from New Orleans to New England knew what they were expected to do, were ready to do it and, in the event, did it.

The Coast Guard assures its readiness and responsiveness by promoting four principles that underlie a culture of preparedness:

1. *Have a Clear Objective.* The Coast Guard delivers "general instructions" in a mission and also details specific responsibilities. After Katrina, the general objective was to safeguard the coast. The specific task was to conduct search and rescue operations.

2. *Maintain an Effective Presence.* The Coast Guard wants to be sure its people can do its job effectively in any situation. In a crisis, people behave in unexpected and unhelpful ways that can get in the way of the Coast Guard operatives doing their job. So, in addition to the captains and pilots and swimmers, the Coast Guard also deployed security personnel to make sure its people were safe.

3. *Take On-Scene Initiative.* According to the US Government Accountability Office report, "Coast Guard personnel [are] given latitude to act quickly and decisively within the scope

of their authority, without waiting for direction from higher levels in the chain of command." One Coast Guard pilot, for example, set out on a mission to conduct an environmental inspection but soon learned that search and rescue helicopters nearby did not have the ability to communicate with ground personnel who were stationed at hospitals and landing areas. She adapted her mission and established her aircraft as a communication platform.

4. *Seek System Flexibility.* The Coast Guard encourages individual flexibility and strives to build flexibility into its structure so that it can quickly deliver "surge" capacities as it did in New Orleans. To do this, the guard "pursues multiple missions with the same people and assets . . . adjusting to a wide variety of tasks and circumstances."[8]

When members of the Coast Guard are called, their readiness skills and protocols do not have to be applied in a specific way for each type of emergency—they have learned resilience skills in general. Nor are their skills site specific. When, for example, personnel from Massachusetts are called to respond to a hurricane in New Orleans, they are capable of providing the services needed. This flexibility allows for continued function throughout the guard, even when surge capacities have limited resources in other locations.[9]

Being prepared requires constant learning, and, to this end, the Coast Guard conducted an investigation of the Katrina mission. In the report that resulted, USCG rear admiral Robert F. Duncan, commander of USCG District 8, talked about how the service members who responded in New Orleans—especially those in junior grades—would one day have significant responsibility and would apply the lessons learned in that operation. "They're Katrina veterans. They know how it was done. They know the kind of centralized command, decentralized execution that worked very well." Duncan concludes that the work in New Orleans and the analysis of it would make for "a better Coast Guard" in the long run.[10]

AN INTERESTING COMPARISON in New Orleans to the Coast Guard's capacity to respond so successfully and resiliently despite highly unpredictable and unforeseen situations can be seen in the response at Memorial Medical Center Hospital—now called Ochsner Baptist—located in the Freret neighborhood of New Orleans, where emergency plans fell apart, flooded basement generators led to a loss of power, and patients who were not evacuated died from heat and lack of medical services, and a doctor was indicted, although not convicted, on criminal charges that some patients had been euthanized.

How did things get so out of hand at this health-care facility?

The Coast Guard is often described as having a culture of preparedness—which allowed them to generate rapid situational awareness, make smart assessments, and take immediate action without a specific action plan and without the go-ahead from higher ups. What Memorial Hospital had was quite the opposite: twenty distinct emergency plans amounting to 273 total pages—more than any single person could wrap his or her head around or utilize in the midst of the crisis.[11] What's more, there was little coordination among the plans, and they did not account for the worst-case scenario—what we now know was Hurricane Katrina.

How the crisis at Memorial Hospital escalated into a disaster is poignantly documented in Sheri Fink's book, *Five Days at Memorial: Life and Death in a Storm-Ravaged Hospital.* Fink writes, "The hospital's preparedness plan for hurricanes did not anticipate flooding. The flooding plan did not anticipate the need to evacuate. The evacuation plan did not anticipate a potential loss of power or communications. Most critically, the hurricane plan relied on the assumption that the hospital's generators would keep working for a minimum of seventy-two hours, although they were never tested to run that long."[12] Although the hospital had a plan—many plans—it was not *prepared,* exhibiting an alarming lack of awareness about the potential devastation caused by a catastrophic storm.

While being prepared invariably involves having some kind of a plan, readiness is about the capacity and capability to become and grow more aware, to adapt, and to utilize certain sets of skills and knowledge in uncertain, changing environments. As Fink summarizes, "Underlying the official response to the crisis at [Memorial Hospital] was a lack of situational awareness—a view of the larger picture of what was happening and what needed to be done."[13] Without situational awareness, it's unlikely there will be an effective response.

New Vulnerabilities Create New Gaps in Response

Now let me return to Surat for a look at a second disruption, in 2006. It, too, involved flood, but had it not been for a different vulnerability—conflicted governance—could probably have been avoided. Since 1994, Surat had done a good deal of self-assessment and taken a number of steps to improve its readiness and enable a better response if such a disruption should come again. The flood and plague crisis had turned out to be a "precipitating event," as Dr. Desai calls it, that spurred the city into action.[14] They implemented a disease surveillance program, which made it possible to learn of outbreaks faster and develop responses more quickly. They installed a flood warning system, with sirens that sound when a flood is expected, which increased Surat's readiness. The health department, city government, and private hospitals coordinated planning, reporting, and treatment protocols, including colleagues from local academic institutions in their discussions, to better integrate the city's response. Sanitation, sewage, and water delivery systems were expanded to better handle the needs of the populations they served, and maintenance procedures were established to more rapidly respond to blockages and other disruptions in normal functioning.

The transformation was, in large part, credited to a strong local leader, S. R. Rao, who had become commissioner of Surat Municipal Corporation in May 1995. Upon entering office, Rao swiftly devised better garbage collection and cleaning systems, temporarily shuttered unsanitary food establishments, demolished structures that had been illegally built on municipal land, and enforced rules and regulations.[15]

These efforts helped restore the public's trust in Surat's authorities, and the city had a much stronger sense of itself as a community. It began making remarkable progress. In 1996, the Indian National Trust for Architectural and Cultural Heritage named Surat the second-cleanest city in India.[16] Industrial growth resumed and the city prospered. By 2006, Surat's GDP was $22 billion, and the city boasted one of the country's highest per capita incomes.[17]

During this period of growth and success, however, Surat developed new vulnerabilities. As business boomed, informal settlements along the river banks continued to expand, exposing a greater number of people to the threat of flood. New public health issues emerged, such as an increase in the incidence of HIV. New industrial facilities were built on landfill in floodplain areas.[18] So although Surat had better readiness, increased protection, and improved response mechanisms in place, the city's very success had increased its vulnerability in certain ways. This is not unusual, and it is the reason awareness and continuous monitoring and learning are so important to building resilience.

There was another factor that had grown increasingly important over the years, an infrastructural element that was a major asset and also a concerning threat: the dam.

THE UKAI DAM, one hundred kilometers upriver from Surat, was built for three purposes: irrigation, power generation, and flood control. Its primary purpose is to control the flow of water to downstream fields for irrigation and to communities for drinking. The dam collects water from the catchment area of the Tapi River, which can be released through sluice gates in controlled amounts as needed to meet demand throughout the year. This is essential because rainfall in India is not steady: there is the rainy monsoon season (May through October) and the dry months in between. The dam is also a mechanism to manage the flow of the Tapi River to avoid flooding downstream.[19]

Effective management of the dam is particularly important and tricky during the monsoon season. That is the time when dam managers have the opportunity to collect the water they will need to ensure supply for the coming dry months, and the goal is to have a full reservoir at the end of the rainy season. However, there is risk in collecting too much water, because it can overtax the dam and threaten its structural integrity. If the water rises too high, it can overtop the dam and rush downstream at its own pace, although the dam itself may not fail. Far worse than overtopping, however, would be a breach, a collapse of the structure such that a gaping hole is created and the contents of the reservoir can gush through. The Ukai Dam is susceptible to breach because upper portions of the structure are constructed of earth and covered in vegetation. Mice, rats, and other rodents tunnel into the earth and make their homes deep inside the wall. Should water rise to the level of these entryways, it would sluice into the tunnels and eat away at the dam's earthen structure, and the enormous pressure of the reservoir against the weakened wall could cause the dam to blow open, causing a catastrophic breach.[20]

The challenge is to maintain an optimal water level, but water doesn't flow into the reservoir in a steady or reliable way. Depending on rainfall, soil conditions, levels in dozens of tributaries, and runoff in the dam's catchment area, water may trickle in or it may come in a surge. Rainfall, too, is hard to predict, particularly in monsoon season. Storms pounce, and rainfall can accumulate quickly. So the level in the dam can rise unpredictably, which means that maintaining the proper level is not as simple as allowing the water to collect to a certain point and then gently letting some go. To help guide water-release decisions, the Central Water Commission, responsible for managing the dam and its twenty-one sluice gates, sets a "rule level" for the reservoir—a water height that must not be exceeded and at which water must, without fail, be released.[21]

But making decisions about when to open the sluice gates is not quite so straightforward as responding mechanically to the rule level. That's because, although the dam serves the state of Gujarat, its catchment area and part of the reservoir is in two other states: Madhya Pradesh and Maharashtra. Management of the dam, therefore, involves a number of authorities at the national, state, and municipal level, and coordination among them is key. Decisions about water releases that are made lightly or unilaterally can threaten the safety and needs of other stakeholders. All constituencies are supposed to be consulted. And, when a release is to be made, the dam's operators are to give adequate warning to all those potentially affected. But the Surtis' concerns about flooding often took a back seat to the need to release water for irrigation or to protect the dam.

The vulnerability, then, is not so much a matter of the hard infrastructure of the dam but of the decision-making process that controlled it, as was revealed in 2006. On August 4, strong storms in the Ukai area blew in, high tides approached in the Arabian Sea, and there was a waxing gibbous moon—factors that exacerbate flooding. The Surti authorities, aware of all this, knew the Ukai Dam was nearing capacity and were concerned that it might overtop or that the managers would wait too long and would have to make too large a release, which would inevitably cause flooding in Surat. Accordingly, Surat's collector (chief administrative and revenue officer) made a request to the dam's managers to make a limited release of water, but the engineers did not think it was necessary.[22] Because the Surtis did not have a strong enough voice in the decision-making process, their fears about flooding were set aside; the operators wanted to continue accumulating water in the dam. A state official made a public announcement that the water was still three feet below the rule level and more than ten feet below the danger level, so no release would be made immediately.[23]

Surat's collector made another request for a contained release, this time in conjunction with the commissioner of the Surat Municipal Corporation, and, on Saturday, the engineers acceded and made a small release. That might have been enough to alleviate the threat as it stood, but the next morning a surge of water rushed into the reservoir, raising the water line three feet above the rule level and approaching the danger zone.[24] That evening, Surti authorities, anticipating the inevitable, activated the flood warning system, sending SMS alerts to some 600,000 mobile phones and broadcasting alerts on TV and radio.[25] Surat residents scrambled to make whatever preparations they could and move to whatever higher ground they could find, even if only the top floors in their homes.

With the dam in danger of overtopping, its engineers—without giving further warning or engaging consultation—finally opened the sluice gates and left them open, releasing a torrent of water that boiled downstream. Around noon, Surat's thirty-six flood-warning sirens began to shriek. Three hours later, water began to flow into the city's low-lying areas.[26] Although the sirens performed as they were meant to, people did not always choose the wisest course of action—many gathered on bridges to watch the water level rise, putting themselves at risk.

Within seventy-two hours, water had engulfed some 75 percent of the city. Health clinics were inundated. Government offices, too, were underwater. The cell phone network was compromised.[27] The Central Water Commission's district office, which analyzes flood risk data, was under ten feet of water.[28] More than 120 people died.[29] Some 20,000 people were trapped on rooftops, balconies, or the upper floors of their homes. Entire settlements of migrants on the riverbanks were washed away. Food and drinking water were in short supply. Businesses closed down. Just as they had in 1994, people fled the city.

In an investigation that followed, multiple and conflicting explanations for what had happened placed blame on different parties for different reasons. State government officials maintained there was no blame because "nobody could have ever predicted such an unprecedented increase in inflow in such a short span."[30]

In understanding what happened in Surat, it is instructive to look beyond the behavior of individuals or groups to the broader context. First, the decision-making process did not have the necessary integration of the entities involved, nor did it accommodate the diversity of their needs. Just as important, however, the entire water management system was not well integrated, nor was it self-regulating. It did not have the capacity to fail safely, nor was there a redundant mechanism, apart from the sluice gates, for managing an overflow.

Over the years since the dam was first built, and even more intensely since the flood of 1994, Surat's growth and urbanization had made the city more vulnerable to flooding. As industry grew, companies built facilities in low-lying areas and, knowing the risk of flood, built up embankments to keep the water out. This cut off the river's natural floodplain and squeezed its natural course. A new weir had been built across the river to control salt-water intrusion from the Arabian Sea, which it successfully did, but it, too, restricted the river's flow. The construction boom—sparked by Surat's economic growth—had increased the demand for sand, which was being dug out of the river's banks, making them less effective as natural buffers for the river's waters when they rose. Overall, the carrying capacity of the river in Surat had been drastically reduced.[31] In other words, the river had been blockaded, congested, and stripped of some of its natural water management capabilities.

Surat is proof that resilience building is a continuing process, requiring a constant assessment and reassessment of vulnerabilities and threats, and that responding to disruption means making well-integrated decisions and communicating them through diverse channels. And, in Surat, there is another lesson: that an asset, such as a dam and a redundant source of water supply, can also be a source of vulnerability.

Many coastal cities will learn these lessons in the years to come, as the oceans rise and more rain falls. They can avoid the kind of disaster Surat suffered if they recognize the necessity of integrated institutional responses to emergencies and disruptions and the importance of thinking about social-ecological systems in a holistic way.

Taking Responsibility, Not Placing Blame

It is common in situations like the 2006 crisis in Surat for official investigations and unofficial analyses of what happened to seek to place blame, preferably, it would seem, on individuals. It is much easier to point the finger at a person than it is to cogently analyze the failings of a system.

But in crisis situations, as in Surat, individual leaders rarely play a make-or-break role. It is usually more accurate to speak of *leadership* than of individual leaders, because the most effective responses are resilient ones: they involve integration and inclusion, engagement of many and diverse players, and constant adaptation to emerging circumstances, such that no one person or entity can be the final decision maker in every situation. There does not need to be a hierarchy, a "top" person or an individual "hero," but there must be leadership.[32]

Often, leadership of the best and most effective kind in a crisis is established based on prior relationships—rather than on hierarchical lines of authority. Eric McNulty and Barry Dorn of the National Leadership Preparedness Initiative, refer to it as "meta-leadership," and they focus particularly on leadership in complex crises that involve a number of agencies and entities, often on a national level. Meta-leaders, they say, "recognize that achieving genuine national preparedness demands a spirit of cooperation" as well as "inter-agency mechanisms" that fuel a quality they refer to as "jointness."[33]

Dorn, McNulty, and their colleagues have worked with leaders at all levels, and have interviewed and debriefed those involved in crises. When they studied the Boston bombings, which involved so many leaders—including the mayor, the governor, the police commissioner, the FBI, the Secret Service, and others—they asked questions such as, Who is the leader? How do you put this all together? How do you make it work?

They came to the conclusion that what made leadership work in Boston was the relationships the leaders and their groups had been building since at least 2004. "They weren't planning for the Boston Marathon bombings," Dorn said, "but they learned to talk to each other. They learned to communicate with each other. They had respect for each other. In other words, they were thinking about the whole of community." As a result, although there was plenty of opportunity to "screw up," the management of the crisis—from the boom moment to the capture of the suspects—went well. "It wasn't because someone said, 'I'm in charge of this thing.' It was because they had built relationships."

THAT IS HOW GOVERNOR PATRICK recalls the situation during the Boston bombings. His daughter had already called him to say that something had happened when the phone rang again, this time with a call from the head of the emergency management team at the scene. "He said, 'Something bad has happened,'" Patrick remembers. "'There are people down. Body parts. It's chaos.' I said, 'I'm on my way.'"[34] Patrick turned around and headed for his office at the State House.

When the second bomb went off and it became apparent, or likely, that something seriously bad was going on and that other bombs in Boston might be set to go off, Patrick's security team of state troopers didn't want him to go to the State House to set up a command post. They urged him to head for the emergency bunker in Framingham, twenty miles outside Boston. "I said, 'I'm not going to Framingham. I'm going to the State House.'" Eventually Patrick wound up at the Westin Hotel near the finish line, where emergency teams and representatives from the many agencies on scene were gathering.

At the Westin, the agencies involved—the Boston Police Department, the State Police, the FBI, the Bureau of Alcohol, Tobacco, Firearms, and Explosives (ATF), and others—all had to act with limited information. "I got all these agencies into a corner," Patrick recalls, "and said, 'Everybody has a role. We don't know how big or small this is, and in order to sort that out, we need everybody. All hands on deck.'" Still, leadership was needed. Patrick looked at the agency representatives and asked each one who they thought should be in charge. The consensus was that the FBI should take the lead, which they did.

We've already seen how the coordinated response in Boston was the result of readiness and preparation that saved lives, and although the coordination of these many agencies was instrumental in the investigation and manhunt for the suspects that followed, Patrick believed there was an important hole in the response effort that he needed to fill: communication.

"My role was not to call the shots in the investigation," Patrick says, "but to help with the communication, the public messaging—to fill in the gaps around law enforcement. It was a lot of comforting and consoling of people."

To use the pilot's mantra, the aviation and navigation were largely being taken care of by the individual agencies and their heads, so

Patrick could focus on communication. "One lesson from other experiences like this," Patrick says, "is that you have to stand up and talk about what's going on, even when you don't have information. Let people ask their questions and tell them you don't know yet."

When those who are leading through a crisis share information openly and are transparent about what they do and do not know, they build trust. That encourages people to further share information and to limit the spread of rumors and suppositions that can lead to extreme and baseless reactions. These are often played out online, and such "digital wildfires," according to the World Economic Forum, pose a significant risk to system stability in our hyperconnected age.[35]

Tom Frieden, director of the CDC, credits honesty in communication for the organization's good reputation and cites what is known as the "risk seesaw" as the motivation for transparency. "If you tell people, 'Don't worry, everything's fine,' they'll worry," he says. "If you overemphasize the things that could go wrong, they'll say, 'You know, they're really exaggerating. It's not so bad.'"[36] By sharing information you create better situational awareness, which improves responsiveness and builds trust across silos of activity (units or disciplines that are isolated from one another) which makes for better integration. Things then rebound more quickly and more safely.

Governor Patrick held two press conferences on Marathon Monday, not to worry people but to explain what was happening and what officials knew and didn't know. Patrick was also thinking about the bigger picture—how to control the messaging and dialogue around the event and, ultimately, how to maintain the social cohesion that would help the city and its people heal once the crisis had passed. Almost from the beginning, Patrick was thinking about how to help the city to rebound as quickly as possible from this unpreventable shock.

"One of the things I was worried about, before we knew the background of the perpetrators," Governor Patrick says, "is that we would turn *on* each other, when part of the response, rebuilding, and rehealing would require turning *to* each other."

At the second press conference, held that Monday evening, after discussing what was being done and had been done during the day by law enforcement, and what citizens could expect in the coming days (increased security, random bag checks), Patrick confidently emphasized the importance of getting through the tragedy and crisis together:

> I also want to say that there have been a number of stories I've heard this afternoon of residents in Boston and along the route in the cities and towns that the marathon passes of extraordinary kindness shown to runners and others—neighbors and visitors—who are shaken by this experience as we are. . . . We're going to get through this. We do not have all the answers to all of your questions yet. . . . But I can tell you from the President to the members of our congressional delegation to many, many fellow Governors who have called to check in, to all of the leaders in law enforcement here in the state at the local level and at the federal level, we are all coming together to do everything we can to get to the bottom of this.[37]

Patrick did not have, and could not have, all the answers. His confidence, as well as his inclusion of all those who expressed both their confidence and concern, presented an image of a governance group that had stabilized itself (if it had even been destabilized at all) and reminded citizens of Boston that they were not alone in their shock and sadness and would not be alone in creating a response.

Perhaps most important, however, Patrick spoke to the "kindnesses"—the beautiful moments of human compassion and action that occurred throughout the city. He spoke of marathoners who did not stop once they crossed the finish line but kept on running until they reached Mass General Hospital and gave blood. He spoke of Bostonians who opened their doors to runners and visitors alike. Patrick wanted such moments, as much as the explosions themselves, to define the day.[38] Boston's story was not going to be about terror—it was going to be about togetherness.

"There were tremendous acts of grace," says Patrick. "There were so many ways people brought the best of themselves out, and I think lifting that up was key. There's another part of the putting-back-together that goes beyond finding the bad guys or gals and bringing them to justice: How do we come together and acknowledge what happened and grieve together but also, in a way, commit to rebuilding together?"

It is a fundamentally important question to our discussion of resilience—rebuilding, healing, revitalizing as a community—and Patrick's responses, and his capacity to enable the leadership of other necessary actors, served Boston well.

LEADERSHIP LOOKED VERY different during the earthquake, flooding, and plant meltdown in Japan of March 11, 2011—a set of cascading disruptions considerably more complex and far-reaching than the Boston bombings. As a result of the magnitude 9.0 earthquake and the tsunami that followed, nearly 20,000 people were killed or went missing. The Fukushima Daiichi nuclear power plant was so badly damaged it is now recognized as the second-worst nuclear disaster, after Chernobyl. Although no deaths came as a direct result of the nuclear plant dysfunction itself, some 270,000 citizens were made refugees in the disaster, about 100,000 of whom lost their homes.[39]

The Japanese were correctly praised in some quarters for aspects of their preparedness. Analysts argued that lives were saved because of planning measures and strict building codes that prevented additional structures from toppling during the crisis.[40] However, accusations soon were being made about the mishandling and unpreparedness of leadership, including in the Fukushima nuclear power plant, which suffered catastrophic damage and a partial meltdown and its reactors released dangerous quantities of radiation.

In August 2012, the company that operated the plant, Tokyo Electric Power (TEPCO), released 150 hours of video of teleconferences between executives and plant managers, providing a glimpse of the disaster as it unfolded. Hiroko Tabuchi, reporting for the *New York Times,* writes about the communication between workers at the plant and executives at headquarters. The workers were exhorted to check the condition of the reactors but also to "take shelter," although there really was no shelter to take.

Clearly, the workers were not to blame for the disaster, and soon enough the finger pointing began. In a report prepared by the

International Atomic Energy Agency, TEPCO was found to have inadequate safety measures and insufficient backup systems and had also underestimated the threat of tsunamis.[41] Others have criticized the plant operators for underreporting the severity of damage and failing to respond rapidly enough.

One of the most startling revelations concerned the behavior of an important player in the disaster: the prime minister of Japan at the time, Naoto Kan. It seems that he had made a classic mistake in such situations. In an effort to show leadership, he traveled to the plant to "direct the workers who were dealing with the damaged core," as the report by the Fukushima Nuclear Accident Independent Investigation Commission put it, but that action backfired because it "diverted the attention and time of the on-site operational staff and confused the line of command."[42]

Eventually, however, the true leaders emerged. According to William Saito, the plant workers had been ordered by the plant operators to stop pumping seawater into the reactors, which the workers had been doing in an attempt to keep the reactors cool and avoid a meltdown. The operators were concerned, however, that the water would destroy the reactors and create an enormous commercial loss. At last, the plant workers ignored the order and kept on pumping.[43] Saito says their actions demonstrated "the real leadership" that day. "They basically totaled the plant," he says, "but saved the country."[44]

THE TOYOTA MOTOR CORPORATION also suffered extensive damage to its plants in Japan during the 2011 earthquake—a total of 659 of its facilities were impacted by the quake, fire, or flooding—but the response and outcomes were very different than at Fukushima. Most of the facilities were operated by Toyota's suppliers and partners, and together they produced some 1,260 different parts that go into the assembly of an automobile, five hundred that are essential to keep production rolling.

Toyota had experienced disruption from two previous earthquakes—one in 1995 that had damaged thirteen production facilities and another in 2007 that had disabled eight plants—so they had learned a great deal about how to respond to such disruptions and were well prepared. When the March quake struck, Toyota immediately called into action the disaster response task forces that had been established in each of the major operations groups, including purchasing, production, engineering, and information technology. Each task force set up an *obeya,* a designated control center and meeting area equipped with all the diverse communications tools known to the modern corporation, including a video network connecting multiple Toyota offices. People at Toyota and its affiliates quickly integrated their efforts around a set of priorities: saving lives, supporting the recovery of earthquake-impacted areas, and, finally, getting production back into swing.

The company's president, Akio Toyoda, did not attempt to manage the operations personally but rather demonstrated the kind of meta-leadership that Dorn and McNulty describe. He encouraged leadership throughout the company, based on the defined priorities. To that end, he immediately delegated his authority to the people on the ground. He addressed the task forces, saying, "I trust your decisions. I will take full responsibility for your actions, so do whatever needs to be done to get our business back on its feet as quickly as possible."[45] Toyota's philosophy of respecting the knowledge and decisions of those closest to the situation is core to its culture.

By March 12, one day after the crisis, Toyota began delivering emergency supplies and helping to restore facilities in the area. The magnitude of the task was almost overwhelming. With communications systems largely disabled, the task forces did not have any idea which facilities were damaged or how extensively. They were able to reach some, but hardly all, of the suppliers by phone. Their next effort was to conduct the most fundamental form of information gathering of the sort we have seen in San Francisco (walking around) and Nairobi (village enumerations) by dispatching teams into the field, one of them in a well-equipped Toyota Land Cruiser, to visit the production facility sites. They acted as relief workers, delivering aid and supplies, as well as advisers and information gatherers. Within days, the relief activities expanded, two facilities were established as relief logistics centers, and some eighty-seven trucks were dispatched with relief workers and supplies.

Although helping people was the primary goal, Toyota needed to get production up and running again as quickly as possible. As information about the facilities came in, the purchasing division synthesized it to determine which plants could produce which parts. At the same time, the production people were checking inventory against the 1,260 parts affected, creating a monumental spreadsheet of 5,000 rows by 5,000 columns. The various internal groups had to make decisions quickly and in an integrated way about how to proceed. "We didn't have the luxury of time to go through the usual decision process," says one Toyota staff member. "But the executives were also there, and they actively exchanged opinions quickly." Another person who participated in Toyota team meetings remarked, "In a system that normally makes decisions very cautiously, it was done at an unbelievable pace."

Over the next two months, Toyota's people worked across departments, with suppliers, and with dealers to develop alternatives to their normal operating methods and adapt to the situation as it developed. They decided to focus on getting production going for a handful of the most in-demand models. They identified substitute materials that could be used in the manufacture of a number of parts. In one case, they ran into a production bottleneck of the sort Lululemon had faced: a single supplier of an ingredient for a special paint type used in sixty-seven of Toyota's two hundred available colors. The company fiercely guarded the formula for its ingredient and would not allow Toyota personnel into their damaged plant. Toyota had no choice but to develop an alternative. They put together an interdisciplinary team with members from across the company, and within about six weeks the team had created a substitute material that enabled them to match thirty-seven of the colors. These could be used in production until the supplier was back in operation.

Toyota was seriously disrupted by the disaster. It lost production of about 370,000 vehicles, which toppled the company from its position as top global automaker to number 4 on the list.[46] But the company recovered far more quickly and successfully than it had anticipated. Production was completely halted for only two weeks. By the middle of April, all of Toyota's major plants in Japan were running again, although at lower capacity than before the disaster. By the end of June, 90 percent of production had been restored.

Toyota is well known for its Toyota Production System, which is both a philosophy and a set of practices—it stresses the importance of relationships and the participation of everyone in the system to achieve continuous improvement. The production system shares the characteristics of resilience: it is aware, diverse, integrated, self-regulating, and highly adaptive. It is so much a part of the way people at Toyota think and provides such a wealth of tools for them that they have the capacity to respond and adapt to the rapidly changing circumstances that characterize the globalized auto industry. "Our mission is to have the parts ready to deliver the cars to the customers," said a member of the purchasing department. "It is in our DNA." And, as large as Toyota is, with offices, production facilities, partners, and dealers around the world, the company-wide understanding of the "Toyota Way," as it is sometimes called, enabled people at all levels to gather and share information, make decisions, and take action during the disaster without being constricted by hierarchy or bureaucracy—they could take on leadership roles as and where needed. Many of those who helped get Toyota back on its feet during the earthquake and in the months that followed said simply, "We just did what we needed to." That approach has enabled Toyota, over a period of decades, to become one of the most resilient companies in the world. In 2013, just two years after experiencing a crisis from which Japan is still recovering, Toyota regained its top spot as the number 1 automaker.[47]

Crisis as a Step Toward Revitalization

Once the floodwaters had receded in Surat in 2006, it became clear that, this time, things had to be different. It would not be enough to resume basic functioning and recover to the point of "normalcy." Yes, it was necessary to build back what had been destroyed and important to make incremental improvements, but the city was facing too many threats, struggling with too many vulnerabilities, to settle for that. Besides, Surat had considerable assets that it could bring to bear on its problems—including a strong commercial base, a more cohesive sense of community, better local governance, and an estimable reputation. Perhaps, by working together and gaining some outside assistance, the city could tackle its problems.

And so, in the years following the 2006 crisis, the city did seek outside technical support and worked with a number of organizations, supported by The Rockefeller Foundation's Asian Cities Climate Change Resilience Network (ACCCRN). This is an initiative, begun in 2008 and led by managing director Ashvin Dayal, that has been funding a large variety of interventions that are building climate change resilience in forty Asian cities—including Surat—in India, Indonesia, Vietnam, and Thailand.[48] With a more explicit focus on resilience building, Surat now has an improved dam management and hydrology analysis system, a better flood early-warning system that provides flood forecasts two to three days before a potential event, and an expanded disease surveillance system. The city is also pursuing a number of new initiatives, including soft solutions such as rainwater harvesting and the reactivation of water sources that have fallen into disuse to provide more diversity and redundancy in the water supply.[49]

A key issue is getting the governance right. Today, in contrast to 2006, the water management process involves decision makers at all levels. In March, just before monsoon season begins, the major stakeholders in the city of Surat get together with other district collectors, personnel from the three state irrigation departments, private industry players, academics, and officials from the Central Water Commission to plan for the coming vulnerable months ahead. They consider: What has changed in the past year? What new irrigation needs or factory facilities have come online? What new factors might affect the flow of water into the dam and along the river's route?

Technology plays an important role, too. To help them in their assessment of the season ahead, they have developed a hydrology model that crunches data about the catchment area, rainfall, local terrain, and land use so that more accurate predictions can be made about how a storm will impact the flow of water to Ukai's reservoir. They have also created a model that figures in the amount of rainfall in Surat itself, as well as the state of the ocean tides and how those factors will further affect the behavior of the river. Using precipitation forecasts provided by the India Meteorological Department, officials can now predict potential floods two to three days in advance and begin preparations accordingly.

Each morning at 8:00 these hydrology reports are sent to members of the Surat Climate Change Trust. This is an informal advocacy group, composed of many stakeholders, that has a good deal of power and influence as the result of its access to near-real-time information and the prognosis reporting system, according to G. K. Bhat, chair of TARU Leading Edge, one of the ACCCRN implementing partners.[50] This system ensures that if, as in 2006, the irrigation department balks at ordering a needed safe release, these actors can sound the alarm and pressure officials to take action. The involvement of private industry players is particularly important. If the lead-up to the 2006 scenario were to happen today, those business leaders could, in a worst-case scenario, ask for intervention from the highest level of political and administrative authorities—and would not be ignored.

In Surat, people have significantly increased their awareness and knowledge such that they can make much better assessments of their vulnerabilities, risks, and the seriousness of the threat. No longer do they rely solely on a single, crude "rule-level" at the dam. And the multistakeholder group ensures the irrigation department no longer makes unilateral judgments about dam releases without oversight. In this way, Surat's municipal government and private sector have worked with the state government to create a self-monitoring and self-regulating system, which can reduce the incidence of floods.

Surat has also accepted that, even with more information and better management, they can never completely rule out the possibility of flood. There is just too much water and too many factors to contend with: rainfall, storms, tide, catchment conditions, river inflow, and the possible amplification of floods as a result of climate change. So they have made improvements to their warning system. Now that the Meteorological Department has the capability to predict floods two to three days in advance, the goal is to warn the people of Surat as soon as the predictions are available and confirmed. Now Surtis will have as much as three days to prepare, a great improvement over the three-hour warning they had become accustomed to. That's enough time to secure homes and commercial buildings, stock up on supplies, organize people and groups, and evacuate if necessary.

To alert people, the city has taken the route of diversity to make sure there are multiple ways to get the word out. Almost everyone has a voice-and-text cell phone, so in 2013 the police department launched an SMS service called Setu ("bridge" in Sanskrit), so citizens can receive extensive water alerts and other relevant information. It is designed to be scaled up during a crisis, providing an important and reliable communication channel for the city's agencies and residents. Large digital displays have been placed in prominent locations throughout Surat to provide data on rainfall, dam water levels, and other information—all of which are also available on Surat Municipal Corporation's website. The final element of the warning system is the most basic: a fleet of vehicles equipped with loud speakers to patrol the streets, broadcasting advisories, alerts, information, and instructions.

And, to integrate all of these elements, Surat is developing a disaster management plan that identifies evacuation routes, contact numbers for key organizations and information hotlines, safe refuges and meeting zones, places that can be used to temporarily house people, and coordination and drop-off points for food and other supplies.[51]

The improvements to the water management system proved their worth during the monsoon season of 2013, when the Ukai Dam–served area experienced rainfall similar to that of 2006. In fact, there was more water in Surat in 2013 due to heavy local rains and fluvial floods, but the outcomes were significantly different. This time, thanks to better information, greater awareness, and integrated decision making, the dam's managers were able to do a number of smaller water releases earlier in the periods of heaviest water collection and were thus able to avoid the last-minute, high-volume releases that had caused such trouble in 2006. Floodgates in Surat were closed. Warning was given. As a result, although the level of the Tapi rose, Surat avoided a catastrophic flood. Residents did their best to protect valuable assets (they parked their cars on bridges and hung their motorcycles out of the water's reach) and moved to safe locations. Businesses continued operations with few interruptions. The disturbance—although trying—did not turn into a disaster.

Surat has also addressed its vulnerabilities related to disease, through the establishment of the Urban Health and Climate Resilience Centre, which The Rockefeller Foundation helped fund. The center will focus on issues at the juncture of public health and climate change adaptation, an area of investigation that is both new and important. One of the organization's main initiatives is the creation of a "climate-informed disease surveillance system,"[52] which will analyze vulnerabilities and threats and evaluate the success of adaptation measures. The hope is that the project will also lead to the development of a public health working group, research pioneered by multidisciplinary teams focusing on urban health, policy measures that help vulnerable residents, and an educational outreach program so that other cities around the world can benefit from Surat's findings, clearly providing Surat with a resilience dividend from its leadership role.

The objective is to create an improved, data-rich surveillance system that will enable Surat and other cities to better plan for, predict, and avert potential epidemics; respond with preventive measures and smart operating procedures; and reduce the spread of infectious and vector-borne diseases—particularly in its poorest neighborhoods where outbreaks tend to start. This would improve the health of the entire city, particularly its most vulnerable populations and those who live near them, and ease the burden on Surat's health system.

Surat has taken more basic measures in the quest to ensure a higher state of public health. Since the city's experience with plague in 1994, authorities there have come to realize that public health can take strange, unpredictable, and highly disruptive turns—and that the cause for an illness may lie with some seemingly unrelated issue. As Dr. Desai puts it, "Poor health is the outcome of the failure of other sectors." And, of course, a lack of basic services.

So, in addition to its research and development initiatives, Surat is also attending to nuts and bolts activities. City organizations have improved their knowledge assessment and tracking of vulnerable populations, the ones most likely to be affected by flood or other crises, and included that knowledge in the citywide disaster plan. Through its outreach, establishment of feedback loops and information-delivery methods, residents have become more aware of the health risks associated with floods and are more likely to keep the right medications and treatments in store. The city has plans to install pumps to evacuate water from the city when the city floodgates are closed and to improve its response practices so that drainage blockages are cleared within twenty-four hours of a flood to reduce water pooling and thus the breeding of disease-bearing mosquitoes. The city has also tested an SMS program that enables residents to inform the city when there is a problem with a basic service, such as water delivery.

Over the past several years, a new sense has developed in the city—that Surat should and will never again have to suffer shame as it had during the years it was known as "plague city." Indeed, people have even begun to believe that Surat could take itself to a whole new level. It could become a model not just for India but for the developing world. It might even be able to build its resilience to the point that knowledgeable people throughout India, and even around the world, would refer to Surat as a *world-class* city. If Surat can accomplish that—given its history as a city historically known for filth, flooding, and disease—it would be a remarkable story of revitalization.

11

AFTER THE CRISIS
Bouncing Forward

The post-crisis period is different from the experience of getting through, and helping others get through, a severe disruption. After the crisis, threats are not as urgent as they were before, when the floodwaters were rising, the disease was spreading, the explosion still echoed through the streets. Nor are the objectives so concrete as in a time of acute disruption, when the goals are sharply defined: save yourself, help others, protect assets. The post-crisis time scale, too, is tougher to get a handle on. A storm can last only so long and a pandemic will run its course, but how do you delineate what comes after?

Experts in disaster management define three phases of post-crisis: relief, restoration, and recovery. Relief involves the alleviation of acute crisis conditions, including search, evacuation, and rescue; delivery of basic supplies; and provision of essential services. Restoration can include many activities, including the bringing back of utilities, communications networks, and transportation systems—and the repair and return to service of damaged facilities and infrastructure. Recovery is a broader concept, usually referring to human or other natural systems, including bringing organizations, communities, and environments back to successful functioning.

These definitions are useful, but they don't fully encompass the process of resilience building. Relief, restoration, recovery—these terms suggest the return to a previous state. We often hear people say their main concern after a disruption is to "get back to normal" or to resume functioning as it has "always been." This is understandable. People, communities, and systems want to stabilize themselves and, as much as possible, do so under their own steam. They want to clean things up, fix what's broken, and get on with their lives and work.

At the same time, people may come to look back at the eye of a crisis with awe and admiration, as a kind of pinnacle experience. As Rebecca Solnit, author of *A Paradise Built in Hell*, writes of disaster, "When all the ordinary divides and patterns are shattered, people step up—not all, but the great preponderance—to become their brothers' keepers."[1] We have seen the truth of this in many of the stories in this book—Oakland residents looking after the ambulance crews, strangers tending to victims of the Boston bombings, the actors of Halifax setting up a relief station. We all have heard such stories, and many of us have lived through such times.

Bouncing back, however, is very different kind of experience. The period of weeks or months (sometimes years) after a severe disruption like those in Surat, at Fukushima, or in New Orleans can be exceptionally difficult for individuals, families, organizations, and societies. The reality of the disruption sets in. Infrastructure is damaged and systems are harmed. Social cohesion may be affected. Livelihoods are threatened or destroyed. Ecosystems may be disturbed. For people and places where there are already significant vulnerabilities, where there is insufficient awareness and readiness, and where response is slow or inadequate, crisis can only make matters worse. Fundamental problems may be laid bare in the post-crisis period as never before. There is no resilience dividend, but rather a deficit.

But resilient entities—those with high levels of awareness, sufficient readiness, and the capacity to effectively respond—move on. Not only do they bounce back to a functioning state, they bounce forward: they nurture natural systems, improve structures, and strengthen social ties.

Still, the process of bouncing forward is never easy. It requires planning, rebuilding, and often reinventing. It is not enough to forge ahead with unconsidered action to put things back into a known order. New assessments must be made, analysis conducted, lessons articulated, narratives developed. What really happened during the crisis? What caused it? What vulnerabilities were revealed? What did we learn? Decisions must be made and priorities set. What are we going to do? When? Who and what should get priority? People must assume responsibility and actions must be taken. Who is "we"? Who will be involved in the work? Who will lead it? Who will benefit? How many resources can we muster? What are we willing to invest? Whose money should it be? Plans need to be developed and acted upon. New types of tools and processes used. How will we move ahead? How will we measure our progress and success? Aspirations must be stated and visions for a possible transformation expressed. What do we really want for ourselves? What might our future look like?

"Never let a good crisis go to waste," Winston Churchill is famously credited with saying, and the same admonition has been iterated in many forms by people in disparate domains, including politics, economics, business, psychology, and sports. From bad emerges good. From crisis comes opportunity. Disaster can be a kind of positive reset button.

Too often, however, people *do* "waste" a crisis, by which I mean they do not take the opportunity to address their vulnerabilities nor do they take action to make positive change and improvement. But fortunately we have many good examples of entities that have successfully bounced forward—including the city that suffered one of the most intense and wide-ranging disruptions of any community in the history of the United States, a crisis that came close to destroying it, New Orleans.[2]

AFTER THE FEDERAL FLOOD

Hurricane Katrina was one of the worst weather-related disasters the United States has experienced. It caused flooding that affected 80 percent of the city, with water reaching as high as eight feet in some neighborhoods (although residents argue it was more like twelve feet in places).[3] Aerial footage from the days after the storm captured images of entire city blocks under water, with only the roofs of homes visible.[4] In Katrina's wake, the city's essential services, facilities, and systems were destroyed or disrupted—water, sanitation, health care, education, utilities, transportation, governance—and, within a few days after the flooding began, the place was virtually empty. The population, nearly half a million before the storm, fell to a few thousand people.[5]

The catastrophe not only demonstrated how vulnerable the city was to flooding because of its location on low-elevation land; it revealed many other vulnerabilities as well. The first and most obvious of these was the hurricane defense system—the essential infrastructural element—which proved to be woefully inadequate. The system was designed, built, and maintained by the US Army Corps of Engineers, which is why New Orleanians often place the blame for the system's failures on the federal government and refer to the storm as the "federal flood."

But New Orleans also suffered from poor social cohesion and was not far from crisis in many ways even before the disaster. The poverty rate was one of the highest in the United States. Median household income was low, $27,000, compared to the national average of $41,000. Home ownership was at 46 percent, in comparison to the US average of 68 percent. Most significant, perhaps, the population had long been in decline. In 1960, New Orleans was a city of about 630,000 people; in 2000 there were fewer than 500,000 residents. Not surprisingly, there were some 40,000 vacant lots throughout the city.[6] This combination of declining population, low home ownership, and abundance of unoccupied properties—along with a struggling educational system and a high crime rate—made revitalization particularly difficult for New Orleans.

Would New Orleans see the Katrina crisis as an opportunity? It was clear that building back, even building back better—just with infrastructural improvements—would not be enough. As the popular saying goes in New Orleans, "You can't pump your way to a solution." Planning would be required.

PLANNING: THE UNGLAMOROUS PART

Planning is not a glamorous activity. It can be tedious, it takes time, it usually does not involve colorful action, and it can be expensive. As we have seen, it took some twenty-three years to develop the Community Action Plan for Seismic Safety and Earthquake Safety Implementation Program in San Francisco. No wonder that, after a crisis, people may prefer to skip the assessment and planning process and get right to the *doing*. They want to rebuild and restore things as quickly as possible, almost as if that would neutralize the power of the crisis and enable them to avoid facing what it has revealed.

Planning is essential not only because of the plan that results but because it is in the process of planning that you build greater capacity to take effective action. During the planning process, all the characteristics of resilience building come into play. The people involved have to become aware of and acknowledge their strengths and weaknesses. They have to consider diverse alternatives and disparate ideas. They have to collaborate to reach solutions that benefit many constituencies. They have to self-regulate—the groups must be functional, able to debate and disagree and still move forward. They may need to adapt their attitudes, behaviors, and actions to suit the plan. After Superstorm Sandy struck the New York area in 2012, for example, New York State developed a revitalization plan called NYS2100, which focused on how to make the state more resilient.[7] (Felix Rohatyn and I were cochairs of the commission established by New York governor Andrew Cuomo to prepare the plan.) The report was developed with the participation of a remarkable group of people, including experts from the public and private sectors. There were government officials, academics, real estate developers, engineers, leaders of conservancy groups and public utilities, and members of the financial community. Our charge was to make recommendations to transform the state's infrastructure and systems with a time horizon of 2100.

Our first task was to identify vulnerabilities that had put the entire system at risk during Sandy and that continued to do so, but the overall goal was much more comprehensive than just finding vulnerabilities and recommending fixes and improvements. As we wrote in the report, "If done right, we have a tremendous opportunity not only to mitigate future damage and subsequent economic losses, but to invigorate New York's economy with a robust green technology sector and to enhance quality-of-life for all New Yorkers."[8] In other words, we were working toward the creation of a resilience dividend.

Ultimately, we made nine meta-recommendations (cutting across sectors) that addressed infrastructure, information systems, land use planning, restoration of the natural environment, and social cohesion. In each area, we made specific recommendations for physical improvements and systems replacements or upgrades, including the development of smart-grid technologies and the implementation of better systems for the analysis of data as well as for mapping and visualization. It was shocking to learn how much data the state had while it lacked the analytic tools to use it more effectively in crisis, to integrate it with city-level systems, and to provide the transparency required by other stakeholders. The recommendations also included enhancing institutional coordination, developing a homeowner buy-out program for homes situated on the most vulnerable land, instituting insurance reform, and streamlining the permitting process for rebuilding. I was particularly concerned that the use of green and natural infrastructure solutions be encouraged, and the report indeed includes a number of such recommendations, such as the use of wetlands and dunes as natural buffers against storm surges.

In addition to recommendations for actions to take, the best plans contain a good deal of discussion of what happened during a disruption, an analysis of what went wrong, and, most important, an exploration of the fundamental issues that contributed to the making of the disaster. The NYS2100 Commission addressed the issues of poverty, population growth, and other demographic pressures—as well as climate change risks such as sea-level rise, changing temperatures and precipitation patterns, and extreme weather events—and how they contributed to the devastation wreaked by Sandy. We also called attention to our vulnerable and aging infrastructure—including pipelines, substations, electric lines, wastewater treatment plants, and hard flood-protection measures—which is not sufficiently resilient and will not be able to protect our communities against severe storms and flooding. These challenges will pose more and more threats over the next several decades. We have little choice but to address them, and quickly.[9]

I should add that, apart from the state plan, New York City has its own comprehensive plan for building resilience called PlaNYC, a "sustainability and resiliency blueprint," which was launched in 2007 and championed by then Mayor Michael Bloomberg. It focuses on adaptation and climate change with the goal of "ensuring quality of life for generations of New Yorkers to come."[10] The plan comprises 257 projects and programs that address physical, environmental, and social issues—from plastics recycling and bicycle lanes to land use and food supply—which are being systematically budgeted for and implemented. After Superstorm Sandy hit, the city augmented PlaNYC with an additional plan focused specifically on "actionable recommendations based on the best available science to protect our city's coastline, buildings, infrastructure, and communities from future climate risks."[11]

ANOTHER COMPREHENSIVE AND particularly intriguing postdisaster report was issued by the Fukushima Nuclear Accident Independent Investigation Commission (NAIIC). It came out in July 2012, about fifteen months after the earthquake-tsunami and nuclear plant disaster of March 2011. Unlike many such reports, this one caused a sensation precisely because it addressed Japan's vulnerabilities in no uncertain terms. It was both an analysis of what had happened in the crisis and a recommendation for what should happen in response.

William Saito, a successful entrepreneur, worked for ten months as a special adviser to the cabinet office for the government of Japan, helping the NAIIC develop its report. Saito was an interesting choice because he is also a well-known observer and critic of Japanese culture, particularly what he refers to as its "moral hazards."[12]

The NAIIC report, which focuses on what happened at the Fukushima Daiichi plant (not on the tsunami), is remarkable in many ways. Most important to understand is that it is the product of the first-ever investigative commission to be chartered by the national Diet, the Japanese legislature. It was conducted by an independent body, composed of and led by people outside the government bureaucracy. "That was groundbreaking," Saito says. The report makes clear that it "was the first independent commission created in the history of Japan's constitutional government."[13]

Not surprisingly then, members of the Diet seemed unsure of what to expect. The commission was led by Kiyoshi Kurokawa, a doctor and professor emeritus at the University of Tokyo, and a distinguished and influential Japanese figure. "The chairman made it very, very clear," Saito says, "there wouldn't be any censoring or any holding back." Even with all of this expertise and brainpower on board, Saito got the sense early on that the politicians did not expect them to "take the job seriously," but rather to toe the official line.

The scope of the investigative work was extensive, and the process included a diverse range of people and groups. The commission presided over hundreds of hours of hearings, conducted more than a thousand interviews, held many town hall meetings, and made numerous site visits. Through additional interviews and surveys, they received comments from more than 10,000 people. Many voices were heard: government officials, regulators, TEPCO executives, evacuees, workers, and contractors. The commission held open meetings that were also shown live online and simultaneously translated into English. People could follow the investigation on Facebook and Twitter and made some 170,000 comments. The commission also sent investigative teams to confer with experts in five other countries.[14]

Then came the writing of the report. Saito and his team had approximately 4,500 pages of material, which they whittled down to 600 pages and, ultimately, to a 23-page summary version. "The editing process was difficult," Saito says, "because a lot of the writers became emotional." They wanted the report to get into a wide range of related issues—such as national policy, recommissioning, compensation processes, effects on the stock market, and the possible abolition of nuclear power in Japan—that were outside the scope of the commission's inquiry. This is a loss for those of us who take a systems approach to building resilience, because the breadth of these issues is indeed highly relevant. Nonetheless, the issues they chose to focus on were crucial.

The report describes the accident in detail, lays out several conclusions, and makes seven recommendations. What is most striking about the report is its directness and transparency about the nature of the accident. In his opening message, the chair writes that the accident at the power plant "was a profoundly manmade disaster—that could and should have been foreseen and prevented." Then comes the truly remarkable statement: "What must be admitted—very painfully—is that this was a disaster 'Made in Japan.' Its fundamental causes are to be found in the ingrained conventions of Japanese culture: our reflexive obedience; our reluctance to question authority; our devotion to 'sticking with the program'; our 'groupism'; and our insularity."[15]

That single paragraph, Saito says, took several days to write, and you can understand why. "It went through multiple edits. Each of those words was selected very specifically," Saito remembers. "And I think they are still right on the mark." Some of the politicians who assumed the commission would not take its work seriously were startled that it went above and beyond what they expected. "A lot of the Japanese were very, very surprised in that the report was very hard on Japan itself," Saito says.

Yes, but what effect has the report had? According to Saito, most of the specific recommendations have not been followed—or, at least, not yet. There was a sense of, "this is nice, great, thank you, now put it on the shelf," Saito says. But that does not mean the report has had no effect at all. Saito believes there have been two important outcomes. First, the NAIIC report can serve as a template for future investigations. "We were able to show how an investigation commission can be run," Saito says, "and how such a report could be done on an evidence-based, nonemotional, open basis." The second benefit is that the existence of such an independent report can be used as a "stick." Government ministers and company executives will now have the prospect of such an investigation in the back of their minds as they make decisions and take actions. They will not want their company or agency to become the subject of such an investigation. "There probably should have been more of these reports in the past," Saito says, and there will probably be more of them in the future. "This put things on record." And that, in and of itself, is an essential characteristic of resilience building: being aware, having data and knowledge to draw upon when making decisions and taking actions.

In New Orleans, the process of planning for revitalization began in late September 2005, about a month after the storm, with the formation of the Bring New Orleans Back Commission. The name of the commission is telling—the focus was on "bringing back"—highlighting the view of government officials that one of the first orders of business was to bring back the people who had been displaced and, in general, rebuilding the population.

But how does one go about repopulating a city with the vulnerabilities that New Orleans had? And where do you start? The greater New Orleans area comprises five parishes, and the city itself is divided into thirteen planning districts, seventeen wards, and seventy-two neighborhoods. The extent of storm damage varied widely from parish to parish and neighborhood to neighborhood. Given this diversity of districts and neighborhoods, the commission faced an almost insurmountable task of integration. How best to establish a citywide repopulation plan?

The planning process quickly ran into problems. One example: the commission determined that more parks and green spaces were needed in New Orleans, primarily to help with flood control and reduce residential risk of flooding but also to make the city more appealing to residents. To that end, the commission determined where these parks and green spaces *could* be located in the city and created a map identifying each of these areas with a green dot. The now infamous "green dot map" was published in the *New Orleans Times-Picayune,* without sufficient explanation. Although the commission had intended the green dots to be seen as "potential areas for future parkland," the paper described them as areas "expected to become parks and greenspace."[16] When residents of those green-dotted neighborhoods saw the map in the *Times-Picayune,* all hell broke loose. Who selected those locations? What would happen to the homes there and the people who lived (or had lived) in them? What about the land? Did the residents or owners have a say in the matter? Why did Lakeview, a predominantly white and upscale neighborhood, have no green dots at all? (The planners said that it was because Lakeview, despite having experienced severe flooding, already had plenty of green areas and open spaces.[17])

The situation only got worse. The commission couldn't secure funding for its citywide plan or for the creation of individual neighborhood plans they had intended to support. So forty-nine neighborhoods developed their own plans, but there was little cohesion among them and they did not amount to a comprehensive vision for a revitalized New Orleans.[18] According to Robert B. Olshansky and Laurie A. Johnson, who studied the storm and its aftermath and wrote about it in *Clear as Mud: Planning for the Rebuilding of New Orleans,* the situation in the spring of 2006 was dire: "After approximately five months of intensive planning efforts and tough negotiations with Washington, virtually all the best efforts of the city and state had gone up in flames. The city had no viable plan, and the draft plan it had was still too controversial to touch. The most contentious issues were punted to the neighborhood planning process, which was subsequently dealt a deathblow. . . . Two months earlier, New Orleans had optimistically dreamt of having both a plan and the money to realize it; now it had neither."[19]

Clearly, the planning process needed a new approach and some outside help. The Rockefeller Foundation had already been active in New Orleans—partnering with the Greater New Orleans Foundation to support displaced residents in the storm's immediate aftermath— so, when we were asked by the Louisiana Recovery Authority (LRA) to step in, we agreed to help restart the planning process. The goal was to create a single, unified plan that would go beyond the tasks of recovery and rebuilding and focus on long-term resilience-building activities. It is a testament to our board of trustees that they supported our engagement in such a politically charged atmosphere.

To coordinate the development of the Unified New Orleans Plan (UNOP), Carey Shea, an experienced community developer and a former resident of New Orleans, was brought on board to coordinate and integrate the planning effort. The situation, she found, was fraught. People were very concerned for their neighborhoods and for the city as a whole. Should New Orleans be rebuilt? Should it *not* be rebuilt? Which neighborhoods should be revitalized? Could New Orleans ever fully recover?[20]

Shea and her team, along with local partners, outside experts, and neighborhood planners worked to align the varied political and expert-driven needs and instituted a series of public outreach activities—from a website to large group meetings—to ensure that the people of New Orleans had a voice in the process. This involved connecting with people who were still displaced and living in cities such as Houston and Atlanta. They were able to participate through the Internet and via satellite.[21] A great deal of the work was organized and executed by a group called America Speaks, a nonpartisan and nonprofit organization whose "mission is to reinvigorate American Democracy by engaging citizens in the public decision-making that most impacts their lives."[22] (The group also facilitated the huge town hall meetings held in New York City after 9/11.)

The findings of these outreach activities were clear. Residents ranked better flood protection as the number 1 issue in the revitalization of New Orleans. In addition to returning to a safer and better-protected city, they wanted to make sure the neighborhoods they came back to were "stable," and, very importantly, they wanted to be near "their former neighbors." They definitely did not want to be subject to mandatory relocation to other parts of the city.[23]

As a result, the UNOP focused on three main issues: population return, flooding, and funding. (Other social issues, such as the economy and education, were addressed in separate plans developed later.) When Shea presented the plan at a board meeting of the LRA in June 2007 she called it "the most extensive and complicated urban redevelopment plan ever attempted."[24]

Rebuilding Hard Infrastructure:
Effective but Not Invincible

In New Orleans, improvements to the hurricane defense system infrastructure clearly had to come first. The system that was in place in 2005 had been conceived in 1965 and had been constructed by the US Army Corps of Engineers. The original design called for some 350 miles of levees and floodwalls but, when Katrina hit, the system was not finished, because of many complications including matters of design, the environment, and funding. As a result, some areas of the city that should have been protected were not.[25]

The American Society of Civil Engineers called the failure of the New Orleans hurricane defense system "one of the nation's worst infrastructure disasters ever."[26] The levees were breached or overtopped in more than fifty places.[27] Floodwalls bent, buckled, and toppled. The system's pumps, which help keep New Orleans dry on your average Tuesday, were overwhelmed and incapacitated. And one failure led to another in a cascade. Levee failure led to pumping failure, which led to more flooding, which caused the failure of electrical and communications systems and on and on.

Water from Lakes Pontchartrain and Borgne surged into New Orleans neighborhoods. Half of New Orleans homes—more than 100,000 of them—were flooded by at least four feet of water.[28] A week passed before successful stopgaps had been implemented at the most devastating breaches.[29] Water lingered in the neighborhoods for three weeks or longer.[30] All told, 225 billion gallons of water had to be pumped out of New Orleans, a task that took until mid-October.[31]

The UNOP made recommendations for better defense against flooding, and the Army Corps of Engineers, mandated and funded by Congress, drew up a 606-page implementation plan, the *Hurricane and Storm Damage and Risk Reduction System Design Guidelines*.[32] It called for levee repairs, improvements, and additions and the building of the world's largest pumping and drainage station, the West Closure Complex. With eleven pumps, the complex is capable of filling an

Olympic swimming pool in four seconds—a rate of 165,000 gallons per second. The total coast of the pumping complex was $1 billion.[33]

The system was completed in the fall of 2012, seven years after Katrina. Although the improved hurricane protection system has yet to undergo a test as brutal as Katrina, it performed well in 2012 when Hurricane Isaac hit southeastern Louisiana. The updated defense system should significantly reduce, if not eliminate, flooding from a hundred-year event. The corps believes it would be sufficiently self-regulating such that it would not suffer catastrophic failure even in the face of a five-hundred-year storm.[34] In terms of storm defense infrastructure, then, New Orleans has been successful in bringing itself back far better than before.

THERE IS MUCH PRECEDENT for creating these hard solutions to storm protection and flooding defense and other natural hazards. The Dutch are the acknowledged masters in devising infrastructure for the successful management of water threats, and their expertise is dramatically expressed in the Delta Works, a complex system of dams, floodgates, storm surge barriers, and other hard features along the coasts and waterways of the Netherlands.

The Dutch, like the people of New Orleans, have an existential relationship with water—although theirs goes back quite a bit further in time. The word "netherlands" means "low lands," and, beginning in the early Middle Ages, the Dutch began to reclaim land from under the North Sea for farming and settlement.[35] As we've seen, creating land where there was none before introduces risk, and, indeed, records of catastrophic flooding in Holland date back to the year 838. To keep the water out, dikes were constructed. When water did intrude, pumps powered by windmills (and later by steam) sucked it out. God created the world, so the saying goes, but the Dutch created Holland.

The Netherlands established its first water authority as far back as 1200, according to Henk Ovink, acting director general of spatial planning and water affairs for the Netherlands. "We didn't turn our back to the water because we have to live with it and because we want to," he says.[36] "Water is an asset, our basis for connecting to the world. It is the base for our cities and economy and the connector between economy and ecology. Water was our culture, is our culture, and will always be." Indeed, today, about 9 million Dutch citizens live, work, and play below sea level, and two-thirds of the nation's gross national product is generated there.[37] Cees Veerman, the chair of the Delta Committee, echoes Ovink's sentiment: "Whatever social or economic hardship this country faces, water runs through it."[38]

All of those people and all of that activity are now protected by the Delta Works flood defenses, a system so sophisticated the American Society of Civil Engineers refers to it as one of the seven wonders of the modern world.[39]

Unfortunately, as is so often the case, it took a major disruption to spur its creation. In 1953, a massive storm blew up in the North Sea. High winds coupled with a spring tide pushed water levels higher than many of the dikes were able to withstand. By the time the storm subsided, it had damaged 187 kilometers of sea defenses. Thousands of people were stranded on rooftops or clung to trees. Some 72,000 had to be evacuated, and more than 1,800 people died. Hundreds of farms were destroyed, and tens of thousands of cattle, horses, and pigs perished. Some areas took a year to pump dry.[40] All told, the storm caused losses of more than 5 percent of the country's GDP.[41]

Soon after the worst was over, the Dutch government formed the Delta Committee and charged it with drawing up a large-scale, long-term plan to protect densely populated areas without interfering with sea traffic in and out of Rotterdam, one of the world's busiest ports. The goal was to come up with innovative ways to manage both sea and fresh water to meet the needs of the Dutch people and the country's economy. It would be a resilience-building effort, an opportunity born of crisis.

The plan included dams, weirs, and storm surge mechanisms that would compartmentalize the region into controllable segments and enable the most-populated areas to withstand a 10,000-year surge level.[42] Not only would the Delta Works prevent flood or mitigate its effects, it would enhance quality of life and commerce. The committee justified the enormous price tag by conducting a cost-benefit analysis that showed the cost of improving the sea defenses was far less than the cost of dealing with the effects of flood.

Delta Works was completed in 1997 and now protects a vast amount of coastline. It has reduced the country's risk of flooding, decreased its dependence on dikes, reduced salt water intrusion, and brought improvements that contribute to social cohesion as well—including more availability of drinking water, better recreational facilities, and a greater feeling of safety and sense of place.[43]

When it came to governance, the decision-making process to determine when to shut the sluices, the Dutch did something that the operators of the dam in Surat did not do—they removed human assessments from the equation. "Science runs our safety," Ovink says. "There's no political decision needed to close that thing, which is ideal."

Delta Works has also delivered a resilience dividend by accelerating economic growth. Infrastructure such as roads and modified waterways improved transportation and access to previously isolated parts of the country. Tourism increased—a 1996 estimate suggested that Delta Works had spurred an additional 760 million guilders in sightseeing revenue. It became possible to sail from Antwerp to Rotterdam without having to wait for the tide, which reduces shipping costs and increases efficiency. And in the western province of Zeeland (an area with slow economic growth prior to the 1950s), business flourished once new roads were built over the Delta Works in the 1960s.[44]

"'Resilience' is a progressive term," says Ovink. "It's not about bouncing back. It's actually about the learning process—a steep learning curve that brings you back far better than where you were before."

HOWEVER, EVEN AS EFFECTIVE as the Dutch and New Orleans water threat systems are, "no matter what protection you build, there will someday be an event that overwhelms it," says Guy Nordenson, the advocate of living-with-water strategies.[45] Even so, people continue to put their faith in hard infrastructure without accepting that none can be invulnerable, without paying enough attention to the human factors involved, and, just as important, without considering the wide variety of soft infrastructure solutions available.

This belief in the invincibility of hard infrastructure has led to the concept of "threat-proofing"—the notion that you can earthquake-proof, flood-proof, fire-proof, or even future-proof a building or a system. Nordenson argues that this is not realistic, and designers and engineers tend to avoid using the term. Earthquake engineers, for example, generally don't claim they can make buildings that are "earthquake-proof," says Nordenson. The goal is, instead, to design earthquake-*resistant* buildings so they protect lives by not collapsing or blocking safe exit when an earthquake strikes. A building that doesn't collapse in an earthquake is self-regulating—it may, for example, withstand moderate earthquake tremors to a certain point without losing function, but in a severe earthquake it will lose function without suffering catastrophic failure, such as a collapse.

The focus on hard solutions and threat-proof design can lead to the creation of structures that, although fulfilling their role as protection, introduce new elements that decrease resilience in other ways. Nordenson cites the new World Trade Center Tower One in Lower Manhattan, which is constructed with a two-hundred-foot base of solid concrete. Across the street stands the Goldman Sachs headquarters building with a lobby surrounded by glass. "Both buildings actually are designed to provide an equivalent amount of protection in the event a terrorist were to explode a truck bomb," says Nordenson, "but they are done in a totally different way, with a totally different attitude to people." The concrete base makes the World Trade Center building seem like a bunker. It decreases, through lack of visibility, the situational awareness of people inside and on the street. It reduces the integration of the building with the streetscape. The Goldman Sachs building does the opposite and is therefore more resilient.

A different design philosophy, performance-based design, avoids the concept of proofing and, instead, focuses on how a building or bridge or system needs to perform in defined situations or circumstances. A large manufacturing company, for example, might want to create a facility that can withstand a set of defined disruptions—storm, explosion, earthquake—and continue functioning or be back in operation the following day, like the General Electric plant in North Carolina. Architects and engineers who espouse a performance-based design philosophy calibrate their designs so that critical structures may be able to continue operations even after severe earthquakes although normal structures may be damaged. "Performance-based urban design allows cities to bounce back from disasters by protecting critical facilities and functions and safeguarding lives, while accepting degrees of damage commensurate with the severity of the disaster," says Nordenson. He is optimistic that this approach is catching on.

REINVENTING:
HARD, SOFT, AND COMBINATION SOLUTIONS

Although hard solutions, especially performance-based ones, will continue to play an essential role in building resilience, people are increasingly seeking to better live with water (and other threats) through combinations of hard and soft infrastructure solutions. There is a wide range of methods and tools being developed and put to use around the world to support this approach, and they often employ soft measures and natural elements—such as vegetation, wetlands, parklands, and coastal berms and buffers—brought together with processes and activities. It's important, when working to build resilience in any given situation, to seek out the best combination.

This was the goal of an initiative called Rebuild by Design, developed as part of President Obama's Hurricane Sandy Rebuilding Task Force: to find the most effective ways to rebuild and reimagine areas in New York and New Jersey, using the full range of solutions, so they would be less vulnerable to future storms and shocks. To tap into the best thinking and gain the participation of the most experienced practitioners around the world, Rebuild by Design took the form of a competition, open to all. (The Rockefeller Foundation, led by our managing director for resilience, Nancy Kete, helped to support the initiative.) The response was extraordinary—148 teams from more than fifteen countries submitted proposals. Rebuild by Design "captured the imagination of the world's best," says Eric Klinenberg, who in addition to his position as head of New York University's Institute for Public Knowledge is research director of Rebuild by Design as well as a juror.[46] This initiative was much needed, says Klinenberg, because the United States is "shockingly behind much of the world" when it comes to increasing its readiness for weather-related disruptions. The competition has "allowed the region in the northeast to benefit from knowledge that's already been produced in other parts of the world," he says, while spurring innovation that can be applied to, adapted for, and scaled up in other regions worldwide. Kete sees Rebuild by Design as a way to experiment, learn, and share new ways to build resilience. "Just as cities are hubs for innovations and investments that expand opportunities," she believes, "they are also living laboratories forced to confront challenges of increasing complexity."[47]

Although the many areas in New York and New Jersey hit by Sandy face similar challenges, the solutions proposed by the Rebuild by Design applicants are wonderfully diverse in their approaches.

One project focuses on the urgent issue of food security. The Hunts Point Food Distribution Center—a crucial link in New York's food supply chain—is located on the Hunts Point peninsula in the Bronx borough of New York. A large percentage of the metropolitan area's supply of meat and fish, and as much as 60 percent of its produce, flows through this facility.[48] "It's as critical as critical infrastructure gets," says Klinenberg, and "it's totally vulnerable." Although the center was not affected by Sandy, it might well have been inundated had the storm struck just a few hours earlier when the tide was high. The food security of some 22 million people would have been put in jeopardy.[49]

A team led by PennDesign (of the University of Pennsylvania School of Design), and OLIN, a landscape architecture firm, developed a solution called Hunts Point Lifelines. It integrates a flood protection system along the area's waterfront greenway that would protect the Hunts Point distribution center and market and that incorporates a research lab that would create jobs, integrate local communities in planning processes, and increase flood and storm awareness. The addition of marine highways and a logistics base for maritime emergency supply chains as well as new pier infrastructure would provide a flexible and redundant transportation system so food and supplies can still be shipped to other boroughs if roads flood.

The team also is developing a plan for alternative sources of energy (critical, given the area's refrigeration needs) that include a micro–grid program and plant that can provide backup power in case of an outage. These measures would save millions of dollars worth of food from spoiling, create a self-regulating energy solution, and decrease the market's energy costs and greenhouse gas emissions. All these improvements create a resilience dividend that would improve daily life and strengthen the community's capacity to withstand shocks. The project demonstrates "that adaptation and mitigation need not be set against one another," says Klinenberg. "They can enhance each other when they're properly designed."

Another Rebuild by Design team, led by MIT and the urban design firm Urbanisten, approached their work in an impressively holistic way: water management and community development are intertwined. The plan, called New Meadowlands: Productive City + Regional Park, is for the revitalization of New Jersey's Meadowlands, a flood-prone marshland between Newark and New York City that was inundated by several feet of Sandy's storm surge. The goal is to integrate transportation, ecology, and development to transform the Meadowlands basin to "address a wide spectrum of risks, while providing civic amenities and creating opportunities for new redevelopment."[50] At the heart of the project is a natural reserve, the Meadowpark, open to the public and connecting to other marshland restoration initiatives already planned or under way. The Meadowpark would be protected from storm surges by an "intricate system of berms and marshes" (berms are raised barriers, usually constructed of earth and typically with a flat top) that would also collect rainfall to ease the burden on drainage systems in surrounding towns. The Meadowpark would be engirded by the Meadowband, which offers a range of recreation and transportation services, including a bus rapid transit line and various public-use spaces. The plan also calls for a new approach to zoning to allow for a more urban feel, including residential and commercial developments that would "enhance the brand and identity" of the Meadowland basin and also bring in more tax dollars.

The Rebuild by Design competition gives a sense of the range of innovative design approaches for building resilience being pursued by forward-thinking cities and communities around the world.

In Indonesia, for example, the coastal village of Lamnga was hard hit by the tsunami of 2004. An important feature of the landscape had been its mangrove forest, which acted as a storm buffer but also played a critical role in supporting the fish, shrimp, and crab population—essential to the villagers' livelihoods. The tsunami destroyed much of the mangrove forest, leaving the village and the shoreline vulnerable to the next storm. With help from Mercy Corps and supported by The Rockefeller Foundation, a group of villagers pursued an initiative to replant the mangrove forest with seedlings. The venture has been successful enough that the villagers have developed a new enterprise for themselves: selling seedlings to other vulnerable communities along the coast to generate additional income. As a result, the villagers are gaining greater protection for their geography, ensuring their traditional livelihoods, and creating a new enterprise—another example of the resilience dividend.[51]

In densely populated urban spaces, human beings interact very differently with the natural environment than they do in the coastal villages of Indonesia, but some city-based property developers are developing new and exciting ways to bring together natural, social, and technological systems and build resilience. For example, the New York–based developer Jonathan Rose collaborated with Phipps Houses, a not-for-profit developer of affordable housing, to create Via Verde (The Green Way), a remarkable housing development in New York's South Bronx. Via Verde serves a diverse population, with a variety of building forms and a range of housing options, from duplexes to live-work units (combining living space and a working area). It is integrated into the South Bronx community of Melrose, with prox-imity to the public transportation system and the downtown area.

Via Verde is designed with a series of stepped green roofs that are "inspired by the integration of nature and city," as its website asserts. "At the heart of the project is a dynamic garden that serves as the organizing architectural element and spiritual identity for the com-munity."[52] Residents can tend the gardens and harvest the fruits and vegetables, activities that promote physical activity and healthy eat-ing. The gardens provide a soft solution to climate change mitigation by dissipating heat and absorbing water runoff. The building com-plex also has a system that reclaims water and recycles it to irrigate the gardens.[53] "Buildings have impacts on both nature and on human health," says Rose. "Designing buildings to reduce their environmen-tal impacts and to enhance human well-being—versus being toxic to people—helps the resilience of people and societies."[54] With this goal in mind, the hope is that Via Verde will help its residents and its com-munity realize the resilience dividend in economic, health, and social gains.

There are many other intriguing ideas for hard and soft solutions for mitigating issues of climate change in urban areas. In cities such as New Orleans, Chicago, and, as we've seen, San Francisco, city planners and developers have been testing a promising technology for urban water management: permeable pavement. The porous sur-face aids in storm-water drainage and helps reduce flooding, because the water seeps through the pavement into the ground rather than pooling or running off into streets or basements. In Japan, "recovery parks" are built on recovered street properties and have facilities that can be used during good times—for gathering and cooking meals—and also as relief stations during a storm or, for that matter, any kind of disruption. Designers have planned for Hoboken, New Jersey, underground parking garages that convert to storm and flood water storage containers in an emergency. And Lower Manhattan is rebuild-ing with a new system for pilings to replace the aging and cracking ones that support the city's docks and piers, known as "digital con-crete" and produced of a stone/concrete-like material with a massive

3-D printer.[55] Flexible, adaptive, and strong, they bend in response to wave action, rather than trying to withstand it, making them far more resilient and cost effective in the long run.

Eric Klinenberg sees all this activity as encouraging evidence of a silver lining to the threat of planetary disruption: we must become united in our response to it. Outside of alien invasion, Klinenberg says, no other endeavor has the potential to bring out so much energy for innovation and such a willingness to work across disciplines and domains. "It is the most urgent issue we face," Klinenberg says. "We have no choice but to adapt."

ADAPTING A SYSTEM IS USUALLY MORE DIFFICULT than creating a new one (by starting with a clean slate or a green field), especially with such an expansive and complex system as the railway network.

As we've seen, the Euro rail system has significant vulnerabilities—among them a lack of integration of many of its elements—and this has taken its toll. The railways have suffered shocks and disruptions of their own making, as well as from competitive forms of transport, which they have had difficulty rebounding from. Although railroads in the EU-27 still account for about €60 billion turnover in the economy and generate approximately 900,000 jobs, rail is no longer the driver of European economic growth it once was.[56] Rail's share of both the land freight transportation and land passenger markets has dropped significantly over the past several decades.[57]

However, with urbanization and globalization and the focus on climate change—especially as it impacts new approaches to energy use—railroads have the possibility of revitalization. Despite its current vulnerabilities, rail has several important advantages over its rival forms of transport. The movement of freight by rail is more fuel-efficient than sending goods by road.[58] Rail has lower CO_2 emissions than either air or road transportation.[59] Travel by rail remains twenty-four times safer than travel by car and is nearly fifty percent safer than bus transportation.[60] And with high-speed trains transporting passengers from Paris to Brussels in under ninety minutes—and the development of high-speed systems in countries around the world—rail is poised to become an effective competitor to air and car travel.[61] This is all good news for an EU community exposed to fuel price shifts and global climate change.

For improved management of infrastructure, the engineering firm Arup envisions the use of intelligent robots to inspect track and other components, especially in hard-to-reach spots such as tunnels and bridges.[62] A Dutch company is already using drones equipped with infrared sensors to monitor switch point heating systems. If it's found that these mechanisms aren't functioning properly, maintenance services can be alerted.[63] Advanced technology for real-time monitoring of tracks (feedback loops, remember, are a critical feature of resilience), along with ERTMS and electronically controlled braking, will be critical for high-speed rail systems, where the margin of error is narrow.[64]

To better anticipate and prepare for the current and potential effects of climate change, railway systems are looking for solutions that may be in use in other geographies where the climate is already in a similar state. To this end, Arup is conducting "analogy" studies, looking for successful practices in places that might be analogous to future conditions in Europe—areas with high rainfall, for example, or extreme heat.

An initiative known as MOWE-IT (Management of Weather Events in the Transport System) is also focused on identifying best practices and developing both hard and soft solutions, specifically to enable train lines to bounce back faster after severe storms of the kind that Europe is increasingly experiencing. The soft approaches include improved weather modeling, better flood response planning, and the development of strategies for rapid clearing of post-flood debris from tracks. Hard solutions include movable flood walls to protect stations, better drainage methods, elevated track, inflatable dams, as well as more redundancy—such as situating reserve diesel engines in places where electrical lines are likely to be damaged by high winds.[65]

Ultimately, such initiatives will contribute to the creation of a more integrated system that will enable a more seamless travel experience—the "integration of rail, with road, with cycling, with walking," says Armitage. Already, some of the big transport players in Europe—including railcar maker Bombardier and automaker BMW—are positioning themselves as contributors to the transport ecosystem, as providers of mobility rather than just as suppliers of specific transport elements. In the future, says Armitage, you will be able to "buy a journey" rather than purchase a collection of tickets and transfers from a variety of vendors.

As every traveler knows, any journey—whether it's a city commute or a global circumnavigation—is subject to disruption, and every disruption comes at a cost. The more resilient the transport system—more integrated, with better and diverse alternatives—the greater chance we have of realizing the dividends that mobility provides.

12

REVITALIZATION
Energizing, Affirming, Sharing a Vision

Revitalization is the process of bringing new life and vigor to an individual, an organization, or a community after it has been through a disruption, a crisis, a disaster. Revitalization goes beyond the achievement of bouncing forward. It suggests that natural systems surge toward greater robustness than ever, that infrastructure performs to high expectations, that communities gain strength, people are energized, identity is enriched, and a shared vision takes shape. As a community revitalizes, it increases its capacity of reaping the resilience dividend.

As New Orleans came to recognize, revitalization cannot be achieved without people's intense commitment and engagement. Jane Jacobs was profoundly right when she argued, "Cities have the capability of providing something for everybody, only because, and only when, they are created by everybody."[1] The plan for improving the infrastructure of the hurricane defense system in New Orleans was essential, therefore, but not sufficient to address the more fundamental problem of bringing people back, energizing them, and creating lasting social cohesion. Nor would people return just because basic services were restored or because accommodations were available. To revitalize a community, people have to want to come back and take pride in strengthening it.

STRENGTHENING NEIGHBORHOODS

Jeffrey Hebert, a Louisiana native, was one of those who came back. An expert in neighborhood development, he was living in Brooklyn, New York, in 2005. When he learned about the situation in New Orleans, he knew he "needed to come home."[2] Hebert took a job with the Louisiana Recovery Authority, a body created after Katrina to manage and oversee the state's recovery from the disaster, primarily through the distribution and allocation of federal funding. Hebert later became executive director of the New Orleans Redevelopment Authority.

At first, people like Hebert trickled back into the city. Most of the early repopulation occurred in areas least impacted by flooding, such as the French Quarter and other riverfront neighborhoods, which were built on high ground. By February 2006, six months after the storm, the city population had risen from the few thousand who had stayed through the storm to more than 130,000, a significant increase but still far below the number needed.[3]

Rebuilding neighborhoods in the low-lying areas most impacted by the storm proved much more difficult. One of the main problems was achieving enough density of home ownership. Not only do you need a mass of people to re-establish a neighborhood, their homes need to be in proximity to one another in order to build and maintain relationships, establish organizations, and pursue group activities. (This is precisely the issue that Detroit is facing, as of this writing.) You need a few bold souls to lead the way, as well as a quantity of early followers. They may need encouragement, incentives, and other outside help.

One element of the Unified New Orleans Plan was the Neighborhood Stabilization Program, which addressed the density issue in "areas of the City with the slowest rates of repopulation, lowest natural elevations, and high risk of future flooding."[4] The proposed method of repopulation was to establish "sustainable neighborhood clusters"—groups of occupied homes that could function as mini-neighborhoods within the larger area. To nurture these clusters, the Neighborhood

Stabilization Program proposed that new housing be built to FEMA's revised flood guidelines, incorporate "sustainable/green building practices," and be made available to returning residents.[5]

A number of new entities sprang up to facilitate the neighborhood development work. Carey Shea, after her work with UNOP was complete, became director of Project Home Again, a nonprofit organization established with start-up funding from the Leonard and Louise Riggio Foundation. Its goal is to "restore community, hope and housing" particularly to low- and moderate-income families.[6] (There were, and still are, many individuals, groups, and organizations that contributed to the revitalization of New Orleans, specifically its neighborhoods, in many ways. The Riggios and Project Home Again are two of many.)

Project Home Again began the process of creating neighborhood clusters by purchasing an undeveloped parcel of land in Gentilly, a middle-class, culturally diverse neighborhood in the northern part of the city, bordering Lake Pontchartrain. They built twenty houses on the land and invited Gentilly residents who had left the city to apply to live in them. The incentives were attractive: If the new resident maintained the house as a primary residence, paid the homeowner's insurance, flood insurance, and property taxes, Project Home Again would forgive 20 percent of the mortgage each year for five years, at which point the resident would own the home without having invested any capital up front. In exchange for this deal, the new owner would hand over ownership of their existing property to Project Home Again—a swap. Project Home Again would demolish any existing structures on that property and build another new home in its place, to be offered to other prospective residents, on the same conditions. This approach had a number of benefits not only for the homeowner but for the city. It encouraged former residents to return. It improved the housing stock, because the new houses would be flood protected and green built. And, by facilitating home purchase, it helped to increase the rate of home ownership.

Although this approach did bring people into the clusters of new, sustainable, flood-protected homes, there was a problem—the properties that Project Home Again received as swaps were scattered all over the Gentilly area, many of them in sections that were not good candidates for clustering. So the challenge of swapping and building and repopulating became, as Shea describes it, a "reverse game of musical chairs." That is, given the uncertain rates of people's return, "we knew there were going to be more chairs than people to sit in them," Shea says.[7]

This is where integration of the various groups involved in the repopulation of New Orleans proved essential. As it turned out, the New Orleans Redevelopment Authority had a large stock of properties in its possession through a repopulation program of the Louisiana Recovery Authority. This one offered people a number of incentives to return to their existing homes and receive a grant or to sell their home to the LRA. Most chose to return, but enough sold out that the state amassed a surplus of vacant properties throughout the city.

By partnering with the New Orleans Redevelopment Authority, Project Home Again had a much greater diversity of properties with which they could play the reverse game of musical chairs. As a result, Project Home Again was able to build two housing clusters in the Saint Anthony neighborhood, one of thirteen houses and another of twenty-five, the latter of which was funded through a grant from the Salvation Army.

"You can see what happened to those blocks," says Oji Alexander, of Project Home Again.[8] "Neighbors who were on the fence, deciding what they were going to do, said, 'OK, well, now I have four new houses on my block. I'm going to rebuild. I'm going to reinvest.' And so we not only were able to facilitate, we actually watched this neighborhood reach its tipping point." As of early 2014, Project Home Again had built a hundred homes in Gentilly and thirty more in other New Orleans neighborhoods, with another seventy projects either under construction or in development.

This is what revitalization looks like—beyond bouncing back or even bouncing back better. These neighborhood rebuilding initiatives address old vulnerabilities—unsustainable building practices, low home ownership rates, high flood insurance costs—head on.

Today, people are returning to New Orleans at a faster rate. In the 2012 census, the population of New Orleans was 370,000—a little more than 80 percent of what it was before the 2005 flooding. In some areas, the growth rate is particularly strong. Between April 2010 and July 2012, Orleans Parish had the highest growth rate among urban centers in all US counties.[9] As the repopulation continues and neighborhoods strengthen further, New Orleans has increasingly greater potential to realize the resilience dividend.

"Recovery begets recovery," as Alexander says.

BUILDING COMMUNITIES is an essential aspect of revitalization and long-term resilience building, but a community does not always look like the ones in the New Orleans neighborhoods.

In Kenya, for example, ethnic communities were severely disrupted and then displaced, not by a natural event or flooding but by political upheaval and violence surrounding the 2007 presidential elections. The situation was so bad that some 600,000 people throughout Kenya were forced to flee their homes.[10]

The circumstances are complicated. The incumbent president, Mwai Kibaki, a member of the Party of National Unity, was declared by the elections committee to have won the contest, beating Raila Odinga of the Orange Democratic Movement. Many believed the elections had been rigged, and, whether or not that is true, long-simmering tensions—fueled by inequity and perceived injustices, particularly around land use and ownership—boiled over, with members of opposing political parties (often antagonistic ethnic groups) attacking each other.

"They broke shops. They raped women. They killed people," says Paul Thingo, a member of the Kikuyu ethnic group.[11] He had to run away from his home in the Great Rift Valley, the beautiful stretch of lowland north of Nairobi that lies along the Cherangani Hills, where two ethnic groups, the Kikuyu and the Kalenjin, had long lived in an uneasy relationship that often erupted in acts of violence. By the time the worst of the postelection violence was over, 1,300 people were dead.[12]

People still debate the causes of the disruption, but whatever the source the people of Kenya were profoundly affected. "At the end of the day, the trust was broken completely," says Irene Ngatia, founder of Volunteer International Community Development Africa, an NGO that works with communities of what is known as internally displaced people.[13]

Thingo, just one of the people displaced by the violence, took refuge for nine months in the Kenyan equivalent of the New Orleans Superdome, the A. S. K. Nakuru Showground, in the city of Nakuru, the capital of the Rift Valley Province. The showground is little more than an oval, race-track sized plot of grass, surrounded by small buildings.

In an attempt to resettle people and repopulate disrupted neighborhoods, the Kenyan government gave displaced families 25,000 Kenyan shillings—about $285—and encouraged them to use it to travel back to their homes and get resettled. Thingo was not interested. He had left home with nothing, and the money wasn't enough to return or to start a new life somewhere else. What's more, the underlying ethnic tensions had not been addressed, let alone resolved. There was no guarantee that he wouldn't be a victim of continuing violence if he returned. He did not wish to return to the status quo.

Thingo talked with other internally displaced people at the showground who were thinking along the same lines. "We didn't know each other," he says. "But after the government decided we had to go back, people started coming together and talking. We had one conclusion: buy land." They decided to pool their money from the government grants, purchase property, and establish a community while the government worked on a better resettlement plan for all displaced people. Thingo and his future neighbors organized themselves into two groups—almost a thousand households in total—and together they bought about sixteen acres of land near Nakuru. They worked with government officials to subdivide the property into 21' × 27' plots—just enough room for a house and a tiny yard. They called their new community Pipeline.

Psychologist Laurie Leitch visited Pipeline and several other such camps in 2009. What she found impressed her. Unlike other camps, where people lived in limbo, waiting for the next step, the people of Pipeline had established a community. They had formed a governance group to represent their interests. They took good care of their small homes and improved them as they could, adding rooms, extending water lines, building community toilets. They planted and tended gardens. They started small cottage industries. One woman, Margaret Wangare, wove baskets and shoulder bags from recycled plastic containers. The people of Pipeline were "willing to invest" in their community, Leitch says.[14]

Although Pipeline is by no means an ideal solution—many families still live in tents—Thingo and his like-minded neighbors have been able to imagine a new way of living after a severe disruption and plan further for their revitalization. They developed a shared vision of a community that would stick together and improve their situation without waiting for outside help—but would also work with outside agencies, primarily the government, to align their needs with those of the larger society. Other displaced people took much different routes. Some migrated to the slums of Nairobi. Others went back to their original situations with all the same vulnerabilities. To bring together a group of a thousand people, most of whom had no previous connections, and form a thriving community was, as Leitch puts it, "a great example of resilience."[15]

MOBILIZING PEOPLE'S ENERGIES

In the revitalization period in resilient communities, institutions and their leaders play crucial roles, newcomers step up in intriguing ways, and champions and supporters abound. Some communities, however, do not have established institutions or agencies in place, nor do they have sufficient social cohesion such that enough organizations can spring up. There are no strong advocates who step forward, few established routes along which leaders can emerge. The informal settlements of the world, for example—the slums, favelas, shack cities, and pavement communities—are often without a political or civic voice. This is sometimes because they have no formal representation in any government or official body (which, as I described, is often because they aren't counted in government censuses) and also because slum dwellers are not accustomed to, or experienced in, the complex tasks of governance and leadership. Many people who live in slums have little formal education, not much in the way of economic means or tangible assets, little awareness of the processes of organization and governance, and few connections with people who can help them.

In such situations, it is often necessary to form a new organization, and that takes a spark of leadership. This was the case with the pavement dwellers of Mumbai, who have suffered chronic stresses and frequent shocks for decades and who have been unable to cohere as a community, even though some people have lived in the same place for years, hold jobs (often in the government), and raise families on the street.

In the 1970s, Jockin Arputham, who was raised in the slums of Mumbai and received no formal education, founded a community organization called the National Slum Dwellers Federation of India.[16] He worked with leaders of similar groups to found Shack/Slum Dwellers International (SDI) in 1996 to provide "successful mobilisation, advocacy, and problem solving strategies," and SDI has grown into a federation "of community-based organizations of the urban poor in 33 countries."[17] One of the important feeder organizations for SDI is a group called the Society for Promotion of Area Resource Centres, founded in 1984 by Sheela Patel, now leader of SDI, specifically to advocate and support women pavement dwellers in India.[18]

In Kenya, more than 60,000 slum dwellers in eleven cities, including Nairobi, belong to SDI's Kenyan affiliate known as Muungano wa Wanavijiji, more simply referred to as Muungano (pronounced muhn-GAH-no), which means "union" or "fusion" in Swahili.[19] Meetings of these groups in Nairobi are often peppered with the use of the word "muungano" as a greeting and a call and response. Muungano! *Muungano.*

Muungano typically gets started in a slum community through a savings group or by doing enumerations. As they work, they seek to identify and cultivate people in the community who might become organizers. In Kambi Moto, for example, Pauline Manguru and Michael Njuguna had no organizational or leadership skills when they got started with Muungano but gradually gained expertise, built their knowledge, martialed community resources, and eventually took on leadership roles.

This is how Muungano, and SDI in general, builds leadership throughout the organization—starting with local, hands-on projects. The savings groups form and elect their own leaders. These groups are very simple and may meet once a week or so to review contributions and the bank balance—the handwritten records are kept in softcover notebooks and often displayed in chalk on a big board in a community meeting room. The savings group then selects a representative to the community and to the larger settlement (which, like Kibera, can have populations in the hundreds of thousands) and, further, to the region or country. Some of leaders who started off in a community savings group eventually join the Kenyan federation's national council, where leaders can collectively discuss challenges and ways forward to strengthen both regional and national progress.[20]

The effect that Muungano has had on the resilience of communities like Kambi Moto is manifested in many ways. Most important, the residents now have the ability to organize and govern themselves, and everyone speaks the language of group collaboration. If you attend a meeting of a savings group or a gathering of community leadership, the proceedings are not greatly different from those you would experience at a well-run committee meeting anywhere in the world. The capacity to collaborate and govern enables them to communicate and problem-solve as they never have before.

Having achieved goals beyond their prior imagining, these groups build their tenacity and commitment. In the community of Kambi Moto, in the Huruma slum, the Muungano group members were the ones who protested before and engaged with the Nairobi City Council, unthinkable in years past, to fight for land tenure. They built thirty-four new homes and are in the process of building twenty-eight more. The buildings are far above the standard of the wooden and tin structures that surround Kambi Moto on all sides, and so there are fewer fires than before. The community has electricity, water, and sewer services, so the residents are less vulnerable to public health threats. This is clearly a resilience dividend. You cannot continue to improve in a place that constantly needs rebuilding or with people who are not well enough to contribute.

The city did not fully adhere to its promise and developed a portion of the slum area, and Kambi Moto has not won tenure for their land. However, the residents have not given up. They are now a recognized organization in the city. One of their own actually serves on the city council. They are prepared to take on new challenges and have developed the skills to do so.

AFFIRMING A SENSE OF IDENTITY

Another element of social cohesion that's important to revitalization is one of the least tangible and also one of the most important: a sense of identity. This is key to bringing people back to a place or an organization after a crisis, helping them make sense of what has happened, and fueling their capacity to recover and revitalize.

Many factors contribute to a sense of identity, including values, physical characteristics, history, and narratives. Residents who had left New Orleans were drawn back to the city—and new people are drawn to come there for the first time—largely because of its distinctive identity. People wanted to return to the New Orleans they knew and understood and loved—the city where they had roots that couldn't be flooded away—and they were worried it might have been fundamentally harmed through displacement and disruption and that rebuilding and redevelopment might radically alter the city's character.

So, after a crisis, it's important that people engage in activities that celebrate their identity and also that bring the crisis into that identity rather than ignore or negate it. Disruptions become important themes in stories that individuals, families, businesses, institutions, and communities tell themselves. Resilient entities create narratives that are positive, aspirational, and forward looking without ignoring past difficulties or venturing into the realm of fantasy.

The New Orleans identity and how it has been affected by Katrina has been endlessly explored, in a wide range of media, including the book *Clear as Mud*, by Robert Olshansky and Laurie Johnson, Sheri Fink's *Five Days at Memorial: Life and Death in a Storm-Ravaged Hospital*, Spike Lee's TV documentary *When the Levees Broke*, personal narratives such as Phyllis Montana-Leblanc's *Not Just the Levees Broke*, the popular television series *Treme*, and works of magical realism such as the independent feature film *Beasts of the Southern Wild*. Each of these narratives expresses some aspect of the New Orleans or Louisiana identity or some view of the experience of the storm, although no one can claim to tell the whole or true New Orleans story.

New Orleans has long been characterized by a narrative told largely by outsiders, non-natives (and no doubt many who have never been to the city), which is generally disliked by locals and long-term residents—the New Orleans of booze, Bourbon Street, Mardi Gras, and parties. "It aggravates a lot of us," says Jeff Hebert, in part because the familiar Mardi Gras story is inaccurate and incomplete. It centers on the raucous doings in the French Quarter and excludes the more intimate, culturally vibrant aspect of the carnival celebration, "the family-oriented piece," Hebert says, "which you don't see on TV. We have tons of parades. They're family-based. People are on their front lawns. It's a time to be with family and friends."

Robert Lyall, director of the New Orleans Opera Company—the oldest such organization in the United States—sees this narrative as largely a product of the city's own marketing and promotional efforts. "When they actually spent the millions of dollars on an advertising campaign, it was still heavily weighted toward: *Come to the French Quarter and enjoy the fun and festivities*." Lyall says that New Orleans offers a much richer experience to its residents and visitors. "And yet," he says, "this is what we sell. Because it is the safest path . . . the course of least resistance."[21] It works—tourism is the city's biggest industry—but the party-focused identity does not come close to conveying the cultural legacy, vibrancy, and history of the Mardi Gras celebration, as well as New Orleans and Louisiana culture at large.

Hebert also acknowledges that Katrina has had a significant effect on the perceived identity of New Orleans. He is shocked at how many people think the city remains underwater and if they were to visit, they would find "people still travelling by boat," he says. The incredible economic development ongoing in New Orleans proves it—the city, and its people, are thriving. Hebert sees Katrina's effect as adding another thread to the New Orleans narrative that runs alongside the party-loving, anything-goes Mardi Gras image—of a place that is not the most "efficient, most above board, most business-friendly" city to live or work in.

The disruption of Katrina brought with it an opportunity to revitalize the city's identity and transform its narrative. Yes, it is still a city that loves to party, but the city, Mayor Mitch Landrieu, its residents—and those who visit—are also reshaping its identity and starting to adjust the narrative: of a city that has learned from its disruptions, is building business, and is beginning to reap the resilience dividend as a burgeoning center of cultural excitement and business innovation.

BOSTON BEGAN DEVELOPING its narratives around the bombings almost immediately. By Tuesday, April 16, Boylston Street, although still closed to traffic, had been cleared, and an investigation and manhunt for the perpetrators were under way. Boston and its citizens, in various forms and fashions, rallied around one another, supporting each other and reaffirming whatever it was about the city they loved, that made it special for them.

An awareness of the past and caring about the effects of current events on future realities perhaps can be credited for the way Bostonians reacted to the bombs on Boylston Street. Boston, founded in 1630, is one of the oldest cities in America and a state capital. At an interfaith memorial service held Thursday, April 18, just three days after the attacks, Governor Patrick made so bold as to claim that "Massachusetts invented America."[22]

Bostonians are well aware of their city's place in American history, from the original Old South Church (then called the Old South Meeting House) from which colonists set out to dump British tea in protest of taxation without representation to the line of red bricks that cuts through the city's sidewalks marking the Freedom Trail.

Bostonian and author Dennis Lehane—whose novels *Gone, Baby, Gone* and *Mystic River* are both set in Boston—spoke the words that many Bostonians had in their hearts in a *New York Times* op-ed, titled "Messing with the Wrong City." He wrote:

> Two different friends texted me the identical message yesterday: They messed with the wrong city. This wasn't a macho sentiment. It wasn't "Bring it on" or a similarly insipid bit of posturing. . . . What a Bostonian means when he or she says "They messed with the wrong city" is "You don't think this changes anything, do you?" . . . When the authorities find the weak and terminally maladjusted culprit or culprits, we'll roll our eyes at whatever backward ideology they embrace and move on with our lives. . . . The community will eulogize the dead and provide care and solace for the injured. And, no, we'll never forget. But what we'll cling tightest to is what the city was built on—resilience, respect and an adoration for civility and intellect. Boston took a punch on Monday—two of them, actually—that left it staggering for a bit. Flesh proved vulnerable, as flesh is wont to do, but the spirit merely trembled before recasting itself into something stronger than any bomb or rage.[23]

As Rocky Balboa, the famous movie character, put it, it isn't about how hard you can hit, but about how hard you can get hit and not fall down, not give up, and keep moving forward.[24] Lehane's editorial framed the narrative and vision of Boston's approach to revitalization. His was a voice of the community encouraging the community not to devolve into anger and rage but to search for compassion, to fight for one another and for the preservation of what it is about Boston that makes so many so proud to call it home.

IN ADDITION TO STORIES DELIVERED through popular media, the world is dappled with physical reminders of crises past that become part of that place's identity and can create awareness far into the future. Sometimes these memorials are created by happenstance. St. Paul's Church in Halifax still stands, and a shard of a wooden window frame blown away from a neighboring building in the *Mont Blanc* explosion is there for all to see. The streetscape of Medellin's Comuna 13 includes painted markings on buildings representing the invisible barriers that used to divide neighborhoods.

Sometimes people create memorials spontaneously and publicly. In the aftermath of the Boston bombings, Reverend Taylor of the Old South Church received outpourings of sympathy and compassion from churches around the country. The most poignant was the gift of a thousand paper cranes hand-delivered by a representative from the Newtown Congregational Church in Newtown, Connecticut. Newtown received the cranes in December 2012, after the mass shooting at its Sandy Hook Elementary School, from a church in Chardon, Ohio, where three were killed in a shooting in February 2012 at the high school there. And Chardon had received the cranes from Sheboygan, Wisconsin, where the cranes originated, crafted on the tenth anniversary of the 9/11 attacks.[25] "We are now the guardians of the paper cranes," says Taylor. The church will keep the cranes until another act of violence disrupts a community and the cranes—representing a thousand prayers for peace—are needed elsewhere.

The cranes are a striking way of remembering, sharing, sympathizing, and reminding similarly affected communities throughout the country that they are not alone and do not have to feel alone. Commemoration is a means by which we share and distribute the pain and sadness of tragedy, lessening the burden for all. "We found we were ministering to people who were ministering to us," Taylor says, "by being attentive to what they sent us."

The scars of such tragedies do not disappear, and it is in this kind of collective commemoration that communities build their resilience—their enduring commitment to one another and to remembering, a constant and repeated awareness of the importance of moving forward from disruption together.

SOMETIMES THESE MEMORIALS ARE CAREFULLY PLANNED, and the act of their creation becomes part of the recovery process—such was the case with the Oslo Memory Wound designed to memorialize the July 22 attacks.

Starting almost immediately after the attacks, spontaneous actions of memorialization sprang up. People laid flowers and lit candles at the bomb site and on the shore across from Utøya. On the first anniversary of the attacks, people came together in an event that came to be called the Rose Rally. Tens of thousands of people turned out to walk through the streets, listen to speakers, lay flowers, connect with one another, and speak of Utøya and what it meant. Everybody in Norway knew somebody who had been directly affected. Four students in the high school that Aage Borchgrevink's daughter attended, for example, had been at the camp and survived. "They brought the experience very close to the other students," he says.[26] A stone was erected and inscribed with a Tweet that had become famous after the attacks, roughly translated: "If one man can have so much hatred, think how much love we can create together." Bruce Springsteen, at a concert in Oslo on the memorial date, dedicated a rendition of "We Shall Overcome" to "the families that lost their loved ones" on Utøya.[27]

But something more permanent, loftier, more accessible to a greater number of people—because Utøya had become a symbol to people throughout Europe—was deemed necessary. In the summer of 2013, the Norwegian government sponsored a competition to design a permanent memorial, and in March of 2014 selected designs submitted by Jonas Dahlberg, a Swedish artist. The most striking of the three memorials he proposed is called Memory Wound, a 3.5-meter slice to be cut through the stone of the Sørbråten Peninsula, which faces Utøya, leaving a gaping separation, as if the strip of land had been sliced through with a giant, keen blade. The one hundred cubic meters of stone that will be removed to create the gap will be used to create a second memorial in Oslo.[28]

The massacre at Utøya is a wound in the country's past, deep and painful. Memory Wound is a scar that is intended to persist into the country's future. If the memorial is constructed as intended (which depends on getting local approval and support from many affected groups), future generations will see the cut in the landscape and re-member—feel—the effect of the event on the country's identity. However, not everyone is convinced of the necessity of a formal me-morial. "The spontaneous memorials, or expressions of grief and sol-idarity, were hugely important," says Borchgrevink, "as indeed were the trial and the report, both important steps in the healing and deal-ing process. The top-down initiatives, for all their good intentions, have been a harder sell—perhaps due to the nature of our society."

However, this view may change as time passes. The disruption caused by the mass killing took a heavy toll on Norway and its peo-ple. To memorialize it by mirroring the loss in the land itself may prove to be a striking work of art that effectively brings a new dimen-sion to a landscape that more than one camper, including the former prime minister, has described as "paradise." From this heinous act of violence may emerge an unexpected dividend—a symbol of how a society can come together to gain new strength from an unimagined disruption.

MEMORIALIZATIONS TEND TO SUSTAIN THE AWARENESS of a disruption over time, so that people continue to communicate about the experi-ence, learn from it, and connect around it. In Rwanda, for example, formal museums and makeshift memorials dot the country, com-memorating the 1994 genocide that killed 800,000 people, mostly Tutsis and some moderate Hutus, in a period of just one hundred days.[29] The largest of these, the Kigali Memorial Centre, opened on April 7, 2004, the tenth anniversary of the genocide. It serves as a research facility, a museum, a memorial, and a graveyard—more than 250,000 victims are buried on the grounds, many of whom are unidentified, along with many whose bodies have been brought to the site by friends and family.[30]

Inside, three permanent exhibitions tell the story to visitors. One documents the Rwandan genocide, a second traces the history of genocide worldwide, and a third memorializes the children who were murdered.[31] Out of the darkness of that last room, visitors emerge onto a balcony overlooking a rose garden, encouraging contemplation and hope for a brighter, peaceful future.

The Kigali Memorial Centre is not a static memorial. Even as visitors flow through the building, research continues and the archives expand. Names, photographs, documents, videos, and the locations of mass graves and roadblocks are collected and filed. With these data, the stories of the dead live on, honoring the victims and educating future generations so similar atrocities are not repeated.[32]

This mind-set of awareness extends beyond the Kigali Memorial Centre and infuses facets of everyday life in Rwanda, where official policy now prohibits people from referring to themselves divisively as "Hutus" or "Tutsis." Rather, everyone is a "Rwandan." Two annual holidays also serve as national days of reflection: Genocide Memorial Day on April 7 begins a week of collective mourning, and Liberation Day celebrates freedom, strength, and a hopeful future.

Through these and other memorials and commemorations, Rwandans have used the genocide narrative to rebuild social cohesion, spur economic development, and create new legal procedures such as the International Criminal Tribunal for Rwanda. The horror of the genocide will be felt for a long time, but, as Rwandans continue to unite through testimony, education, reflection, and learning, they forge a new future—one that's stronger together.

THE STORY OF CHRISTCHURCH, New Zealand, has not yet been so widely told in the academic and popular media, but it very likely will, because it's a remarkable tale of a city working to create a whole new narrative for itself.

It began with an earthquake. In February 2011, a 6.3 magnitude aftershock of an earlier earthquake that occurred in September 2010 caused a disastrous disruption to Christchurch—killing nearly 200 people, injuring 10,000 more, and leading to the demolition of more than 70 percent of the buildings in the city's central business district, which were deemed unsafe to remain standing.[33] In the 2010 quake, no deaths were recorded, and significantly less damage was done.

The 2011 quake was remarkable in that it was just one of thousands of aftershocks from the September rupture—as of March 2014, the city of Christchurch has experienced more than 12,000 aftershocks—but none like the tremor that forever changed the way Christchurch will think about its vulnerability to earthquake and, potentially, the way the community sees itself more broadly—as a resilient city.[34]

That, at least, is the goal of Christchurch's mayor, Lianne Dalziel, who signed Christchurch's application to become a part of the 100 Resilient Cities network in October 2013, less than a week after being sworn in. In the first week of November, Dalziel hosted a forum with more than eighty participants from local communities and governments to discuss how they could work together to make Christchurch a more resilient city.

"When I saw The Rockefeller Foundation's call for expressions of interest to [join the 100 Resilient Cities] initiative, I knew that this was what I wanted for the city," she said at the city's first 100 Resilient Cities workshop in March 2014. For Dalziel, becoming a resilient city is all about "participatory democracy" and "collective governance."[35]

"Reclaiming the word resilience in its broadest sense will enable us collectively to reclaim the power that rightly resides within our neighbourhoods and communities," she said.[36] One way Dalziel intends to support community development is by letting communities redefine themselves, even setting their own boundaries, an important political distinction—indeed, this would be almost unthinkable in the United States, where voting districts are elaborately drawn to keep like-minded constituencies together, at least on paper. "Communities need to be allowed to make sense of their own identities if people are going to want to vote and influence how their cities are run," Dalziel said.[37]

The mayor talks about cocreating a new Christchurch through grassroots community building and efforts to strengthen social cohesion. These factors will also facilitate the awareness, acceptance, and mitigation of community-specific risks (such as development in liquefaction zones, where soil has been weakened due to stress, or where there is a high density of buildings that are vulnerable to earthshake) and use top-down governance to identify and achieve outcomes that are grounded in the collective good and shared identity. There are things communities can do for themselves that government cannot, but there are also things governments can do that communities cannot. Thus, Dalziel emphasizes the importance of creating partnerships and networks that bring stakeholders, decision makers, and experts—with both local and generalized knowledge—together to take prioritized, resilience-based action. "Resilience is not a destination," she said at the 100 Resilient Cities workshop. "It is a means by which we can determine our destination as well as providing us with the means of getting there."[38]

Christchurch is already on a path of transformation, and it can be seen most clearly in initiatives that are, surprisingly—resiliently—taking advantage of the destruction that the earthquake caused. Take, for instance, Gap Filler—an organization dedicated to finding creative, innovative, and communally significant ways to use and develop vacant lots throughout the city, of which, considering the ongoing demolitions of seismically unsafe buildings, there are plenty. Gap Filler's projects include a miniature golf course, spreading hole by hole on abandoned lots throughout the city, and the Pallet Pavilion, an outdoor performance venue pieced together out of shipping pallets. (The pavilion was so well liked that roughly $70,000 was raised through crowdsourcing to keep the space in operation for another year).[39] Greening the Rubble and Life in Vacant Spaces are two similarly minded organizations, working to provide "transitional" function to the lots and areas in the city destroyed or otherwise disrupted in the quake until something more long-term moves in. You can imagine the effect such initiatives can have, promoting and encouraging social cohesion by re-enlivening Christchurch's streets, creating activity—and *fun*—where there were once only grim reminders of the earthquake and the toll it took.

There's a new furniture company in Christchurch, Rekindle, that uses wood salvaged from the rubble to create chairs, tables, and more. There's a new bar, Revival, that serves customers out of a shipping container. A new cathedral—which has a resemblance to Christchurch Cathedral, badly damaged in the quake and yet to reopen—is made in part from cardboard tubing.[40] Creativity and willpower are two major assets in Christchurch, and they may, in the long run, prove more valuable than any concrete or steel structure.

As we've seen before, crisis and disaster can be powerful opportunities for revitalization. After the February 2011 earthquake, a new community in Christchurch is beginning to emerge, just as it has in New Orleans, and may well do in the area around Fukushima—the young, the creative, the innovative, the entrepreneurial—who will be sorely needed in the years and decades ahead if Christchurch is going to continue on and sustain its path to creating a new identity as a resilient city.

A BRIEF FINAL NOTE on the city of Halifax. Stories of revitalization are often long and complex, but Halifax achieved a transformation with remarkable speed.

Samuel Henry Prince surveyed how the city fared in the two years after the explosion in 1917, and what he found encouraged him in his thesis: that catastrophe can bring about positive social change. Prince writes that the catastrophe transformed the city from a traditional, backward-looking place to a progressive one. "The spell of the past is broken," he writes. And he goes so far as to say that, as sad as the day of the explosion might have been, it may also be seen as "the greatest day in the city's history."[41]

Prince ticks off his proof for that supposition. In the years between 1917 and 1920, housing construction boomed (and well beyond just the replacement of demolished structures), and home values soared. Businesses came surging in. A new shipyard was constructed, and Halifax became a major port for oil distribution. Sidewalks were laid.

Telephone links were established between Halifax and cities as far away as New York and Chicago. Population swelled. A town planning board was formed and a comprehensive plan for the town developed, including changes to the waterfront. The problem of public health was addressed such that, by 1920, Prince claims, "Halifax has the finest public health program and the most complete public health organization in the Dominion."[42] Education was not forgotten. Dalhousie University was able to expand and improve, thanks to efforts and funding of many people and groups.

All of this work led to greater social cohesion. New committees were formed and people joined them. More people voted on Election Day. Prince notes that people were better at cooperating with one another. "There has been a new sense of unity in dealing with common problems," he writes. "The number of things which perforce had to be done together during the catastrophe was great. This doing of things together will be continued."[43]

Leap ahead by almost a century, and we find that the gains Halifax made—largely as the result of how it revitalized in response to catastrophe—endure. Halifax is a strong economic center, home to government agencies and private industries. In 2012, *MoneySense* magazine ranked Halifax as the fourth-best place in Canada to live, and in 2014 it was ranked ninth for midsize "cities of the future" in North and South America.[44]

Halifax, Prince concludes, "has been galvanized into life through the testing experience of a great catastrophe. She has undergone a civic transformation, such as could hardly have happened in fifty years. She has caught the spirit of the social age."[45]

DEVELOPING A SHARED VISION

There is one more aspect of the revitalization process I would like to discuss: the development of a vision. By vision I mean the articulation of a desired future condition. A vision imagines a new and often transformed way of being, for an individual, an organization, a city, even a country. A vision may begin with an individual or a small group—just as the engineers in Medellin had a vision of a neighbor-hood transformed by an escalator. A vision, however, must become a collective goal, a shared idea of a future possibility.

A vision, by its nature, implies fundamental change—beyond building back better. It suggests that the people who share the vision want to think of themselves and their environment in a new way and want others to do so too, and they want to act in very new ways as a result. A vision is particularly important for people, groups, and places that have not built much resilience yet, are struggling with se-rious vulnerabilities, face many threats, are short on assets, and are a long way from realizing their full potential.

NEW ORLEANS, THROUGH its numerous programs and the con-tributions of many individuals and groups, has developed a shared vision for a new city, one that goes well beyond the issues of storm defense and builds on the community development work. The vision addresses three main issues: education, environmental adaptation, and economic growth.

It was clear before the storm that the New Orleans educational system was in need of serous improvement. The state of Louisiana described the majority of the 128 schools as "academically unaccept-able."[46] Ninety-six percent of students scored below levels of basic proficiency in English; 94 percent below basic proficiency in math. Only one in four New Orleans residents had completed high school. What's more, the public school system was struggling with a debt of $300 million.[47] After Katrina, all but 35 percent of the public school system's buildings were rendered "completely unusable."[48]

Rather than rebuild a system that had been so far below standard, the state embarked on a course of bold action. It took responsibility for most of the public schools out of the hands of the local school board, placed them in a state-run recovery school district, and over a period of eight years (with leadership from Scott Cowen, president of Tulane University) converted them into independent charter schools.

In the 2013–2014 school year, 91 percent of the public school stu-dents attended charter schools, according to Leslie Jacobs, an advocate for educational reform in the city. In 2014–2015, close to 95 percent of the students will attend charter schools, and there will be just five traditionally run public schools in the city. It is no longer a centrally run school system but what Jacobs calls a "system of schools"—and has greatly improved.[49]

There are statistics to prove it. Between 2005 and 2012, New Orleans's district performance scores (a relative measure of a school's success)—for all students, all tests, and all performance levels—rose from 56.9 to 93.7, the highest rate of improvement in Louisiana. In 2005, fifty-two out of one hundred students graduated on time with a diploma; in 2012, the number jumped to seventy-eight of one hundred. The dropout rate in New Orleans, which was 11.4 percent in 2005, by 2011 had fallen to 4.1 percent, the state average. In 2005, 62 percent of students in New Orleans were attending failing schools. In 2013, only 5 percent were.[50]

The importance of good education to the repopulation and revitalization of New Orleans cannot be underestimated. If you want families to come back (and new ones to settle too), you must have schools. "You need your house, your job, and your school," says Jacobs. "You can't really come back as a family until you have all three." The difference between the pre-Katrina school system and the one the city has today, according to Jeff Hebert, who serves on the board of one of the city's charter schools, is "night and day." When you think about how to build community resilience, Hebert says, "public education, that's the future."

The second aspect of the vision for a revitalized New Orleans concerns its relationship with the environment, and it is articulated in a coastal master plan, *Louisiana's Comprehensive Master Plan for a Sustainable Coast*, created by the state of Louisiana and issued in 2012. The $50 billion, fifty-year plan does not call for an even more extensive water defense system but rather focuses on environmental adaptation, a version of living with water. There will be less attention paid to flooding and more to root causes, the most fundamental of which is land loss.[51]

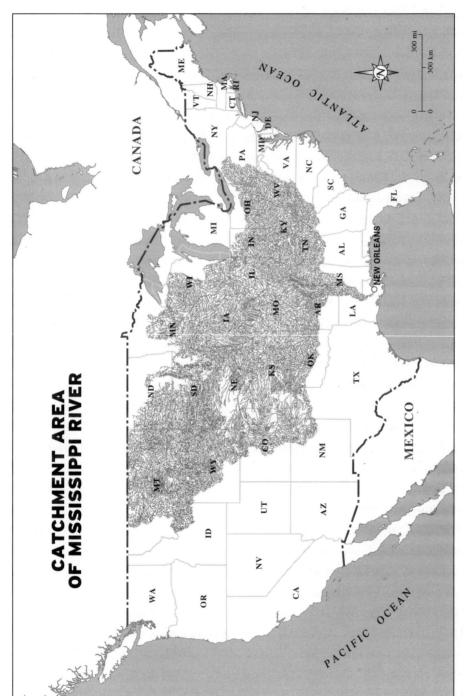

CATCHMENT AREA OF MISSISSIPPI RIVER

Source: USGS

Land loss has been an issue for the gulf for a long time. "Louisiana is in the midst of a land loss crisis that has claimed 1,880 square miles of land since the 1930s," according to the master plan, and the US Geological Survey estimates that if the land loss continues at its present rate, the wetland habitat will be gone in two hundred years.[52] A healthy wetlands is fundamental to flood protection and defense—and, indeed, it was highlighted by UNOP's Community Congresses as a priority for the city's recovery. Healthy wetlands can also act as an economic buffer. According to the Royal Swedish Academy of Sciences, citing findings from a 2008 study using data from thirty-four hurricanes since 1980, a loss of one hectare "of wetland . . . corresponded to an average $33,000 increase in storm damage from specific storms."[53]

One of the major causes of land loss and the disappearance of the wetlands is the Mississippi River, which is one of the greatest assets of New Orleans and also poses the city's most formidable threat. Some $15 billion worth of cargo travels along the Mississippi through the Port of New Orleans annually.[54] However, as author John McPhee argues, the Mississippi would prefer *not* to run through New Orleans at all. Like all rivers, the Mississippi seeks the path of least resistance to the sea. The Mississippi, if it had its way, would shift its path dramatically, merging into the Atchafalaya, a river that empties into the gulf at Morgan City, eighty-five miles southwest of New Orleans. "The consequences of the Atchafalaya's conquest of the Mississippi would include," McPhee writes, "the virtual destruction of New Orleans."[55] The city, with its reliance on the river for industry and integration with the rest of the country's economy, could not survive next to the former mighty river that would become, instead, a "tidal creek."[56]

The desire to control the Mississippi to maintain the city's viability is what originally led to the construction of the entire Mississippi River levee system. Although it protects riverside communities from flooding and helps keep the Mississippi running its current course, it also has contributed to land loss. Wetlands are created by the layering up of sediment deposited by the river as it flows. But the levees contain the river so that the sediment cannot flow beyond its banks and, instead, runs the entire course of the river, depositing itself miles offshore in the Gulf of Mexico.

Another contributing factor to land loss is subsidence—the gradual sinking of land. In New Orleans, the major cause is the draining of swamps and wetlands to create stable land for development. This creates underground pockets of air into which soils gradually sink, further lowering land below sea level and increasing vulnerability to flooding and storm surge. Between 2002 and 2005, the three years prior to Katrina, New Orleans subsided an average of eight millimeters per year.[57]

The goal of Louisiana's coastal protection and restoration plan, then, is not only to reduce the threat of flooding but to mitigate the fundamental environmental threats to the assets of the Gulf Coast—including the river-born cargo and the facilities and services that support the oil industry. Damage to essential infrastructure in the region could substantially increase consumer energy costs annually, and if coastal flooding continues to worsen, damage costs could increase tenfold.[58] In the language of the coastal protection plan, "These outcomes are wholly unacceptable."[59]

In addition to an improved education system and a new approach to environmental issues, the vision for a revitalized New Orleans is one of innovation and economic growth. Not only is the population growing; there has been a "brain gain," an influx of smart, energetic entrepreneurial people who are attracted to the area because of the opportunities it presents. In 2006 and 2007, moving to New Orleans was like "committing to the wild, wild West," says Leslie Jacobs.

As a result, the pace of economic activity in New Orleans has picked up remarkably, and the goal is to become a hub of innovation along the lines of San Francisco and Silicon Valley. In 2011, the rate of business start-ups was 56 percent higher than the national average, with 501 out of every 100,000 individuals starting a business, compared to the national average of 320. ("Aspiration metro" areas average about 376.) That figure represents a 129 percent increase compared to pre-Katrina levels.[60] The city has become nationally recognized as a hotbed for business, creativity, and innovation, named by *Forbes* as the number 1 "brain magnet." *Inc.* magazine ranks New Orleans as the "coolest startup city" in the country.[61]

As a vivid demonstration of the resilience dividend, New Orleans is looking into all kinds of new areas of economic activity. In 2013, the New Orleans Business Alliance—established in 2010 by Mayor Landrieu as a public-private, nonprofit body focused on economic development (with major stakeholders including the City of New Orleans, Entergy, Chase, and Harrah's New Orleans)—released a plan, *ProsperityNOLA,* with initiatives to drive economic growth through 2018. The plan focuses on strengthening existing industries, while ensuring opportunities for growth in three important fields: bioinnovation and health services, creative digital media, and sustainable industries.[62]

Still, success has created new vulnerabilities, as it always does—one of which is a workforce shortage. According to Robin Barnes, executive vice president and COO of Greater New Orleans, Inc., the economic development organization for southeast Louisiana, a number of factors—including an energy boom and growing information technology and medical and bioscience sectors, as well as the onset of the nation's most significant investment in coastal restoration—have created a demand for talent that far exceeds the number of people suitable for the available jobs. "Ensuring and resourcing adequate workforce training is critical so that we can keep up and grow," Barnes says.[63]

The transformation in progress has had an effect on how New Orleans thinks about itself. In many ways, prior to Katrina, New Orleans was an insular place, not particularly receptive to new or outside ideas and hardly seen as an innovation hub. Katrina forced it into resilience building, such that the city is now more diverse in ideas and integrated in activity.[64] Now, New Orleans has an "ability to demand what we want—to be strategic and smart—and not be quiet about it," says Barnes. She notes that in a report called *The New Orleans Index at Five,* from the Brookings Institution Metropolitan Policy Program and the Greater New Orleans Community Data Center, New Orleans is rated high on its ability to organize quickly when things happen. From the Brookings report: "Greater New Orleans has become more 'resilient,' with increased civic capacity and new systemic reforms, better positioning the metro area to adapt and transform its future."[65] Hebert agrees. "There is a renewed spirit," in New Orleans, he says. "We want to be here, so let's make it better."

CREATING A SHARING ECONOMY

Just as the disaster of New Orleans brought a new spirit to the city, Superstorm Sandy provided valuable lessons for the city and state of New York in evaluating, managing, and—looking down the road— envisioning a potential and different future. One element of this vision includes a factor I touched on briefly before, in regards to New York's latent housing stock and Airbnb's response to Sandy, that could prove important in the transformation of cities, communities, and individuals around the world: the sharing economy. The Airbnb response to Sandy was just one indicator of the extent of the hidden surplus, or latent assets, that surround us and of which we are almost completely unaware.

In 2011, *Time* magazine called the sharing economy one of ten ideas that could change the world.[66] The basic idea? You don't own everything you'll ever need—and don't need to—but someone does, and more value can be created for everyone by sharing our goods, our skills, and our services, rather than everyone trying to own everything. "Sharing is not new," says April Rinne, chief strategy officer at the Collaborative Lab in San Francisco, a consultancy that advises governments, businesses, and investors on how to best utilize aspects of collaborative consumption for more sustainable and citizen-engaging growth. "Sharing is the oldest thing known to mankind."[67]

"What *is* new," Rinne says, "is our ability to use technology to connect what some people have to what other people need in a way that's efficient. In the context of emergency management and disaster planning and disaster relief," she says, "the role of the sharing economy could be transformational."

The contemporary sharing economy as a whole—as well as many of the most successful start-ups and companies in that space— was born in San Francisco, and that's where Rinne's vision of its transformational capacities might first be tested. In 2013, San Francisco mayor Ed Lee announced a partnership between the city and BayShare—a network of San Francisco sharing-economy companies. These include Airbnb, NextDoor, RelayRides (which offers privately owned cars for rent), and yerdle (which enables users to trade unwanted belongings for points with which they can make other "purchases"), as well as nonprofit media outlets such as Shareable and think tanks such as the Collaborative Lab. The goal of the BayShare initiative is to help the city prepare for, respond to, and recover from the next Great San Francisco Earthquake or any other serious disruption.

By partnering with BayShare, San Francisco hopes to tap into the latent surplus of goods, services, and space and to leverage the networks these sharing-economy companies create. "One of the elements of the sharing economy that's so interesting for emergency response and recovery," says Alicia Johnson, San Francisco's resilience and recovery manager, "is being able to connect people who need something specifically with someone who actually has the infrastructure or the capability to give it." Airbnb, as we've seen, can provide shelter to displaced residents. An organization like yerdle could help receive and redistribute donated items. A service such as TaskRabbit (a site which enables people to hire helpers for odd jobs) could call up volunteers willing to assist in restoration and rebuilding efforts.[68] With these online networks and communities already in place, the transition from everyday business to postdisruption operation could be seamless, facilitating a more rapid response. "With so many sharing economy companies and communities here in the Bay Area willing and interested to see how they can help in a disaster," says Alicia Johnson, "I'm very excited to see where we're going."

THE RISE OF THE SHARING economy has implications for resilience building beyond preparing for and responding to disruption, namely in how we measure societal, national, and city growth and productivity. When April Rinne sat down with her financial adviser to discuss plans for her future, she recalls saying, "I'd love to spend time each year in another country, and I'll swap the house. I want to travel, and I'll do it on Airbnb. I would love to take a holiday, but I don't need to own a car. I'll share one. He looks at the numbers," she says, "and he's like, 'You're breaking my model. There's no way. This needs to cost a lot more.'"

That Rinne's utilization of the sharing economy breaks the model says less about how she wants to live her life than it does about the model itself. "Traditional economists have a hard time with what this whole thing is," says Rinne. "Much of what's happening in the sharing economy doesn't end up in GDP." GDP is a measurement of the market value "of goods produced and services provided in a country, excluding transactions with other countries" and is commonly used to indicate a country's financial health and prosperity.[69] But, says Rinne, it is also a "blunt, two-dimensional, clumsy, awkward tool to measure the kinds of value we need to measure today." GDP measures only new production; it includes a new car but not a shared car. For example, GDP would be five times as high if five people bought new cars than if those five people shared a car—despite the benefits that car sharing yields, such as lower congestion and pollution. It would also save each person a lot of money and probably improve their health. So, what kinds of value do we need to measure? What metrics can be indicative of a nation's progress toward resilience and not merely of its economic growth?

One framework that embodies a more resilience-minded perspective is the social progress index (SPI), a measurement that pits GDP alongside other metrics of national progress (as opposed to merely financial production) in three categories: access to and fulfillment of basic human needs, foundations of well-being, and opportunity. It has submeasures, which include nutrition and basic medical care and shelter; access to basic knowledge and ecosystem sustainability; personal rights, tolerance, and inclusion; and access to advanced education. Released by the Social Progress Imperative, a group founded by the Skoll Foundation, which now has added other foundations including The Rockefeller Foundation, the 2014 index does indicate a trend between GDP and SPI but reveals the former to be an inconsistent measure of the latter.

The United States, for example, which ranks second in GDP per capita at $45,336, ranks sixteenth on the SPI scale, with a score of 82.77. What is most useful about the SPI is that it provides details about a nation's strengths—the United States, for instance, scores very high in access to advanced education (89.37)—as well as weaknesses, such as the relatively low US score of 53.78 in ecosystem sustainability (that is, out of 132 countries studied, the United States was 69th in this measure).[70] The Netherlands, with its advanced strategy for living with water, ranked 18th in the same category, and 1st (with a score of 100) in terms of water and sanitation.

New Zealand, which scored highest overall on the index at 88.24 (and is where we find Christchurch) also received a perfect score for water and sanitation. But where New Zealand separates itself from the field—primarily in the category of "opportunity"—is highly telling for the utility of a measure such as SPI. New Zealand ranked 1st overall in the categories of personal rights (98.80) and personal freedom and choice (94.00), while ranking 4th in both tolerance and inclusion (82.41) and access to advanced education (76.84).[71]

But New Zealand's GDP per capita is relatively low: $25,857, 25th overall. Norway, the study country with the highest GDP per capita, $47,547, ranked 5th on the SPI, also scoring high on measures of opportunity—2nd on personal freedom and choice (93.27) and 9th on personal rights (87.96). Norway also scored high on measures in the category "foundations of well-being," 3rd overall on access to basic knowledge (99.44), 2nd on access to information and communications (98.45), and 8th on health and wellness (81.60). In all of these rankings, the United States—with the second largest GDP—failed to crack the top 10.[72] Although some will disagree with the measures produced or the methodology that produced them, the SPI goes a long way toward indicating that a country's successes—and its failures—are about much more than economic factors.

This kind of broad-focused assessment, taking a holistic view of a country's well-being and vitality, enables more knowledge-based growth, allowing nations to focus resources where its citizens need them most. Whether a single metric can be decided upon or created to assess the resilience of a country, city, or community is yet to be determined, but future measurements and assessments of cities and nations should similarly focus on the many components, networks, and services that underlie a resilient system.

Measuring the impact of the sharing economy "isn't rocket science," says Rinne. "But we're going to have to dismantle a lot of the ways we've come to think about value and wealth creation and returns, and the big picture." That traditional economic and business models may undergo substantial changes in the coming years is not solely an opinion held by those in sharing-economy companies or start-ups or by millennials as a group. The multinational corporation Unilever—one of the world's largest producers of consumer household goods, with brands such as Dove, Vaseline, and Ben & Jerry's—had turnover of nearly €50 billion in 2013 and was ranked 135 on *Fortune*'s Global 500 list.[73] But Paul Polman, Unilever's CEO, knows that to stay successful in the years to come, the company—and business in general—must adapt to address the threats of the twenty-first century.

Though officially formed into a corporate group in 1930, the companies that merged to create Unilever have been operating successfully since the late 1880s and have survived countless disruptions large and small—two world wars, the Great Depression, the Great Recession, market competition, and globalization—so it is not surprising that long-term planning, a vital element of the resilience mind-set, would be at the center of their business strategy.

"We need a different approach to business," writes Polman in a blog hosted by McKinsey & Company, "a new model led by a generation of leaders with the mind-set and the courage to tackle the challenges of the future."[74] The challenges, as we've seen, have few, if any, simple solutions.

"Interestingly," Polman continues, "the challenge [for business] is likely to encourage a much more collaborative form of capitalism. Companies will have to work with each other, not just governments, nongovernmental organizations (NGOs), and civil society . . . growth strategies will have to be more inclusive. . . . In a world of scarcity," he writes, "there will be greater pressure to ensure that wealth is created not just for the few, but that the benefits are spread more widely."[75]

In other words, the benefits of the future economy must be shared. Because we are all inhabiting a single planet and will inevitably suffer the consequences of misused resources and of civil unrest sparked by inequality and poverty, we must find ways to share the benefits of responsible business strategies and sustainable growth. We need to think, therefore, much less about short-term financial gain and much more about resilience and the dividends it can bring.

CONCLUSION
Realizing the Resilience Dividend

S haun Donovan, the former US secretary of housing and urban development, keeps a sponge in the shape of the Netherlands in the family bathroom of his home. It reminds him of how his thinking about resilience has evolved.

When Donovan served as commissioner of the New York City Department of Housing Preservation and Development, his focus was largely (and necessarily) on fundamental issues of affordable housing development: adherence to regulations and codes, ensuring proper standards for structure and infrastructure. His thinking, in other words, ran more or less along the lines of development financing and risk management.

When he became HUD secretary in 2009, Donovan began to think more broadly. Soon after taking the job, he traveled with Janet Napolitano, then secretary of homeland security, to New Orleans. There, he saw how badly the recovery was going, three and a half years after the storm. Some 30,000 families, displaced by Katrina, were still living in temporary housing, and one reason was that the government's response had been so ineffective. The physical conditions were bad enough. The social situation was worse—for the individuals affected, the city, the economy, and the nation as a whole. "I was so angry after that trip," Donovan says.[1]

In March 2009, he gained further awareness of the ways in which a disruption can affect people and their communities. He visited Cedar Rapids, Iowa, which had also experienced severe flooding just a year earlier. Donovan trudged through neighborhoods and talked with homeowners who were facing agonizing choices about whether to repair or rebuild, sell out, leave the neighborhood, or even depart the city. His experiences helped him "understand our vulnerability in a fundamentally different way."

Then came a revelation. Donovan traveled with his family to the Netherlands and, with Henk Ovink as guide, toured The Hague, Rotterdam, Amsterdam, and the country's coasts and waterways. Donovan inspected the measures the Dutch have taken to deal with the challenge of water—including the elements of the audacious Delta Works, designed to withstand a 10,000-year flood. More important, he came to understand that the Dutch had developed a fundamentally different social approach to living with water—and to disruption in general. Resilience, he realized, could become "part of a culture," not just the responsibility of experts and professionals or a matter of structures and protections. Resilience could be about the "way you live." Donovan brought the sponge home as a kind of talisman of a certain view of resilience: that it is both a technical and social concept.

My own thinking about resilience has also evolved—through my early work with the West Philadelphia community when I was president of Penn, my involvement in New Orleans in the years after Katrina, my service as cochair of the NYS2100 Commission, and, of course, through our many resilience-focused endeavors at The Rockefeller Foundation, including the ACCCRN, Rebuild by Design, and 100 Resilient Cities initiatives. I believe that building resilience is of paramount importance today, especially as we see that the problems of the world are growing increasingly threatening. In report after report, study after study, in domain after domain, we learn about the challenges facing us in the years ahead, from the deleterious effects of climate change on human health to the threats of breakdown in political governance to the explosive social dynamics of fast-populating cities to the vulnerabilities of aging and inadequate infrastructure.

But I have also become convinced that the resilience dividend is real and achievable, and provides great opportunities to improve lives and livelihoods in the good times as well.

However, once we agree that resilience building is essential, there certainly will be disagreement about how to go about it—where we should focus our energy and how we should allocate our resources. We can't fix everything. Should we focus on reducing vulnerabilities so as to reduce risk? And, if so, which ones? In what order? Or should we put more energy into building up our response capabilities, knowing that bad things will undoubtedly happen and we must be prepared? Or perhaps we should leap right to innovation and revitalization, in hopes that new activity will drive out old vulnerabilities.

All three phases of resilience building are important, but our tendency is to focus attention most keenly on response. That's because we can't ignore a disruption. We must respond to a crisis and deal with disaster. We have little choice.

It's more difficult, in many ways, to focus on increasing readiness or on developing a path to revitalization. That's partly because there is less urgency to act in relatively stable times, when the stresses are accustomed and the shocks are small and manageable. It's also because all the entities that must be involved—individuals, organizations, communities, and cities—are complex and diverse. They all have differing points of view, assets and vulnerabilities, goals and aspirations, and these elements can come into conflict because considerations of complex human concerns come into play, including politics, ethics, and faith. Simply put, it is difficult for us as individuals, and for groups as well, to focus on preparing for bad things that *might* happen when it seems, at the moment, that things are going pretty well.

But taking action before a disruption occurs is essential to resilience building. If we do not assess our situations when life is calm, if we do not take actions and commit resources to reduce our vulnerabilities and potential threats when things are relatively stable, we will always be in a reactive mode—acting only after things have gone wrong. Yes, it may be easier to mobilize people and to martial resources in the wake of a crisis, but there are at least two problems with the reactive approach to resilience building. First, you may be forced into actions that might not necessarily be optimal—such as constructing a new building when an existing one could have been made more able to withstand a disruption. Second, the cost is always higher to take action postcrisis than it is when relief and recovery are not part of the agenda. By cost, I of course refer to the toll crisis takes on human beings and social cohesion, as well as on tangible assets.

Determining what actions to take in noncrisis times—to articulate the points of conflict, develop alternatives and solutions, and make decisions about trade-offs—almost always requires a process that is inclusive and integrated. The trade-offs must be assessed and difficult questions must be raised. Are some choices better or more important for building resilience than others? Can we articulate resilience-building priorities as we make individual and collective choices?

An inclusive process involves a wide range of stakeholders engaging in the conversation about tensions and trade-offs. It is essential to include individuals, groups, or organizations that are particularly vulnerable—such as the socially marginalized and those with few assets—because they typically suffer the most intense impacts of disasters or crises. When numerous people and groups are involved and the trade-offs are complex, the process can often be lengthy and sometimes messy. Be that as it may, the process can be navigated and superb results can be obtained, as I hope I have demonstrated with the many stories in this book.

NECESSARILY, SUCH A PROCESS will and should include a lot of diversity—of people, opinions, and, as a result, thinking styles. So, as I've discussed, it's important that the process be well managed in order to avoid the disarray that can come from an abundance of approaches and to ensure that ideas are well synthesized and that you arrive at integrated solutions.

Michael Berkowitz, head of The Rockefeller Foundation's 100 Resilient Cities initiative, is well aware of the complications involved in influencing how people think and how communities take action with regard to resilience, and he says that one of the main areas of difficulty is that there is often a significant disconnect between how large a threat actually is and how strongly people feel about it. He cites the work of Peter Sandman, an expert in "risk communication," who refers to the "incredibly low correlation" between the scale of a hazard and what he calls people's "outrage" toward it.[2] In the United States, for example, people see terrorism as a grave threat although it claims far fewer lives than do commonplace disruptions like car accidents. When people feel great outrage about a very real threat, Sandman says, they are most likely to commit to taking action. That is one reason it so often takes a crisis to catalyze change and improvement. Feeling runs high. The need is obvious. The urgency is there.

This phenomenon has long been studied by psychologists and social scientists. Gustave Le Bon, a French sociologist working in the late nineteenth and early twentieth centuries, studied why groups of people—or, in his parlance, "crowds"—come to place greater or lesser importance on certain types of disruptive events. It is not the facts of the crisis that "strike the popular imagination," he writes, "but the way in which they take place and are brought under notice." A "startling and very clear image" is key, he says, as are dramatic moments. "A hundred petty crimes or petty accidents will not strike the imagination of crowds in the least, whereas a single great crime or a single great accident will profoundly impress them, even though the results be infinitely less disastrous than those of the hundred small accidents put together."[3] This is certainly one reason the Halifax explosion had such a lasting impact on that city and why images of the airplanes striking the Twin Towers have become iconic.

There are many cognitive biases at play as we humans go about making decisions in circumstances involving disruption, risk, and uncertainty. Perhaps the most pertinent to our discussion of anticipating the effects of a potential disruption is the *availability heuristic,* first posited by cognitive psychologists Amos Tversky and Daniel Kahneman in 1973. When estimating future outcomes or, more generally, thinking about frequency and probability, "the ease with which instances or associations could be brought to mind"—that is, their cognitive availability—has a significant effect on our estimations and leads to "systematic biases," the psychologists write.[4] For instance, if you were trying to guess whether the driver of a pickup truck in front of you were a man or a woman, frequency would play an important role: How many times do you recall having seen men at the wheel of similar trucks in comparison to how many women you've seen driving them? Salience, too, will affect your judgment—that is, how prominent in your awareness is some aspect of the estimation? For example, you might recently have seen an advertisement for that brand of truck. The availability heuristic, therefore, is useful because it facilitates rapid assessments in reasonably simple situations, even though it is not integrated with statistics, data, and baseline probabilities (such as, in this case, the total number of male and female truck drivers or owners).

But for unique, complex, or hard to imagine predictions, according to Kahneman and Tversky, the availability heuristic can be powerfully disadvantageous. "Many of the events whose likelihood people wish to evaluate depend on several interrelated factors. Yet it is exceedingly difficult for the human mind to apprehend sequences of variations of several interacting factors." So, the authors suggest, "in evaluating the probability of complex events only the simplest and most available scenarios are likely to be considered. In particular, people will tend to produce scenarios in which many factors do not vary at all, only the most obvious variations take place, and interacting changes are rare."[5]

In the context of resilience, then, it is very hard for us to imagine, and nearly impossible to predict, how a disruption will play out and what a disaster might look like. This is one reason it is so difficult to get people to focus on things that *might* go wrong or to make decisions about how to deal with threats, especially when they involve multiple vulnerabilities and multiple stakeholders. That's why it's important to move as swiftly as possible in the revitalization process. Because the disruption and its effects are highly available, it is more likely that people will be able to focus on them and be willing to devote energy to looking for solutions. If you wait too long, something else will come along and overshadow the availability of the disruption.

Never let a good crisis go to waste.

LIVING IN THE FORELOOP

Certainly some elements of the "improvement-by-crisis" approach do work—that is largely how the National Transportation Safety Board has dramatically improved the safety of air travel over the years—but is hardly the optimal, most productive, or most salutary way to live. It is also incredibly costly, in both financial and human terms, and drains resources away from more productive endeavors. According to the World Bank, for example, about 20 percent of all humanitarian aid is spent on responding to disaster, while less than 1 percent is spent on preventive measures that could have kept disruption from becoming disaster in the first place.[6]

Maybe we could tolerate this approach to threats in the past—lurching from disruption to disruption, weathering crises, making slow, incremental improvements to reduce our vulnerabilities—but today the disruptions are too varied and too great, too frequent and too severe, too interconnected and too wide-ranging to continue this way. The risks are too great and the costs too high. At the same time, we are much more aware of our vulnerabilities than ever before and have much more knowledge and expertise about how to mitigate threats, how to make ourselves and our institutions stronger and more adaptive to any kind of challenge (seen and unforeseen), and therefore have tremendous capacity to make change—but much of it is, as yet, untapped.

To proactively build resilience—without waiting for disaster to push us into it—we need to live, as much as we possibly can, in the *foreloop* of the adaptive cycle. You may remember that the adaptive cycle, the concept that comes from systems theory (particularly as applied to ecological systems), has four phases and is often described as a loop. The first two phases—rapid growth and conservation—make up the foreloop. The third and fourth phases—release and reorganization—constitute the backloop. Release has the effect of rattling the status quo and presenting an opportunity for change.

Living in the foreloop simply means that we spend as much time as possible in the periods of growth and conservation and as little time as possible in the release and reorganization phases. Building resilience enables us to do that by improving our readiness and responsiveness. Living in the foreloop also implies, and this is a key point, that *we take control* of when and how we respond to a release, or disruption.

What's more, when we develop greater resilience, we may even deliberately create disruptions to force positive change. Such deliberate, positively intended disruptions are simply well-calculated risks—the kind of planned and intentional risks that individuals, companies, organizations, cities, and even countries have always taken to grow, improve, and realize the great benefit that can come with revitalization and transformation.

For example, a city takes a deliberate risk when it hosts an Olympic Games, because it disrupts the normal functioning of the place but can bring about positive social change; Barcelona, the capital city of Catalonia, Spain, is often cited as the most positive example of this. Located on the northwest coast of the Mediterranean Sea, the city hosted the 1992 summer games and more than two decades later is still reaping the dividends.

Barcelona deliberately set out to leverage the games to create an "urban transformation," as a 2002 report declares. Barcelona proceeded with "institutional unity" and secured "mixed public-private funding" following a process that was inclusive, integrated, and animated by a shared vision of widespread, long-term positive change.[7]

In preparation for the games, Barcelona devoted more than 85 percent of its total spending to infrastructural and facility improvements, but only 9 percent of that total went to *athletic* facilities. Between 1986—when the International Olympic Committee (IOC) selected Barcelona—and 1992, the city built new roads and sewage systems, and increased green and beach areas by 78 percent.[8] New residential housing was built for the Olympic Village and then opened up for commercial sale after the games.[9] Hotel capacity was increased by 38 percent.[10] Barcelona saw the Olympics as an opportunity to strengthen the entire city for the long term, not just spruce it up for the games to realize a short-term gain.

The effects of Barcelona's work were immediate, long-lasting, and dramatic. The infrastructural work created tens of thousands of jobs such that unemployment dropped from 18.4 percent in October 1986 to 9.6 percent in August 1992. Although many of those jobs were specific to construction work before the games, more than 20,000 people found permanent employment as a direct result of investments made for the event.[11]

Since the Olympic Games, Barcelona has become an enterprising and attractive European city. According to the IOC, "Twenty years on, Barcelona was the 12th most popular city destination in the world and was ranked 5th amongst European cities."[12] In 1990 Barcelona welcomed about 2 million tourists; in 2012, nearly 7.5 million people visited the city.[13] And, in a ranking of the business confidence in Barcelona—"as reflected by the willingness of foreign companies to establish there (a combination of attractiveness, availability of services, workers, market, and competitiveness) improved notably in the aftermath of the Games"—the city jumped from 11th in 1990 to 6th in 2001.[14]

The public health of the nation and its standing as an athletic power were improved. By 1995, more than half of the Spanish population engaged in some kind of sport at least once a week, an increase of 15 percent from 1983.[15] The 1992 Olympic Games have often been credited with Spain's current reign in several sports.[16] Spain is home to two powerhouse, profitable soccer clubs, Real Madrid and FC Barcelona, and its national team won the World Cup in 2010 (although they failed to advance in 2014). Rafael Nadal, the world's number 1 ranked tennis player as of this writing, was born and lives on the island of Majorca, just off the coast of Barcelona.

Of course, there were unintended consequences. A 2014 documentary, *Bye Bye Barcelona,* questions whether Barcelona's rampant tourism has taken away from the city's cultural heritage and identity.[17] And unemployment in Barcelona has since risen to 21.74 percent.[18]

But, unlike many cities that bring on the intentional disruption of the Olympics, Barcelona did so planning for the long-term, making investments and improvements that would develop the city for continued growth and prosperity, not for a one-off, month-long event. And, given the obvious improvements to the city and the country's well-being after the games, although things aren't perfect, it raises the question: how would Barcelona be faring had it *not* taken the risk?

BARCELONA IS HARDLY THE ONLY CITY TO TAKE THE RISK of a major intentional disruption. Glasgow, buoyed by the success of its 1990 European Capital of Culture, continued to host major festivals and improve its status in the world. In 1999, Glasgow was named the UK City of Architecture and Design—with an estimated economic benefit of £34 million—and in 2003 it won the designation as the European Capital of Sport.[19]

In 2006, the city, confident of its ability to leverage its diverse skills and capabilities (and with the memory of the 1990 Capital of Culture success still in its mind), submitted a bid to host the 2014 Commonwealth Games. The eleven-day sporting event—which would involve hosting some 6,500 athletes from seventy-one countries and territories and providing infrastructure for seventeen categories of competition and selling more than 1 million tickets[20]—would cost at least a half billion pounds to stage and would create a major disturbance for the city and its people.[21] However, it was not a pipe dream. Glasgow had been on the path of revitalization for well over a decade. Thanks to its experience with the multitude of activities of a number of high-profile, large-scale events of international significance, Glasgow had accumulated significant resilience assets: strong leadership, the ability to integrate diverse groups and coordinate multiple activities, and new facilities and infrastructural elements that represented some seventy percent of what would be needed to host the Commonwealth Games.[22] There was risk, yes, but the Games also represented a major opportunity. In 2007, Glasgow won the bid.[23]

From the outset, Glasgow understood what was at stake and took a long view. As stated in its application, hosting the Commonwealth Games would "contribute to the economic, social, cultural and environmental development of the city and the country."[24] Chief resilience officer Alastair Brown says that the effort has been about using the Commonwealth Games to "bring up the social benefits for the people of Glasgow." The city developed a comprehensive plan, the *Glasgow 2014 Legacy Framework*, which details how the Games activities and initiatives will play out through 2019.[25] "We expect to see clear advantages and benefits coming from the Commonwealth Games," says Brown.

The Games were also viewed as a way to bring new vitality to areas of the city that had suffered most during the period of decline—the East End, in particular. The area continued to be stressed, even as much of the rest of Glasgow prospered. Residents struggled to find regular work, and life expectancy was five years less than the national average.[26] Dalmarnock, one of the East End's districts, had been hit particularly hard when manufacturing jobs dried up, shrinking from a community of 50,000 in the 1950s to one of less than 2,000 today.[27] The Games, stated the application, would facilitate "significant regeneration of the East End of Glasgow, making effective use of otherwise derelict land and creating employment opportunities for local people."[28]

After winning the bid, the city of Glasgow spent seven years preparing for the Games. The multi-partner, government-funded Clyde Gateway Project was created to manage the regeneration efforts in the East End.[29] Some of the key new infrastructural elements were sited there, including the Emirates Arena, the renovated Sir Chris Hoy Velodrome, and the crown jewel of the Games' built environment, the low-carbon Athletes' Village, located near the river Clyde. It was designed to accommodate all 6,500 competitors during the Games[30] and then to become housing for 700 Glaswegian families in the years that followed. (Four hundred of the townhouse units will be priced so they are affordable to lower-income families.) The development, described as "one of the most significant new urban housing developments in the UK,"[31] benefits from an upgraded transit station and new roads, plenty of green spaces, and soft solutions for the management of river water intrusion, including gardens and floodable areas.[32] Future plans call for the development of a 120-bed senior housing facility, community center, and retail outlets.[33] "Just five years ago, if you went to parts of the East End of Glasgow, you would leave with a bad impression of the place," Brown says. "If you went back to the same places today, you wouldn't recognize it. They have reinvented themselves."

The changes in the East End Dalmarnock district in the name of revitalization have not come without controversy. Entire tenement blocks and a local community center were demolished to make way for the new structures, and many have expressed skepticism that the current residents of the East End will be the people who reap the benefits of the city's investment. In an article in the *Guardian*, reporter Oliver Wainwright did not mince his words when he criticized the Games' development policy in Dalmarnock, calling it a "broad-brush approach" that "follows a long tradition of crass planning."[34] And many followed the story of Margaret Jaconelli, a longtime resident of Dalmarnock who was evicted in 2011 from the flat she and her family had lived in since 1976, which was razed shortly after to make way for the Athletes' Village. Her protracted legal battle with the city attracted significant media attention, including coverage in *Commonwealth City*, a BBC documentary about the Games' impact.[35] (The Jaconellis eventually received more than £80,000 in compensation.[36])

But many people, including the majority of the East End's current inhabitants, believe the long-term benefits will outweigh the negatives. A survey conducted in the summer of 2012 by the University of Glasgow showed that eighty-one percent of East End residents believed the Games would improve their local area[37] and 44.5 percent reported their neighborhood had benefited in the previous three years,[38] aided by the cultural, physical fitness, and job programs serving the area. Just as important, more than one third of those polled felt they had participated in the Games' preparations and had influenced the decisions made about their area.[39]

Even before the Games began, Glaswegians had realized some of the planned economic benefit. While the long-term impact of the initiative can't be calculated yet, about £200 million in contracts has been awarded to local companies and has created thousands of jobs.[40]

As we've seen, the city of Glasgow has come a long way from the sooty place it was before 1990 and is more like the stately urban gem that Nathaniel Hawthorne so admired in the mid-nineteenth century. Not only is Glasgow a player on the international stage, it has become a case study used by planners and analysts as a model of urban renewal and a trailblazer in urban technology. Indeed, in 2013, Glasgow won the Technology Strategy Board's Future Cities Demonstrator competition and received a £24 million prize. The award money has been used to pilot smart technologies, including an integrated operations center that better manages the city's safety and traffic and which served as the operations base for the Commonwealth Games. Glasgow is also becoming a major player in the renewables sector. According to Alastair Brown, the Scottish government has set high targets for the increased use of renewable energy sources. The three universities in Glasgow have been particularly ambitious in pushing to establish Glasgow as a hub for activity in renewable energy initiatives. "There are more renewable sector jobs in Glasgow than anywhere else in Scotland now," says Brown.

Over a period of twenty-five years, Glasgow has taken smart, calculated risks to build greater resilience, but there remain significant vulnerabilities. The unemployment rate is too high. Some communities are impoverished. There is a disproportionate number of elderly in the population. "It's not that we don't have our problems and our difficulties," Brown says. "But we are much more capable of being able to overcome, or certainly address, many of those problems—which wasn't the case in the early '80s." No city erases all its problems. But, through an integrated set of planned, disruptive actions, Glasgow has revitalized itself, reduced its vulnerabilities, increased its assets, and created a more equitable and livable city for all its residents. As it built its resilience, Glasgow was also able to open new opportunities—hosting international events, welcoming tourists, becoming a center of renewable technology development. Revitalization does not mean attaining perfection—no city can do that. But Glasgow has clearly, and in multiple ways, realized the resilience dividend.

BUSINESSES, TOO, TAKE intentional, foreloop risks by launching new products or entering new markets that may disrupt their operations, cause shifts in relationships, put a burden on finances, but, more importantly, bring opportunity for growth and improvement. Andrew Winston, a business strategy expert, suggests that taking risks is especially important for businesses today, given the world's "megachallenges," including climate change, urbanization and demographic shifts, commodity price increases, limits on resources, and the possibility of financial collapse.[41] He argues that they call for a fundamentally different strategy that focuses on building resilience.

"An extreme world calls for extreme change," Winston writes, and he suggests that businesses find new ways to deal with megachallenges by asking what he calls "heretical questions." These should challenge the most fundamental strategic and operating assumptions and should be framed in the light of specific global challenges. Winston cites the example of Nike, which, he says, asked "whether it would be possible to dye clothes—a very water-intensive process—without water."[42] The question was asked in the context of the very real threat of water shortages, or lack of access to water, especially in facilities in developing countries. If the threat materialized and Nike had developed a waterless dying system, then the water stoppage would not constitute a disruption, making the company far more resilient.

Companies are also seeking to make "dramatic improvements in operational efficiency and cuts in material and energy use, waste, and carbon emissions," Winston writes, so they can "become much more flexible and antifragile."[43] ("Antifragile" is Nassim Taleb's term to define entities that "gain from disorder."[44]) This is why companies are seeking to develop and manage their own sources of energy and increase their use of renewable energy sources. Walmart, for example, intends to increase its use of "onsite renewable energy 600% by 2020." According to one Walmart executive, that will enable the company to keep "stores up and running no matter how bad the weather is or who else might be shut down."[45]

Coca-Cola, too, is thinking hard about the management of important resources, in particular its product's key ingredient: water.

Today, the company sells nearly two billion bottles of Coke every day and has plans to double its business by the year 2020.[46] To accomplish this goal, Muhtar Kent, chair and CEO, knows that resilience must be at the forefront of the company's thinking. "In some corner of the world," he says, "there is always an external disruption that can have bearing on our business."[47]

The central component of Coca-Cola's resilience and sustainability strategy necessarily focuses on water stewardship, with an ambitious goal of the company becoming "water neutral" by 2020. As part of this mission, Coca-Cola has conducted some four hundred community water-focused projects in ninety-four countries, partnering with groups including the Nature Conservancy, the World Wildlife Fund, CARE, USAID, and local government groups.

Additionally, Coca-Cola has embarked on a long-term partnership for clean water worldwide with world-renowned innovator Dean Kamen, founder of DEKA R&D, developer of the Segway, and inventor of a water purification system called Slingshot. This new technology can filter and purify water from any source —including rivers, oceans, and even, amazingly, sewage—so that it is potable. One Slingshot filtering unit—using less electricity per hour than an ordinary hairdryer—can produce eight hundred liters of clean water daily, which is enough water to meet the needs of three hundred people. In 2013, one hundred Slingshot units were placed in schools and health facilities in countries throughout Africa and Latin America.

Slingshot may well be a successful water filtration technology for rural areas. It can be connected to a local power grid or to any number of other types of energy sources, including batteries or solar cells. Another source of power could be an electric generator developed by DEKA R&D that runs on biogas, such as methane, which can often be conveniently sourced from nearby waste facilities. This will undoubtedly help Coca-Cola and its partners reach their goal of delivering 100 million liters of clean drinking water to 45,000 people in twenty countries by 2015.[48]

For Kent, these initiatives relate directly to the economic viability of the company's supply chain and its customers that span the globe.

"The multinational corporation will always have a role to play in driving sustainable economic development," he says.[49]

In addition to the kind of initiatives that companies such as Walmart and Coca-Cola are pursuing, Andrew Winston also suggests that a large industry is now in the making, one that will create and commercialize products and services that help customers of all kinds be more efficient, less susceptible to disruptions from the world's megachallenges, and less dependent on nonrenewable energy sources over which they have no control. The Economist Intelligence Unit, for example, found that 63 percent of the companies it polled saw opportunities to generate value from disaster risk reduction.[50] Mori Building, a privately held construction company, has successfully invested in earthquake-resistant housing developments in Japan, where earthquake resistance has become the most important criterion for 92 percent of companies choosing new offices.[51]

But efficiency and self-reliance alone will not likely produce growth. "The principles of resilient systems include diversity," and, to achieve that, Winston argues that companies should pursue a "near-religious avoidance of risk for the vast majority of the business, coupled with extreme risk taking with pilot programs or small parts of the enterprise."[52]

THIS BRINGS US TO A REFINEMENT of the concept of living in the foreloop: while the larger system (the company or the city as a whole) chugs along in the growth and conservation phases, small parts of the system (a unit or project) can create a disruption that will provoke change and do so *without* destabilizing the entire system or causing it to lose its ability to self-regulate. As the smaller element grows, it too will move into the conservation phase, perhaps resulting in the transformation of the entire company. This concept is well known in business, and the example of Apple is often cited. It kept its computer business growing while starting up its iPod and iPhone initiatives, which eventually became the core of the company without destabilizing the business.[53]

Individuals, like cities and business, regularly take risks that bring with them disruptions—such as moving to a new city, committing to an innovative project, or taking on a new job—but that enable them to grow and thrive and be more resilient in the face of still more challenges.

Pauline Manguru, for example, who lives in the Nairobi community of Kambi Moto, took what for her was an enormous risk several years ago. She describes herself as a person who used to spend her time doing nothing more than "cutting vegetables on the street." She had little education and not much work experience. Her friends called her "little Pauline," and she says she was too shy to speak English with strangers. Fed up with her situation, and with children to look after, Pauline took what seemed to her like a big risk at the time: she joined the Kambi Moto savings group.

She then created a series of deliberate disruptions to her life that have transformed her. She learned organizational skills and took on a leadership role with the savings group, eventually serving as treasurer and chair. She became so aware of the vulnerabilities of living on land without ownership that she was finally able to summon the courage to speak up, protest before the city council, and help improve the community's integration with the city. She was able to save enough money to finance the building of a two-story home and looks forward to the day when she can add a third.

Pauline has worked as a Muungano representative and mentor for more than a decade, offering guidance and support to other slum dwellers in her neighborhood and around the country. Her impact even extends beyond the borders of Kenya. In September 2012, Pauline flew to the World Urban Forum in Naples, Italy, and shared the stage with SDI president Jockin Arputham, as well as various mayors and ministers, participating on a panel about inclusive urban governance.[54]

By taking on a series of deliberate disruptions, Pauline has grown so that she is hardly recognizable to herself and her friends. "I have seen I'm a leader," says Pauline. Her friends say she's now the "Pauline who can fight for something, who can own something. The Pauline who can make people come together with one idea and a dream that becomes a reality."[55]

Barcelona, Nike, Pauline—they have all sought to spend as much of their time as possible in the foreloop—taking deliberate risks and controlling disruption (a.k.a. release) as skillfully as possible—where they can best reap the resilience dividend.

THE RESILIENCE DIVIDEND

Building resilience creates two aspects of benefits: it enables individuals, communities, and organizations to better withstand a disruption more effectively, and it enables them to improve their current systems and situations. But it also enables them to build new relationships, take on new endeavors and initiatives, and reach out for new opportunities, ones that may never have been imagined before. This is the resilience dividend.

We can see how resilience pays dividends in many ways and situations—for example, the difference between how well two large retail stores fared during and after Superstorm Sandy. Fairway, a supermarket, and Ikea, the household goods supplier, occupy large buildings in the Red Hook section of Brooklyn and are situated within a stone's throw of the bay and one another. The Ikea store, which opened in 2008, was built to be resilient. It was constructed on pilings, with a ground floor garage and the show floors and inventory on the upper floors; the building also has an emergency generator. When the storm hit, the Ikea building was not unaffected. Its elevators ceased to function when city power went out, some of its outside benches were torn away, and the parking lot was awash with floodwater and debris. But the store recovered quickly and reopened for business after the storm, and soon after it became headquarters for FEMA representatives as well as a neighborhood hub for the distribution of food, clothing, and other supplies for the thousands of neighborhood residents affected by the flooding.[56]

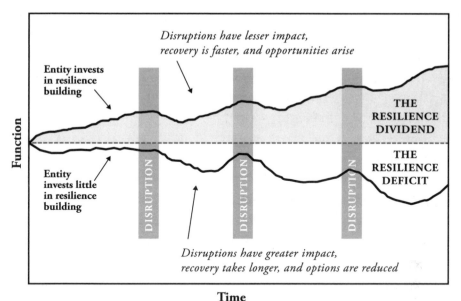

Figure C.1. The Resilience Dividend

Fairway, however, did business in a nineteenth-century warehouse building, which was seriously flooded in the storm. Fairway had to close its doors during the storm and did not reopen. It finally had to gut the building, renovate, and restock its entire inventory—a process that took four months. Fairway, a nearly $1 billion company, was able to survive the loss, although a smaller operation might well have failed. However, the hit was significant to the company as well as to the neighborhood, where it is the only full-service grocery store. Fairway had not made itself more resilient, especially necessary because it was in an old building.

Ikea, however, reaped the resilience dividend: its business was only briefly disrupted by the storm *and* it took advantage of a new opportunity—it strengthened its neighborhood connections by taking on a new and important role in the relief efforts. It can be difficult for a chain retailer to integrate itself into a community because ownership is distant, employees may not live in the area, and the company will have protocols for the way it engages with community activities. Ikea came into a different and improved relationship with its community, largely because of its resilience-building efforts. By contrast, Fairway lost business and lost its connection with the neighborhood during a critical time.[57] (A telling statistic: 25 percent of businesses do not reopen at all after a major disaster.[58])

Resilience can also pay a great dividend in noncrisis situations— that is, when we are living in the foreloop. It can, for example, create a competitive advantage for a company or a city. This is what happened in Pune, India, a city that has made a considerable investment in resilience building in the past several years. The city is highly aware of the chronic stresses and vulnerabilities that can disrupt the operations of large companies that do business in India, including interruptions to basic services such as electric power and transportation, as well as an unreliable supply of educated, committed workers. Pune has taken many actions to build its resilience, including improvements to its transportation and utility systems and the integration of government and citizen groups—and not as a direct result of an acute crisis or disaster. Its degree of social cohesion is high.

Pune realized the dividend on this investment in resilience when Deutsche Bank chose to locate a large operations center there rather than in any of the several other Indian cities it had considered. The bank's leaders could clearly see that it would benefit from Pune's approach to resilience building. Disruptions were less likely to occur and, if they did, would be less likely to lead to dysfunction and difficult recovery. For Pune, the resilience dividend manifests in the form of an increase in jobs, greater opportunities for partnerships, a boost to its international reputation, and an enhanced sense of place—as a city that is attractive to sophisticated, world-class business organizations.

The resilience dividend can bring benefits that accrue to multiple groups within a system—just as Ikea's dividend was shared with the neighborhood—and can result in wonderfully unexpected results.

The global brewing and beverage company SABMiller, for example, realized a resilience dividend for itself, the people of a community where it was located, and the local ecosystem, as well.

Water is essential to SABMiller's operations, and if supply is interrupted or the cost of supply varies, it can seriously affect its business. In Bogota, Colombia, SABMiller's brewery purchases water from a local utility and found that the cost of water was rising precipitously. What was happening? SABMiller discovered that the utility's cost of water treatment was going up because the amount of sediment in its river source was increasing as the result of the actions of upstream dairy farmers who were clearing land so their cows could graze. The process disrupted the river banks and freed soil, which traveled downstream. The situation could easily have led to a crisis—pressure on the utility and the potential loss of a major local business for Bogota.

SABMiller joined with the water utility and the Nature Conservancy to support and underwrite the dairy farmers in adopting new practices—specifically purchasing higher-producing cows, keeping smaller herds, and not disturbing vegetation on the riverbanks—in return for the farmers' commitment to preserve their natural areas for the long term. Through this investment in watershed protection, the water utility saved $4 million a year. SABMiller saved money on water purchase. The dairy farmers developed more efficient farms. The ecology of the river system was improved.

The potential for achieving a resilience dividend should be an important factor in the plans and investments we consider in the foreloop. Ideally, any action we take to build resilience will do more than just reduce a vulnerability or mitigate a threat—it will also bring benefit to multiple groups in the form of economic, social, and infrastructure gains. We saw how the investment in the Metro system in Medellin helped reduce violence, created new economic opportunities, increased social cohesion, and greatly enhanced the city's sense of itself as a model of resilience building for Latin America and beyond. The city has built its resilience and is now reaping the dividends.

The resilience dividend not only enables people and communities to rebound faster from disasters or deal with stresses; it spurs economic development, job creation, environmental sustainability, and social cohesion. It brings benefit to people, organizations, and communities when things are going right as well as when they go wrong.

WHAT WE CAN DO

Finally, I want to focus on the contributions that we—as individuals, as members or leaders of organizations, and as citizens of a community and a society—can make to the process of resilience building and achieving the resilience dividend. Everywhere I look, I see people and groups engaged in actions and activities, initiatives and programs, that build resilience in some way, although they may not think of or talk about it in that way. They do so in one or more of the multiple roles that we all play—as members of families, institutions and businesses, neighborhoods and communities, cultures and nations. They are champions of resilience, and I am constantly impressed by the impact they can have.

I think, for example, of Stefania, Adriana Restrepo's teenage daughter living in the San Javier neighborhood of Medellin. She got involved in a program designed to reduce the threat of violence in her city. She and other teens visited a prison in Medellin to meet with inmates and see for themselves just where a life of violence and crime would lead. Stefania was so affected by the potential to steer kids away from drug trafficking and street crime that she traveled to Brazil as an ambassador for the program to discuss how to dissuade kids from engaging in criminal activities. Stefania's engagement, and the work of the program, not only helps lessen the threat of youths getting involved with crime, it creates new opportunities for them and integrates them with groups across the city. An individual, a group, a program, a city, and a country—all are involved in resilience building.

John Peterson is an architect in San Francisco who built a successful private practice focused on what he thinks of as "design for design's sake." Then he won a project to design a neighborhood development that would include a grocery store, a library, and housing. He realized that the development would have an enormous impact on the neighborhood—how people interacted, how they got to work, their sense of the place—and he was awakened to the impact of the built environment on social cohesion and the effect of social cohesion on resilience. As a result, he founded a new organization, Public Architecture, devoted to design for the sake of social function. He went further, creating The 1% Program, the goal of which is to encourage designers and architects around the country to give at least 1 percent of their time—twenty hours a year—to pro bono work that will help "build cities and communities, or alter them, so that the design of the built environment can be a catalyst for social change," as Peterson puts it.[59] Today, more than 1,300 firms in the United States donate more than $50 million in design services every year. Peterson hopes to keep raising awareness, changing the conversation in the design community about how best to create designs that achieve resilient, social, and infrastructural outcomes, without the need for a disruption or crisis to catalyze thinking and drive action. An individual, a practice, and a whole discipline—contributing to our understanding and the development of resilience.

My colleague Peter Madonia and his family have owned a bakery in the Bronx for nearly a hundred years. When Peter first began running its operations, he quickly realized the lessons of diversity, adaptive capacity, and redundancy, installing a second (smaller) oven and training his staff so they could handle any one of the key tasks of the business in case of equipment failure or if an employee was unavailable. For Peter, resilience building was intuitive. "You run a business," he says, "and your livelihood depends on it. The livelihoods of the people who work for you depend on it, too. And you start to think, OK, what happens *if*?"[60] A family business whose output contributes to food security throughout the region: thinking about resilience.

I FIND THAT ONCE YOU EMBRACE the concepts of resilience, they become relevant in almost every aspect of your life. As your understanding increases, you reach a threshold and see what a disproportionately large role disruption plays in our lives. As I write, the worldwide news is filled with accounts of air and sea disasters, disease outbreaks, political unrest, cyber threats, food and energy insecurities, mass violence, business failure, and natural calamities. Many of these disruptions were foreseeable and could have been prevented or their effects reduced. What if we could reduce the incidence of disruption by even a fraction? We could shift our attention away from the immediate demands of responding to crisis and to the more positive efforts of readiness and revitalization.

Although some disruption can create positive change, how much *unintended* disruption do we need to add to our knowledge and build our resilience? Much less than we now live with.

What's more, intentional disruption—the kind that does not create crisis or disaster and that I am advocating for—is not a smooth or easy path. There will be plenty of struggle and anxiety as we deliberately take on the thorny challenges of new endeavors. Just ask the executives and engineers at BMW, who set themselves the challenge of developing—in just thirty-eight months—a super-lightweight, electric-powered vehicle that would meet social, political, and regulatory demands and would act as a standard for a whole new class of vehicles. It was a deliberate disruption taken in advance of the crisis that is surely coming as the demand for cars skyrockets in developing countries and the pressures on reducing emissions increase with equal urgency. According to the leader of the project, Carsten Breitfeld, there were "nights when we went to bed not sure how to go forward."[61]

Or ask Jeff Williams, manager of corporate environmental initiatives for Entergy, the big utility, about the process the company engaged in to develop a way to help ensure the economic viability of the communities the company serves along the Gulf Coast. To understand the vulnerabilities, risks, and assets of the communities they served throughout the region, Entergy partnered with America's Wetland Foundation to fund and execute a comprehensive study and analysis of some seventy-seven counties and eight hundred zip codes. They found that the region could, in the long-term, face losses of 2–3 percent of the area's $634 billion GDP from wind, sea-level rise, and storm surge alone, but that a $50 billion upfront investment in coastal infrastructure improvements of both the hard and soft variety—between now and 2050—could avert future losses of up to $135 billion.[62] Although the necessary initiatives would entail disruption, it would be deliberate, it would be known, and it would result in a resilience dividend: new opportunities and benefits.

They took the information to communities throughout four states, hosting Blue Ribbon Resilient Communities forums that were open to local leaders, community representatives, and concerned citizens. "All of the conversations we had with our communities," Williams says, "began by talking about shared values—enhanced prosperity, safety, quality of life."[63] Even so, he says, it was a "tough dialogue," because habits would have to change and livelihoods would be affected.

As a result of the panels, each of the eleven communities that participated developed its own set of values and prioritized solutions for the threats they faced, while the Wetlands Foundation released a summary report outlining five recommendations for building resilience along the Gulf Coast.[64] Developing the report, conducting the panels, and holding conversations with stakeholders across the region was a process of two years. "The hardest thing in the world," Williams concludes, "is to be proactive."

Any of the people I have featured in this book would agree. Dr. Desai in Surat, who, with her colleagues, seeks to get ahead of climate-related public health problems. Patrick Otellini and Rob Dudgeon and so many others in San Francisco who are working against time to make the city more resilient in the face of multiple threats—especially the earthquake that is inevitable. Juliana Rotich, who, through Uchaguzi, the information-mapping platform her company Ushahidi has developed, hopes to make elections safer and fairer worldwide.

And ask yourself: What have I done to build resilience for the people and places I care about? What more can I do?

There is no ultimate or end state of resilience. But, by working together to build resilience to the greatest degree possible, we can reduce our reliance on crisis as a driver of change and, instead, deliberately take the future into our own hands—for the well-being of our families, our communities, our cities, and, indeed, the planet we all share.

ACKNOWLEDGMENTS

This book is the culmination of the contributions of many people, not only to the book itself—an undertaking of some three years' duration—but also to the comprehensive work on resilience at The Rockefeller Foundation over the last decade. The book has my name on the cover, but it is truly the result of the efforts of hundreds of individuals and institutions, in many domains and disciplines, and in countries around the world. Individually, and through collaborations and partnerships, we are all working to deepen our understanding of resilience and to improve its practices and extend them into new fields and initiatives. There is still a great deal of research, analysis, and application to be done, however, so I am heartened that so many have chosen to join the effort of building resilience for ourselves, our institutions, our communities, and our societies. I am grateful for the knowledge, perspective, time, energy, and experience that I have been able to draw upon as we have developed this book. People have responded with incredible grace and enthusiasm to our requests for knowledge and assistance. Indeed, I feel that we have created a community around this endeavor, one that I hope will only gain strength and add new members as the book takes its place in the world. Here, I offer my heartfelt thanks and deep gratitude to those who made direct contributions to the book. In addition, I want to acknowledge the many people who have influenced resilience thinking and practice more generally but who are too numerous to name individually.

My thanks to:

THOSE WHO GENEROUSLY AGREED TO BE INTERVIEWED during the research phase of the book. Some two hundred people, in countries around the world, were interviewed by telephone or in person. Many others provided research materials and helpful context. The range of expertise and depth of knowledge was extraordinary. My research team spoke with people in academia, business and industry, government, faith-based institutions, nongovernmental organizations, the military, the arts, and philanthropy. We benefitted from the perspective of people at all levels, from senior-most leaders to volunteers working in the field for the first time. We heard from world-renowned experts in a wide range of disciplines and from ordinary people with deep understanding of resilience building from their experiences. Everyone added superb insights and stories, new perspectives and intriguing references, all of which added to our understanding and enriched the narrative.

To the following people, and their colleagues and institutions, I offer my thanks: Eric Abrahamson, President and Principal Historian, Vantage Point Historical Services, Inc.; Roger Anderson, PhD, Senior Research Scientist, Columbia University; Tim Armitage, Associate Director, Arup; Jainey Bavishi, Executive Director, Asia Pacific Disaster Risk Reduction and Resilience (APDR3) Network; Sofia Belay, Manager R4 Rural Resilience Initiative, Oxfam America; Dr. Mick Blowfield, Senior Visiting Research Fellow, Head of the Business and Sustainability Research at the Smith School of Enterprise and the Environment, University of Oxford; Dr. George Bonanno, Professor of Clinical Psychology, Teachers College, Columbia University; Gene Boniberger, Senior Vice President–Director of Operations, Rudin Management Co., Inc.; Aage Borchgrevink, writer and journalist, Oslo; Margot Brandenburg, Fellow at Nathan Cummings Foundation and former Senior Associate Director of The Rockefeller Foundation; Alastair Brown, Head of Sustainability, Land & Environmental Services, Glasgow City Council; Don Callahan, Head of Technology and Operations at Citi; Jenny Chung, Eighth-Grade Social Studies Teacher at Putnam Avenue Upper School in Cambridge, Massachusetts; Richard Concannon, Operations Manager of Rudin Management Co., Inc.; Jo da Silva, Director of Arup International Development; Benjamin de la Peña, Director, Community and National Strategy at John S. and James L. Knight Foundation and former Associate Director, The Rockefeller Foundation; Shaun Donovan, Director of the White House Office of Management and Budget and former Secretary of the US Department of Housing and Urban Development (HUD); Barry Dorn, MD, Associate Director of the National Preparedness Leadership Initiative and

Associate Director of the Program on Health Care Negotiation and Conflict Resolution, Harvard School of Public Health; Ken Feinberg, Director of One Fund Boston and September 11 Victim Compensation Fund and founder and Managing Partner of Feinberg Rozen LLP; Brian Fishman, Philanthropic Engineer at Palantir Technologies; Adam Frank, Palantir Technologies; Tom Frieden, MD, MPH, Director, US Centers for Disease Control and Prevention (CDC); John J. Gilbert IV, Rudin Management Co., Inc.; John Gilbert III, Executive Vice President and Chief Operating Officer of Rudin Management Co., Inc.; Janine Händel, CEO, the Roger Federer Foundation; Leslie Jacobs, founder of Educate Now!; Alex Kaplan, Vice President, Global Partnerships, Swiss Re; Alex Karp, PhD, CEO of Palantir Technologies; J. M. Kind, Senior Natural Resource Economist, Deltares, the Netherlands; Eric Klinenberg, PhD, Professor of Sociology and Director of the Institute for Public Knowledge at New York University; Michiel Kool, Executive Vice President, Safety, Environment, and Social Performance, Royal Dutch Shell; Mayor Mitch Landrieu, City of New Orleans; Laurie Leitch, PhD, Cofounder of Threshold GlobalWorks; Ky Luu, Executive Director, Disaster Resilience Leadership Academy, and Clinical Associate Professor, Tulane University; Kate Lydon, Public Sector Portfolio Director, IDEO; Kelly Mason, Manager, Global Communications and Public Affairs, Google; Eric McNulty, Director, Research and Professional Programs, National Preparedness Leadership Initiative, Harvard School of Public Health; Osamu Nagata, President and CEO, Toyota Motor Engineering and Manufacturing North America; Guy Nordenson, Partner, Guy Nordenson and Associates; Henk W. J. Ovink, Principal, Rebuild by Design, and Senior Advisor to former Secretary Shaun Donovan, HUD; Martyn Parker, Chair, Global Partnerships, Swiss Re; Governor Deval Patrick, Commonwealth of Massachusetts; Ann Patton, former Director of Project Impact Tulsa and founding Director of Tulsa's Citizen Corps, Medical Reserve Corps, and Tulsa Partners, Inc.; Josh Penn, Producer, *Beasts of the Southern Wild*; Henry Posner III, Chairman, Railroad Development Corporation; April Rinne, sharing economy and shareable cities expert, most recently Chief Strategy Officer, Collaborative Lab; Jonathan F. P. Rose, President, Jonathan Rose Companies; Michael Rudin, Vice President of Rudin Management Co., Inc.; William H. Saito, Chief Technology Officer of the Fukushima Nuclear Accident Independent Investigation Commission (NAIIC), President and CEO of InTecur, and Special Advisor to the Cabinet

Office for the Government of Japan; David Satterthwaite, former Deputy Director Private Sector Department, Oxfam America; Barry Scanlon, President and Cofounder, Witt Associates, and former business liaison and corporate outreach official for Project Impact; F. E. Schasfoort, Environmental Economist, Deltares, the Netherlands; Astrid Scholz, PhD, President of EcoTrust; Richard Schulze, founder, former CEO, and Chair, and Chair Emeritus of Best Buy Company, Inc.; Meryl Stone, Partnership Development Manager, Google Crisis Response; retired Army Brig. Gen. Loree Sutton, MD, Cofounder of Threshold GlobalWorks; Nancy Taylor, Senior Minister and CEO of the Old South Church in Boston; Mark Tercek, President and CEO of the Nature Conservancy; Molly Turner, Director of Public Policy, Airbnb; Lawrence Vale, PhD, Ford Professor of Urban Design and Planning, Department of Urban Studies and Planning, Massachusetts Institute of Technology, and Director, Resilient Cities Housing Initiative; Brian Walker, PhD, Retirement Fellow, the Commonwealth Scientific and Industrial Research Organization (CSIRO) Ecosystem Sciences, Australia; and Daniel Zarrilli, PE, Director of Resiliency, Long-Term Planning and Sustainability, Office of the Mayor of New York City.

Below, I have grouped interviewees by cities and countries where field visits were made.

DELHI AND SURAT, INDIA

G. K. Bhat, Chair of TARU Leading Edge Private Limited; Madhav Chavan, Cofounder and CEO–President, Pratham; Lalit Dashora, TARU Leading Edge Private Limited; Dr. Vikas Desai, Technical Director of Urban Health and Climate Resilience Center in Surat; A. K. Gosain, PhD, Professor, Department of Civil Engineering, Indian Institute of Technology Delhi; Kavneet Kaur, Program Manager, Development Alternatives Group; Ashok Khosla, PhD, Founder, Development Alternatives Group; Mehul Patel, Consultant, TARU Leading Edge Private Limited; Sandhya Rao, PhD, Executive Director of Integrated Natural Resources Management (INRM) Consultants Pvt. Ltd.; Aromar Revi, Director of the Indian Institute for Human Settlements (IIHS); Saumyaranjan Sahoo, Research Associate, TARU Leading Edge Private Limited; Shailendra Sharma, Delhi Program Head, Pratham; Virendra Singh Shekhawat, Consultant, TARU Leading Edge Private Limited; Sunandan

Tiwari, Deputy Director of ICLEI—South Asia Secretariat; and Kamlesh Yagnik, President, Southern Gujarat Chamber of Commerce and Industry.

MEDELLIN, COLOMBIA

Mariano Norman Cavajal Guerrero, Guide in Comuna 13; Daniela Mejía Rios, Communications and Public Relations, Empresa de Transporte Masivo del Valle de Aburrá, Metro de Medellín Ltda; Braulio Eduardo Morera, Associate at the International Development Team, Arup; Eyleen Natalia Ospina, Consultant, Agencia de Cooperación e Inversión de Medellín y el Área Metropolitana (ACI); Catalina Echavarria Ramirez, Executive Director, Fundación Bancolombia; María José Ramirez, Consultant, ACI; Marinella Ramirez Gomez, Metro de Medellín Ltda; Adriana Restrepo, resident of Comuna 13; Ana Maria Ruiz Montoya, Consultant, ACI; Santiago Uribe, Chief Resilience Officer, City of Medellin; Ana Maria Villa Zapata, Consultant, ACI; Martin Zapata Roman, Translator and Guide; and the many people from San Javier, La Loma, and other communities in Medellin who shared their stories.

NAIROBI AND NAKURU, KENYA

Dr. Alex O. Awiti, Director, East African Institute of the Aga Khan University; Cary S. Farley, PhD, Chief of Party, Resilience, and Economic Growth in the Arid Lands–Accelerated Growth (REGAL-AG); Linda Kamau, Developer, Ushahidi; Irene Karanja, Executive Director, Muungano Support Trust (MuST); Josiah Mugambi, Executive Director, iHub; Irene Ngatia, Executive Director, VICDA, Kenya; Juliana Rotich, Executive Director, Ushahidi; Jane Weru, Executive Director of Akiba Mashinani Trust (AMT); Ronald Yona, Founder of Zetu Deals and Curator for Collaborative Lab–Kenya; Shack and Slum Dwellers International and Muungano wa Wanavijiji members and personnel, including Peter Chege, Gabriel Kabue, Pauline Manguru, Rashid Mutua, Joseph Muturi, Michael Njuguna, Wilberforce Onyango, John Te, Florence Wairimu, Joyce Wairimu, Mary Wanjira, Susan Wanjiru, Jason Warelu, and the many others who joined the conversations in Kambi Moto, Kiandutu, Kibera, Kosovo, Pipeline, Giwa Farm, Lemolo A, and beyond, including Peter Jenga, Florence Kitoni, Leonard Korgoren, Peter Mutunga, Jane

Nyambura, Paul Thingo, Julia Wacera, Anastasia Wairimu, Margaret Wangare, and Anderson.

NEW ORLEANS, LOUISIANA

Robin Barnes, Executive Vice President and Chief Operating Officer, Greater New Orleans, Inc.; Carol Bebelle, Cofounder and Executive Director, Ashé Cultural Arts Center; Michael J. Burns, Corporate/National Media Relations, Entergy Corporation; Gary Cecchine, PhD, Director, RAND Gulf States Policy Institute, Senior Natural Scientist; Anita Chandra, DrPH, Senior Policy Researcher and Director, Behavioral and Policy Sciences Department, RAND Corporation; Jan Gilbert, Artist; Harmon Greenblatt, Director, Arts Administration Program, the University of New Orleans; David Groves, PhD, Senior Policy Researcher, RAND Corporation; Cherice Harrison-Nelson, Educator, Artist, and Curator of the Mardi Gras Indian Hall of Fame; Jeffrey Hebert, Executive Director, New Orleans Redevelopment Authority (NORA); David Johnson, PhD, Associate Mathematician, RAND Corporation; Baty Landis, PhD, Executive Director, YAYA; Robert Lyall, Director, New Orleans Opera Association; Stephanie McKee, Artistic Director, Junebug Productions; Gene Meneray, Director, Artist Services, Arts Council of New Orleans; Tony Micocci, Assistant Director, Graduate Program in Arts Administration, the University of New Orleans; Carey Shea, Executive Director, Project Home Again; Martha Savitzky, Media Professional, Martha Savitzky Creative Direction; and Jeff Williams, Director, Climate Consulting, Entergy Corporation.

SAN FRANCISCO BAY AREA, CALIFORNIA

Michael D'Orazi, Fire Chief, Alameda, California; Tamsen Drew, Deputy Director, Legislative and Government Affairs, City and County of San Francisco; Rob Dudgeon, Deputy Director, Division of Emergency Services, San Francisco Department of Emergency Management (SF DEM); Adina Glickman, LCSW, Director, the Resilience Project, Stanford University; Daniel Homsey, Director of Neighborhood Resilience, Neighborhood Empowerment Network; Alicia Johnson, Resilience and Recovery Manager, SF DEM;

Wendy Kwong, Coordinator, EcoCenter; Alexander Nguyen, Assistant City Manager, Alameda, California; Patrick Otellini, Chief Resilience Officer, San Francisco; John Peterson, AIA, Founder and President of Public Architecture; Maria Raff, Fire Administration Supervisor, Alameda, California; and Francis Zamora, Public Information Officer, SF DEM.

Additionally, I would like to thank the many people who helped my team coordinate interviews and review manuscript segments, including Shin Aoyama, Toyota Motor North America, Inc.; Margie Boone, CDC; Melissa Bruns, HUD; Catalina Cano Zapata, Grupo Bancolombia; Christina Cue, HUD; Russell Eisenstat, TruePoint; Lina María Gómez Parra, ACI; Juli Hanscom, Office of Governor Deval Patrick; Julie Hamp, Toyota Motor North America, Inc.; Jen Hensley, Association for a Better New York; Naomi Kelly, City and County of San Francisco; Katsuhiko Koganei, Toyota Motor North America, Inc.; Christine Levesque, RLM Finsbury; Anand Mahindra, Mahindra & Mahindra; Natalie Manning, NORA; Michele Mansilla, Office of Governor Deval Patrick; Kelly Maze, Palantir Technologies; Jesse Mermell, Office of Governor Deval Patrick; Barbara Reynolds, PhD, CDC; Melanie Roussell, HUD; Michael J. Ruffin, Office of Mayor Mitch Landrieu; Sue Samuda, Citi; Brooke E. Smith, Office of Mayor Mitch Landrieu; Emily C. Strong, Office of Mayor Mitch Landrieu; Javier Dario Ramirez Arango, Metro de Medellín Ltda; Marissa Wan, Office of Governor Deval Patrick; Ariane Wiltse, Disaster Resilience Leadership Academy at Tulane University; and Malcolm Wolf, TruePoint.

THE GRANTEES OF THE ROCKEFELLER FOUNDATION whose work is proof of the importance of resilience building and of the reality of the resilience dividend. We are privileged to work with individuals, organizations, and groups around the world who, every day, do the work of building resilience through initiatives of many kinds. The goals of The Rockefeller Foundation can only be realized through the diligence and innovation of the thousands of people who commit themselves to helping others confront the issues and vulnerabilities that are described in this book, including the challenges of urbanization and climate change, food security, health and nutrition, infrastructure development, governance and leadership, and so much more.

I speak for The Rockefeller Foundation when I sincerely acknowledge the Mayors and Chief Resilience Officers in the 100 Resilient Cities network; the 2013 100 Resilient Cities Centennial Challenge Judges: President Bill Clinton, President Olusegun Obasanjo, Ricky Burdett, Dr. Peter Head, Dr. Helene Gayle, Anshu Jain, and David Miller; Felix Rohatyn and all the members of the NYS2100 Commission; Michael Bloomberg, former Mayor of New York City; Andrew Cuomo, Governor of New York State; Shaun Donovan and his team at HUD; the teams that participated in Rebuild by Design; Raj Shah, Administrator of USAID and his team; our partners in the Asian Cities Climate Change Resilience Network (ACCCRN), including Mercy Corps, ICLEI, Verulam Associates, Intellcap, ADPC, APCO, IIED, ISET and IC-CCAD; my former colleagues who worked in New Orleans: Darren Walker and Nick Turner; and the team at Arup.

THE STAFF AT THE ROCKEFELLER ARCHIVE CENTER for their superb research skills. The Rockefeller Archive Center is an extraordinary repository of documents that pertain to The Rockefeller Foundation, the Rockefeller family, other Rockefeller philanthropic endeavors, and many other foundations, nonprofit organizations, and individuals. The staff of the Archive Center provided valuable support to the research team.

ALL MY WONDERFUL COLLEAGUES AT THE ROCKEFELLER Foundation for advancing the thinking and action on resilience globally. I am honored to work with a staff of incredibly knowledgeable, experienced, committed, and engaged people who hail from a wide variety of backgrounds and experiences. In our headquarters in New York and offices around the world, we do our best to embody the characteristics of resilience in our culture and processes. My thanks and grateful recognition go to the individuals and teams whose work has inspired and provided material cited in the book: Tara Acharya, Amy Armstrong, Jose Baptista, Michael Berkowitz, Pallavi Bharadwaj, Mamadou Biteye, Maria Blair, Fred Boltz, Sundaa Bridget-Jones, Anna Brown, Samuel Carter, Paksupa Chanarporn, Michael Criscuolo, Ashvin Dayal, Julie De Guia, Ayishah Ferrer-Lang, Leah Flax, Lily Fu, C. D. Glin, Hunter Goldman, Kippy Joseph, Kimberly Junmookda, Nancy Kete, Betty Kibaara, Bryna Lipper, Peter Madonia, Saadia Madsbjerg, Robert Marten,

Zuhura Masiga, Kathryn Maughan, Elizabeth Mercer, Stefan Nachuk, Michael Odermatt, Kitima Praphandha, Alyssa Rhodes, Carmella Richards, Scott Rosenstein, Cristina Rumbaitis del Rio, Andrew Salkin, Natakorn Satienchayakorn, Aaron Spencer, Suman Sureshbabu, Michele Tall, John Thomas, Gary Toenniesssen, Edwin Torres, Fern Uennatornwaranggoon, and Maxwell Young.

My colleagues at The Rockefeller Foundation who provided invaluable support to the researching and writing of the book—I thank Jereme Bivins, Robert Bykofsky, Pam Foster, Jay Geneske, Laura Gordon, Heather Grady, Erica Guyer, Claudia Juech, Zia Khan, Kanitha Kongrukgreatiyos, Carey Meyers, Achieng' Otieno, Shari Patrick, Selina Patton, Erissa Scalera, and Iracel Rivero.

Thanks to Neill Coleman and Traci Carpenter in The Rockefeller Foundation Communications Office, who made me believe this book was doable and then worked to make it a reality.

The team in my office, who enthusiastically engaged with the research and publishing team and expertly supported me throughout the process. Thanks to Patrick Brennan, Louise Lopez, Joshua Murphy, Alexandria Phillips, and Keisha Senter.

The Board of Trustees of The Rockefeller Foundation not only encouraged the development of the book; they offered extremely valuable counsel and guidance along the way. As always, the Trustees asked probing questions and made incisive comments that immeasurably improved the book. My respectful appreciation to David Rockefeller Jr., Ann M. Fudge, Helene D. Gayle, Alice S. Huang, Martin L. Leibowitz, Yifei Li, Monica Lozano, Strive Masiyiwa, Diana Natalicio, Ngozi Okonjo-Iweala, Richard D. Parsons, John W. Rowe, and Ravi Venkatesan.

The publishing team who helped bring this book from initial concept to reality. To John Butman, who was my thought partner and research leader par excellence, and his great team at Idea Platforms, Inc.: Anna Weiss, Henry Butman, John De Lancey, and Patricia Lyons, for their research and development work, drafting and editing, and publishing support. Our publishers, who provided expert guidance and thoughtfully helped to shape the book and give it form: John Mahaney and his colleagues in the United States, including Jaime Leifer, Peter Osnos, Clive Priddle, Melissa Raymond, Melissa Veronesi, Carrie Watterson, and Susan Weinberg; and, in the United Kingdom, Andrew Franklin, Nick Sheerin, Anne-Marie Fitzgerald, Penny Daniel and Paul Forty. And thanks to our literary agent, Todd Shuster, and his colleagues at ZacharyShusterHarmsworth, for finding a good home for the book and seeing it through to completion.

Finally, thanks to my husband, Paul Verkuil, and son, Alex Niejelow, who constantly asked me tough questions about this work that continued to sharpen my thinking, who were always pointing out new and interesting ideas I should consider, and who lovingly enabled my personal resilience to grow under the stress of doing this book while fulfilling the demands of a complicated job. Their love and support provided my own resilience dividend.

NOTES

CHAPTER 1:
THE RESILIENCE FRAMEWORK

1. A crowd-sourced initiative sponsored by Citi, WSJ.com, and the Urban Land Institute.

2. Luis Fernando Suarez Velez, "Medellin Ciudad Resiliente" (100 Resilient Cities presentation), slide 6, provided by Agencia de Cooperación e Inversión de Medellín y el Área Metropolitana via e-mail on February 24, 2014.

3. Calculation based on 2012 New York City population estimate of 8.337 million: https://www.google.com/webhp?sourceid=chrome-instant &ion=1&espv=2&ie=UTF-8#q=new%20york%20city%20population &safe=off.

4. "Medellin Ciudad Resiliente."

5. All quotations from Martin Zapata Roman come from an interview conducted on January 31, 2014.

6. City of Medellin, Colombia, "Application for 100 Resilient Cities," The Rockefeller Foundation. Proprietary information of The Rockefeller Foundation's 100 Resilient Cities Initiative.

7. Shelley H. Carson and Ellen J. Langer, "Mindfulness and Self-Acceptance," *Journal of Rational-Emotive and Cognitive-Behavior Therapy* 24, no. 1 (2006): 29–43.

8. Ellen J. Langer, *Mindfulness,* Kindle ed. (Cambridge, MA: Da Capo Press, 1989), location 673.

9. Unless otherwise noted, all quotations from Daniel Homsey come from an interview conducted on January 14, 2014. This segment is primarily informed by that interview.

10. IRIN, "In-Depth: Kenya's Post-Election Crisis," January 7, 2008, http://www.irinnews.org/in-depth/76116/68/kenya-s-post-election-crisis.

11. Anand Giridharadas, "Africa's Gift to Silicon Valley: How to Track a Crisis," *New York Times,* March 13, 2010, http://www.nytimes.com /2010/03/14/weekinreview/14giridharadas.html?_r=0/.

12. Rhoda Omenya, *Uchaguzi Kenya 2013 Monitoring & Evaluation,* iHub Research, http://www.ihub.co.ke/ihubresearch/jb_UchaguziMEFinal Reportpdf2013-7-5-14-24-09.pdf.

13. Ibid., 10.

14. Bryan Walsh, "10 Years After the Great Blackout, the Grid Is Stronger—but Vulnerable to Extreme Weather," *Time,* August 13, 2013, http://science.time.com/2013/08/13/ten-years-after-the-great-blackout-the -grid-is-stronger-but-vulnerable-to-extreme-weather/.

15. Unless otherwise noted, all quotations from Rudin executives and Roger Anderson come from an interview conducted on March 14, 2014.

16. Roger Anderson, "Di-BOSS: The World's First Digital Building Operating System," *State of the Planet: Blogs from the Earth Institute* (blog post), August 16, 2013, http://blogs.ei.columbia.edu/2013/08/16/38968/.

17. William H. Saito, "Weak Signals or Willful Failure to Perceive Them?" *William H. Saito Securtiy Blog* (blog post), March 6, 2013, http://saitohome.com /2013/03/06/weak-signals/.

18. "Lewiston, Maine Population: Census 2010 and 2000 Interactive Map, Demographics, Statistics, Quick Facts," CensusViewer, http:// censusviewer.com/city/ME/Lewiston.

19. National Civic League, "Lewiston, Maine," http://www.ncl.org /index.php?option=com_content&view=article&id=205:lewsiton&catid=49: success-stories-diversityinclusion&Itemid=189.

20. Jesse Ellison, "Lewiston, Maine, Revived by Somali Immigrants," *Newsweek,* January 16, 2009, updated March 13, 2010, http://www .newsweek.com/lewiston-maine-revived-somali-immigrants-78475.

21. Jonathan Riskind, "Lewiston Mayor Testifies on Immigrants' Impact," *Kennebec Journal,* July 26, 2011, http://www.kjonline.com/news /Lewiston-mayor-testifies-on-immigrants-impact-.html.

22. Maggie Jones, "The New Yankees," *Mother Jones,* March/April 2004, http://www.motherjones.com/politics/2004/03/new-yankees.

23. Ellison, "Lewiston Revived."

24. Ibid.

25. National Civic League, "Lewiston."

26. Matthew L. Wald, "How N.Y.U. Stayed (Partly) Warm and Lighted," *New York Times* (blog post), November 5, 2012, http://green.blogs.nytimes

.com/2012/11/05/how-n-y-u-stayed-partly-warm-and-lighted/?_php
=true&_type=blogs&_r=0.

27. Jesse Hardman, "Radio in Chile: Voice of Recovery," *Dart Center for Journalism and Trauma,* May 4, 2010, http://dartcenter.org/content /it-has-to-be-radio-community-broadcasters-respond-to-chile-quake# .U2OiYqLiiKg.

28. Arup, "City Resilience Framework," The Rockefeller Foundation, April 2014, http://www.rockefellerfoundation.org/uploads/files/0bb537c0 -d872-467f-9470-b20f57c32488.pdf.

29. Lululemon Athletica, "Black Luon Pants Shortage Expected," March 18, 2013, http://investor.lululemon.com/releasedetail.cfm?Release ID=749315; Jonathan Stempel and Joseph Ax, "Update 3—Lululemon Prevails in Lawsuits over Yoga Pants Recall," Reuters, April 4, 2014, http:// www.reuters.com/article/2014/04/04/lululemon-lawsuit-yogapants -idUSL1N0MW0Q220140404.

30. EDGAR Online, "Lululemon Athletica Inc.," United States Securities and Exchange Commission, March 20, 2013, http://files.shareholder.com /downloads/LULU/3190377536x0x677637/64A2CB6B-0B78-41FD -A536-B99C8245F022/2012_Annual_Report.pdf.

31. Suzanne Kapner, "Lululemon's Problem Might Just Be Sell-Through, Not See-Through," *Corporate Intelligence* (blog post), *Wall Street Journal,* March 26, 2014, http://blogs.wsj.com/corporate-intelligence/2014/03/26 /lululemons-problem-might-just-be-sell-through-not-see-through/.

32. Andria Cheng, "Retailers' Top Worries in 2014: Interest Rates, Security Breaches, Minimum Wage," *Wall Street Journal,* May 16, 2014, http://online.wsj.com/news/articles/SB10001424052702304547704579566 233927962334.

33. Unless otherwise noted, all quotations from Tom Frieden come from an interview conducted on November 22, 2013.

34. Louis S. Thompson, "A Vision for Railways in 2050" (International Transport Forum, 2010), http://www.internationaltransportforum.org/pub/ pdf/10FP04.pdf, 7.

35. This section is informed by an interview with Henry Posner III, chairman of Railroad Development Corporation, conducted on July 22, 2014.

36. Union des Industries Ferroviaires Européennes (UNIFE), "A Unique Signalling System for Europe: The Long Journey to an Interoperable Railway

System," www.ertms.net/wp-content/uploads/2013/09/ertms-facts-sheet-9-a-unique-signalling-system-for-europe.pdf.

37. The European Commission Directorate-General for Energy and Transport, *Modern Rail, Modern Europe* (Luxembourg: Office for Official Publications of the European Communities, 2008), http://ec.europa.eu/transport/media/publications/doc/modern_rail_en.pdf, 7; Siemens, "Technical and Administrative Barriers for Rail Traffic," http://www.mobility.siemens.com/mobility/global/en/interurban-mobility/rail-solutions/locomotives/vectron/boundlessness/technical-barriers/pages/technical-barriers.aspx; UNIFE, "A Unique Signalling System for Europe."

38. Unless otherwise noted, all quotations from Tim Armitage come from an interview conducted on July 23, 2014.

39. *Railway Safety Performance in the European Union* (European Railway Agency, 2014), http://www.era.europa.eu/Document-Register/Documents/SPR2014.pdf, 15.

40. *Central European Floods 2013: A Retrospective*, Risk Nexus (Zurich Insurance Company Ltd, 2014), http://www.zurich.com/internet/main/sitecollectiondocuments/insight/risk-nexus-may-2014-central-european-floods-2013-en.pdf, 8.

41. "Deadly Floods Hit Germany and Central Europe," *Deutsche Welle*, February 6, 2013, http://www.dw.de/deadly-floods-hit-germany-and-central-europe/a-16854599.

42. *Central European Floods 2013*, 15.

43. *Transport Resilience Review: A Review of the Resilience of the Transport Network to Extreme Weather Events* (Department for Transport, July 2014), https://www.gov.uk/government/uploads/system/uploads/attachment_data/file/335115/transport-resilience-review-web.pdf.

44. Lynne Goulding and Marcus Morrell, *Future of Rail 2050* (Arup, July 2014), www.arup.com/~/media/Publications/Files/Publications/F/Arup_Future_of_Rail_2050.ashx, 5.

45. Ibid., 5–7.

46. UNIFE, "ERTMS Levels: Different ETMS/ETCS Application Levels to Match Customers' Needs," demo.oxalis.be/unife/ertms/wp-content/uploads/2013/09/ertms-facts-sheet-3-ertms-levels.pdf.

47. Ibid.

48. UNIFE, "From Trucks to Trains: How ERTMS Helps Making Rail Freight More Competitive", www.ertms.net/wp-content/uploads/2014/07/ERTMS_Factsheet_1_From_trucks_to_trains.pdf; "ERTMS Benefits,"

The European Rail Traffic Management System, 2014, http://www.ertms. net/?page_id=44.

49. Marsha Walton, "Scientists: Sumatra Quake Longest Ever Recorded," *CNN*, May 20, 2005, http://edition.cnn.com/2005/TECH/science/05/19 /sumatra.quake/index.html; "Indonesia Quake Toll Jumps Again," *BBC News*, January 25, 2005, http://news.bbc.co.uk/2/hi/asia-pacific/4204385.stm.

50. Unless otherwise noted, all quotations from Cristina Rumbaitis del Rio come from an interview conducted on October 16, 2013.

51. Quotations from Anand Mahindra, as well as some background information, come from an interview with Anand Mahindra conducted by Malcolm Wolf, of TruePoint, on August 5, 2009, used with permission. The interview was originally the basis of the story told by Michael Beer, Russell Eisenstat, Nathaniel Foote, Tobias Fredberg, and Flemming Norrgren in *Higher Ambition: How Great Leaders Create Economic and Social Value* (Boston, MA: Harvard Business Review Press, 2011), 89–94.

52. Ada Louise Huxtable, "Why One Remained Standing," *Wall Street Journal*, May 10, 2011, http://online.wsj.com/news/articles/SB1000142405 27487038593045763052436671190 26.

53. Ibid.

54. Ibid.

55. National Police Agency of Japan, "Damage Situation and Police Countermeasures Associated with 2011 Tohoku District—off the Pacific Ocean Earthquake," June 10, 2014, http://www.npa.go.jp/archive/keibi /biki/higaijokyo_e.pdf.

56. Quotation from an interview with Richard M. Schulze, May 30, 2014. Material for the Best Buy story is also based on several interviews with Richard Schulze as well as material from his book, *Becoming the Best: A Journey of Passion, Purpose, and Perseverance* (privately published, 2011).

57. "The World's Billionaires: #789 Richard Schulze," *Forbes*, June 9, 2014, http://www.forbes.com/profile/richard-schulze/#.

58. Karen J. Leong, Christopher A. Airriess, Wei Li, Angela Chia-Chen Chen, and Verna M. Keith, "Resilient History and the Rebuilding of a Community: The Vietnamese American Community in New Orleans East," *Journal of American History* 94 (2007): 770–779.

59. Wei Li, Christopher A. Airriess, Angela Chia-Chen Chen, Karen J. Leong, and Verna Keith, "Katrina and Migration: Evacuation and Return by African Americans and Vietnamese Americans in an Eastern New Orleans Suburb," *Professional Geographer* 62, no. 1 (2009): 103–118.

60. Lung Vu, Mark J. VanLandingham, Mai Do, and Carl L. Bankston III, "Evacuation and Return of Vietnamese New Orleanians Affected by Hurricane Katrina," *Organization & Environment*, 22 no. 4 (2009): 422–436.

61. Li et al., "Katrina and Migration," 112.

62. Vu et al., "Evacuation and Return," 427.

63. Cain Burdeau, "Last FEMA Trailer Leaves New Orleans, Home to More Than 23,000 of the Shelters After Katrina," *Star Tribune,* February 15, 2012, http://www.startribune.com/nation/139400188.html.

64. Lance Hill, "The Miracle of Versailles: New Orleans Community Rebuilds," *Organización Auténtica,* January 17, 2005, http://www.autentico.org/oa09808.php; Eric Tang, "A Gulf Unites Us: The Vietnamese Americans of Black New Orleans East," *American Quarterly* 63, no. 1 (2011): 117–149.

65. Hill, "The Miracle of Versailles."

66. Li et al., "Katrina and Migration," 107.

67. Tang, "A Gulf Unites Us," 124.

68. Li et al., "Katrina and Migration," 107.

CHAPTER 2: A MINDSET

1. Brian Walker and David Salt, *Resilience Thinking* (Washington, DC: Island Press, 2006), xiii.

2. Harvard University, "Mission," *Harvard Forest,* http://harvardforest.fas.harvard.edu/mission.

3. Conversations with Brian Walker at Bellagio, November 25–26, 2013.

4. Walker and Salt, *Resilience Thinking,* xiii.

5. Unless otherwise noted, all quotations from Jo da Silva come from an interview conducted on November 20, 2013.

6. Unless otherwise noted, all quotations from George Bonanno come from an interview conducted on October 15, 2013.

7. Martin E. P. Seligman, "Building Resilience," *Harvard Business Review*, April 2011, http://hbr.org/2011/04/building-resilience/ar/pr.

8. Ibid.

9. Ibid.

10. Jay W. Forrester, *Urban Dynamics* (Cambridge, MA: Massachusetts Institute of Technology Press, 1969).

11. Donella Meadows, *Thinking in Systems: A Primer,* Kindle ed. (White River Junction, VT: Chelsea Green, 2009), 462.

12. Forrester, *Urban Dynamics,* 25.

13. Ibid., 9.

14. Ibid.

15. Ibid.

16. Ibid., 10.

17. C. S. Holling, "Resilience and Stability of Ecological Systems," *Annual Review of Ecology and Systematics* 4 (1973): 1–23, http://www.jstor .org/stable/2096802.

18. Ibid., 1.

19. Ibid., 14.

20. Ibid., 1.

21. Walker and Salt, *Resilience Thinking,* 53.

22. City of Christchurch, New Zealand, "Application for 100 Resilient Cities," The Rockefeller Foundation. Proprietary information of The Rockefeller Foundation's 100 Resilient Cities Initiative.

23. Joseph Schumpeter, *Capitalism, Socialism, and Democracy* (New York: Harper and Brothers, 1942), 81.

24. Peter Senge, *The Fifth Discipline: The Art and Practice of the Learning Organization* (New York: Doubleday, 1990), 7.

CHAPTER 3: A PRACTICE

1. "Mayor Menino Announces Urban Shield: Boston Simulated 24-Hour Public Safety Exercise" (press release), City of Boston, October 31, 2012, http://www.cityofboston.gov/news/default.aspx?id=5837.

2. Ibid.

3. Federal Emergency Management Agency (FEMA), "Boston Marathon Bombings: The Positive Effect of Planning and Preparation on Response," *US Department of Homeland Security Lessons Learned Information Sharing,* August 2, 2013, https://www.llis.dhs.gov/content/boston-marathon -bombings-positive-effects-planning-and-preparation-response-0.

4. FEMA, "Boston Marathon Bombings: Medical Response Activities at the Incident Site," *US Department of Homeland Security Lessons Learned Information Sharing,* July 10, 2013, https://www.llis.dhs.gov /content/boston-marathon-bombings-medical-response-activities -incident-site.

5. Ibid.

6. Ibid.

7. Ibid.

8. Unless otherwise noted, all quotations from Governor Deval Patrick come from an interview conducted on November 4, 2013.

9. FEMA, "Medical Response Activities."

10. FEMA, "Boston Marathon Bombings: Hospital Readiness and Response," *US Department of Homeland Security Lessons Learned Information Sharing*, August 23, 2013, https://www.llis.dhs.gov/sites/default/files /Boston%20Marathon%20Bombings%20Hospital%20Response.pdf.

11. FEMA, "Medical Response Activities."

12. Correspondence and interview with Eric McNulty and Barry Dorn, November 19, 2013. McNulty and Dorn, from Harvard University's National Leadership Preparedness Initiative, conducted extensive interviews with officials and first responders after the marathon bombings.

13. Leonard Roy Frank, ed., *Quotationary* (New York: Random House, 2001), 472.

14. Jon Keller, "Boston Sees Surge in Tourism Since Marathon Bombing," *CBS Boston*, July 3, 2013, http://boston.cbslocal.com/2013/07 /03/boston-sees-surge-in-tourism-since-marathon-bombing/.

15. "Interfaith Service for Bombing Victims in Boston," *C-SPAN*, April 18, 2013, http://www.c-span.org/video/?312222-1/interfaith-service -bombing-victims-boston.

16. Unless otherwise noted, all quotations from Nancy Taylor come from an interview conducted on November 14, 2013.

17. Jason Mastrodonato, "Boston Stronger: Sox Pay Tribute to Victims," *MLB.com*, April 20, 2013, http://boston.redsox.mlb.com/news/article .jsp?ymd=20130420&content_id=45300030&c_id=bos.

18. David Filipov, "A Pause to Pay Tribute, to Weep at Marathon Finish Line," *Boston Globe*, November 3, 2013, http://www.bostonglobe .com/metro/2013/11/02/finish-line-fans-gathered-celebrate-red-sox -and-remember-marathon/ycEyTbgpZAiVIWF3KvhAWO/story.html.

19. Giuseppe Macri, "Creepy Autonomous AI CCTV Surveillance Network Watches All of Boston," *Daily Caller*, April 17, 2014, http:// dailycaller.com/2014/04/17/creepy-autonomous-surveillance-network -watches-all-of-boston/.

20. Katharine Q. Seelye, "For Boston, a New Beginning After a Safe Ending to Its Marathon," *New York Times*, April 21, 2014, http://www .nytimes.com/2014/04/22/us/boston-marathon.html.

21. Garrett Hardin, "The Tragedy of the Commons," *Science* 162 (1968): 1243–1248, http://www.sciencemag.org/content/162/3859/1243.full.

22. Unless otherwise noted, all quotations from Rob Dudgeon come from two interviews, conducted on November 20, 2013, and January 14, 2014.

23. "San Francisco City and County," *Bay Area Census,* http://www.bayareacensus.ca.gov/counties/SanFranciscoCounty70.htm.

24. Jason E. Eberhart-Phillips, Theresa M. Saunders, Amy L. Robinson, Douglas L. Hatch, and R. Gibson Parrish, "Profile of Mortality from the 1989 Loma Prieta Earthquake Using Coroner and Medical Examiner Reports," *Disasters* 18, no. 2 (June 1994): 160–170, http://onlinelibrary.wiley.com/doi/10.1111/j.1467-7717.1994.tb00298.x/abstract;jsessionid=C2F7AA9075941BF35A68D19211C9883D.f04t01.

25. Patricia Grossi and Robert Muir-Wood, "The 1906 San Francisco Earthquake and Fire: Perspectives on a Modern Super Cat," *Risk Management Solutions*, 2006.

CHAPTER 4: DISRUPTION

1. Jeremy Egner, "A Bit of Britain Where the Sun Still Never Sets," *New York Times,* January 3, 2013, http://www.nytimes.com/2013/01/06/arts/television/downton-abbey-reaches-around-the-world.html?_r=0.

2. United Nations (UN) Department of Economic and Social Affairs, Population Division, *World Population Prospects: The 2012 Revision* (New York: United Nations, 2013), http://esa.un.org/wpp/.

3. Adam Cole, "Visualizing How a Population Grows to 7 Billion," *NPR,* October 31, 2011, http://www.npr.org/2011/10/31/141816460/visualizing-how-a-population-grows-to-7-billion.

4. UN, *World Population Prospects.*

5. World Health Organization (WHO), *Global Health Observatory (GHO): Urban Population Growth,* http://www.who.int/gho/urban_health/situation_trends/urban_population_growth_text/en/.

6. Claire Provost, "Nigeria Expected to Have Larger Population Than US by 2050," *Guardian,* June 13, 2013, http://www.theguardian.com/global-development/2013/jun/13/nigeria-larger-population-us-2050.

7. This segment is informed by an interview with Ashvin Dayal conducted on September 10, 2013.

8. Asian Cities Climate Change Resilience Network (ACCCRN), *ACCCRN City Projects* (Bangkok: The Rockefeller Foundation, May 2013),

http://www.rockefellerfoundation.org/uploads/files/8ff925b8-2254-4b71
-a7fb-6082464b844e-acccrn-cities.pdf.

9. UN Department of Economic and Social Affairs, Population Division, *World Urbanization Prospects: The 2011 Revision: Highlights* (New York: United Nations, March 2012), http://esa.un.org/unup/pdf/WUP2011 _Highlights.pdf.

10. Arthur C. Nelson, "Toward a New Metropolis: The Opportunity to Rebuild America," Brookings Institution, December 2004, http://www .brookings.edu/~/media/research/files/reports/2004/12/metropolitan policy%20nelson/20041213_rebuildamerica.pdf.

11. These estimates are tallies of the recognized metropolitan area of the given city, and they also include populations living in the city's immediate suburbs. "Largest Cities of the World (by Metro Population)," *WorldAtlas,* 2012, http://www.worldatlas.com/citypops.htm.

12. NYS2100 Commission, *Recommendations to Improve the Strength and Resilience of the Empire State's Infrastructure,* 2013, http://www.governor .ny.gov/assets/documents/NYS2100.pdf, 119.

13. Medellín Departmento Administrativo de Planeación, *Perfil Sociodemográfico 2005–2015 Comuna 13 San Javier,* August 2013, http://www.medellin.gov.co/irj/go/km/docs/wpccontent/Sites/Subportal %20del%20Ciudadano/Planeaci%C3%B3n%20Municipal/Secciones /Indicadores%20y%20Estad%C3%ADsticas/Documentos/Proyecciones %20de%20poblaci%C3%B3n%202005%20-%202015/Perfil%20 Demografico%202005-2015%20Comuna%2013.pdf.

14. "Steepest Ski Resorts in the World," thread posted by mogulover, *Epicski,* April 26, 2013, http://www.epicski.com/t/120210/lightbox /post/1582650/id/118681.

15. Muchiri Karanja, "Myth Shattered: Kibera Numbers Fail to Add Up," *Daily Nation,* September 3, 2010, http://www.nation.co.ke/News /Kibera%20numbers%20fail%20to%20add%20up/-/1056/1003404 /-/13ga38xz/-/index.html.

16. Neil Espinova, Anita Pugliese, and Julie Ray, "381 Million Adults Worldwide Migrate Within Countries," Gallup, May 15, 2013, http://www .gallup.com/poll/162488/381-million-adults-worldwide-migrate-within -countries.aspx.

17. World Bank, *World Development Report 2010: Development and Climate Change,* 2010, http://siteresources.worldbank.org/INTWDR2010 /Resources/5287678-1226014527953/WDR10-Full-Text.pdf.

18. Gordon G. Chang, "China's Maoist Vision: A City of 260 Million People," *Forbes,* June 23, 2013, http://www.forbes.com/sites/gordonchang /2013/06/23/chinas-maoist-vision-a-city-of-260-million-people/.

19. World Bank, *World Development Report 2010,* 110.

20. This segment is informed by an interview with Aromar Revi on December 10, 2013.

21. Shirish Sankhe et al., McKinsey Global Institute, *India's Urban Awakening: Building Inclusive Cities, Sustaining Economic Growth, Executive Summary*, McKinsey & Company, April 2010, 12, http://www.mckinsey .com/insights/urbanization/urban_awakening_in_india.

22. Intergovernmental Panel on Climate Change (IPCC), *Climate Change 2013: The Physical Science Basis: Summary for Policymakers* (Cambridge: Cambridge University Press, 2013), http://www.climatechange 2013.org/images/report/WG1AR5_SPM_FINAL.pdf. The Fifth Assessment Report (AR5) from the Intergovernmental Panel on Climate Change consists of three Working Group (WG) reports. In 2013, WG1 produced *Climate Change 2013: The Physical Science Basis,* which includes assessment and analysis of scientific research and observation into the physically changing global environment. In 2014, WG2 produced *Climate Change 2014: Impacts, Adaptation and Vulnerability,* which considers how climate change has impacted and will impact human populations, as well as how we might adapt. Also in 2014, WG3 produced *Climate Change 2014: Mitigation of Climate Change,* which assesses mitigative actions that governments and policy makers might take in the coming years. Both contributions of WG2 and WG3 based their assessments and recommendations on the data provided by WG1.

23. IPCC, *Physical Science Basis.*

24. US Global Change Research Program, "Overview: Climate Change Impacts in the United States," *US National Climate Assessment,* http://nca2014.globalchange.gov/highlights/overview/overview.

25. National Oceanic and Atmospheric Administration, "State of the Climate: Global Summary Information—May 2014," National Climatic Data Center, July 15, 2014, http://www.ncdc.noaa.gov/sotc/.

26. Center for Naval Analyses Military Advisory Board, *National Security and the Accelerating Risks of Climate Change* (Alexandria, VA: CNA Corporation, 2014), 2, 24.

27. World Bank, *World Development Report 2010.*

28. Sara Hoverter, *Adapting to Urban Heat: A Tool Kit for Local Governments* (Washington, DC: Georgetown Climate Center, August 2012).

29. IPCC, *Managing the Risks of Extreme Events and Disasters to Advance Climate Change Adaptation: Summary for Policy Makers* (Cambridge: Cambridge University Press, 2012), http://ipcc-wg2.gov/SREX/images/uploads/SREX-SPMbrochure_FINAL.pdf.

30. Jane E. Brody, "Too Hot to Handle," *Well* (blog), *New York Times,* June 23, 2014, http://well.blogs.nytimes.com/2014/06/23/too-hot-to-handle/?_php=true&_type=blogs&_php=true&_type=blogs&_r=1&.

31. "The European Heat-Wave of 2003 Caused Damages of $15 Billion in the Farming, Livestock and Forestry Industry from the Effects of Drought, Heat Stress and Fire," World Preservation Foundation, (blog post), March 31, 2010, http://www.worldpreservationfoundation.org/blog/climate/the-european-heat-wave-of-2003-caused-damages-of-15-billion-in-the-farming-livestock-and-forestry-industry-from-the-effects-of-drought-heat-stress-and-fire/#.Uw9DhPRdUqo.

32. J. M. Robine, S. L. Cheung, S. Le Roy, H. Van Oyen, and F. R. Herrmann, "Report on Excess Mortality in Europe During Summer 2003" (paper presented to the EU Community Action Programme for Public Health, under Grant Agreement 2005114, February 28, 2007).

33. Ibid.

34. Terry Devitt, "Forget Blizzards and Hurricanes, Heat Waves Are Deadliest," *University of Wisconsin–Madison News,* August 1, 2012, http://www.news.wisc.edu/20929.

35. Candy Sagon, "Heat Wave Threatens Older Americans," *AARP Bulletin,* July 21, 2011, http://www.aarp.org/health/conditions-treatments/info-07-2010/heat_wave_threatens_older_americans.html.

36. A. de Bono, G. Giuliana, S. Kluser, and P. Peduzzi, "Impacts of Summer 2003 Heat Wave in Europe," *United Nations Environment Programme,* March 2004, http://www.preventionweb.net/files/1145_ew heatwave.en.pdf.

37. Ibid.

38. IPCC, *Climate Change 2013.*

39. US Global Change Research Program, "Overview."

40. IPCC, *Climate Change 2013.*

41. US Global Change Research Program, "Overview."

42. Unless otherwise noted, all quotations from Guy Nordenson come from an interview conducted on November 7, 2013.

43. Benjamin Strauss and Robert Kopp, "Rising Seas, Vanishing Coastlines," *New York Times,* November 25, 2012, http://www.nytimes.com/2012/11/25/opinion/sunday/rising-seas-vanishing-coastlines.html?_r=0;

"What Could Disappear," *New York Times* (multimedia), http://www
.nytimes.com/interactive/2012/11/24/opinion/sunday/what-could
-disappear.html?ref=sunday.

44. Michael Kimmelman, "Going with the Flow," *New York Times,*
February 13, 2013, http://www.nytimes.com/2013/02/17/arts/design
/flood-control-in-the-netherlands-now-allows-sea-water-in.html.

45. World Bank, *World Development Report 2010,* 91.

46. National Oceanic and Atmospheric Administration, "The U.S.
Population Living at the Coast," *State of the Coast,* March 14, 2013,
http://stateofthecoast.noaa.gov/population/welcome.html.

47. US Global Change Research Program, "Overview."

48. US Environmental Protection Agency, "Future Precipitation and
Storm Events," *Future Climate Change,* http://www.epa.gov/climatechange
/science/future.html#Precipitation.

49. Thomas R. Knutson, John L. McBride, Johnny Chan, Kerry
Emanuel, Greg Holland, Chris Landsea, Isaac Held, James P. Kossin, A.
K. Srivastava, and Masato Sugi, "Tropical Cyclones and Climate Change,"
Nature Geoscience 3 (2010): 157–163, http://www.nature.com/ngeo/journal
/v3/n3/full/ngeo779.html.

50. National Hurricane Center, *Introduction to Storm Surge,* http://www
.nhc.noaa.gov/surge/surge_intro.pdf.

51. IPCC, *Climate Change 2007: Work Group II: Impacts, Adaptation,
and Vulnerability: 3.4.3 Floods and Droughts,* 2007, http://www.ipcc.ch
/publications_and_data/ar4/wg2/en/ch3s3-4-3.html.

52. IPCC, *Managing the Risks,* 2012.

53. US Department of Agriculture, "U.S. Drought 2012: Farm and
Food Impacts," http://www.ers.usda.gov/topics/in-the-news/us-drought
-2012-farm-and-food-impacts#.Uw9gjfRdUqo.

54. World Bank, "Severe Droughts Drive Food Prices Higher, Threatening
the Poor" (press release), August 30, 2012, http://www.worldbank.org/en/news
/press-release/2012/08/30/severe-droughts-drive-food-prices-higher
-threatening-poor.

55. World Food Programme, "Sahel Crisis: 8 Questions Answered,"
http://www.wfp.org/stories/sahel-crisis-8-questions-answered; Matthew
Newsome, "Sahel Food Crisis Overshadowed by Regional Conflict," *Inter
Press Service,* March 28, 2014, http://www.ipsnews.net/2014/03/sahel-food
-crisis-overshadowed-regional-conflict/.

56. Thomas L. Friedman, "Wikileaks, Drought, and Syria," *New York Times,* January 21, 2014, http://www.nytimes.com/2014/01/22/opinion /friedman-wikileaks-drought-and-syria.html.

57. Ibid.

58. Barbara Surk, "Death Toll in Syria's War Tops 160,000: Activists," *Associated Press* on *Huffington Post,* May 19, 2014, http://www .huffingtonpost.com/2014/05/19/syria-war-death-toll_n_5353021.html.

59. Xan Rice, "Kenya Evicts Thousands of Forest Squatters in Attempt to Save Rift Valley," *Guardian,* November 18, 2009, http://www.the guardian.com/world/2009/nov/18/kenya-forest-squatters-evicted.

60. Amnesty International, *Kenya: Nowhere to Go; Forced Evictions in Mau Forest* (briefing paper), May 2007, http://www.amnesty.org/en/library /asset/AFR32/006/2007/en/64050754-d392-11dd-a329-2f46302a8cc6 /afr320062007en.pdf.

61. Unless otherwise noted, all quotations from Leonard Korgoren come from an interview conducted on December 18, 2013.

62. Unless otherwise noted, all quotations from Alex Awiti come from an interview conducted on December 19, 2013.

63. Megan Gambino, "Alfred W. Crosby on the Columbian Exchange," *Smithsonian,* October 4, 2011, http://www.smithsonianmag.com/history /alfred-w-crosby-on-the-columbian-exchange-98116477/?no-ist.

64. "The Second City of the Empire—19th Century," *Glasgow City Council,* https://glasgow.gov.uk/index.aspx?articleid=3475.

65. Ibid.

66. Gerry Mooney and Mike Danson, "Beyond 'Culture City:' Glasgow as a 'dual city'," in Transforming Cities: Contested Governance and New Spatial Divisions, ed. Nick Jewson and Susanne MacGregor (Abingdon, UK: Routledge, 1997), 78.

67. Clement Bezold, Craig Bettles, Claudia Juech, Evan Michelson, Jonathan Peck, and Katilyn Wilkins, "Foresight for Smart Globalization: Accelerating and Enhancing Pro-Poor Development Opportunities," Institute for Alternative Futures (report presented at The Rockefeller Foundation Bellagio Center, Bellagio, Italy, March 15–20, 2009), http://www.rockefeller foundation.org/uploads/files/cf248c9f-3d6c-434a-9d1e-7909bb4c1feb.pdf.

68. Barbara Starfield, "Is US Health Really the Best in the World?" *Journal of the American Medical Association* 284, no. 4 (2000): 483–485, http://www.drug-education.info/documents/iatrogenic.pdf.

69. "Heart Disease Health Center," WebMD, http://www.webmd.com /heart-disease/guide/heart-disease-risk-factors.

70. Centers for Disease Control and Prevention, "Obesity and Overweight," May 14, 2014, http://www.cdc.gov/nchs/fastats/overwt.htm.

71. Debra Bruno, "China Confronts Problem of Obesity," *Independent,* January 1, 2013, http://www.independent.co.uk/news/world/asia/china-confronts-problem-of-obesity-8434421.html.

72. "Global Burden of Diseases, Injuries, and Risk Factors Study 2013," *Lancet,* May 2, 2014, http://www.thelancet.com/themed/global-burden-of-disease.

73. Bill Gates, "The Deadliest Animal in the World," *Gatesnotes* (blog post), April 25, 2014, http://www.gatesnotes.com/Health/Most-Lethal-Animal-Mosquito-Week.

74. WHO, "WHO Statement on the Meeting of the International Health Regulations Emergency Committee Concerning the International Spread of Wild Poliovirus," May 5, 2014, http://www.who.int/mediacentre/news/statements/2014/polio-20140505/en/.

75. World Economic Forum, *Global Risks 2013: Eighth Edition* (Geneva, Switzerland: World Economic Forum, 2013), http://www.weforum.org/reports/global-risks-2013-eighth-edition.

76. Jennifer Duggan, "China's Air Pollution Blamed for 8-Year-Old's Lung-Cancer," *China's Choice* (blog), *Guardian,* http://www.theguardian.com/environment/chinas-choice/2013/nov/07/china-air-pollution-eight-year-old-cancer.

77. WHO, "7 Million Premature Deaths Annually Linked to Air Pollution" (news release), March 25, 2014, http://www.who.int/mediacentre/news/releases/2014/air-pollution/en/.

78. Susan S. Lang, "Water, Air and Soil Pollution Causes 40 Percent of Deaths Worldwide, Cornell Research Survey Finds," *Cornell Chronicle,* August 2, 2007, http://www.news.cornell.edu/stories/2007/08/pollution-causes-40-percent-deaths-worldwide-study-finds.

79. Unless otherwise noted, all quotations from Fred Boltz come from an interview conducted on June 12, 2014.

CHAPTER 5: HOW CRISIS BECOMES DISASTER

1. Samuel Henry Prince, *Catastrophe and Social Change: Based upon a Sociological Study of the Halifax Disaster* (New York: Longmans, Green, 1920), 27.

2. Ibid., 26–30.

3. Ibid., 31.

4. Havidan Rodríguez, Enrico L. Quarentelli, and Russel R. Dynes, eds., *Handbook of Disaster Research* (New York: Springer, 2007), xviii.

5. Prince, *Catastrophe and Social Change,* footnote p. 26.

6. Rebecca Solnit, *Paradise Built in Hell: The Extraordinary Communities That Arise in Disaster* (New York: Penguin, 2009), 74.

7. Stella Kim, Jason Hanna, and Ed Payne, "Ferry Disaster: Too Much Cargo Contributed to Sinking, Police Say," *CNN,* May 7, 2014, http://www .cnn.com/2014/05/06/world/asia/south-korea-ship-sinking/.

8. Losses reported are total losses (as opposed to insured losses). Munich Re, *Significant Natural Catastrophes 1980–2012,* March 2013, https://www .munichre.com/touch/site/touchnaturalhazards/get/documents_E16085 56616/mr/assetpool.shared/Documents/0_Corporate%20Website /_NatCatService/Significant_natural_catastrophes/2012/natcatservice _significant_eco_touch_en.pdf.

9. World Bank, *Building Resilience: Integrating Climate and Disaster Risk into Development,* 2013, http://documents.worldbank.org/curated /en/2013/11/18513435/building-resilience-integrating-climate-disaster -risk-development-world-bank-group-experience-vol-1-2-main-report.

10. Pascal Fletcher, "Haiti Reconstruction Cost May Near $14 Billion: IADB," *Reuters,* February 16, 2010, http://www.reuters.com /article/2010/02/16/us-quake-haiti-cost-idUSTRE61F43Z20100216.

11. Eduardo Porter, "Recession's True Cost Is Still Being Tallied," *New York Times,* January 21, 2014, http://www.nytimes.com/2014/01 /22/business/economy/the-cost-of-the-financial-crisis-is-still-being-tallied .html.

12. City of Tulsa, "Our City," https://www.cityoftulsa.org/our-city /our-city-overview.aspx.

13. US Census Bureau, "Oklahoma," http://www.census.gov/population /cencounts/ok190090.txt.

14. City of Tulsa, "Flooding History: Flood Control and Drainage," https://www.cityoftulsa.org/city-services/flood-control/flooding-history.aspx; "Inflation Calculator," *John Williams's Shadow Government Statistics,* http:// www.shadowstats.com/inflation_calculator.

15. City of Tulsa, "Flooding History."

16. Ibid.

17. Unless otherwise noted, all quotations from Ann Patton come from an interview conducted on October 11, 2013.

18. City of Tulsa, "Flooding History."

19. Ibid.

20. Ibid.

21. City of Tulsa, "Flood Control and Drainage," https://www.cityof tulsa.org/city-services/flood-control.aspx.

22. Ibid.

23. Alexandra Bech Gjørv et al., *NOU 2012: 14, Rapport Fra 22. Juli-Kommisjonen*, Norges Offentlige Utredninger (Oslo: Departementenes Servicesenter Informasjonsfor Valtning, August 13, 2012), http://www.regjeringen.no/pages/37994796/PDFS/NOU201220120014000DDDPDFS.pdf; Alexandra Bech Gjørv et al., *Report of the 22 July Commission: Preliminary English Version of Selected Chapters*, Norges Offentlige Utredninger (Oslo: Departementenes Servicesenter Informasjonsfor Valtning, August 13, 2012), http://www.regjeringen.no/smk/html/22julikommisjonen/22JULIKOMMISJONEN_NO/EN/CONTENT/DOWNLOAD/475/3689/VERSION/3/FILE/COMPLETE_COMBINED_ENGLISH_VERSI.PDF. This segment draws significantly on the 22 July Commission Report, which runs to nearly five hundred pages. It contains extensive information about the events of July 22 as well as background information on government, police, security and related issues. The report draws on extensive interviews, surveys, and other sources but, even with its thoroughness, the authors state there are uncertainties about exactly what happened and how. The report was written in Norwegian, with some sections translated into English. Other sections have been cited here from an unofficial translation, so may not match the original wording exactly. The English translation does not contain page numbers, but does have section numbers, which are noted when a citation is made. This segment also draws on the extensive international coverage of the attacks, several books including Aage Borchgrevink's "A Norwegian Tragedy", cited below, as well as two video documentaries, particularly the BBC production, "This World—Norway's Massacre" also cited below. There are many discrepancies from account to account. Where facts have been drawn from a specific source, they are noted. When facts have generally been agreed across a number of sources, they are not cited.

24. "This World — Norway's Massacre," BBC, YouTube video, uploaded as "BBC Documentary on Anders Behring Breivik" by om86xx, May 27, 2012, https://www.youtube.com/watch?v=xjVD0ztWaKA, 0:32.

25. United Nations Office on Drugs and Crime (UNODC) Research and Trend Analysis Branch, Division of Policy Analysis and Public Affairs,

Global Study on Homicide 2013: Trends, Contexts, Data (Vienna: United Nations publication, 2013), http://www.unodc.org/documents/gsh/pdfs/2014_GLOBAL_HOMICIDE_BOOK_web.pdf, 131.

26. Gjørv et al., *Report of the 22 July Commission: Preliminary English Version of Selected Chapters*, Chapter 1: Introduction with Conclusions, 8.

27. Helen Pidd, "Anders Behring Breivik Spent Years Training and Plotting for Massacre," *The Guardian*, August 24, 2012, http://www.theguardian.com/world/2012/aug/24/anders-behring-breivik-profile-oslo.

28. Åsne Seierstad, *One of Us: A Tale of Norway*, (London: Little Brown, 2015).

29. Gjørv et al., *NOU 2012: 14, Rapport Fra 22. Juli-Kommisjonen*, Section 15.5.

30. Unless otherwise noted, all quotations from Aage Borchgrevink come from an interview conducted on July 29, 2014.

31. "The Oslo Bombing," *The Breivik Timeline*, https://sites.google.com/site/breiviktimeline/timelines/the-oslo-bombing.

32. Aage Borchgrevink, *A Norwegian Tragedy: Anders Behring Breivik and the Massacre on Otøya* (Cambridge, England: Polity Press, 2013), 227.

33. Gjørv et al., *NOU 2012: 14, Rapport Fra 22. Juli-Kommisjonen*, Section 7.6.

34. Interview with John Ouchterlony conducted on July 17, 2014.

35. Gjørv et al., *Report of the 22 July Commission: Preliminary English Version of Selected Chapters*, Section 19, 15.

36. Ibid., Chapter 1: Introduction with Conclusions.

37. Ibid., Chapter 1: Introduction with Conclusions and Section 19.

38. Ibid., Chapter 1: Introduction with Conclusions and Section 19.

39. Ibid., Section 19.8.

40. Simon Hollis and Magnus Ekengren, *Country Study: Norway* (Analysis of Civil Security Systems in Europe (ANVIL), August 2013), http://anvil-project.net/wp-content/uploads/2014/01/Norway_v1.0.pdf, 25.

41. Kjetil Malkenes Hovland, "Norwegian Police Prepared for Terrorist Attack: Norway Beefs Up Security Following Warning of Syria-Linked Terror Attack," *Wall Street Journal*, July 25, 2014, http://online.wsj.com/articles/norwegian-police-prepared-for-terror-attack-1406302948.

42. Gjørv et al., Report of the 22 July Commission: Preliminary English Version of Selected Chapters, Chapter 1: Introduction with Conclusions.

43. "Norway Stands Strong: Oslo and Utoya Massacres A Year On," RT News, July 22, 2012, http://rt.com/news/norway-massacres-memorial-services-breivik-772/.

44. Borchgrevink refers to work described in an article by Dag Wollebæk published in the book *Tillit I Norge* (published in Norwegian; the title translates as "Trust in Norway" or "Confidence in Norway"). Helge Skirbekk and Harald Grimen, eds., *Tillit I Norge*, (Oslo: Res Publica, 2012).

45. Aage Borchgrevink, "Has Norway Reclaimed Utoya?," *Al Jazeera*, July 22, 2014, http://www.aljazeera.com/indepth/opinion/2014/07/utoya-massacre-201472195635499950.html.

CHAPTER 6: AWARENESS

1. United States Geological Survey (USGS), "2008 Bay Area Earthquake Probabilities," http://earthquake.usgs.gov/regional/nca/ucerf/images/2008 probabilities.pdf.

2. Thomas M. Brocher, Jack Boatwright, James J. Lienkaemper, Carol S. Prentice, David P. Schwartz, and Howard Bundock, "The Hayward Fault: Is It Due for a Repeat of the Powerful 1868 Earthquake?" (Menlo Park, CA: USGS, 2008), http://pubs.usgs.gov/fs/2008/3019/fs2008-3019.pdf.

3. Ibid.

4. Multidisciplinary Center for Earthquake Engineering Research, "Earthquake's Impact on Building Codes," http://mceer.buffalo.edu/1906 _Earthquake/industry_impacts/impact-building-codes.asp.

5. Brocher et al., "Hayward Fault."

6. Jack London, "The Story of an Eyewitness: The San Francisco Earthquake," *Collier's Magazine*, May 5, 1906. Made available by the Virtual Museum of the City of San Francisco, http://www.sfmuseum.net/hist5 /jlondon.html.

7. USGS, "The Great 1906 San Francisco Earthquake," *Earthquake Hazards Program*, http://earthquake.usgs.gov/regional/nca/1906/18april/.

8. Patricia Grossi and Robert Muir-Wood, "The 1906 San Francisco Earthquake and Fire: Perspectives on a Modern Super Cat," Risk Management Solutions, 2006, https://riskinc.com/Publications/1906 _SF_EQ.pdf.

9. London, "Story of an Eyewitness."

10. Renee Montagne, "Remembering the San Francisco Earthquake," *NPR*, April 11, 2006, http://www.npr.org/templates/story/story.php?storyId =5334411; Grossi and Wood, "1906 San Francisco Earthquake and Fire."

11. London, "Story of an Eyewitness."

12. A. C. Lawson and H. F. Reid, *The California Earthquake of April 18, 1906: Report of the State Earthquake Investigation Commission,* 2 vols., publication 87 (Washington, DC: Carnegie Institution of Washington, 1908).

13. Ibid., 2:13.

14. Ibid., 2:17–18.

15. USGS, "Historic Earthquakes: Santa Cruz Mountains (Loma Prieta), California," *Earthquake Hazards Program,* http://earthquake.usgs.gov/earth quakes/states/events/1989_10_18.php.

16. Unless otherwise noted, all quotations from Patrick Otellini come from an interview conducted on January 13, 2014.

17. City of San Francisco, "Application for 100 Resilient Cities," The Rockefeller Foundation. Proprietary information of The Rockefeller Foundation's 100 Resilient Cities Initiative.

18. Unless otherwise noted, all quotations from Ann Patton come from an interview conducted on October 11, 2013.

19. Unless otherwise noted, all quotations from Shaun Donovan come from an interview conducted on October 30, 2013.

20. Unless otherwise noted, all quotations from Fred Boltz come from an interview conducted on June 12, 2014.

21. Joan Lowy and Mike Baker, "AP Impact: Many US Bridges Old, Risky and Rundown," *AP The Big Story,* September 15, 2013, http://bigstory .ap.org/article/ap-impact-many-us-bridges-old-risky-and-rundown-0.

22. Jim Yardley, "Report on Deadly Factory Collapse in Bangladesh Finds Widespread Blame," *New York Times,* May 22, 2013, http://www.nytimes .com/2013/05/23/world/asia/report-on-bangladesh-building-collapse-finds -widespread-blame.html.

23. Mary C. Comerio, "Housing Repair and Reconstruction After Loma Prieta," *National Information Service for Earthquake Engineering* (Berkeley: University of California, December 9, 1997), http://nisee.berkeley.edu /loma_prieta/comerio.html.

24. Applied Technology Council (ATC), *Here Today—Here Tomorrow: The Road to Earthquake Resilience in San Francisco: A Community Action Plan for Seismic Safety,* San Francisco Department of Building Inspection, City and County of San Francisco, Under the Community Action Plan for Seismic Safety (CAPSS) Project, 2010.

25. Ibid.

26. Ibid.

27. Unless otherwise noted, all quotations from Michael Njuguna come from an interview conducted on December 15, 2014.

28. Jane Weru, "Community Federations and City Upgrading: The Work of Pamoja Trust and Muungano in Kenya," *Environment and Urbanization* 1, no. 1 (April 2004): 50, http://pubs.iied.org/pdfs/G00472.pdf.

29. Ibid., 52.

30. According to Alex Awiti, interviewed on December 19, 2013.

31. Cristina Rumbaitis del Rio, "Inclusive Blue Growth?" *Expiscor* (blog post), *WorldFish,* June 3, 2014, http://blog.worldfishcenter.org/2014/06/inclusive-blue-growth/.

32. Elizabeth Matthews, Jamie Bechtel, Easkey Britton, Karl Morrison, and Caleb McClennen, *A Gender Perspective on Securing Livelihoods and Nutrition in Fish-Dependent Coastal Communities* (report of the Wildlife Conservation Society to The Rockefeller Foundation, Bronx, NY, December 2012), 12, http://anewcourse.org/wp-content/uploads/2013/04/WCS-Gender-Fisheries-2012.pdf; Food and Agriculture Organization of the United Nations, *The State of World Fisheries and Aquaculture 2012* (Rome, 2012), 5, www.fao.org/docrep/016/i2727e/i2727e.pdf.

33. National Oceanographic and Atmospheric Administration (NOAA), "Atlantic Cod," *FishWatch,* http://www.fishwatch.gov/seafood_profiles/species/cod/species_pages/atlantic_cod.htm.

34. Angela Herring, "Better Science for Better Fisheries Management," *news@Northeastern,* http://www.northeastern.edu/news/2014/05/grabowski/.

35. Shelly Dawicki, "North Atlantic Fish Populations Shifting as Ocean Temperatures Warm" (research communication), Northeast Fisheries Science Center, 2009, http://www.nefsc.noaa.gov/press_release/2009/SciSpot/SS0916/.

36. Rowan Jacobson, "Something Is Seriously Wrong on the East Coast—and It's Killing All the Baby Puffins," *Mother Jones,* May/June 2014, http://www.motherjones.com/environment/2014/04/gulf-maine-puffin-climate-change.

37. Ibid.

38. Marjorie Mooney-Sues, "States Reach Consensus on Plans to Distribute New England Groundfish Disaster Funds," NOAA, May 28, 2014, http://www.nero.noaa.gov/mediacenter/2014/states_reach_consensus_on_plans_to_distribute_new_england_groundfish_disaster_funds.html.

39. Unless otherwise noted, all quotations from Cristina Rumbaitis del Rio come from an interview conducted on October 16, 2013.

CHAPTER 7: READINESS

1. San Francisco Department of Emergency Management, "2013 San Francisco Lifelines Interdependencies Tabletop Exercise," http://sfgsa.org /modules/showdocument.aspx?documentid=10952.

2. Unless otherwise noted, all quotations from Tom Frieden come from an interview conducted on November 22, 2013.

3. Centers for Disease Control and Prevention (CDC), "Updated CDC Estimates of 2009 H1N1 Influenza Cases, Hospitalizations and Deaths in the United States, April 2009–April 10, 2010," May 14, 2010, http://www .cdc.gov/h1n1flu/estimates_2009_h1n1.htm.

4. CDC, "First Global Estimates of 2009 H1N1 Pandemic Mortality Released by CDC-Led Collaboration," June 25, 2012, http://www.cdc.gov /flu/spotlights/pandemic-global-estimates.htm.

5. Unless otherwise noted, all quotations from Ky Luu come from an interview conducted on November 22, 2013.

6. Samuel Loewenberg, "Thirsty Cities: Nairobi's Fast Growing Slums Still Lack the Basics," *Pulitzer Center on Crisis Reporting*, October 31, 2012, http://pulitzercenter.org/reporting/kenya-thirsty-cities-nairobis-slums-food -security-malnutrition-aid-high-mortality.

7. AkiraChix, http://akirachix.com/index.html.

8. Unless otherwise noted, all quotations from Linda Kamau come from an interview conducted on December 19, 2013.

9. Unless otherwise noted, all quotations from Michiel Kool come from an interview conducted on February 25, 2014.

10. United States Environmental Protection Agency, "Ground Level Ozone," http://www.epa.gov/groundlevelozone/.

11. D. T. Max, "Green Is Good: The Nature Conservancy Wants to Persuade Big Business to Save the Environment," *New Yorker*, May 12, 2014, 56, http://www.newyorker.com/reporting/2014/05/12/140512fa _fact_max.

12. Unless otherwise noted, all quotations from Mark Tercek come from an interview conducted on June 11, 2014.

13. Unless otherwise noted, all quotations from Fred Boltz come from an interview conducted on June 12, 2014.

14. Robert W. Herdt, "The Life and Work of Norman Borlaug, Nobel Laureate" (speech delivered at College Station, Texas, January 14, 1998), http://www.rockefellerfoundation.org/uploads/files/40e4f901-005d-425b -bd36-7c5913a5ac4d-98borlaug.pdf.

15. "A Timeline of Dr. Norman Borlaug's Work Involving the Rockefeller Foundation," http://www.rockefellerfoundation.org/uploads/files/ff61301b -15d4-4783-8109-78e0e1b930ab-norman.pdf.

16. US Government's Global Hunger and Food Security Initiative, "Rice," Feed the Future, April 1, 2014, http://www.feedthefuture.gov/sector/rice.

17. International Rice Research Institute, "Seeds: Sharing Rice," http:// irri.org/our-work/seeds.

18. Judith Rodin, speech delivered at "Digital Technologies for 21st Century Democracy," Club de Madrid 2011 Annual Conference and Gala Dinner, New York, November 8–9, 2011, http://www.clubmadrid.org/2011 conference/?page_id=2131.

19. Corine Hegland, "An Africa like Iowa," *National Journal,* June 7, 2008, http://www.nationaljournal.com/magazine/an-africa-like-iowa -20080607; Judith Rodin, "Mobilizing the Next Green Revolution: Alleviating Poverty in the Age of Climate Change" (speech delivered at 2008 World Food Prize—Norman Borlaug International Symposium's Laureate Luncheon, October 17, 2008), http://www.rockefellerfoundation.org /uploads/files/05a4b4a6-25bd-4e40-b2a9-5d4bbf2f0bc2.pdf.

20. Unless otherwise noted, all quotations from Barry Scanlon come from an interview conducted on October 10, 2013.

21. Federal Emergency Management Agency, "Chapter 3: Mitigation," http://training.fema.gov/EMIWeb/downloads/Case%20Study%20 Chapter%203.doc.

22. "European Capitals of Culture," *European Commission,* http:// ec.europa.eu/culture/tools/actions/capitals-culture_en.htm.

23. Glasgow City Council, *Glasgow 1990: European City of Culture* (Documentation Centre on European Capitals of Culture), http://ecoc-doc-athens.eu/attachments/472_Glasgow%201990%20European%20City%20 0f%20Culture.pdf, 4.

24. John Myerscough, *Monitoring Glasgow 1990* (Report prepared for Glasgow City Council, Strathclyde Regional Council, and Scottish Enterprise, December 1991), http://www.understandingglasgow.com/ assets/0000/5038/MONITORING_GLASGOW_1990_vpdf.pdf, 53.

25. Myerscough, *Monitoring Glasgow 1990,* iii.

26. Glasgow City Council, *Glasgow 1990,* 4.

27. Derek Douglas, "Greater Glasgow 'But It Still Has Miles To Go,'" *Herald Scotland,* March 8, 1990, http://www.heraldscotland.com/sport/spl/ aberdeen/greater-glasgow-but-it-still-has-miles-to-go-1.587262.

28. Glasgow City Council—Cultural and Leisure Services, *Glasgow's Cultural Strategy* (Glasgow City Council, March 2006), http://www.glasgowlife.org.uk/policy-research/cultural-strategy/documents/glasgowsculturalstrategymaindoc.pdf, 7.

29. Myerscough, *Monitoring Glasgow 1990*, iii.

30. Ibid., iv.

31. Beatriz Garcia, "Learning from Glasgow 1990: Interrogating the European Culture Capital Title As Impulse for Cultural and Creative Development" (PowerPoint presented at the 2009, EU Year of Creativity and Innovation: Creative Cities Seminars, Amsterdam, September 23, 2009), http://www.liv.ac.uk/impacts08/Papers/BG%282009–09%29Amsterdam-Glasgow%26CommunityLegacy.pdf, slide 9.

32. "Factsheets," *Glasgow City Council*, https://www.glasgow.gov.uk/index.aspx?articleid=3014.

33. City of Glasgow, Scotland, "Application for 100 Resilient Cities," The Rockefeller Foundation. Proprietary information for The Rockefeller Foundation 100 Resilient Cities Initiative.

34. "Billy Connolly's History & Culture Of Glasgow: Made in Glasgow," YouTube video, uploaded by Glasgow20140C, November 19, 2012, https://www.youtube.com/watch?v=sJqB2bW336k.

CHAPTER 8: GETTING AHEAD OF THREATS

1. Applied Technology Council (ATC), *Here Today—Here Tomorrow: The Road to Earthquake Resilience in San Francisco: A Community Action Plan for Seismic Safety,* San Francisco Department of Building Inspection, City and County of San Francisco, Under the Community Action Plan for Seismic Safety (CAPSS) Project, 2010.

2. Metro de Medellin, "History," https://www.metrodemedellin.gov.co/index.php?option=com_content&view=article&id=53&Itemid=1&lang=en.

3. "Medellin Slum Gets Giant Outdoor Escalator," *Telegraph,* December 27, 2011, http://www.telegraph.co.uk/news/newstopics/howaboutthat/8978929/Medellin-slum-gets-giant-outdoor-escalator.html.

4. Conversations with San Javier residents in Medellin, January 29, 2014.

5. Tom Parfitt, "Georgian Woman Cuts off Web Access to Whole of Armenia," *Guardian,* April 6, 2011, http://www.theguardian.com/world/2011/apr/06/georgian-woman-cuts-web-access.

6. Carlotta Gall and James Glanz, "U.S. Promotes Network to Foil Digital Spying," *New York Times,* April 20, 2014, http://www.nytimes .com/2014/04/21/us/us-promotes-network-to-foil-digital-spying.html?_r=0.

7. Munich Re, "Significant Natural Catastrophes 2012," NatCatSERVICE, 2013, https://www.munichre.com/touch/site/touch naturalhazards/get/documents_E-382661941/mr/assetpool.shared /Documents/0_Corporate%20Website/_NatCatService/Annual_Statistics /2012/2012_mrnatcatservice_natural_disasters2012_ordered_by_eco _touch_en.pdf; Munich Re, "Loss Events in 2013," NatCatSERVICE, 2014, http://www.munichre.com/site/corporate/get/documents_ E113504877/mr/assetpool.shared/Documents/0_Corporate%20Website /6_Media%20Relations/Press%20Releases/2014/2014_01_07_munich _re_natural-catastrophes-2013-overview_en.pdf.

8. Jeff Masters, "Super Typhoon Haiyan: Strongest Landfalling Tropical Cyclone on Record," Weather Underground, November 7, 2013, http:// www.wunderground.com/blog/JeffMasters/super-typhoon-haiyan—strongest -landfalling-tropical-cyclone-on-recor.

9. United States Department of Commerce, Bureau of Economic Analysis, "Economic Growth Widespread Across Metropolitan Areas in 2012" (news release), September 17, 2013, http://www.bea.gov/newsreleases /regional/gdp_metro/2013/pdf/gdp_metro0913.pdf.

10. World Bank, "Data: Philippines," 2014, http://data.worldbank.org /country/philippines.

11. Unless otherwise noted, all quotations from Martyn Parker come from an interview conducted on October 10, 2013.

12. These data were provided by Martyn Parker and Alex Kaplan via e-mail correspondence. This information comes from Swiss Re Economic Research and Consulting.

13. "Hurricane Sandy Fast Facts," *CNN,* July 13, 2013, http://www.cnn .com/2013/07/13/world/americas/hurricane-sandy-fast-facts/.

14. RAND Corporation, *The Rising Cost of Flood Insurance: Effects on New York City After Hurricane Sandy* (research brief), 2013, http://www .rand.org/content/dam/rand/pubs/research_briefs/RB9700/RB9745 /RAND_RB9745.pdf.

15. Ibid., 4.

16. Ibid.

17. Ibid.

18. Oxfam America, *R4 Rural Resilience Initiative: Quarterly Report October–December 2013,* 4, http://www.oxfamamerica.org/static/media/files /R4-October-to-December-2013.pdf.

19. Ibid., 11.

20. Securities Industry and Financial Markets Association (SIFMA), "Cybersecurity Exercise: Quantum Dawn 2," http://www.sifma.org/services /bcp/cybersecurity-exercise--quantum-dawn-2/.

21. SIFMA, "SIFMA Announces Key Findings of Quantum Dawn 2" (press release), October 21, 2013, http://www.sifma.org/newsroom/2013 /sifma-announces-key-findings-of-quantum-dawn-2/.

22. Ibid.

23. Unless otherwise noted, all quotations from Don Callahan come from an interview conducted on January 10, 2014.

24. Paul Krugman, "A Can't-Do Government," op-ed, *New York Times,* September 2, 2005, http://www.nytimes.com/2005/09/02/opinion/02k rugman.html?_r=0.

25. Unless otherwise noted, all quotations from Barry Scanlon come from an interview conducted on October 10, 2013.

26. Committee on Homeland Security and Governmental Affairs, S. Rept. No. 109-322, *Hurricane Katrina: A Nation Still Unprepared* (2006), 110, http://www.gpo.gov/fdsys/pkg/CRPT-109srpt322/pdf/CRPT-109 srpt322.pdf.

27. Ibid., 112.

28. Select Bipartisan Committee to Investigate the Preparation for and Response to Hurricane Katrina, H. Rept. No. 109-377, *A Failure of Initiative: The Final Report of the Select Bipartisan Committee to Investigate the Preparation for and Response to Hurricane Katrina* (2006), 81, http:// katrina.house.gov/.

29. Ibid., 82.

30. Committee on Homeland Security, *Nation Still Unprepared,* 112.

31. Committee to Investigate the Preparation for and Response to Hurricane Katrina, *Failure of Initiative.*

32. Unless otherwise noted, all quotations from Alicia Johnson come from two interviews, conducted on November 20, 2013, and January 14, 2014.

33. Unless otherwise noted, all quotations from Kate Lydon come from an interview conducted on November 5, 2013.

34. San Francisco Department of Emergency Management, SF72, http://www.sf72.org/home.

CHAPTER 9: RESPONSIVENESS

1. Duarte Barbosa, *A Description of the Coasts of East Africa and Malabar: In the Beginning of the Sixteenth Century,* trans. Henry E. J. Stanley (London: T. Richards, 1866).

2. John F. Burns, "Thousands Flee Indian City in Deadly Plague Outbreak," *New York Times,* September 24, 1994, http://www.nytimes.com/1994/09/24/world/thousands-flee-indian-city-in-deadly-plague-outbreak.html.

3. Centers for Disease Control and Prevention (CDC), "Plague: Frequently Asked Questions," http://www.cdc.gov/plague/faq/.

4. Unless otherwise noted, all quotations from Vikas Desai come from an interview conducted on November 12, 2013.

5. Burns, "Thousands Flee Indian City in Deadly Plague Outbreak."

6. Unless otherwise noted, all quotations from Ashvin Dayal come from an interview conducted on September 10, 2013.

7. Institute for Social and Environmental Transition, *Asian Cities Climate Change Resilience Network (ACCCRN): Surat: Health Impact and Adaptation,* 2010, 82, http://www.acccrn.org/sites/default/files/documents/5%20Surat%20Health%20Sector%20Study.pdf.

8. The National Preparedness Leadership Initiative is a joint program of the Harvard School of Public Health and the Center for Public Leadership at Harvard's Kennedy School of Government. Unless otherwise noted, all quotations from Barry Dorn and Eric McNulty come from an interview conducted on November 19, 2013.

9. Dorn and McNulty acknowledge that Sigmund Freud was likely the first to use the term "basement" to refer to the deep subconscious. The terms "the basement" and "the toolbox" were introduced to them by their former colleague, Dr. Isaac Ashkenazi.

10. "Stress: The Fight or Flight Response," *Psychologist World,* http://www.psychologistworld.com/stress/fightflight.php.

11. Dorn and McNulty credit Daniel Goleman, author of *Emotional Intelligence,* for bringing the role of the amygdala to their attention.

12. Unless otherwise noted, all quotations from Alicia Johnson come from two interviews, conducted on November 20, 2013, and January 14, 2014.

13. Shelly E. Taylor, Laura Cousino Klein, Brian P. Lewis, Tara L. Gruenewald, Regan A. R. Gurung, and John A. Updegraff, "Behavioral Responses to Stress in Females: Tend-and-Befriend, Not Fight-or-Flight," *Psychological Review* 107, no. 3 (2000): 411–429.

14. This story is informed by an interview with Jenny Chung conducted on February 13, 2014. Unless otherwise noted, all quotations from Chung come from this interview.

15. Eric Klinenberg, "Adaptation: How Can Cities Be 'Climate-Proofed'?" *New Yorker,* January 7, 2013, 32.

16. Henry Anderson Lafler, "How the Army Worked to Save San Francisco: Being of a Supplementary Nature to 'How the Army Worked to Save San Francisco', Personal Narrative of the Acute and Active Commanding Officer, by Frederick Funston, Brig.-Gen., U.S.A," unpublished letter to the editor, *Argonaut,* 1906, Bancroft Library, University of California, Berkeley, http://content.cdlib.org/view?docId=hb7w1008 vb&brand=calisphere&doc.view=entire_text.

17. Ibid.

18. 9/11 Commission, *The 9/11 Commission Report: Final Report of the National Commission on Terrorist Attacks upon the United States* (New York: W. W. Norton, July 22, 2004), 396, http://www.9-11commission.gov /report/911Report.pdf.

19. Courtney Hutchison, "9/11 First Responders Plagued by Health Problems from Toxic Dust and Debris," *ABC News,* September 1, 2011, http://abcnews.go.com/Health/Wellness/911-responders-plagued-cancer -asthma-ptsd/story?id=14427512; *9/11 Commission Report,* 311.

20. Katharine Herrup, "Boatlifters: The Unknown Story of 9/11," Reuters (blog post), September 11, 2011, http://blogs.reuters.com/katharine -herrup/2011/09/09/boatlifters-the-unknown-story-of-911/; "Boatlift— An Untold Tale of 9/11 Resilience (HD Version)," YouTube video, posted by eyepopproductions on September 6, 2011, https://www.youtube.com /watch?v=18lsxFcDrjo.

21. Samuel Henry Prince, *Catastrophe and Social Change: Based upon a Sociological Study of the Halifax Disaster* (New York: Longmans, Green, 1920), 133.

22. Ibid., 60.

23. Ibid., 60–61.

24. "Hurricane Sandy: One Year Later," *NY Daily News,* October 26, 2013, http://www.nydailynews.com/new-york/hurricane-sandy/hurricane-sandy-year-breezy-point-article-1.1494576.

25. Graham T. Beck, "The Neighborhood Hurricane Sandy Couldn't Flood," *Next City,* February 13, 2014, http://nextcity.org/daily/entry/the-neighborhood-hurricane-sandy-couldnt-flood.

26. Rockaway Beach Surf Club, "About Us," http://www.rockawaybeachsurfclub.com/about-1/.

27. Laura Lorenzetti, "Cultural Hub on the Shore Plans Reopening Bash," *Crain's New York,* August 16, 2013, http://www.crainsnewyork.com/article/20130816/HOSPITALITY_TOURISM/130819915/cultural-hub-on-the-shore-plans-reopening-bash#.

28. Ibid.

29. Nick Corasaniti, "Waves Are Different After Sandy, and Some Surfers Say Better," *New York Times,* April 28, 2013, http://www.nytimes.com/2013/04/28/sports/after-sandy-surfers-return-to-rockaway-to-find-better-waves.html?_r=0.

30. Airbnb, "About Us," https://www.airbnb.com/about/about-us.

31. Unless otherwise noted, all quotations from Molly Turner come from an interview conducted on October 25, 2013.

32. Malcolm Jones, "What to Do with the Thousands Displaced by Hurricane Sandy?" *Daily Beast,* November 8, 2012, http://www.thedailybeast.com/articles/2012/11/08/what-to-do-with-the-thousands-displaced-by-hurricane-sandy.html.

33. Patrick McGeehan and Griff Palmer, "Displaced by Hurricane Sandy, and Living in Limbo," *New York Times,* December 6, 2013, http://www.nytimes.com/2013/12/07/nyregion/displaced-by-hurricane-sandy-and-living-in-limbo-instead-of-at-home.html?_r=0.

34. "Airbnb's Hurricane Sandy Story," YouTube video, posted by Airbnb on June 12, 2013, https://www.youtube.com/watch?v=LJgRwdIGyRs.

35. Simon Baker, "George Lawrence: A Giant in Kite Aerial Photography," http://robroy.dyndns.info/lawrence/kitelines94.html.

36. Ibid.

37. "Arkansas Tornado Damage Aerial Video 4-27-2014," YouTube video, posted by Brian Emfinger on April 27, 2014, https://www.youtube.com/watch?v=c7s2lzDtjew.

38. USAID, *Philippines—Typhoon Yolanda/Haiyan,* Fact Sheet #21, February 18, 2014, http://www.usaid.gov/sites/default/files/documents/1866/philippines_ty_fs21_02-18-2014.pdf.

39. Unless otherwise noted, all quotations from Brian Fishman come from an interview conducted on November 21, 2013.

40. "Iridium Everywhere: About Iridium," http://www.iridium.com/About.aspx.

41. Unless otherwise noted, all quotations from Meryl Stone come from an interview conducted on January 23, 2014.

CHAPTER 10: LEADERSHIP EMERGES

1. Samuel Henry Prince, *Catastrophe and Social Change: Based upon a Sociological Study of the Halifax Disaster* (New York: Longmans, Green, 1920), 60.

2. Ibid.

3. US Government Accountability Office (USGAO), *Coast Guard: Observations on the Preparation, Response, and Recovery Missions Related to Hurricane Katrina,* July 2006, 7, http://www.uscg.mil/history/docs/Katrina GAO06903.pdf.

4. US Coast Guard, *The U.S. Coast Guard & Hurricane Katrina: Historical Index,* http://www.uscg.mil/history/katrina/katrinaindex.asp.

5. USGAO, *Coast Guard.*

6. Ibid., 16–17.

7. Ibid., 3.

8. Ibid., 10–13.

9. Ibid.

10. Scott Price, *A Bright Light on the Darkest of Days: The U.S. Coast Guard's Response to Hurricane Katrina,* http://www.uscg.mil/history/katrina/docs/DarkestDay.pdf.

11. Sheri Fink, *Five Days at Memorial: Life and Death in a Storm Ravaged Hospital* (New York: Crown, 2013), 71.

12. Ibid.

13. Ibid., 348.

14. Unless otherwise noted, all quotations from Vikas Desai come from an interview conducted on November 12, 2013.

15. Raaj Desai, "Rebirth of a City," *Women's Feature Service*. Provided by G. K. Bhat on July 28, 2010.

16. Ibid.

17. TARU Leading Edge Private Limited and the Asian Cities Climate Change Resilience Network, *Surat City Resilience Strategy,* April 2011, http://acccrn.org/sites/default/files/documents/SuratCityResilienceStrategy _ACCCRN_01Apr2011_small_0.pdf. Unless otherwise noted, facts and figures related to Surat in the following segment can be found in this strategy booklet.

18. Dileep Mavalankar and Amit Kumar Srivastava, *Lessons from Massive Floods of 2006 in Surat City: A Framework for Application of MS/ OR Techniques to Improve Dam Management to Prevent Flood*, Indian Institute of Management working paper no. 2008-07-06, Adhedabad, India, July 2008, 6.

19. Unless otherwise noted, information about Surat's water management and resilience initiatives comes from interviews with G. K. Bhat conducted on April 30, 2014; Lalit Kumar Dashora, Dr. Sandhya Rao, and Professor A. K. Gosain on December 11, 2013; and Dr. Vikas Desai on December 12, 2013.

20. Interview with G. K. Bhat conducted on April 30, 2014.

21. Mavalankar and Srivastava, *Lessons from Massive Floods of 2006 in Surat City*, 8–10.

22. Ibid.

23. *People's Committee Report: 2006 Gujarat Floods: Dam Made Disasters,* SANDRP, July/August 2007, 1, http://sandrp.in/floods/People _Committee_Report_on_Gujarat_Flood_Aug07.PDF., 2.

24. Ibid., 9.

25. GoI-UNDP Disaster Risk Management Programme, United Nations Development Programme India, *Towards a Disaster Resilient Community in Gujarat,* August 2007, 8.

26. Ibid.

27. Ibid., 7, 10.

28. Mavalankar and Srivastava, *Lessons from Massive Floods of 2006 in Surat City,* 10.

29. The estimated death toll varies, from a low of 120 to the "People's Committee Report," which estimates 150 people died; the cited *New York*

Times article reports 400 by flood, then another 60 by disease. See Somini Sengupta, "Often Parched, India Struggles to Tap the Monsoon," *New York Times,* October 1, 2006, http://www.nytimes.com/2006/10/01 /world/asia/01india.html?pagewanted=all&_r=0 accessed.

30. *People's Committee Report.*

31. Mavalankar and Srivastava, *Lessons from Massive Floods of 2006 in Surat City,* 6–7.

32. The distinction between a single resilient leader and resilient leadership comes, in part, from the thinking of Loree Sutton, MD, a retired Army brigadier general, and Laurie Leitch, PhD, a psychotherapist, who have been working in the field of social and individual resilience through their organization Threshold GlobalWorks. Interview conducted October 1, 2013.

33. National Preparedness Leadership Initiative, "Meta-Leadership," Harvard Kennedy School of Government, http://npli.sph.harvard.edu/meta -leadership/.

34. Unless otherwise noted, all quotations from Governor Deval Patrick come from an interview conducted on November 4, 2013.

35. World Economic Forum, *Global Risks 2013: Eighth Edition,* 2013, http://www3.weforum.org/docs/WEF_GlobalRisks_Report_2013.pdf.

36. Unless otherwise noted, all quotations from Tom Frieden come from an interview conducted on November 22, 2013.

37. "Press Conference Updates Boston Marathon Explosions, Says FBI in Charge of Investigation," YouTube video, uploaded by PBS NewsHour, April 15, 2013, https://www.youtube.com/watch?v=ZBkPFRY9VTY.

38. Annie Colbert, "10 Touching Acts of Kindness at the Boston Marathon," *Mashable,* April 16, 2013, http://mashable.com/2013/04/16 /boston-marathon-acts-of-kindness/.

39. New York Times Editorial Board, "Fukushima's Continuing Tragedy," *New York Times,* March 11, 2014, http://www.nytimes.com/2014/03/12 /opinion/fukushimas-continuing-tragedy.html.

40. Martin Fackler, "Powerful Quake and Tsunami Devastate Northern Japan," *New York Times,* March 11, 2011, http://www.nytimes.com /2011/03/12/world/asia/12japan.html?pagewanted=all&_r=0.

41. Martin Fackler, "Report Finds Japan Underestimated Tsunami Danger," *New York Times,* June 1, 2011, http://www.nytimes.com/2011/06 /02/world/asia/02japan.html.

42. Fukushima Nuclear Accident Independent Investigation Commission (NAIIC), *The Official Report of The Fukushima Nuclear Accident Independent Investigation Commission: Executive Summary* (National Diet of Japan, 2012), 18, https://www.nirs.org/fukushima/naiic_report.pdf.

43. Justin McCurry, "Fukushima Boss Hailed as Hero Dies," *Guardian*, July 10, 2013, http://www.theguardian.com/world/2013/jul/10/fukushima -plant-boss-hero-dies.

44. Unless otherwise noted, all quotations from William Saito come from an interview conducted on January 8, 2014.

45. Unless otherwise noted, all data, quotations, and information for this story derive from Team Toyota "Road to Recovery: Toyota Associates Band Together in the Aftermath of the March 11 Disaster," (no. 50) July– September 2011, 3–16, as well as conversation with Toyota executives on Sunday, June 29, 2014.

46. "A Year After Quake, Japan's Auto Industry Recovers," *USA Today*, March 11, 2012, http://content.usatoday.com/communities/driveon /post/2012/03/a-year-after-japans-quake-nissan-thrives/1#.U7Vr4hbF_ww.

47. Ma Jie and Masatsugu Horie, "Toyota Beats GM in 2010 as 10 Million Vehicles Seen," *Bloomberg*, January 24, 2014, http://www.bloom berg.com/news/2014-01-23/toyota-beats-gm-vw-in-2013-car-sales-sees -3-growth-this-year.html.

48. The Rockefeller Foundation, *ACCCRN City Projects Catalogue: Asian Cities Climate Change Resilience Network*, August 2012, www.acccrn.org/sites /default/files/documents/ACCCRN%20Cities%20Project%20Catalogue. pdf; "Rockefeller Foundation Extends US$1.75 Million Grant to Expand Climate Change Resilience Programme to 30–40 New Cities" (press release), ACCCRN, November 1, 2012, http://www.acccrn.org/sites/default/files/ documents/11%2001%2012%20ACCCRN%20Expansion.pdf.

49. TARU, *Surat City Resilience Strategy.*

50. Unless otherwise noted, all quotations from G. K. Bhat come from an interview conducted on April 30, 2014.

51. Interview with Lalit Dashora, Dr. Sandhya Rao, and Professor A. K. Gosain conducted on December 11, 2013.

52. The Rockefeller Foundation, *ACCCRN: City Projects*, May 2013, http://www.rockefellerfoundation.org/uploads/files/8ff925b8-2254-4b71 -a7fb-6082464b844e-acccrn-cities.pdf.

CHAPTER 11: AFTER THE CRISIS

1. Rebecca Solnit, *A Paradise Built in Hell: The Extraordinary Communities That Arise in Disaster* (New York: Penguin, 2009), 3.

2. White House, *The Federal Response to Hurricane Katrina: Lessons Learned* (Washington, DC: February 2006), 5, http://library.stmarytx.edu /acadlib/edocs/katrinawh.pdf.

3. Federal Emergency Management Agency (FEMA), "Overview of Hurricane Katrina in the New Orleans Area," *Hurricane Katrina in the Gulf Coast: Mitigation Assessment Team Report,* http://www.fema.gov/media -library-data/20130726-1520-20490-4521/549_ch8.pdf.

4. "Hurricane Katrina," *History Channel,* http://www.history.com/topics /hurricane-katrina.

5. Kevin F. McCarthy, D. J. Peterson, Narayan Sastry, and Michael Pollard, "The Repopulation of New Orleans After Hurricane Katrina," RAND Corporation, http://www.rand.org/pubs/technical_reports/TR369.html.

6. Robert B. Olshansky and Laurie A. Johnson, *Clear as Mud: Planning for the Rebuilding of New Orleans* (Chicago, IL: American Planning Association Planners Press, 2010), 11–13.

7. NYS 2100 Commission, *Recommendations to Improve the Strength and Resilience of the Empire State's Infrastructure,* 2013, http://www.governor .ny.gov/assets/documents/NYS2100.pdf.

8. Ibid., 10.

9. Ibid., 10, 20–23.

10. PlaNYC, http://www.nyc.gov/html/planyc/html/home/home.shtml.

11. PlaNYC, "About PlaNYC," http://home.nyc.gov/html/planyc/html /about/about.shtml.

12. This section is informed by a telephone interview with William Saito on January 8, 2014. Unless otherwise noted, all quotations from William Saito come from this interview.

13. Fukushima Nuclear Accident Independent Investigation Commission (NAIIC), *The Official Report of the Fukushima Nuclear Accident Independent Investigation Commission: Executive Summary* (National Diet of Japan, 2012), 10.

14. Ibid., 11.

15. Ibid., 9.

16. Olshansky and Johnson, *Clear as Mud,* 57.

17. Ibid.

18. Ibid., 67.

19. Ibid., 71.

20. This section is informed by an interview with Carey Shea conducted on January 16, 2014. Shea was instrumental in informing the segments on the New Orleans planning process, as well as the repopulation efforts, post-Katrina.

21. Unified New Orleans Plan (UNOP), *Citywide Strategic Recovery and Rebuilding Plan*, April 2007, 14–15.

22. America Speaks Facebook page, https://www.facebook.com/America Speaks/info.

23. UNOP, *Citywide Strategic Recovery and Rebuilding Plan*, 15.

24. Olshansky and Johnson, *Clear as Mud*, 212.

25. David E. Daniel et al., "Hurricane Katrina External Review Panel," *The New Orleans Hurricane Protection System: What Went Wrong and Why*, American Society of Civil Engineers, 2007, http://www.asce.org /uploadedfiles/publications/asce_news/2009/04_april/erpreport.pdf.

26. American Society of Civil Engineers, "Hurricane Katrina: Five Years Later," http://www.asce.org/Featured-Images/Hurricane-Katrina --Five-years-later/.

27. Olshansky and Johnson, *Clear as Mud*, 5.

28. Ibid., 8.

29. Ibid., 5.

30. FEMA, "Overview."

31. Olshansky and Johnson, *Clear as Mud*, 6.

32. United States Army Corps of Engineers (USACE), *Hurricane and Storm Damage Risk Reduction System Design Guidelines*, New Orleans District Engineering Division, revised June 2012, http://www.mvn.usace.army.mil /Portals/56/docs/engineering/HurrGuide/EntireDocument.pdf.

33. USACE, *The Times Picayune, New Orleans Area Hurricane Protection*, (infographic), http://media.nola.com/hurricane_impact/other/hurricane -protection-graphic-2012.pdf.

34. Mark Schleifstein, "Upgraded Metro New Orleans Levees Will Greatly Reduce Flooding, Even in 500-Year Storms," *NOLA.com*, August 16, 2013, http://www.nola.com/hurricane/index.ssf/2013/08 /upgrated_metro_new_orleans_lev.html; John Schwartz, "Vast Defenses Now Shielding New Orleans," *New York Times*, June 14, 2012, http://www .nytimes.com/2012/06/15/us/vast-defenses-now-shielding-new-orleans .html?pagewanted=2&_r=0, 2.

35. Delta Programme Commissioner, "Working on the Delta: Investing in a Safe and Attractive Netherlands, Now and in the Future" (video), September 21, 2010, http://www.deltacommissaris.nl/english/news/videos /workingonthedelta.aspx.

36. Unless otherwise noted, all quotations from Henk Ovink come from an interview on March 20, 2014.

37. Michael Kimmelman, "Going with the Flow," *New York Times,* February 13, 2013, http://www.nytimes.com/2013/02/17/arts/design /flood-control-in-the-netherlands-now-allows-sea-water-in.html?page wanted=all&_r=0.

38. "Dutch Draw up Drastic Measures to Defend Coast Against Rising Seas," *New York Times,* September 3, 2008, http://www.nytimes.com /2008/09/03/news/03iht-03dutch.15877468.html?_r=1&.

39. Deltacommissie, *Working Together with Water: A Living Land Builds for Its Future. Findings of the Deltacommissie 2008: Summary and Conclusions,* 2008, http://www.deltacommissie.com/doc/deltareport_summary.pdf; American Society of Civil Engineers, "Seven Wonders," www.asce.org /content.aspx?id=2147487305.

40. Kees d'Angremond, "From Disaster to Delta Project: The Storm Flood of 1953," *Terra et Aqua* 90 (March 2003): 3–10, http://www .iadc-dredging.com/ul/cms/terraetaqua/document/1/2/4/124/124/1 /terra-et-aqua-nr90-01.pdf.

41. Private memo from Femke Schasfoort and Jarl Kind, "Benefits of the Dutch Delta Works—Rockefeller Foundation Resilience Book," May 8, 2014, 1.

42. d'Angremond, "From Disaster."

43. Schasfoort and Kind, private memo.

44. Ibid.

45. Unless otherwise noted, all quotations from Guy Nordensen come from an interview conducted on November 7, 2013.

46. Unless otherwise noted, all quotations from Eric Klinenberg come from an interview conducted on April 23, 2014.

47. Nancy Kete, "A Framework for Articulating City Resilience," The Rockefeller Foundation (blog post), April 10, 2014, http://www. rockefellerfoundation.org/blog/framework-articulating-city-resilience.

48. MIT CAU + ZUS + URBANISTEN, "Hunts Point Lifelines," Rebuild by Design (winning project), http://www.rebuildbydesign.org /project/penndesignolin-final-proposal/#details.

49. Ibid.

50. PennDesign/OLIN, "New Meadowlands: Productive City + Regional Park," Rebuild by Design (winning project), http://www.rebuildbydesign .org/project/mit-cau-zus-urbanisten-final-proposal/.

51. Mercy Corps, "Precious Seedlings," December 20, 2006, http://www .mercycorps.org/articles/indonesia/precious-seedlings.

52. Jonathan Rose Companies, "Via Verde / The Green Way: Bronx, New York," http://www.rosecompanies.com/all-projects/via-verde-the-green-way.

53. Center for Active Design, "Via Verde," http://centerforactivedesign .org/via-verde/.

54. Unless otherwise noted, all quotations from Jonathan Rose come from an interview conducted on November 20, 2013.

55. New York City Economic Development Corporation, "NYC Waterfront Construction Competition," http://www.nycedc.com/Waterfront Competition; D-Shape, http://www.d-shape.com/index.htm.

56. The European Commission Directorate-General for Energy and Transport, *Modern Rail, Modern Europe* (Luxembourg: Office for Official Publications of the European Communities, 2008), http://ec.europa.eu/ transport/media/publications/doc/modern_rail_en.pdf, 3.

57. The European Commission Directorate, *Modern Rail, Modern Europe,* 2.

58. Lynne Goulding and Marcus Morrell, *Future of Rail 2050* (Arup, July 2014), www.arup.com/~/media/Publications/Files/Publications/F/Arup_ Future_of_Rail_2050.ashx, 5.

59. Union des Industries Ferroviaires Européennes (UNIFE), "A Unique Signalling System for Europe: The Long Journey to an Interoperable Railway System," www.ertms.net/wp-content/uploads/2013/09/ertms-facts-sheet-9-a-unique-signalling-system-for-europe.pdf.

60. *Railway Safety Performance in the European Union* (European Railway Agency, 2014), http://www.era.europa.eu/Document-Register/Documents/ SPR2014.pdf, 13.

61. "About Thalys," *Thalys,* https://www.thalys.com/be/en/about-thalys/ presentation.

62. Goulding and Morrell, *Future of Rail 2050,* 23.

63. Goulding and Morrell, *Future of Rail 2050,* 45.

64. Louis S. Thompson, "A Vision for Railways in 2050" (International Transport Forum, 2010), http://www.internationaltransportforum.org/pub/ pdf/10FP04.pdf, 16.

65. David Jaroszweski et al., "Guidebook for Enhancing Resilience of European Railway Transport in Extreme Weather Events" (Management of Weather Events in the Transport System, March 2014), http://www.mowe-it.eu/wordpress/wp-content/uploads/2013/02/Move_it_Guidebook_Rail_transport.pdf, 8–11.

CHAPTER 12: REVITALIZATION

1. Jane Jacobs, *The Death and Life of Great American Cities* (New York: Vintage Books, 1992), 238.

2. Unless otherwise noted, all quotations from Jeffrey Hebert come from an interview conducted on January 17, 2014.

3. Bruce Katz, Matt Fellowes, and Mia Mabanta, *Katrina Index Monthly Summary of Findings: February 1, 2006,* Brookings Institution, http://www.brookings.edu/~/media/Research/Files/Reports/2011/8/29%20new%20orleans%20index/200602_KatrinaIndexes.PDF.

4. Unified New Orleans Plan (UNOP), *Citywide Strategic Recovery and Rebuilding Plan,* April 2007, 192.

5. Ibid.

6. Project Home Again, http://projecthomeagain.net/.

7. Unless otherwise noted, all quotations from Carey Shea come from an interview conducted on January 16, 2014.

8. Unless otherwise noted, all quotations from Oji Alexander come from an interview conducted on January 16, 2014.

9. Bruce Eggler, "New Orleans Reached 81 Percent of Pre-Katrina Population in 2012, Census Figures Show," *NOLA.com,* March 14, 2013, http://www.nola.com/politics/index.ssf/2013/03/new_orleans_reached_81_percent.html 3-27-14.

10. Kenya National Dialogue and Reconciliation, "Introduction to KDNR," http://www.dialoguekenya.org/.

11. Unless otherwise noted, all quotations from Paul Thingo come from an interview conducted on December 18, 2013.

12. Kenya National Dialogue and Reconciliation, "Introduction."

13. Unless otherwise noted, all quotations from Irene Ngatia come from an interview conducted on December 18, 2013.

14. Unless otherwise noted, all quotations from Laurie Leitch and Loree Sutton come from an interview conducted on October 1, 2013.

15. Laurie Leitch and Loree Sutton, "Laurie Leitch and Loree Sutton: Tapping Social Resilience," PopTech talk, YouTube video, posted by "poptech," October 13, 2013, www.youtube.com/watch?v=auYNy7Oqvic.

16. Skoll World Forum, "Jockin Arputham," http://skollworldforum.org /contributor/jockin-arputham/.

17. Shack/Slum Dwellers International (SDI), "What We Do," http:// www.sdinet.org/about-what-we-do/.

18. SPARC, "About Us," http://www.sparcindia.org/aboutus.aspx.

19. SDI, "Kenya," http://www.sdinet.org/country/kenya/about/.

20. Information gathered from interviews with leaders at Muungano headquarters on December 17, 2013.

21. Quotation from Robert Lyall comes from conversations with a group of New Orleans artists and art and cultural advocates on January 16, 2014.

22. "Interfaith Service for Bombing Victims in Boston," *C-SPAN* (video), April 18, 2013, http://www.c-span.org/video/?312222-1/interfaith-service -bombing-victims-boston.

23. Dennis Lehane, "Messing with the Wrong City," op-ed, *New York Times,* April 17, 2013, http://www.nytimes.com/2013/04/17/opinion /messing-with-the-wrong-city.html?_r=1&.

24. "Rocky Balboa (2006) Quotes," *IMDb,* http://www.imdb.com/title /tt0479143/quotes.

25. John M. Edgerton, "Invisible Fellowship," *Old South Church in Boston* (blog post), May 10, 2013, http://www.oldsouth.org/blog /invisible-fellowship.

26. Unless otherwise noted, all quotations from Aage Borchgrevink come from an interview conducted on July 29, 2014.

27. "We Shall Overcome—Bruce Springsteen @ Memorial Concert 22 July Oslo Norway," YouTube video, uploaded by Tom Rise, July 22, 2012 https://www.youtube.com/watch?v=B1VjFneRVag.

28. Cameron Robertson, "Wounded Landscape: How Norway Is Remembering Its 2011 Utøya Massacre," *The Guardian*, March 6, 2014, http://www.theguardian.com/artanddesign/2014/mar/06/ norway-massacre-memorial-jonas-dahlberg-anders-behring-breivik.

29. Kigali Memorial Centre, "Genocide," http://www.kigaligenocide memorial.org/old/genocide/index.html.

30. Kigali Memorial Centre, http://www.kigaligenocidememorial.org /old/index.html.

31. Kigali Memorial Centre, "The Memorial Centre," http://www
.kigaligenocidememorial.org/old/centre/index.html.

32. Kigali Memorial Centre, "Documentation Centre," http://www
.kigaligenocidememorial.org/old/doccentre/index.html.

33. "Story: Historic Earthquakes," *The Encyclopedia of New Zealand,*
http://www.teara.govt.nz/en/historic-earthquakes/page-13; Charles
Anderson, "Christchurch: After the Earthquake, a City Rebuilt in Whose
Image?," *Guardian,* January 27, 2014, http://www.theguardian.com/cities
/2014/jan/27/christchurch-after-earthquake-rebuild-image-new-zealand
/print.

34. City of Christchurch, New Zealand, "Application for 100 Resilient
Cities." Proprietary information of The Rockefeller Foundation's 100
Resilient Cities Initiative.

35. Lianne Dalziel, "Mayor Welcomes Rockefeller Foundation and
Its Partners to Christchurch" (speech delivered March 24, 2014), http://
resources.ccc.govt.nz/files/TheCouncil/mayor/2014/24Mar2014
WelcomeRockefellerFoundation.pdf.

36. Ibid.

37. John McCrone, "How Does a City Bounce Back?" *Press,* May 4,
2014, http://www.stuff.co.nz/the-press/news/christchurch-earthquake-2011
/9907759/How-does-a-city-bounce-back.

38. Lianne Dalziel, "Mayor's Welcome to Workshop Participants" (speech
delivered at 100 Resilient Cities workshops, March 2014), http://resources.ccc.
govt.nz/files/TheCouncil/mayor/2014/25March100RCWelcomespeech.pdf.

39. Justin Bergman, "After Earthquakes, a Creative Rebirth in
Christchurch," *New York Times,* April 4, 2014, http://www.nytimes.com
/2014/04/06/travel/after-earthquakes-a-creative-rebirth-in-christchurch
.html?_r=2.

40. Ibid.

41. Samuel Henry Prince, *Catastrophe and Social Change: Based upon
a Sociological Study of the Halifax Disaster* (New York: Longmans, Green,
1920), 122.

42. Ibid., 133.

43. Ibid., 138.

44. Matt Lundy, "4. Halifax, N.S.," *Moneysense,* March 7, 2012,
http://www.moneysense.ca/property/top-35-best-places-to-live-in-2012
/attachment/04_halifax; Jacqueline Walls, "American Cities of the Future
2013/14," *fDi Intelligence,* April/May 2013, http://www.tfsa.ca/storage

/reports/American%20Cities%20of%20the%20Future%202013%20 and%202014%20(1).pdf.

45. Prince, *Catastrophe and Social Change,* 139.

46. New Schools for New Orleans, *A Brief Overview of Public Education in New Orleans, 1995–2009,* http://www.newschoolsforneworleans.org /downloads/nsno_%20EducFactSheet.7.09.pdf.

47. Ibid.

48. Ibid.

49. Unless otherwise noted, all quotations from Leslie Jacobs come from an interview conducted on February 5, 2014.

50. Data from Leslie Jacobs received via e-mail, PowerPoint presentation.

51. Coastal Protection and Restoration Authority (CRPA) of Louisiana, *Louisiana's Comprehensive Master Plan for a Sustainable Coast* (Baton Rouge, Louisiana, 2012), 14, http://www.coastalmasterplan.louisiana.gov/2012 -master-plan/final-master-plan/.

52. Ibid.; USGS, "Louisiana Coastal Wetlands: A Resource at Risk," *Coastal and Marine Geology Program,* http://pubs.usgs.gov/fs/la-wetlands/.

53. Robert Costanza, Octavio Perez-Maqueo, M. Luisa Martinez, Paul Sutton, Sharolyn J. Anderson, and Kenneth Mulder, "The Value of Coastal Wetlands for Hurricane Protection," *Ambio* 37, no. 4 (2008): 241–248, http://seagrant.noaa.gov/Portals/0/Documents/what_we_do/social_science /ss_tools_reports/value_hurricane_protection.pdf.

54. Robert Dean, "New Orleans and the Wetlands of Southern Louisiana," *The Bridge: Linking Engineering and Society* (National Academy of Engineering, Washington, DC) 36 (Spring 2006): 35–42, http://www .nae.edu/File.aspx?id=7393.

55. John McPhee, *The Control of Nature* (New York: Macmillan, 2011), 6–7.

56. Ibid., 6.

57. NASA, "Subsidence in New Orleans," Earth Observatory, June 3, 2006, http://earthobservatory.nasa.gov/IOTD/view.php?id=6623.

58. CRPA, *Louisiana's Comprehensive Master Plan,* 16–19.

59. Ibid., 21.

60. Greater New Orleans Data Center, *The New Orleans Index at Eight,* August 2013, 20.

61. Bobby Jindal, "New Orleans Is America's Comeback City," op-ed, *NOLA.com,* August 11, 2013, http://www.nola.com/opinions/index.ssf /2013/08/new_orleans_is_americas_comeba.html.

62. New Orleans Business Alliance, *ProsperityNOLA: A Plan to Drive Economic Growth for 2018: Executive Summary,* 2013, http://nolaba.org/wp-content/uploads/2013/06/Executive-Summary_Booklet.pdf.

63. Unless otherwise noted, all quotations from Robin Barnes come from an interview conducted on January 16, 2014.

64. Charles Davidson, "The Big Busy: A Radical Reset After the Katrina Catastrophe Is Transforming the Economy of New Orleans," *EconSouth,* Third Quarter, 2013, http://www.frbatlanta.org/documents/pubs/econsouth/13q3_big_busy.pdf.

65. Amy Liu and Allison Plyer, *The New Orleans Index at Five: An Overview of Greater New Orleans: From Recovery to Transformation* (Brookings Metropolitan Policy Program and Greater New Orleans Community Data Center, August 2010), http://www.brookings.edu/~/media/research/files/reports/2011/8/29%20new%20orleans%20index/08neworleansindex.pdf.

66. Bryan Walsh, "Today's Smart Choice: Don't Own. Share," *Time,* March 17, 2011, http://content.time.com/time/specials/packages/article/0,28804,2059521_2059717_2059710,00.html.

67. Unless otherwise noted, all quotations from April Rinne come from an interview conducted on November 8, 2013.

68. Jill Tucker, "SF to Tap 'Sharing' Firms in Next Disaster," *San Francisco Chronicle,* June 11, 2013, http://www.sfchronicle.com/bayarea/article/SF-to-tap-sharing-firms-in-next-disaster-4592803php?t=049116571 8459eab13.

69. "Gross: Gross Domestic Product," *OED.com,* http://www.oed.com/view/Entry/81765?redirectedFrom=gross+domestic+product#eid134037825.

70. Social Progress Index, "United States," Social Progress Imperative, 2014, http://www.socialprogressimperative.org/data/spi/countries/USA.

71. Social Progress Index, "New Zealand," Social Progress Imperative, 2014, http://www.socialprogressimperative.org/en/data/spi/countries/NZL.

72. Social Progress Index, "Norway," Social Progress Imperative, 2014, http://www.socialprogressimperative.org/en/data/spi/countries/NOR#data_table/components/NOR/USA,NZL. This URL will lead to a page comparing Norway, New Zealand, and the United States on the reported measures.

73. Unilever, "Unilever Facts," http://www.unilever.com/aboutus/introductiontounilever/unileverataglance/; "Unilever N.V./ Unilever PLC," *Fortune,* http://fortune.com/global500/unilever-n-v-unilever-plc-135/.

74. Paul Polman, "The Remedies for Capitalism," McKinsey & Company (blog post), http://www.mckinsey.com/features/capitalism/paul_polman.

75. Ibid.

CONCLUSION

1. Unless otherwise noted, all quotations from Shaun Donovan come from an interview conducted on October 30, 2013.

2. Peter M. Sandman, "Introduction to Risk Communication and Orientation to this Website," The Peter Sandman Risk Communication Website, http://www.psandman.com/index-intro.htm.

3. Gustave Le Bon, *The Crowd: A Study of the Popular Mind,* Kindle edition (New York: Dover, 2002), locations 672–719.

4. Amos Tversky and Daniel Kahneman, "Availability: A Heuristic for Judging Frequency and Probability," *Cognitive Psychology* 5 (1973): 207–232.

5. Ibid., 229.

6. "Counting the Cost of Calamities," *Economist,* January 14, 2012, http://www.economist.com/node/21542755.

7. Ferran Brunet, *The Economic Impact of the Barcelona Olympic Games, 1986–2004: Barcelona: The Legacy of the Games, 1992–2002* (Barcelona: Centre d'Estudis Olimpics, Universitat Autònoma de Barcelona, 2005), http://olympicstudies.uab.es/pdf/wp084_eng.pdf.

8. Ibid.

9. International Olympic Committee (IOC), *Factsheet: Legacies of the Games; Update—December 2013,* http://www.olympic.org/Documents /Reference_documents_Factsheets/Legacy.pdf.

10. Ibid.

11. Brunet, *Economic Impact.*

12. IOC, *Factsheet.*

13. Feargus O'Sullivan, "Is Tourism Ruining Barcelona?" *CityLab,* April 21, 2014, http://www.theatlanticcities.com/jobs-and-economy/2014/04 /tourism-ruining-barcelona/8918/.

14. Brunet, *Economic Impact.*

15. IOC, *Factsheet.*

16. Adam Taylor, "How the Olympic Games Changed Barcelona Forever," *Business Insider,* July 26, 2012, http://www.businessinsider.com /how-the-olympic-games-changed-barcelona-forever-2012-7.

17. O'Sullivan, "Is Tourism Ruining Barcelona?"

18. "Catalonia Leads Unemployment Reduction with a 7.9% Drop in 2013," *Catalan News Agency,* January 23, 2014, http://www.catalannews agency.com/business/item/catalonia-leads-unemployment-reduction -with-a-7-9-drop-in-2013.

19. "Regeneration—The New Millennium," *Glasgow City Council*, https://glasgow.gov.uk/index.aspx?articleid=3702.

20. "Glasgow 2014: Tickets For Popular Events Still Available," *BBC News*, July 14, 2014, http://www.bbc.com/news/uk-scotland-28293223.

21. Produced for The Scottish Government by APS Group Scotland, *An Evaluation of Legacy from the Glasgow 2014 Commonwealth Games: Pre-Games Report* (The Scottish Government, April 28, 2014), files.scotgov. publishingthefuture.info/the-scottish-government-an-evaluation-of-legacy-from-the-glasgow-2014-commonwealth-games-pre-games-report.epub, 10.

22. Ibid., 9.

23. "Glasgow – The Host City of the 2014 Commonwealth Games," Commonwealth Games Federation, http://www.thecgf.com/games/2014/glasgow2014-bid.asp?yr=2014.

24. Glasgow 2014 Commonwealth Games Candidate City, "People, Place, Passion: Glasgow 2014 Commonwealth Games Candidate City File," http://www.thecgf.com/media/games/2014/G2014_CCF_V011–3.pdf, 8.

25. Glasgow 2014 Legacy Framework (Glasgow City Council), http://www.glasgow.gov.uk/CHttpHandler.ashx?id=7770&p=0.

26. Oliver Wainwright, "Glasgow Faces Up To Reality of A Divided Commonwealth Games Legacy," *Theguardian.com*, March 3, 2014, http://www.theguardian.com/cities/2014/mar/03/glasgow-faces-reality-commonwealth-games; Julie Clark and Ade Kearns, *Go Well in Glasgow's East End: Baseline Community Survey 2012—Report One: Headline Indicators* (GoWell, May 2013), http://www.gowellonline.com/assets/0000/0499/GoWellEast_Baseline_Community_Survey_2012_-_1_Headline_Indicators. pdf, 20. (This survey, which covered part of the East End, showed residents had a forty-eight percent employment rate in 2012, a distance away from Glasgow City's sixty-one percent employment rate and the seventy-one percent Scottish average.)

27. Wainwright, "Glasgow Faces Up To Reality of A Divided Commonwealth Games Legacy."

28. Glasgow 2014 Commonwealth Games Candidate City, "People, Place, Passion," 8.

29. Ibid., 11.

30. "Athletes' Village," *Glasgow 2014—Commonwealth Games*, http://www.glasgow2014.com/your-games/venues/athletes-village.

31. "Athletes' Village," *Glasgow City Council*, http://www.glasgow.gov.uk/index.aspx?articleid=5089.

32. Wainwright, "Glasgow Faces Up To Reality of A Divided Commonwealth Games Legacy."

33. Produced for The Scottish Government by APS Group Scotland, *An Evaluation of Legacy from the Glasgow 2014 Commonwealth Games*, 12; Lisa Summers, "Glasgow 2014: Margaret Jaconelli's Story," *BBC News*, March 26, 2014, http://www.bbc.com/news/uk-scotland-glasgow-west-26740648.

34. Wainwright, "Glasgow Faces Up To Reality of A Divided Commonwealth Games Legacy."

35. Chris Leslie, "Jaconelli—Fighting Eviction," (video on blog post "Commonwealth City") *Chris Leslie: Photo/Film*, May 20, 2014, http://www.chrisleslie.com/commonwealth-city/.

36. Summers, "Glasgow 2014: Margaret Jaconelli's Story."

37. "University News: Impact of Commonwealth Games on East End," *University of Glasgow*, May 2013, http://www.gla.ac.uk/news/archiveofnews/2013/may/headline_279097_en.html.

38. Clark and Kearns, *Go Well in Glasgow's East End*, 2.

39 Jamie Rodney, "Commonwealth City," *Herald Scotland*, July 13, 2014, http://www.heraldscotland.com/business/company-news/commonwealth-city.24728286.

40 Ibid.

41. Andrew Winston, "Resilience in a Hotter World," *Harvard Business Review*, April 2014, 56–64, http://hbr.org/2014/04/resilience-in-a-hotter-world/ar/1.

42. Ibid.

43. Ibid.

44. Nassim Nicholas Taleb, *Antifragile: Things That Gain from Disorder* (New York: Random House), 2012.

45. Winston, "Resilience."

46. "Coca-Cola Company Statistics," Statistic Brain, http://www.statisticbrain.com/coca-cola-company-statistics/.

47. Muhtar Kent, "The Coca-Cola Company and Resilience," The Rockefeller Foundation (blog post), January 28, 2013, http://www.rockefellerfoundation.org/blog/coca-cola-company-resilience.

48. Coca-Cola Company, "Slingshot™: How It Works," September 24, 2013, http://www.coca-colacompany.com/stories/slingshot-how-it-works.

49. Kent, "Coca-Cola Company."

50. United Nations, *Global Assessment Report on Disaster Risk Reduction*, 2013, http://www.preventionweb.net/english/hyogo/gar/2013/en/gar-pdf/GAR2013_EN.pdf.

51. Judith Rodin, "The Transformation of Medellín Provides a Model for Cities Worldwide," The Rockefeller Foundation (blog post), April 16, 2014, http://www.rockefellerfoundation.org/blog/transformation-medelln-provides-model.

52. Winston, "Resilience."

53. Clark Gilbert, Matthew Eyring, and Richard N. Foster, "Two Routes to Resilience," *Harvard Business Review,* December 2012, 67–73.

54. Irene Karanja, "Kenya SDI Affiliate Reports on the World Urban Forum," *SDI,* September 19, 2012, http://www.sdinet.org/blog/2012/09/19/kenya-sdi-affiliate-reports-world-urban-forum/.

55. Unless otherwise noted, all quotations from Pauline Manguru come from an interview conducted on December 15, 2013.

56. Sarah Goodyear, "Why IKEA, a New Urbanist Development and a Park-in-the-Making All Withstood Sandy," *Next City,* October 29, 2013, http://nextcity.org/daily/entry/why-ikea-a-new-urbanist-development-and-a-park-in-the-making-all-withstood-.

57. Cara Buckley, "Small Shops Shiver in Gloom of a Shuttered Red Hook Market," *New York Times,* November 8, 2012, http://www.nytimes.com/2012/11/09/nyregion/in-red-hook-closure-of-fairway-leaves-nearby-shops-anxious.html?pagewanted=1&_r=3&ref=nyregion.

58. US Small Business Administration, "Disaster Planning," http://www.sba.gov/content/disaster-planning.

59. Unless otherwise noted, all quotations from John Peterson come from an interview conducted on January 13, 2014.

60. Unless otherwise noted, all quotations from Peter Madonia come from an interview conducted on October 16, 2014.

61. Dan Neil, "BMW Plots Sustainable Supercar with the i8 Project," *Wall Street Journal,* May 3, 2014.

62. Entergy Corporation, *Building a Resilient Energy Gulf Coast: Executive Report* (Entergy Corporation with America's Wetland Foundation and America's Energy Coast, 2010), http://www.entergy.com/content/our_community/environment/GulfCoastAdaptation/Building_a_Resilient_Gulf_Coast.pdf.

63. Unless otherwise noted, all quotations from Jeff Williams come from an interview conducted on January 17, 2014.

64. Blue Ribbon Resilient Communities, *Beyond Unintended Consequences: Adaptation for Gulf Coast Resiliency and Sustainability* (America's Wetland Foundation, 2012), http://www.futureofthegulfcoast.org/AmericasWETLANDFoundation_Beyond.pdf.

INDEX